CINEPHEMERA

CINEPHEMERA

ARCHIVES, EPHEMERAL CINEMA, AND NEW SCREEN HISTORIES IN CANADA

Edited by

ZOË DRUICK

and

GERDA CAMMAER

McGill-Queen's University Press

Montreal & Kingston • London • Ithaca

ISBN 978-0-7735-4446-8 (cloth)
ISBN 978-0-7735-4447-5 (paper)
ISBN 978-0-7735-9675-7 (ePDF)
ISBN 978-0-7735-9676-4 (ePUB)

Legal deposit fourth quarter 2014
Bibliothèque nationale du Québec

Printed in Canada on acid-free paper that is 100% ancient forest free (100% post-consumer recycled), processed chlorine free

This book has been published with the help of a grant from the Canadian Federation for the Humanities and Social Sciences, through the Awards to Scholarly Publications Program, using funds provided by the Social Sciences and Humanities Research Council of Canada. Funding has also been received from the Simon Fraser University Publications Fund.

McGill-Queen's University Press acknowledges the support of the Canada Council for the Arts for our publishing program. We also acknowledge the financial support of the Government of Canada through the Canada Book Fund for our publishing activities.

Library and Archives Canada Cataloguing in Publication

Cinephemera : archives, ephemeral cinema, and new screen histories in Canada / edited by Zoë Druick and Gerda Cammaer.

Includes bibliographical references and index.
Issued in print and electronic formats.
ISBN 978-0-7735-4446-8 (bound).— ISBN 978-0-7735-4447-5 (pbk.).—
ISBN 978-0-7735-9675-7 (ePDF).— ISBN 978-0-7735-9676-4 (ePUB)

1. Motion pictures—Canada—History. 2. Motion pictures—Preservation—Canada. 3. Motion pictures—Canada—Archival resources. I. Druick, Zoë, author, editor II. Cammaer, Gerda, author, editor

PN1993.5.C3C56 2014 791.430971 C2014-905363-0
C2014-905364-9

CONTENTS

ACKNOWLEDGMENTS

THIS PROJECT WAS inspired by a fortuitous meeting of a group of Canadians at NYU in 2008. Around the original table were Joseph Clark and JoAnne Stober, whose enthusiasm was instrumental in getting this project off the ground. Clark deserves special mention for coining the title, *Cinephemera*, a catchy portmanteau if ever there was one.

Research assistants Davina Rimmer (Ryerson) and especially Itrath Syed (SFU) were instrumental in tracking the project and compiling the manuscript, and we would like to formally offer them our deepest thanks. Jonathan Crago of McGill-Queen's University Press is a stalwart promoter of Canadian media studies. We count ourselves lucky that he took this project under his wing and thank him for his support.

We would also like to acknowledge with thanks the Dean's Office of the Faculty of Communication and Design and the Office of Research Services at Ryerson University, and the SFU University Publication Fund for their generous aid. Finally, we would like to acknowledge the commitment to uncovering media history undertaken by archivists, artists, and scholars around Canada. In this moment of media transition, we hope that there will be even more collaboration between these groups. Without a common sense of the value of media history, efforts at preservation are even less likely. We hope that this volume contributes to this important discussion for many years to come.

CINEPHEMERA

INTRODUCTION
CANADIAN CINEMA, EPHEMERAL CINEMA

Zoë Druick and Gerda Cammaer

WHAT DOES THE digital turn mean for cinema studies? This question has taken on increasing urgency over the past decade as media makers and scholars of all stripes grapple with the material, epistemological, aesthetic, and economic shifts brought about by digital convergence. Along with cheaper production costs, digital promises to preserve and make accessible myriad films that would otherwise ferment in archives, basements, and obscure collections. And certainly initiatives like the Prelinger Archive in the United States, and even the embarrassment of riches available on demand on YouTube and Vimeo, seem to make this a reality. But what, specifically, does the digital turn mean for cinema studies in Canada? Does it make our media history more accessible to the public, to scholars, to filmmakers? Will it preserve our media heritage? The research collected in this book shows that it both does and does not. While major resources have been put into preserving, distributing, and making accessible important parts of our media history, the high cost of conversion means that not everything can be saved. Or perhaps it has just made us more aware of what has already been lost or is on the verge of disappearing forever. Thus it seems useful – and timely – to study these recent developments of moving image technology with a Janus-faced regard for media history.

This anthology brings together a range of impressive new research that in different ways engages with this question of ephemerality in Canadian cinema (or *cinephemerality*, to coin a portmanteau[1]). The diverse meanings of ephemera and ephemerality within film studies seem to offer productive avenues for scholarship, from the study of the impermanence of moving image media themselves to the inclusion of marginalized film genres to the use of ephemeral research material. Less specific than *orphan cinema*, the contributors to this collection suggest that ephemeral can be used as a category of study and even an emerging ethico-critical methodology to rethink media history, making, and archiving in Canada.

The ephemeral as a critical concept in film studies comes along with a growing interest in media archaeology, a relatively new area that offers potentially productive ways to think about film history and cultural memory. Media archaeology opens up the possibility of a non-linear understanding of media history, one that allows for multiple variants and numerous turning points. Most media archaeologists share Siegfried Zielinski's conviction that media historians must abandon ideas of linear development from simple to more sophisticated technologies.[2] Rather, this perspective highlights the way in which a progression of media have insinuated themselves into everyday life to augment and otherwise change ways of perceiving and recording the world. In short, the change in dominant platforms has inspired a new look at the taken-for-granted aspects of our media history, including conventional national narratives.

In the United States, one response to the realization of the fragility and multiplicity of audio-visual history in the digital age has been the emergence of the concept of orphan films, which has taken hold since the 1990s.[3] In its most general meaning, *orphans* – a term librarians and archivists use for all media – refers to works for which the copyright holders cannot be identified or located. Both text-based and audio-visual materials include substantial numbers of works, especially older materials, with unclear copyright status.[4] For film, the term gained interest in North America thanks to the National Film Preservation Plan in the United States, and the public hearings for this plan initiated by David Francis for the Library of Congress.[5]

The wide interest in the National Film Preservation Plan meant that orphan film quickly became a common term in archival and scholarly discourse.[6] In the broadest sense, orphan films include those that lack clear copyright holders as well as those that lack commercial potential. In the American national context, orphan films refer to media that exist outside of mainstream commercial systems: amateur, alternative, educational, ethnographic, experimental, governmental, industrial, independent, medical, non-theatrical, training, sponsored, small-gauge, silent, student, obsolescent, unreleased, and underground. In short, an orphan film is any that has been abandoned, neglected, or almost lost; is ephemeral, but also, in this naming, ripe for rescue and rediscovery. This idea of orphan films and (more broadly defined) an ephemeral cinema justifies the preservation of cinematic archival objects from outside the traditional focus of film studies on narrative fiction. For this volume, we have adopted this broader definition of orphan films, and include the notion that cinema refers to moving images in general, not solely those recorded on celluloid.

If anything, the situation for all types of ephemeral cinema is even more pronounced north of the border. Canadian strengths in film production have historically been the very genres championed by orphan film networks: educational, non-mainstream, non-theatrical, small gauge. Our film archives, like our university film production and film studies programs, work with barely adequate funding. Our independent filmmakers and film exhibitors struggle just to make, circulate, and screen films; resources for archiving tend to run a distant fourth. All media outside the commercial mainstream are in even greater need of scholarly and archival attention here, since there may be little or no written historical record of their existence; these valuable media, which provide traces of the texture of everyday life and potentially carry critical parts of our cultural history, risk disappearing altogether in the face of digitization.

Operating as a media archaeologist, the Canadian cinema historian must become something of a sleuth. This anthology offers numerous examples of precisely such careful investigations yielding important film history finds. It also illustrates the heterogeneity of instruments and inspirations that media historians are using, and an exciting new openness to what may formerly have languished on the margins of the national media story. Indeed, this volume reflects developments in film studies that put film historians in the same conversation with experimental filmmakers and archivists, and highlights common interests around the material circulation and preservation of films and videos and their related technologies and archival material.

In the past few years, these ideas have been workshopped on panels at the annual conference of the Film Studies Association of Canada as well as at a number of dedicated events. In 2010, André Habib (a contributor to this volume) organized a conference called L'avenir de la mémoire (The future of memory) with Michel Marie at the Cinémathèque Québécoise in Montreal.[7] Gathering film scholars, film archivists, and filmmakers to discuss their concerns and exchange ideas, this event centred around the question of how best to preserve our cinematic heritage at a time of digital transition. The conference echoed the ongoing discussions at the annual conference of the Association of Moving Image Archivists and the biannual Orphan Film Conferences in the United

States. Topics that are related to the content of this book were the focus of two other Canadian conferences as well: Useful Cinema, a symposium that professors Charles Acland and Haidee Wasson organized at Concordia University in August 2006[8] and, the next year, Is Film Dead?, a symposium on the state of celluloid organized by the Atlantic Film Cooperative.[9] Indeed, a recurrent feature among all these fora has been the concern for the future of the cinematic past brought on by digital technology.

As the contributors to this collection clearly indicate, the risks to our cinema history are also reinvigorating Canadian film studies with a new imperative. Archival studies are becoming more robust and central to the discipline. Instead of bemoaning the lack of a healthy feature film industry or the paucity of auteurs, as was traditionally the case, scholars are paying increased attention to the abundance of work Canada has actually produced.[10] When the lens shifts away from dramatic sound features, it turns out there is an embarrassment of Canadian cinema to be discovered both inside and outside of archives, very little of which has received much scholarly attention. This archival turn also means a renewed attention to materiality of form.

Experimental films, especially found-footage films and videos, are resurfacing as a key genre for emphasizing the particular qualities of the dwindling film medium through the exploration of all kinds of films past their best-before dates. Many found-footage filmmakers adopt and rework various ephemeral cinema genres, such as travelogues, B-movies, scientific films, government-sponsored service films, advertisements, and industrial films, that are often dismissed as film junk and video trash, recycling and remixing these images with the aim of calling into question the way cinema circulates meaning. Faced with the growing ephemerality of 16 mm film, many film artists have turned their attention to issues linked to the "death of film," using a variety of crumbling film images as their main formal trope while critiquing different aspects of how quickly film has become a residual medium. Several of the contributors in this book draw compelling parallels between found-footage filmmaking and film preservation (see chapters 7, 8, 15, and 16). Film studies, filmmaking, and film preservation have much more in common than has thus far been assumed, especially in light of a growing amount of Canadian "cinephemera."

THE STRUCTURE OF THIS BOOK

This collection aims to cover a wide range of issues surrounding cinema's ephemerality in Canada, including neglected or overlooked histories; footage that has been lost and then rediscovered; the blatant recontextualization of images and sounds, with attendant questions of access and copyright; film preservation; as well as the past, present, and future of audio-visual archives. Proceeding roughly chronologically, the contributions to this volume highlight the vitality of Canadian cinema studies as it moves beyond the canon of dramatic sound features and feature-length documentaries, considering everything from the lost histories (and objects) of silent film to recent experimental film performances.

Through meticulous archival research, previously unknown auteurs and vernacular genres are being uncovered. In chapter 1, examining the production and dissemination of moving images photographed in the early silent era in Quebec as part of the Silent Era Quebec Filmography Project, Louis Pelletier demonstrates how film producers and distributors commonly felt the need to frame or edit actuality footage differently for local and foreign markets, and explores the ways in which non-fiction films were increasingly expected to complete and support fiction films within the newly hegemonic system of theatrical cinema. As a result, "topicals" and newsreels in the transitional era reflected the tensions between their pursuit of originality and novelty on one hand, and the convenience of the new formulas that were beginning to make inroads into cinema on the other. In chapter 2, Peter Lester digs up "the stillborn saga" of *Policing the Plains* (1927). A.D. Kean, a cowboy cum Vancouver-based filmmaker, undertook the project in order to present an "authentic" picture of Canada and its mounted police, an antidote against the growing discontent among Canadian audiences with the plethora of American Westerns. Lester argues that this film represents a classic cautionary tale of independent filmmaking in Canada: a labour of love followed by lack of access to audiences and ending up with a bitter filmmaker living in almost complete obscurity.

In a similar vein, in chapter 3, Charles Tepperman unearths the fascinating history of Leslie Thatcher, a star of the amateur film world in the mid-1930s. Thatcher was making award-winning work during a period in which traditional histories of Canadian cinema do not detect much activity, forcing Tepperman to challenge our received ideas about Canadian cinema history. Performing a similarly impressive feat of archaeology, in chapter 5 Liz Czach opens a window on the wealth of amateur travel filmmaking of the post-war era. Made to be presented in non-theatrical venues and accompanied by lectures, this genre of filmmaking and film exhibition has received scant attention in Canadian cinema history, despite its immense post-war popularity and its importance in presenting images of Canada both at home and abroad. Czach uncovers the story of Melvin and Ethel Ross, a Calgary-based couple who enjoyed a long and successful career as adventurer-filmmakers.

A number of the chapters provide new perspectives on Canadian film institutions. For instance, in his history of Crawley Films in chapter 4, Scott MacKenzie maps the cross-border history of educational film beyond the better-known story of the National Film Board (NFB). MacKenzie's work on 1950s mental hygiene films made by Crawley Films for McGraw-Hill in the United States was facilitated by resources held by Library and Archives Canada, including 30,000 film cans, countless production files, and the help of archivist Bill O'Farrell, demonstrating the centrality of archives and archivists to this kind of film history. Likewise, in chapter 6, Christine York illuminates the operation of the NFB's versioning units in the 1950s and 1960s and emphasizes the importance of the soundtrack for the meaning of films. York demonstrates that more than mere translations, the language versioning at times created radically different films circulating in diverse contexts, at times troubling the NFB's nationalist orientation. York insists that NFB history should concern itself with the "intertwined" histories of French and English production at the board, rather than treating them as distinct.

Tracking the rise of experimental work in Canada, in chapter 7, William C. Wees traces Canada's "first generation" of found-footage filmmakers, conducting close readings of films by Joyce Wieland, Arthur Lipsett, and Jack Chambers, among others. His critical analysis of these films offers an opportunity to rediscover the subjects, formal techniques, sources, and circumstances of production of key films that laid the groundwork for recycled cinema in Canada by tying Cold War apocalyptic scenarios in with critiques of ambient mass media culture.

Found footage is one thing, but incomplete films are another thing entirely. Monika Kin Gagnon was confronted with this conundrum when she discovered *R69*, pieces of an unfinished film by her late father, the Quebec artist Charles Gagnon, and decided to complete it. In chapter 8, Gagnon compares her personal experience with what she terms "posthumous cinema" to the little-known story of *Wendy and Joyce*, a film that Canadian artist Joyce Wieland began in 1967 but never completed. Gagnon offers a compelling case study of how digitization has made it possible to access incomplete works, and so has created new opportunities for creative and scholarly research.

Turning to lost Canadian technological innovations, in chapter 9, Seth Feldman considers the first proto-IMAX film, *Tiger Child* (1970) by Donald Brittain, a nine-screen film that has languished largely unseen since it was first released. Made to be projected in a very particular site – the enormous Fuji Bank Pavilion of the 1970 Osaka Expo – as IMAX subsequently developed into a single-screen format, *Tiger Child* was orphaned by the IMAX brand and written out of the Canadian film canon as well. Unavailable in Canada until 2007 when a new print was struck and shown, the film has been understandably but, Feldman argues, unduly ignored. He reconsiders its importance as an early example of installation documentary and associational storytelling, complementary to a larger reconsideration of the film work of Expo 67.[11]

A number of chapters investigate the place of video in Canadian cinema history. In chapter 10, Jerry White digs up an all-but-ignored story of new wave filmmaker Jean-Luc Godard in Quebec from a neglected chapter of international film history to expose some of the overlooked consequences of his presence in "la belle province." Godard visited the Abitibi region in 1968 and gave a series of lectures at Concordia University in Montreal in 1978. White argues that accounting for these visits can help to clarify not only key moments in Godard's career, but also certain influences on the Quebec media scene.

In another insightful discussion on Quebec cinema, Micky Storey and Jason B. Crawford provide a reading of the unique project of Michel Audy's rural queer educational cinema in chapter 11. Storey and Crawford use Audy's two best-known features, *Luc ou la part des choses* (1982) and *Crever à vingt ans* (1984), as the basis for a case study illustrating the hardships of gay life in Quebec outside of the province's two major cities. By analysing the films as a queer "archive of feelings," the authors describe how this work has become marginal and inaccessible, while its content still has significance for audiences today, particularly for gay youth in rural areas. Their formal analysis of the crumbling state of the few circulating VHS tapes of these films emphasizes how easily non-mainstream content can become ephemeral.

In chapter 12, Jennifer VanderBurgh presents an invaluable chronicle of the archival turn that took place at CBC television in the early 1990s, when the death of magnetic tape as an archival medium was becoming apparent and digital was appearing on the horizon. Although undoubtedly the most mainstream element of Canadian media production, lack of public archiving has paradoxically put television among the most ephemeral of media. VanderBurgh's study is indebted to the work of Ernest J. Dick, the CBC's only corporate archivist (1989–96), once again demonstrating the centrality of archivists for this kind of media study.

In his study in chapter 18, Andrew Burke considers the specificity of lost and found video. Not only does analogue video have a different valence than celluloid film, it particularly lends itself to telling stories of rediscovered pop culture phenomena. The assemblage video *Death by Popcorn* (2008), by the now-defunct Winnipeg collective L'Atelier national du Manitoba, brilliantly uses degraded videotape found in a dumpster to tell a mock-ironic story about Winnipeg's troubled hockey team, the Jets, doomed to endlessly succumb to Wayne Gretzky's Oilers. In the process of reassembling the cast-off cultural artefacts, much is revealed about the culture and local television of 1980s Winnipeg itself. When read together, Burke and VanderBurgh's research highlight the differences between official and unofficial video archives.

Randolph Jordan presents an unusual case of a re-mastered film soundtrack without an original in chapter 13. Often treated as secondary to image, film sound can easily be considered the most ephemeral domain in film studies. In his analysis of Larry Kent's silent short film *The Street* (1962), which was never commercially released, and the sound version of the same film titled *Hastings Street*, which was released in 2000, Jordan depicts the dramatic changes in the soundscape of the city of Vancouver, the local film industry, and the technology of film sound. This story of how a film was rediscovered by its own maker shows on a small scale the dynamics of a fast changing media landscape in Canada over the past four decades, and how easily, without extra attention or effort, films can be abandoned and forgotten.

In chapter 14, Katherine Quanz maps the history of and current struggles around the preservation and distribution of experimental films and videos made by Indigenous artists in Canada. Taking Vtape and IsumaTV as her central sites of analysis, Quanz explores both the centrality of experimental practices to Aboriginal media makers and the importance of alternative distribution networks for the circulation of this often doubly marginalized work. Continuing with the theme of archiving and precarity, in chapter 17 Zoë Druick considers the implications of the NFB's shift to digital for Canadian cinema history. In the past decade, the NFB has committed an ever-increasing proportion of its dwindling budget to making its "heritage" collection available on its website and through the encouragement of sampling in the work of select filmmakers. At the same time, the archive has increasingly restricted its access for scholars and unsanctioned filmmakers. Druick argues that, given its importance, the NFB archive must be seen as a public archive first and digital archive second.

Taking up the current concern about the "ruins of cinema," in chapter 15 André Habib analyses the film performances of Montreal-based artist Karl Lemieux. Habib discusses the close link between experimental film practices and film preservation, as well as various perspectives on the dialectic between destruction and preservation that this work blatantly foregrounds. Lemieux's interventionist "art of the ruins" provides a concrete element to discussions around ephemeral films, while also referring back to the tradition of found-footage films as an art linked to disaster, collapse, destruction, and chaos. In chapter 16, with a similar ethos of preserving that which is rapidly decaying, Gerda Cammaer tells the story of the making of *Stardust* (2009), a joint project with sound-collage artist Randolph Jordan. She reveals how the film's narrative was inspired by the study of ephemeral films and other issues of film preservation. Celebrating the most-despised feature of film – its dust and scratches – *Stardust* raises questions about the positioning of celluloid film as a site of mourning, memories, and loss.

LOOKING FORWARD, LOOKING BACK

As the contributors to this collection make abundantly apparent, Canadian cinema studies has entered a new and productive phase, spurred in part by the changes to technologies of production, viewing, and archiving. With digital convergence, cinema scholars are called upon to make sense of the changes to the social meanings of our once ubiquitous and now obsolete objects of study and of our discipline as a whole. As the impressive and wide-ranging studies in this book show, the media archaeological approach to the history of cinema in Canada – and the recognition of the precarious material state of our cinema history and the implications of platform transition – provides many resources for the present. Canadian cinema history has long been entangled with international as well as local or regional stories. Moreover, cinema has always offered as many possible genres and forms as digital media do today, and was meant to slot into everyday life just as the Internet does now. The study of silent film reminds us that re-editing and remediating footage for different contexts is as old as the medium itself.

Approaching cinema through the ephemeral films and other related objects that remain also demonstrates the extent to which cinema was often made for immediate uses and then jettisoned. This process has become even more amplified today, when finding and moving data has become so effortless. Looking back at the artefacts of lost cinema history in Canada can help us interpret the current overabundance of ephemeral media. There is something poignant about the quantity of media that is now routinely produced and lost on an ongoing and structural basis. In this context, the act of finding media can be an ethical gesture of remembrance while at the same time offering new critical insights about the present-day media field. It is our hope that this simultaneous and complementary regard for the media of both past and future can become an animating feature of a renewed cinema studies in Canada.

NOTES

1 We wish to thank Joseph Clark for this particularly evocative neologism. We use the word *cinema* in its broadest sense to refer to moving images, whether watched in purpose-built auditoriums or non-theatrical settings, as well as in various forms of remediation, that combine to constitute a national aesthetic and political project.

2 Siegfried Zielinski is a German media theorist and one of the founders of Media Archeology. He is the author of *Deep Time of Media: Toward an Archeology of Hearing and Seeing by Technical Means* (Cambridge, MA: MIT Press, 2008). See also Erikki Huhtamo and Jussi Parikka, eds., *Media Archaeology: Approaches, Applications, and Implications* (Berkeley: University of California Press, 2011).

3 In 1999, Dan Streible, currently at New York University but then at the University of South Carolina, organized the first Orphan Film Symposium, Saving Orphan Films in the Digital Age (www.nyu.edu/orphanfilm). More symposia have followed biannually, each one bigger and more successful than the last. Gradually this gathering of archivists, preservationists, curators, scholars, collectors, technology experts, and media artists who come together to study and screen neglected moving images has become a movement with connections around the globe.

4 Register of Copyrights, *Report on Orphan Works* (Washington, DC: United States Copyright Office), http://www.copyright.gov/orphan/orphan-report.pdf.

5 David Francis, hearing before the Panel of the National Film Preservation Board, United States Library of Congress, in *A Study of the Current State of American Film Preservation* (Washington, DC: 1993).
6 Paolo Cherchi Usai, "What Is an Orphan Film? Definition, Rationale and Controversy" (paper presented at Orphans of the Storm: Saving "Orphan Films" in the Digital Age, University of South Carolina, Columbia, South Carolina, 23 September 1999), http://www.sc.edu/filmsymposium/archive/orphans2001/usai.html.
7 See also André Habib and Michel Marie, eds., *L'Avenir de la mémoire: patrimoine, restauration et réemploi cinématographiques* (Villeneuve-d'Ascq, France: Presses Universitaires du Septentrion, 2013).
8 One outcome of this workshop was the volume *Useful Cinema*, edited by Charles Acland and Haidee Wasson (Durham, NC: Duke University Press, 2011).
9 Conference proceedings are published online in *Incite: Journal of Experimental Media and Radical Aesthetics*, no. 1 (2008), http://www.incite-online.net/issueone.html.
10 See, for example, the Canadian Educational, Sponsored, and Industrial Film Archive (www.screenculture.org/cesif); The Early Cinema Filmography of Ontario (Ryerson); the University of Western Ontario's digital re-release of Roy Massacar's *Stars of the Town* series; and Expo 67: Expanded Cinema (www.yorku.ca/filmexpo/index.html).
11 See Expo 67: Expanded Cinema.

1 EARLY QUEBEC ACTUALITIES AND THE EPHEMERAL MEANING OF MOVING IMAGES IN THE TRANSITIONAL ERA

Louis Pelletier

NON-FICTION FILMS have not always been relegated to the margins of cinema. In the early years of animated pictures, actuality films were produced and exhibited just as frequently as fiction films.[1] The marginalization of non-fiction subjects seems to have largely been the result of the institutionalization of film, a process commonly associated with cinema's transitional era. Generally situated by historians somewhere between 1907 and the advent of the classical era in the mid-1910s, this crucial period of film history saw permanent film theatres replace travelling showmen as the dominant mode of exhibition, and multi-reel fiction films become the focal point of the increasingly standardized programs exhibited within these establishments.[2] This hegemonic process simultaneously relegated some strands of non-fiction film production (mainly those associated with what Charles Acland and Haidee Wasson label "useful cinema") to the newly conjured non-theatrical ghetto, and incorporated others (such as newsreels and travelogues) by having them support fiction films in the "balanced programs" the new class of exhibitors so fervently sought.[3] The programs film theatres assembled thus served dual commercial and rhetorical purposes, as they aimed to attract a wide range of patrons while addressing rising concerns over the influence of film. Canadian film history more particularly demonstrates that, in addition to lending some level of cultural capital to film shows, newsreels, topicals, and short documentaries were used to insert some measure of local or national content to programs almost invariably headlined by foreign films.[4]

One of the consequences of the incorporation of non-fiction films into the hegemonic system of commercial theatrical cinema was that many types of non-fiction film productions were affected by the strong push toward rationalization that shaped theatrical cinema in the transitional era. At the time, many producers sought to minimize risks and maximize returns by simultaneously attempting to widen the circulation of their productions – most notably through opening foreign markets – and narrow the scope of their output by having their films conform to an increasingly limited set of ever more strictly defined genres. This two-pronged strategy was complicated, however, by audiences' varying needs, as well as by the fact that moving images often mean different things to different communities and individuals.

Indeed, the analysis of the abundant data pertaining to the production and dissemination of moving images taken in Quebec gathered by the Silent Era Quebec Filmography project demonstrates that film producers and distributors commonly felt the need to frame actuality footage differently for local and foreign markets.[5] This could partly be explained by the fact that by the turn of the 1910s, films were increasingly less likely to be shown accompanied by external agents, such as lecturers, who could emphasize different angles for different publics. Producers and distributors consequently had to intervene in the films themselves in order to make them palatable to a broad range of publics. Most notably, they could do this through using different titles and intertitles, or through recycling the same moving images in multiple films conforming to different genres and formats.

A most eloquent case of such intervention is that of the short Kinemacolor film produced by the Natural Colour Kinematograph Co in Montreal on the day of George V's coronation, 22 June 1911 (see figure 1.1). Photographed on the terrain of the Montreal Amateur Athletic Association, the film depicted a group of Kahnawake Mohawks taking part in the celebrations by performing scenes of a pageant adapted from Longfellow's *Hiawatha* in-between periods of a lacrosse match.[6] When the footage was first exhibited locally in September (the exceptionally long delay can most likely be attributed to the limited exhibition opportunities offered to Kinemacolor films), it was simply introduced to Montrealers as *Caughnawaga Indians on the M.A.A.A. Grounds.*[7] The Natural Colour Kinematograph people seem to have deemed the coronation day footage quite striking, as they recycled it in a Kinemacolor travelogue entitled *Canada: Nova Scotia to British Columbia* released in the United Kingdom more than a year later, in November 1912.[8] This travelogue gave the footage a new slant by introducing it as an authentic document – purportedly photographed on a reservation – showing the Iroquois Indians' ceremonial rites.[9] The producer thus implicitly acknowledged that different markets required different sales arguments: for Montrealers, recognition of a

SHE WILL BE THE STAR AT THE M.A.A.A. GROUNDS TO-DAY.

WARI SOSE,

the Indian girl who will take the principal ladies' part in the tableaux that will be shown by the Caughnawaga actors between the periods of the Montreal-Caughnawaga Coronation Lacrosse match to-day.

1.1 One of the Kahnawake Mohawks performing in the Hiawatha pageant cinematographed by the Natural Colour Kinematograph Co in 1911.

familiar site and, possibly, remembrance of the previous June's festivities were expected to do the trick, whereas for filmgoers living in the old country, exoticism was perceived as more of a selling point. This seemingly simple (if perhaps ethically dubious) strategy actually involved a radical shift in meaning, as the footage shot on the MAAA grounds ceased to be the mere trace of an ephemeral event to become a document purportedly depicting a timeless tradition.

The coronation day film case represents an extreme example of a situation more common than previously thought. The Quebec Filmography project demonstrates that the production of such actuality films was surprisingly common in Montreal during the transitional era, and that a large number of these films circulated in one guise or another outside of the province. Between 1906 and 1915, Léo-Ernest Ouimet, F. Guy Bradford, Bert Mason, and many others produced dozens of "local topicals" – to use the label coined by local film historian Stephen Bottomore – for the city's theatres (see figure 1.2).[10] All of these local filmmakers worked fast to ensure that their films would arrive in theatres while interest for the news events depicted was still high. In some cases, less than eight hours elapsed between the event filmed and the resulting topical's first public screening.[11] The fact that Ouimet, Bradford, Mason, and their peers mostly covered events where large amounts of people could be expected to gather demonstrates they understood that they could increase their films' drawing powers by playing on the moviegoing public's curiosity for its own reflected image. "See yourself as others see you," promised a New Grand advertisement for the exhibition of a Mason topical showing the forced march of the local regiments.[12]

The prominent local element of these topicals did not prevent footage issuing from them from widely circulating outside of Quebec. The Filmography project has documented more than fifty American, British, French, and even Russian newsreels featuring Quebec film segments produced between 1910 and 1915. While some of these had indubitably been photographed by stringers selling footage directly to newsreel producers, theatre advertisements and records from the Quebec Board of Censors demonstrate that a good deal of the footage these Quebec segments contained had first been exhibited locally in topicals.

Period descriptions of these newsreels suggest that a slight shift in emphasis and some edits were often sufficient to make the Quebec footage suited for foreign exhibition. The images of the opening of the

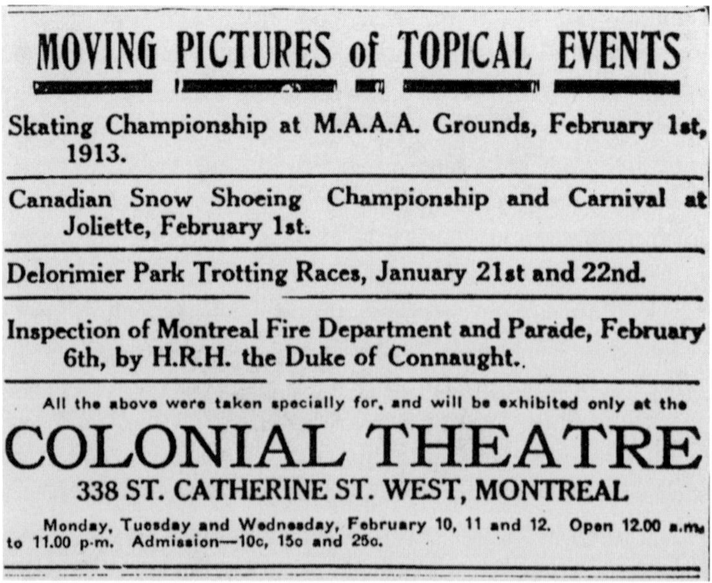

1.2 Montreal film exhibitors wishing to offer balanced programs frequently produced local topicals in the transitional era.

new Montreal dry docks by the Duke of Connaught on 18 November 1912 are a case in point. When this footage was exhibited locally at the Orpheum on 21 November 1912, advertisements emphasized the fact that the film was "showing prominent Montreal people."[13] As both the people and the event depicted were presumably of little interest to foreign moviegoers, the editions of the French *Le film Gaumont-actualités* and American *Gaumont Weekly* that reprised some of this footage in the winter of 1913 simply framed it as sheer spectacle or, to be more precise, colonial pomp (with the published summary of the US newsreel even casually misidentifying the duke as the "Prince of Connaught").[14]

Footage from another local topical depicting the frozen ruins of a major wintertime downtown fire was similarly reduced to an exotic sight when included in an edition of the US *Pathé Weekly* in January 1914. The description of this particular newsreel segment published in the *Moving Picture World*, most likely taken from an intertitle of the now-lost film, gave a sort of contemplative tone to the footage: "When winter blows his chill breath of fire-swept buildings, he rears a crystal palace on the ruins, changing tons of water to glittering walls of ice, many-gabled and of infinite fantasy."[15] The description emphasized the poetic side of the event, but neglected to mention the circumstances behind it: the fire's cause, the firefighters' work, and the loss the building's occupants incurred.

Such repurposing of Quebec footage became routine in the early months of the Great War, when US newsreels such as the *Mutual Weekly*, the *Universal Animated Weekly*, the *Hearst-Selig News Pictorial*, and *Pathé's Daily News* recycled material originating from many local topicals dealing with the mobilization, training, and departure of Canadian soldiers.[16] To Montreal filmgoers, these short views offered one last glimpse at a son, brother, friend, or lover departing for the war. To US producers, however, their main attraction might very well have been that they provided a cheap and trouble-free source of visual material dealing with the most sensational news event of the young century. Charles Musser notes that, while everything war related was obviously very popular with American audiences in the early months of the European conflict, US authorities were banning fiction films too partial or simply too literal in their treatment of the ongoing events in order to enforce the country's neutrality. However, since non-fiction films were not viewed with the same suspicion, recycling Canadian images provided US newsreel producers with a convenient source of in-demand war footage.[17]

To conclude, the analysis of the production and dissemination of early Quebec news films suggests that non-fiction film production became engaged in a sort of contrapuntal relationship with fiction in the transitional era. Non-fiction films were increasingly expected to complete and support fiction films within the new hegemonic system of theatrical cinema. Local actuality films, newsreels, and travelogues could inject the informational and local content generally missing from the fiction features newly promoted to the top of the bill in film theatres. In the process, the exhibition of non-fiction films also helped the Canadian film industry placate its critics by countering, however superficially, the perception of cinema as a harmful foreign influence. This, in turn, may have helped create more screening opportunities for the imported fiction films that Canadians craved to see. Transnational distribution networks then permitted this material to be repurposed in foreign markets. In short, topicals and newsreels – both within themselves and by the mere fact of their existence – reflected the tensions between the lure of the exotic and the need for self-recognition, as well as between novelty and the convenience of established formulas, that continued to shape cinema beyond the 1910s.

ACKNOWLEDGMENTS

This project was funded by research grants from the Social Sciences and Humanities Research Council of Canada and Bibliothèque et Archives nationales du Québec. Many thanks to Paul Moore, who provided some of the documents discussed here.

NOTES

1 See for instance Patrick Loughney's invaluable study of the Library of Congress Paper Print Collection in "A Descriptive Analysis of the Library of Congress Paper Print Collection and Related Copyright Materials" (dissertation, George Washington University, 1988).

2 On cinema's transitional era, see Charlie Keil and Shelley Stamp, "Introduction," in Keil and Stamp, eds., *American Cinema's Transitional Era: Audiences, Institutions, Practices* (Berkeley: University of California Press, 2004), 1–14.

3 Charles Acland and Haidee Wasson, eds., *Useful Cinema* (Durham, NC: Duke University Press, 2011).

4 In the classical era, organizations such as Associated Screen News, the Canadian Government Motion Picture Bureau, and the National Film Board of Canada would provide Canadian exhibitors with a wide range of non-fiction shorts.

5 The Silent Era Quebec Filmography (http://cri.histart.umontreal.ca/grafics/fr/filmo/default.asp) was a project conducted by the Groupe de recherche sur l'avènement et la formation des institutions cinématographique et scénique and funded by the Social Sciences and Humanities Research Council of Canada between 2003 and 2009. It aimed to compile the various films photographed in Quebec up to 1930 as well as to provide data and commentaries on their production, makers, and subjects.

6 "She Will Be the Star at the MAAA Grounds To-Day," "Hiawatha's Story to Be Told at the Lacrosse Match," Montreal *Daily Star* (22 June 1911): 2, 4; "Crowning of Hiawatha by Iroquois Indians," Montreal *Daily Star* (23 June 1911): 2.

7 Princess theatre advertisement and "Au Princess," *La Patrie* (9 September 1911): 6, 17; "Fine Color Pictures Shown at Princess," Montreal *Daily Star* (12 September 1911): 2. Kahnawake was at the time known as "Caughnawaga."

8 *Kinematograph Monthly Film Record* no. 7 (November 1912): 25, 27–8.

9 The Natural Color Kinematograph Co (London), *Catalogue of Kinemacolor Film Subjects* (London: The Natural Color Kinematograph Co, 1912–13).

10 Stephen Bottomore, "From the Factory Gate to the 'Home Talent' Drama: An International Overview of Local Films in the Silent Era," in Vanessa Toulmin, Simon Popple, and Patrick Russell, eds., *The Lost World of Mitchell and Kenyon: Edwardian Britain on Film* (London: British Film Institute, 2004), 38–40.

11 "Une reproduction de l'accident de hier," *La Presse*, 19 September 1913, 17.

12 New Grand theatre advertisement and "Moving Pictures of Forced March at the New Grand and Français," Montreal *Daily Star* (10 November 1913): 2, 15.

13 Orpheum theatre advertisement, Montreal *Daily Star* (25 November 1912): 2.

14 "Le Film Gaumont-Actualités, 4e année, no. 2," *Ciné-Journal* 229 (11 January 1913): 17; *Moving Picture News* 7.6 (8 February 1913): 26.
15 "Pathé's Weekly, No. 8," *Moving Picture World* 19.6 (7 February 1914): 677, 708.
16 "Mutual Weekly, No. 89," *Moving Picture World* 21.12 (19 September 1914): 1692; "Animated Weekly, No. 134," *Moving Picture World* 22.2 (10 October 1914): 246; "Hearst-Selig News Pictorial, No. 62," *Moving Picture World* 22.3 (17 October 1914): 335; "Pathé's Daily News, No. 194," *Moving Picture World* 23.1 (2 January 1915): 125.
17 Charles Musser, "Film, Propaganda and World War I: Images of War in the United States during the First Months of Neutrality," in Roland Cosandey and François Albera, eds., *Cinéma sans frontière 1896–1918* (Lausanne/Quebec: Payot/Nuit blanche, 1995), 264–5.

2 CANADA'S LOST FRONTIER EPIC

THE STILLBORN SAGA OF *POLICING THE PLAINS*

Peter Lester

IN SEPTEMBER 1925, seemingly at the height of popularity of Hollywood's Mountie subgenre, the *Vancouver Province* reprinted a letter to the editor previously published in the *London Daily Mail*. The letter, penned anonymously by "a Canadian," highlights with great concern the travails of the Canadian film industry, and in particular the representations of Canada itself in the American-produced films dominating domestic theatre screens. Lamenting how Canadians are forced "to see their own country caricatured," the author pinpoints some of the dominant misconceptions, with particular attention to that most Canadian of national symbols, the Mountie:

> The American producer is very fond of an alleged "Canadian" background, and so he puts Canada on the screen – in a Hollywood backyard. So we Canadians see "Northwest Mounted Policemen" wearing the most extraordinary uniforms, with their chevrons upside down, American style, with hats that bear no resemblance to the genuine Stetson of the "mountie" than a high hat does to a saucepan lid. We see weird French-Canadians (picturesquely but quite erroneously described as "half-breeds") wearing checkered shirts that never appeared on any Canadian back and talking the strangest argot. We see lumberjacks with their hair marcelled and glued straight. Instead of our beautiful native pine trees and spruces, we see the carefully manicured lawns and tropical shrubbery of Los Angeles.[1]

Furthermore, demonstrating an awareness of the economic structures of the film industry of the era, the author extends his criticism toward those mechanisms that effectively constricted the industry in both Canada and Great Britain:

> What makes it worse is that nearly all the Canadian cinemas are linked together in "chains" controlled by big American syndicates. The Canadian cinema has therefore very little choice in films, for it has to show what is sent it; and because American theatre managers are notoriously unfriendly to imported films, it is almost impossible for either the British or Continental film to get a showing.[2]

I cite these passages at length because they speak to the growing awareness and discontent emerging during this period in Canada with the perceived dominance of the industry by American influences, and because they tap into long-standing mythologies about Canadian film history. Of the various narratives that have come to characterize the Canadian film industry since its inception, perhaps two stand out as particularly prominent and enduring. The first of these, rooted in political economy, emphasizes the themes of American domination and dependence that have historically structured the production, distribution, and exhibition spheres of the industry. The second, operating on a more representational level, laments the colonization and/or appropriation within the content of movies themselves of Canada's landscape and history by the demands of the commercial film industry. The political economic framework has been notably articulated in varying degrees and capacities by scholars such as Peter Morris, Manjunath Pendakur, Ted Magder, and Michael Dorland.[3] The representational narrative on the other hand, while permeating a great deal of scholarly writing about film and Canada, has perhaps found its most public and popular champion in the writings of Pierre Berton, Canada's unofficial chronicler of "official" culture and history.

The historical context of the preceding anecdotal reference is important to my intentions in this chapter, as the publication of the letter happened to coincide with the production of *Policing the Plains* – a film adaptation of the popular text of the same name written by a Presbyterian pastor from Vancouver, Rev R.G. MacBeth. The book, originally published in 1921, is a historical account of the history of the Royal North-West Mounted Police. The director of the adaptation was A.D. "Cowboy" Kean, a Vancouver-based former rodeo rider turned professional filmmaker. As a filmmaker, Kean was well aware of the difficulties and risks associated with film production in Canada (it is entirely plausible that he was the author of the anonymous letter to the *Daily Mail*),[4] and was motivated to effectively offer the "authentic" representation of Canada and its mounted police that seemed to be absent from American producers' genre exercises. Within the history of Canadian filmmaking, *Policing the Plains* is a curious specimen to be sure. Despite its ambitious origins and storied, albeit tragic, production history, the film and its director are little known to Canadians. The film was put into storage shortly after its limited (and only) theatrical run, and seemingly never re-emerged. No remaining copy of the film has surfaced, and the only proof of its initial existence lies in the traces and fragments it left behind in publicity stills, vague shooting diaries, and newspaper reviews – the ephemeral remnants that make up a historian's palette. *Policing the Plains* has even managed to evade much of the writing on Canadian film history. Peter Morris's encyclopedic history of the first few decades of the Canadian film industry, *Embattled Shadows*, includes a few paragraphs on the topic but little more. The most substantial work on Kean has come from Dennis Duffy, who authored a 1989 article along with David Mattison on his career as a filmmaker, and who conducts a similarly oriented ongoing lecture series at the Royal British Columbia Museum and Archives.[5] Yet aside from Duffy and Mattison's work, and the occasional reference or footnote in writings on Canadian cinema, the story of Kean and his film has eluded most Canadian film historiography.[6]

Unlike a great many amateur, industrial, and feature films that enjoyed relative degrees of popularity and healthy circulation during their own era only to become lost or orphaned with the passage of time, no more than a few hundred people could have ever seen *Policing the Plains* in the first place, even upon its lone theatrical engagement during a week-long stint in Toronto in December 1927. However, despite the small audiences the film drew over the course of its stunted lifespan, its ultimate legacy is relatively profound. In a sense, the film represents a classic case of what could have been. Accompanied by optimism and pride, the filmmakers began production with a bold sense of righting the representational wrongs of Hollywood and its romanticized depictions of the Royal North-West Mounted Police. But after three full years in production and post-production limbo, the film barely emerged – its filmmakers beaten down and nearly bankrupt. As such, the tragic saga of *Policing the Plains* speaks to the passions and perils of independent filmmaking in Canada. While the film is historically notable for its brazen attempt to redress the perceived American colonization of "Canadian" themes, sadly its ultimate burden is to serve as a telling object lesson in the political economic framework of control and dependency that governed and characterized the Canadian film industry in the 1920s and 1930s. Rather than offering a challenge, either symbolic or otherwise, to the governing truisms that have come to characterize the history of the Canadian film industry, *Policing the Plains* offers yet another unfortunate example.[7]

What distinguishes *Policing the Plains*, however, from a generic status as yet another piece of historical evidence in the case against a vibrant domestic film industry is tied to its status as a lost film and how our handling of such phenomena shapes how we understand history. Ongoing debates within film studies regarding the relative merits of textual and contextual analysis find their ultimate stumbling block when confronted with the issue of "lost" films. How can we assess the significance of a film that no longer exists in a physical sense? The study of the related concepts of orphaned, lost, and ephemeral cinema has enjoyed considerable scholarly attention in recent years, much of it tied to Dan Streible's popular Orphan Film Symposium and his related work on the subject.[8] One thing that becomes apparent amidst all of the work and research in this vein is that the concept of the "lost" can mean a number of different things depending on the specific contexts of the discussion. For Ina Bertrand, for instance, the concept of the lost extends not merely to films of which no physical copies remain, but rather to any film or filmmaker that has been overlooked or for whatever reasons omitted from the central relevant histories or reference guides – the availability or materiality of the film itself is not necessarily the defining issue.[9] Often, films described as lost are not actually so, in the technical sense. Eric de Kuyper, for instance, discusses the enormous quantity of unknown films that sit unexamined in archives – orphaned, perhaps, but certainly not lost in any material sense.[10] Yet, as David Pierce notes, only a small fraction of films produced during the silent era remain in a physical form: literally thousands of films have simply disappeared over the decades, for reasons such as poor storage conditions, fires, and, perhaps most prominently, outright disinterest and neglect.[11] In certain cultural contexts, such as the history of the Hong Kong film industry, Steven Teo and Vivian Lee reveal the difficulty, but also the necessity, of filling in the gaps of the tremendous quantity of neglected film production.[12] The situation in Canada, however, is considerably different. Given that, historically, feature film production was limited to begin with, particularly during the silent era, one would assume that films and filmmakers that persisted despite their circumstances might retrospectively benefit from an increased sense of historical imperative possibly attributable to, among other things, their unique contextual standing. But aside from the attention previously mentioned, the presence of *Policing the Plains*, and of Kean himself, has been largely absent from the narrative of early Canadian film history, as marginal as that field is to begin with. Much of this marginalization, if not all of it, can be attributed to the film's immaterial or ephemeral status, since no physical copy appears to exist. Historical import is often in no small way determined by the documentation and evidence that remains over time. The absence of such material, most notably the film itself, has correspondingly more often than not meant less critical attention. Yet, despite the unavailability of *Policing the Plains*, there is much to be learned from the film's – and its director's – history.

A.D. Kean began his career as a filmmaker during the early 1910s, after retiring from his successful career as a rodeo competitor. Throughout the decade he worked on a number of varied film projects for institutions such as the Canadian Pacific Railway (CPR) and the BC provincial government, and gained experience as a cameraman working on American-produced westerns. Among his notable productions from this period are *B.C. for the Empire*, a 1916 actuality of Canadian battalions leaving for war; *Whaling: B.C.'s Least Known and Most Romantic Industry*, a 1916 documentary about the whaling industry off Vancouver Island; and *The Adventures of Count E.Z. Kisser*, a short comedy released in 1917. In addition to his work as cameraman and producer, Kean also ran his own film laboratory and distribution company, Kean's Canada Film Exchange.[13] In the early 1920s, much of his work in film was done on a contract basis for the British Columbia Patriotic and Educational Picture Service, a short-lived, government-run film distribution unit.[14] But none of this was as ambitious as the initiative Kean would undertake in 1924, when he began film-making an adaptation of R.G. MacBeth's *Policing the Plains*. MacBeth's book had originally been optioned to a newly minted Canadian production company called Canadian Historic Features, which had been established in Vancouver with an agenda to produce films about Canadian history. The company was short lived, however, and Kean soon took over the project.[15]

It perhaps bears mentioning simply how saturated the film-going market was with American-produced Mountie genre pictures in the 1920s.

In his exhaustive research on the topic, Berton reveals that prior to 1922, the year he identifies as the peak period of the genre's production output, Hollywood had made 188 Mountie movies, forty-eight of them as full features after 1914. In 1922, the year the genre hit its peak (or nadir, depending on the viewpoint), Berton counts twenty-three titles in total.[16] Furthermore, although the production numbers topped out during this year, forty-eight additional Mountie titles were released over the next eight years until the end of the silent era.[17] The popularity of the genre is often attributed to its close affinity with the western. With a little syntactic and semantic tinkering, the films represented little more than slight deviations from the basic structure of this classical genre. The figure of the Mountie, then, in Berton's words, represented little more than "an American sheriff in a scarlet tunic."[18] Reportedly, American studios were so focused on the genre that certain companies even had actors who "specialize[d] in Mounted Police characters."[19]

What troubles Berton, however, is not so much the volume of titles, nor their generic formulae, but rather the "celluloid mountain of misconceptions" that the films collectively represent.[20] Apparently, these misconceptions irked none more than the police force itself. In August 1924, an article in the *Calgary Herald* recounted an anecdote concerning a trip to one such movie by an RCMP officer in Vancouver. Upon exiting the theatre, the officer allegedly quipped: "Why in the name of all that's practical doesn't somebody get out a real historic picture of the police? ... something done by Canadians and acted in the country where the police did their work. Don't you think that people would stand for one movie that was a historical record, rather than a long string of impossible situations, pieced together by a mushy plot and acted in settings that are evidently faked?"[21] This perceived inaccuracy and inauthenticity in large part provided the impetus for the production of *Policing the Plains.* Kean himself cited the musings of this officer as a source of inspiration for the film. From the very start, in terms of promotional rhetoric and the various forms of reportage that tracked its production, *Policing the Plains* was discursively positioned as an "authentic" antidote to the inauthentic Hollywood depictions of the storied police force. Of course, discussions of authenticity and fidelity are highly loaded, contentious, and potentially problematic issues in the study of cinematic representation. What an "authentic" representation of the Mounties would consist of is by no means self-evident, as interpreting the image and "meaning" of the figure of the Mountie is a polysemic endeavour. For many, the Mountie is an enduring symbol of Canadian law and order. Conversely, many would understand it as an outdated symbol of empire, rooted in authority and subjugation and further tainted by more recent contemporary scandals.[22] In the context of the production of *Policing the Plains*, two clear discursive conceptions of the Mounties were in play. On one hand was the purportedly inauthentic and commercialized version of the police force, rooted in stereotypes and genre conventions. On the other hand was a model steeped in the rhetoric of tradition, heroism, and historical detail that MacBeth, Kean, and others associated with the film presented as an alternative. My intent here is by no means to enter this debate, or to evaluate the veracity of these claims about authenticity. Rather, the issue is relevant because those terms clearly motivated the film's genesis and helped shape the various promotional discourses surrounding its production. Furthermore, in a sense, the film's purported commitment to a form of historical realism anticipates the dominant shift toward this mode of representation that would characterize feature film production in Canada decades later.

Duffy and Mattison detail the fascinating yet troubled history of the film's production elsewhere, yet the salient points bear recounting. Aside from its inherent uniqueness as a feature film initiative in 1920s Canada, from the very start, *Policing the Plains* was distinguished by the sheer scale of its ambition. In 1924, during the early stages of production, Kean and MacBeth went into overdrive attempting to muster support for the film. MacBeth apparently had a knack for self-promotion and had in the preceding years circulated his book widely, garnering generally favourable reviews in the United Kingdom, and had begun correspondence with no less a figure than Will Hays of the Motion Picture Producers and Distributors of America about its possible adaptation.[23] Furthermore, likely with more cultural capital to his credit than Kean, MacBeth penned letters to influential individuals and organizations in Canada and was able to secure "unprecedented facilities" from the RCMP, the CPR, and the Hudson's Bay Company.[24] As early as 1923, before Kean had even signed on to direct the film, the RCMP had promised "every assistance possible" for the "pictureisation" of *Policing the Plains*.[25] Much of this support took the form of historically accurate props, in keeping with the film's commitment to historical realism, such as handcuffs, leg irons, revolvers, and, of course, horse riding paraphernalia.[26] The CPR, for its part, responded with hyperbolic enthusiasm typical of the initial period of the film's production with the encouraging observation that, should the production "fling the glamour of Idealism round it," the filmmakers would be able to "back David Griffith and the others off the map."[27] MacBeth also secured rights for footage of the Prince of Wales, shot during his earlier visit and appearance with the police force. Given the declared commitment to historical realism and accuracy, the inclusion of authentic props and equipment and stock actuality footage appears to be altogether in keeping with this intention. This commitment was apparently to be solidified in the opening dedication card, which read: "In whole-hearted admiration of the men, both past and present who have silently but effectively policed the world's widest frontier and made the settlement of the Canadian North-West possible. This picture, true to life, is shown."[28] This declared commitment to historical accuracy combined with a clear sense of patriotism was picked up in the early press coverage of the film's production, which was unanimously positive and optimistic. In a detailed piece published during the first few months of the film's production, the *Vancouver Sun* announced that it was expected to "have a wide circulation throughout the English-speaking world" and that, according to information from British film houses, "the picture will do 'a big business' in the British Isles."[29] Kean himself, needless to say, was equally enthusiastic and excited about the film and its potential for success. In the *Lethbridge Herald* in July 1924, he declared that he thought the film would be "the most fascinating picture of its kind ever produced."[30] *Policing the Plains* was produced through Kean's Western Pictures Company, which secured funding through a syndicate of forty subscribers. The budget was initially $40,000, but by the time the film was completed three years later in 1927, it had ballooned to $125,000.[31] This amount, while certainly not lavish by Hollywood standards, was at the time unprecedented in Canada.[32] The spring and summer months of 1924 appeared to have been largely successful, as principle photography was underway and the early sense of optimism still prevailed. On-location shooting occurred in the Cariboo region of British Columbia's interior and in and around the city of Vancouver during the spring months (see figure 2.1). While in Vancouver, Kean was required to take on many of the duties of a producer, and his personal archives are littered with mundane correspondence and receipts related to such production details as securing shooting permissions and trying to wrangle up horses and American cavalry uniforms.

2.1 A portion of "E" Division of the RCMP, assisting at the filming of *Policing the Plains*; Vancouver courthouse in the background, with Margaret Lougheed as Britannia.

The film industry in Vancouver at that point was a far cry from what it is today, and as such much of the production infrastructure for a film of this scope simply did not exist. Kean's records indicate having to deal with California-based costumers, and film stock delivered from Toronto.

That summer, production was relocated to Macleod, Alberta. Founded in 1874, Fort Macleod served as an early headquarters for the NWMP and, as such, was central to the narrative of *Policing the Plains*. Rather coincidentally, in July 1924, the town was celebrating its fifty-year jubilee. Clearly this was fortuitous for Kean and the production crew, and the town's residents greeted them warmly and enthusiastically. The press in Macleod, Calgary, and neighbouring Alberta municipalities was particularly ebullient about the presence of the film crew and the film's potential for success. Kean further endeared himself to the community by filming the festivities and later presenting them on-screen. Kean's record of the jubilee, claimed the *Macleod Times* in superlative terms apparently typical of the western press of the era, showed "clearly the outside world that a western town put over the biggest thing Canada has ever seen."[33]

While the specific narrative arc of *Policing the Plains* is difficult to piece together, it is known that it highlighted the cornerstone events in the history of the NWMP. The event that historians often single out as directly catalyzing the establishment of the force is the Cypress Hills massacre of 1873. A group of American "wolfers" and whiskey traders crossed the Canadian border pursuing supposedly stolen horses. Blaming a Nakota tribe for the theft, the traders waited until nightfall and opened fire on a camp they came upon, killing roughly twenty people.[34] Furor over this event in eastern Canada led Prime Minister John A. MacDonald to establish the NWMP to safeguard Canadian interests in the west and to maintain order. Clearly a pivotal moment in the history of the police force, the Cypress Hills massacre was to become a major set piece in *Policing the Plains*. The scene was shot with the cooperation of members of the local Blood tribe, who took on the roles of the Nakota. The *Calgary Herald* describes this scene:

> Simulating drunkenness, bucks and squaws, to the number of more than one hundred danced round and round to the frantic measure of the tom-toms … At the climax of the wild dance, the whisky runners sneak back to a vantage point near the camp and begin shooting down the now drunk Indians. The dance goes on and down they go, one by one. Never suspecting that their comrades are being shot down, the crazed braves finish their dance. As the flares die down, the last dancer falls.[35]

Unfortunately, little tangible evidence remains of this scene, and the *Lethbridge Herald*'s prediction that "the scenes that were taken … will in the near future appear on the screen of all the movies throughout Canada and other countries" failed to materialize.[36]

Kean in fact benefitted from the considerable cooperation of local First Nations tribes in the production of the film, beyond the depiction of the Cypress Hills massacre. Clearly, the NWMP's history was intricately enmeshed with Aboriginal history in the west, and available historical accounts indicate an agreeable and cooperative working arrangement between Kean and the Blood and other local tribes. Numerous historical events were filmed over the course of the film's production, such as the signing of various treaties and even Sitting Bull's sojourn north of the American border and his subsequent, peaceful dealings with the NWMP.

2.2 "The Indians of the Blackfoot Confederacy were most intelligent, and gave serious heed to all details of the subject in hand – Treaty Number 7."

The *Calgary Herald*'s report that the film featured "a backdrop of thousands of Indians" may have been an overstatement, but on-location photographs taken during filming certainly indicate that number was likely at least in the hundreds.[37] The imperial and colonial connotations and implications of the film and its production notwithstanding, the degree of collaboration with First Nations communities does appear pronounced and atypical for its time. If we are to believe the press reports on these interactions, the Blood reserve enthusiastically embraced the production (see figure 2.2). Reportedly, there were one or two "aged chiefs" present who, as young men, had attended some of the events that were recreated for the film.[38] Kean was even made an honourary chief within the tribe for his role in bringing the movies to them, and he was given the title Oh-Mack-ke-si-na-Ki, which translates as "the first who writes pictures."[39]

Although the film was not, as originally planned, ready for the British Empire Exposition in England that summer, 1924 was unquestionably the peak of the production's sense of optimism and artistic creativity. Unfortunately, the finish line was still far away, and as production stretched into 1925 things began to sour. While numerous issues plagued Kean and his crew, financing remained the most pressing. MacBeth was apparently again enlisted to help shore up additional production funds, but, perhaps sensing the increasingly risky venture the film was turning into, many potential investors declined the opportunity. Perhaps most notably, in a letter addressed to MacBeth, Grant Hall, the CPR's vice president, politely turned down a request for an investment of $10,000.[40] The production seemed to hit rock bottom in November 1925, when the Hotel Vancouver, where the Western Pictures Company and the *Policing the Plains* Syndicate had set up shop, became increasingly concerned about the outstanding balance they had incurred.[41] Although less is known about the production of the film throughout 1926, Duffy and Mattison suggest it is not unrealistic to assume that it was characterized by intense periods of filmmaking coupled with bouts of both desperate fundraising and inactivity.[42] Amazingly, despite the financial obstacles, the film finally emerged as a finished product in 1927 after three full years of production.

Scholars of Canadian film history have often observed that the fundamental challenge facing the Canadian film industry is one of distribution and exhibition, rather than one of production. For Kean, as if the production of the film were not difficult enough, its exhibition constituted yet another major challenge. Duffy and Mattison reveal that the film was originally supposed to premiere at the Canadian National Exhibition in 1927, but various problems related to the quality of the negative and missing footage meant a screenable print was simply not produced in time.[43] After much haranguing with distributors, the only exhibition Kean was able to secure for the film was at the Royal Alexandra Theatre in Toronto, for the week of 19 December (see figure 2.3). It bears noting that this theatre was, in industry parlance, a "legitimate" theatre, dedicated primarily to live performances rather than film screenings. It therefore operated largely outside of the parameters of the film distribution and exhibition infrastructure in Canada, which Kean maintained he was simply unable to penetrate. Nevertheless, *Policing the Plains* was reasonably well promoted in Toronto, with page two advertisements in the Toronto daily papers. Reviews appeared in the *Globe* and the *Toronto Star* on 20 December, following opening night, and were highly favourable. The *Globe* review was a rave, with particular praise bestowed on the film's "remarkable faithfulness" and its ability to showcase Canadian history "unvarnished and free from all imaginative dramatics." It concluded with no less than an endorsement of the film as "emphatically one of the significant screen achievements which no one can afford to miss."[44] The

2.3 The Royal Alexandra Theatre for the opening of *Policing the Plains* (1927).

Toronto Daily Star was a little more tempered in its enthusiasm but nevertheless full of praise. The reviewer paid attention to the "splendid veracity" of historical detail, and characterized the screening itself as "the most auspicious presentation of an all-Canadian film ever made." However, seen as lacking was the "dramatic technique" of the film, which the reviewer felt was somewhat sacrificed in the name of historical detail.[45]

Despite these rather favourable reviews, once *Policing the Plains* completed its week-long stint in Toronto it was never screened theatrically again.[46] Kean blamed the rigid and oppressive system in place in the Canadian film industry that favoured American studios. In fact, Kean was called to testify during the Combines Investigation Act of 1930, which led an inquiry into monopolistic practices in the industry led by the "cartel" of American business interests.[47] Though little concrete change emerged from these proceedings, they were nevertheless an opportunity for Kean to state his long-held complaints on record.

The example of *Policing the Plains* does not exactly challenge the prevailing mythologies surrounding the Canadian film industry, and in fact it largely reinforces them. However, given how widely documented those narratives are, and how neatly *Policing the Plains* seems to buttress them, its absence from such accounts is all the more curious. This ultimately speaks to the impact and importance placed upon the physical materiality of film and its accessibility to later generations (which is perhaps an irony given the increasing digitization of film). *Policing the Plains* as a historical case study is a telling microcosm for the travails of Canadian filmmaking during the early decades of the industry – an industry as much characterized by absence as by presence. In this sense, that the film no longer exists to be seen by contemporary audiences is perhaps perversely fitting, however tragically unfortunate it may be.

The following anecdote is perhaps an appropriate epilogue for the saga of *Policing the Plains*. In March 1937, Omri J. Silverthorne, the chairman of the Ontario Board of Censors Motion Pictures, wrote a very brief letter to Kean inquiring about some reels of film that had been discovered in the government vaults: "We have in our film vault one parcel containing several thousand feet of standard film, which was submitted by you in December, 1927. Please advise us what you wish to do with this film."[48] A still-embittered Kean responded with a lengthy and verbose retelling of the film's long-standing ordeal, from its initial production period up until his testimony during the Combines Investigation. The correspondence seemingly ended there, with Silverthorne merely curious about what to do with the remaining film reels and apparently uninterested in this unsolicited genealogy of the film. Little has been heard of the film since, and barring any unexpected discoveries, it is considered permanently lost. Also telling is that the following year, 1938, long after Kean had abandoned filmmaking for a career in radio, he filled out a standard promotional questionnaire for the CBC Press Department. When asked if he had any accomplishments of note besides his work in radio, Kean succinctly listed "Professional writer, Horseman, Lecturer."[49] It seems that even Cowboy Kean himself had forgotten, perhaps willingly, both *Policing the Plains* and his own contributions to film history in Canada.

NOTES

1 "*Daily Mail* Airs Canada's Film Grievances," *Vancouver Province*, 20 September 1925.

2 Ibid.

3 Peter Morris, *Embattled Shadows: A History of Canadian Cinema, 1895–1939* (Montreal: McGill-Queen's University Press, 1978); Manjunath Pendakur, *Canadian Dreams and American Control: The Political Economy of the Canadian Film Industry* (Detroit: Wayne State University Press, 1990); Ted Magder, *Canada's Hollywood: The Canadian State and Feature Films* (Toronto: University of Toronto

Press, 1993); and Michael Dorland, *So Close to the States: The Emergence of Canadian Feature Film Policy* (Toronto: University of Toronto Press, 1998).

4 A copy of this clipping remains in Kean's archival files, and although the author of the letter does not mention *Policing the Plains* specifically, it could conceivably be read as an attempt to drum up publicity and interest in his film. A.D. "Cowboy" Kean Papers, Provincial Archives of British Columbia.

5 Dennis J. Duffy and David Mattison, "A.D. Kean: Canada's Cowboy Movie-Maker," *Beaver* 69, no. 1 (1989): 28–41.

6 With a few exceptions, the majority of writing on Canadian film and/or the history of the industry do not reference the film or Kean at all. An exception to this is Colin Browne, who provides a brief but valuable historical discussion of Kean. Colin Browne, *Motion Picture Production in British Columbia: 1898–1940 – A Brief Historical Background and Catalogue* (Victoria: British Columbia Provincial Museum, 1979), 22–3.

7 Of the various attempts to kickstart a Canadian film industry, the most notable failure was undoubtedly Canadian International Films' 1928 production *Carry on, Sergeant*, which was at the time, as Peter Morris describes, the Canadian industry's "most expensive flop." Morris, *Embattled Shadows*, 71.

8 Dan Streible, "The Role of Orphan Films in the 21st Century Archive," *Cinema Journal* 46, no. 3 (Spring 2007): 124–8.

9 Ina Bertrand, "The Mystery of the Missing Director," *Film History* 12 (2000): 215–25.

10 Eric de Kuyper, "Anyone for an Aesthetic of Film History," *Film History* 6 (1994): 100–09.

11 David Pierce, "The Legion of the Condemned – Why American Silent Films Perished," *Film History* 9 (1997): 5–27.

12 Stephen Teo and Vivian Lee, "Introduction: Placing Value in the Missing and the Lost," *Journal of Chinese Cinemas* 4, no. 2: 83–7.

13 Morris, *Embattled Shadows*, 90.

14 Denis J. Duffy, "British Columbia Patriotic & Educational Picture Service, 1920–1925," *Camera West: British Columbia on Film, 1941–1965* (Victoria: Provincial Archives of British Columbia, 1986); and Duffy and Mattison, "A.D. Kean: Canada's Cowboy Movie-Maker," 32.

15 Browne, *Motion Picture Production in British Columbia: 1898–1940*, 19, 22. As perhaps another telling example of the ephemerality that typifies much of the Canadian film industry from this period, Browne notes a number of such production companies that were created "virtually overnight, but none lasted long enough to file their first annual report." Canadian Historic Features was but one of these companies.

16 Pierre Berton, *Hollywood's Canada: The Americanization of Our National Image* (Toronto: McClelland and Stewart, 1975), 112.

17 Berton, *Hollywood's Canada*, 113.

18 Ibid., 121.

19 "Motion Pictures and the Theatres," *Montreal Herald*, 5 December 1925, 9.

20 Berton, *Hollywood's Canada*, 12.

21 "Glorious Record for Screen: Thousands of Indians Help Film Industry," *Calgary Herald*, 16 August 1924.

22 Michael Dawson, *The Mountie from Dime Novel to Disney* (Toronto: Between the Lines, 1998). Dawson traces the evolution of representations of the Mountie throughout the popular culture of the twentieth century.
23 Letter from Will Hays, MPPDA, Inc, to R.G. MacBeth, 28 June 1922, A.D. Kean Fonds, box 1, file 2, R.G. MacBeth Correspondence, 1921–25.
24 Letter from R.G. MacBeth to potential funding sources, A.D. Kean Fonds, box 1, file 2, R.G. MacBeth Correspondence, 1921–25.
25 Letter from Corlandt Starnes, Office of the Commissioner, Royal Canadian Mounted Police, to R.G. MacBeth, 6 April 1923, A.D. Kean Fonds, box 1, file 2, R.G. MacBeth Correspondence, 1921–25.
26 Memo from Royal Canadian Mounted Police to A.D. Kean, list of items on loan, Vancouver, 20 March 1924. A.D. Kean Fonds, box 1, file 3, Miscellaneous Production Memoranda, *Policing the Plains*, 1924.
27 Letter from H.E. Steele, CPR Press Bureau, to R.G. MacBeth, A.D. Kean Fonds, box 1, file 2, R.G. MacBeth Correspondence, 1921–25.
28 Memo for dedication card, A.D. Kean Fonds, box 1, file 3, Miscellaneous Production Memoranda, *Policing the Plains*, 1924. This was the intended opening dedication, but whether it actually appeared or not is unknown.
29 "Work Starts on Film History of Mounted Police," *Vancouver Sun*, 13 March 1924.
30 "Policing the Plains: Jubilee Events Being Filmed," *Lethbridge Herald*, 3 July 1924.
31 Duffy and Mattison, "A.D. Kean: Canada's Cowboy Movie-Maker," 34.
32 This figure would be eclipsed in 1928, when the budget of *Carry on, Sergeant* ballooned to $500,000, making it the most expensive Canadian film of the silent era. Morris, *Embattled Shadows*, 77.
33 "Macleod Gets Big Boost When Jubille Feature Shown," *Macleod Times*, 1 January 1925.
34 Press coverage of *Policing the Plains* lists the casualties as high as one hundred First Nations people, though more recent contemporary accounts of the massacre's numbers vary from sixteen to twenty-three. The massacre was recently dramatized in the CBC's adaptation of Guy Vanderhaeghe's novel *The Englishman's Boy.*
35 "Glorious Record for Screen: Thousands of Indians Help Film Industry," *Calgary Herald*, 16 August 1924.
36 "Film Massacre Scene in Reserve," *Lethbridge Herald*, 2 August 1924.
37 "Indian Movie Actors Finish Work and Turn Back to Farms," *Calgary Herald*, 2 August 1924, and "Glorious Record for Screen: Thousands of Indians Help Film Industry," *Calgary Herald*, 16 August 1924.
38 Ibid.
39 *Lethbridge Herald*, 5 August 1924. Interestingly, this is an honour that has subsequently been shared with such individuals as Pierre Berton and, more recently, Canadian Prime Minister Stephen Harper.
40 Letter from Grant Hill to A.D. Kean, 24 March 1925, and letter from Grant Hill to R.G. MacBeth, 24 March 1925, A.D. "Cowboy" Kean Papers, box 1, file 8.
41 Memo from A.D. Kean, "With Reference to the Outstanding Account of Room 145," A.D. "Cowboy" Kean Papers, box 1, file 10, Correspondence Outwards, *Policing the Plains* Productions, Ltd.

42 Duffy and Mattison, "A.D. Kean: Canada's Cowboy Movie-Maker," 37.
43 Ibid., 38.
44 Review of *Policing the Plains*, *Globe*, 20 December 1927, 12.
45 Augustus Bridle, "Cyclorama of Open Spaces is Film 'Policing the Plains,'" *Toronto Daily Star*, 20 December 1927, 15.
46 Morris suggests that the film "enjoyed a modest release across Canada" and that Kean recouped his investment, but the historical evidence does not appear to support this assertion. Morris, *Embattled Shadows*, 91.
47 Although he does no refer to Kean, Pendakur provides a detailed examination of the Combines Investigation in the film industry.
48 Letter from O.J. Silverthorne to A.D. Kean, 15 March 1937, A.D. "Cowboy" Kean Papers, box 1, file 13, Correspondence A.D. Kean – Ontario Board of Censors of Motion Pictures.
49 CBC Press Department biographical questionnaire, October 1938, A.D. "Cowboy" Kean Papers, box 1, file 17.

3 UNCOVERING CANADA'S AMATEUR FILM TRADITION

LESLIE THATCHER'S FILMS AND CONTEXTS

Charles Tepperman

UNKNOWN IN THE annals of Canadian film history, Leslie Thatcher was a star of the amateur cinema world. In the mid-1930s, Thatcher won numerous international awards, and his well-crafted short films evince a striking aesthetic sophistication. In this chapter I introduce a filmmaker whose amateur work during the 1930s made important but unrecognized contributions to Canadian film history. I also point to some persistent gaps in our understanding of film history in Canada: while recent research contests received accounts of Canadian cinema's late development and art film canon, the field remains full of blind spots and question marks. This is especially the case for the pre-National Film Board (NFB) years, before the best-known traditions of Canadian film production were institutionalized. An examination of Thatcher's films makes a re-consideration of the film production and exhibition contexts in Canada during the 1930s even more pressing. During this decade, Thatcher received international attention and even acclaim for his amateur works; and yet he remains barely a footnote in historical accounts of Canadian film.[1]

The 1930s was not a strong decade for Canadian feature film production, as the high cost of synchronized sound filmmaking remained beyond the economic feasibility of most Canadian commercial producers.[2] The decade presents something of a lull in Canadian film production, between the ambitious silent-era features and government-supported non-fiction film production of the 1920s and the watershed formation of the NFB in 1939. But if the story of Canadian film during the 1930s is not one of commercial feature-film production, then we must look elsewhere to locate its significant, but now mostly forgotten, traces. Most films produced in Canada during the 1930s were of the industrial or sponsored variety, such as the short films directed by Gordon Sparling for Associated Screen News in Montreal. Indeed, Sparling might have been the most important Canadian director of the decade, producing dozens of theatrical shorts and early Canadian sound films. But the period also saw the emergence of several successful amateur filmmakers, such as Thatcher, Frank "Budge" Crawley, and Albert Tessier. Crawley's 1930s amateur productions would stand as his proving ground en route to becoming Canada's most successful non-governmental industrial filmmaker in the post-World War II era. In the few accounts of Crawley's work, however, his amateur activities are unfortunately neglected. Similarly, Tessier was a Québécois priest and educator whose amateur filmmaking was well-known enough to result in the later naming of an award for Quebec filmmaking after him, but his films remain relatively unknown, especially in English-language scholarship. Yet it was precisely this decade, and the amateur cultures that supported Thatcher, Crawley, and Tessier's work, that contributed to the development of individual filmmakers and enabled the growth and later expansion of Canadian film culture.

The tradition and community of amateur filmmaking that Thatcher belonged to is important for several reasons. First, during the 1930s the category of amateur film encompassed a variety of styles, including documentary, experimental, and industrial works. This broad categorization designated an alternative realm of filmmaking from Hollywood's commercial mode of production and circuits of exhibition, fields of activity that were generally closed to Canadian filmmakers. Second, the porousness of the amateur film category allowed for a dynamic and vernacular mode of film expression that drew on examples and styles from elsewhere and infused them with localized significance. Thatcher's amateur films reflect this, as they blend globally circulating art cinema stylistics with their rootedness in local milieu and regional customs. Finally, amateur film culture supported and informed these filmmakers in ways that require further attention: local amateur film clubs gave filmmakers the opportunity to nurture each other's work and to participate in broader, international networks of non-mainstream film exhibition and cinephile culture.

In this chapter I will provide a brief introduction to the work of Toronto filmmaker Leslie Thatcher, commenting on three of his award-winning films in particular: *Mighty Niagara* (1933), *Another Day* (1934), and *Fishers of Grande Anse* (1935).[3] Thatcher's films provide a few key examples among many of how Canadian amateur filmmakers adopted new international stylistic vocabularies and techniques in order to present a visual account of their local surroundings. The films also raise important questions about the status of the vernacular in Canadian film history.

In linguistic terms, the vernacular refers to local usages and permutations of a larger "official" (hegemonic) language. In film studies, Miriam Hansen traces the way that Hollywood film reconfigured modernist visual strategies into a classical style, which was in turn subject to permutations and retranslations in different global contexts.[4] Canadian amateurs provide additional ways to think about vernacular filmmaking, first in terms of their geographical displacement from American and foreign art-film cultures, and second with their amateur appropriations and adaptations of other film styles. Thatcher's films are examples of each of these vernacular uses of cinema, drawing on localized contexts in formal terms that borrow from both commercial and art cinema.

With these ideas of the vernacular in mind, I will also consider the contexts within which Thatcher operated, including the Toronto Amateur Movie Club (TAMC), the Amateur Cinema League (ACL), and other local and international organizations that helped support and shape amateur activities during the 1930s. In the 1930s Thatcher was an *American Cinematographer* prizewinner and a three-time winner of the ACL's annual "Ten Best" honours.[5] More locally, I will examine the aesthetic horizon, or range of possibilities, for filmmaking in Toronto during the mid-1930s. What were the models for alternative or independent film production? What was the "art world" (to borrow Howard Becker's phrase) within which Thatcher's films emerged in Toronto? In the first part of this chapter, I will examine three of Thatcher's award-winning amateur films. Then in a shorter, second part I will sketch out some of the contextual factors around his filmmaking and movie culture in Toronto during the 1930s. Taken together, my discussion of Leslie Thatcher seeks to fill in an important gap in Canadian film history.

MIGHTY NIAGARA

About Leslie Thatcher himself, little information is available. Census records reveal that he was born in England in 1901 and moved to Canada with his family as a child in 1906, and that they settled in downtown Toronto by 1911.[6] According to Toronto city directories, Thatcher worked as a salesman for several different paper and engraving companies during the 1920s and '30s. How and when Thatcher became interested in filmmaking isn't clear, but his earliest extant film, *Mighty Niagara* (1933), is a fourteen-minute silent work that narrates a steamship voyage from Toronto to Niagara Falls. The film is structured as a polished travelogue, reminiscent of theatrical travel shorts by Burton Holmes and James

3.1 This sequence from *Mighty Niagara* is reminiscent of early "phantom ride" films, which simulated travel by positioning the camera, and therefore the spectator, at the front or window of a moving train.

FitzPatrick.[7] Carefully framed as a daytrip, it begins with the ship embarking in Toronto, proceeds to Niagara via Queenston Heights, and concludes with the sun setting as the ship returns to Toronto. In its carefully edited and narrativized form, the film distinguishes itself from the snapshot holiday films more often associated with amateur filmmaking.

But even as travel provides a structure for the film, Thatcher explores other expressive possibilities of the medium, such as the way camera movement can evoke a sensation of motion in the spectator. In one sequence, *Mighty Niagara* places the camera in the optical point of view of a traveller on a moving train. The sequence begins with an intertitle that reads: "We cross to the American side and travel the Niagara Gorge by radial." What follows is a pair of shots taken from the front and side of the radial car as it travels along the river, showing the passing scenery. This is followed by three reverse-angle shots that show the trolley from across the river and then through some trees. Finally there are several more shots taken from the front and side of the radial car, showing the

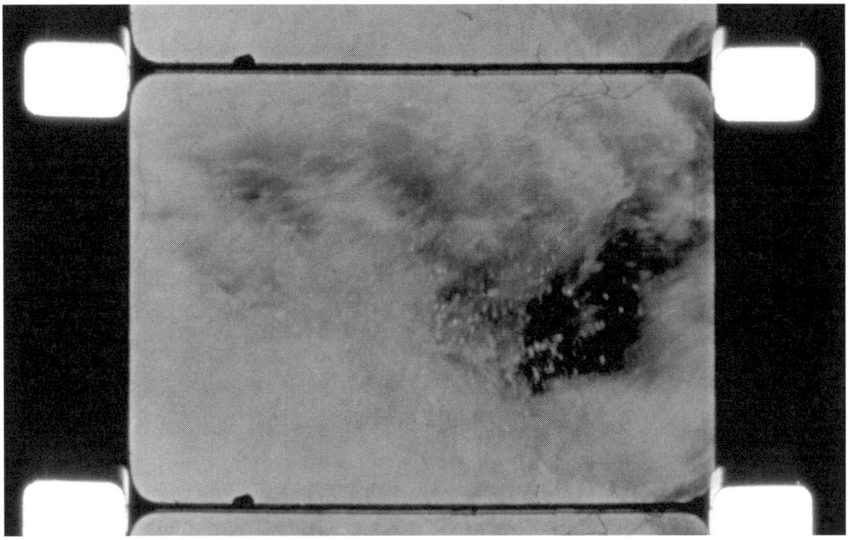

3.2 *Mighty Niagara*: "Turbulent beauty found in the rapids above the Falls."

tracks ahead and the passing rocks and rushing river. The sequence adheres to some continuity editing tenets – its use of reverse-angle shots and a consistent axis of action, for example – but its presentation of travel also evokes a sensory dimension. This sequence is reminiscent of early "phantom ride" films, which simulated travel by positioning the camera, and therefore the spectator, at the front or window of a moving train (see figure 3.1). Thatcher's use of this technique points to one way in which amateur filmmakers were rediscovering some of the earliest elements of film language and spectacle.

Thatcher's film won a silver medal in the travel films category in the 1933 *American Cinematographer* amateur movie competition, and the award citation reports, "Leslie P. Thatcher offered a well edited picture in 'Mighty Niagara' with a preponderance of good photography."[8] Much of the film's good photography is devoted to the spectacle of swirling water and churning rapids around Niagara. One sequence shows what an inter-title describes as the "turbulent beauty found in the rapids above the Falls": beginning with long shots of the river as seen from the shore, the film cuts in to closer and closer views of the swirling and churning water until the entire frame is filled with it (see figure 3.2). Films of the whirlpools at Niagara Falls were among some of the earliest films shot in

Canada, by cameramen for both the Lumière brothers and Thomas Edison, so we know that water, surf, and reflected light have a long-standing appeal to cinematographers. The visual spectacle of light and rushing water also appealed to many amateur filmmakers in the late 1920s and early '30s, most notably Ralph Steiner, whose experimental films *H_2O* (1929) and *Surf and Seaweed* (1931) won awards and circulated widely in amateur circles. Thatcher's film is a more conventional travelogue than Steiner's, but even in this short sequence his interest in using motion pictures to explore the abstract aesthetic qualities of the Falls is apparent.

As these examples demonstrate, Thatcher's film is not just a recorded journey; it is also an effort to present a range of different ways that film can capture the visual impressions of travel through light reflections, motion, and temporal change. In a way, the film provides a microhistory of cinema itself: in its presentation of a spectacle (the Falls), in its production of affect and sensation (through motion and phantom rides), and in its shaping of these materials through the sophisticated aesthetic means of continuity and expressive editing. Tom Gunning argues that many early travel films appealed to a "sensational" approach, provoking the sensation of physical movement through space. As Gunning points out, these panoramic and sensational films – perhaps like moments in Thatcher's film of a trip to Niagara – "promote a truly modern perception of landscape, one mediated by technology and speed."[9] *Mighty Niagara*, like many polished amateur travelogues, shares this preoccupation, embracing the cinema's ability to capture, and technologically aestheticize, elements of scenery, natural spectacle, or everyday life.

ANOTHER DAY

Thatcher's second film, the ten-minute silent short *Another Day* (1934), expanded his aestheticization of the everyday further, presenting a city symphony film of Thatcher's own home town. City symphonies were an early type of non-narrative film that emerged in the 1920s and presented cities like New York or Berlin in montage form, using editing to draw out some of the energy, routines, and rituals of daily life in a big city. The city symphony originated in the United States with Charles Sheeler and Paul Strand's *Manhatta* (1921), but was later seen, following Walter Ruttmann's *Berlin: Symphony of a Great City* (1927), as a primarily European form. Though associated with high-art film practices, the city symphony was also popularized in works like Fox's short film *Manhattan Medley* (1931),

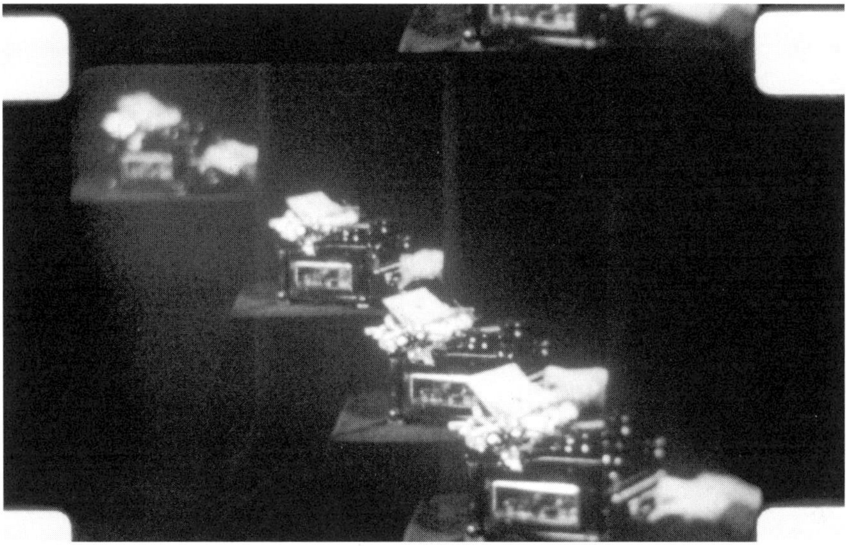

3.3. *Another Day*'s modernist fragmentation and reconstruction is demonstrated in a sequence about Saturday morning at different kinds of work.

and eventually its stylistic influence was evident in Canadian productions as well.[10] Thatcher's film begins with an intertitle that points to the similarity between all "great cities," where "the hustle and bustle which accompanies the demands of commerce ... means "just another day." The film's opening shots show distant vistas of tall buildings and busy streets, revealing that the setting is not "any city," but Toronto. Like other city symphony films, *Another Day* follows the chronology of a day's activity, fragments continuous action, and emphasizes the quotidian objects (the alarm clock, the toaster, the coffee pot) and strangers that residents of big cities encounter. In this, Thatcher appears to be making a film about "the things" that surround us, and edits these parts together in a way that constructs a new meaning.

The film's modernist fragmentation and reconstruction is best demonstrated in a sequence about Saturday morning at different kinds of work (see figure 3.3). The sequence begins with a low-angle close-up shot of the word "Offices" carved on the exterior of a building, before cutting to a shot of hands on a typewriter against a black background. This image of a typewriter is soon joined by a superimposition of itself, and then another and another until four sets of hands and typewriters

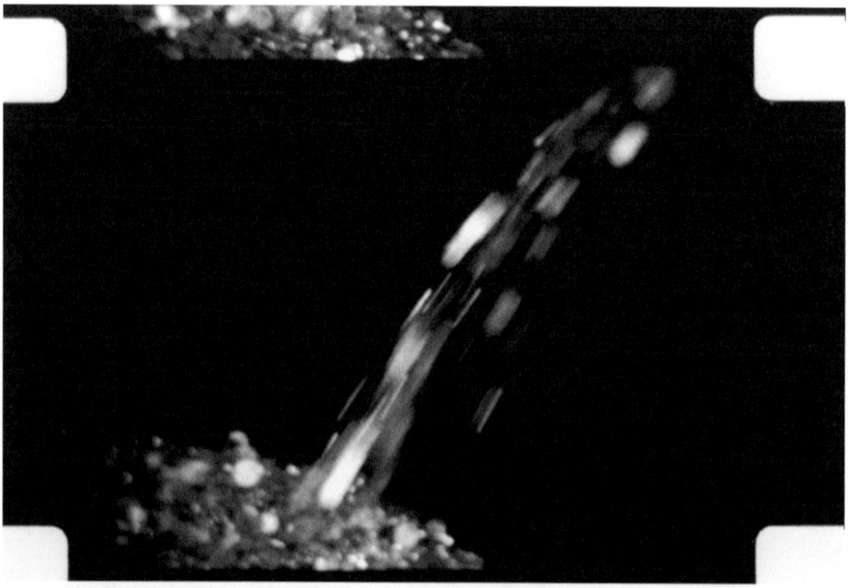

3.4. In this sequence from *Another Day*, we see an increasingly abstract depiction of the events of everyday life, as a shower of coins represents commerce.

are exposed diagonally across the frame. The next two shots duplicate this pattern of alternating exterior signs and abstracted interior actions, this time showing a sign that reads "The Bank of Toronto" before cutting to an image of coins showering into a pile against a black background (see figure 3.4). A final alternation is presented with an exterior shot of the word "Exchanges" on a building, and then a low-angle medium close-up shot of a man writing in a ledger (see figure 3.5); as the shot holds on the image of this man, the word "WORK" appears and grows in size, superimposed over him. The image of the man at his ledger fades to black as "WORK" expands to fill the screen. When the word has reached its maximum size, the film cuts to a series of six increasingly brief shots of a hammer swinging downward and across the frame against a white background (see figure 3.6). Finally, these accelerating abstractions of work give way to a shot of a carpenter swinging a hammer in an actual work situation. In this sequence, we see an increasingly abstract depiction of the events of everyday life, as commerce is represented by a shower of coins and labour by a swinging hammer. But on the other hand, signs and landmarks specify the setting once again: this is Toronto, not just the anonymous city of

3.5. An accountant at a ledger stands in for one kind of work.

3.6. And a swinging hammer represents another.

the film's opening title. Later, the film continues to develop this dialectical relationship between specificity and abstraction – there are abstractions of leisure in superimposed, swirling musical notes at a nightclub; but there are also markers of local specificity in images of Toronto's nighttime streetscape.

Thatcher's film employs modernist techniques to shape a visual record of Toronto. *Movie Makers* magazine named *Another Day* one of the ten best amateur films of 1934, and describes it as "a splendid example of the relatively simple avant garde film, so popular among European amateurs but so seldom attempted by even the advanced workers of the American continent."[11] While it is clear that the film does not present the kind of radical ideological point of view that we expect from avant-garde works, it is definitely engaged in some manner of cultural analysis. In an earlier *Movie Makers* article about montage films, critic Harry Alan Potamkin writes, "Every amateur ought to attempt to film his city or a part of it. It would be interesting to compare the data."[12] Thatcher's film allows us to do just that; on one hand, it raises Toronto to a status that is the aesthetic equivalent of the other "great cities" (like Berlin or New York) chronicled in a similar vein; but on the other hand, it provides specific details about *one* city that can be widely communicated and compared. As a film, *Another Day* might be most productively compared to a similar commercial short about Montreal called *A Rhapsody in Two Languages* (Associated Screen News, 1934). Produced by Gordon Sparling in the same year as *Another Day*, *Rhapsody* has some similar footage and at least a few identical shots, such as the image of superimposed typewriters. Though it is difficult to determine with certainty in which direction the influence flowed, Thatcher and other amateur filmmakers of this period show a propensity for absorbing circulating film styles and occasionally even appropriating entire shots, acting as early forerunners of today's remix culture. Modernist techniques and the city symphony form were evidently well-known in Canadian film circles during the early 1930s, as filmmakers like Thatcher and Sparling employed these tools to envision and analyse life in Canadian cities.

FISHERS OF GRANDE ANSE

Thatcher's third prize-winning film was the twelve-minute semi-ethnographic documentary *Fishers of Grande Anse* (1935). Like the previous two films, this one also employed the structure of "a day" to organize its narration.

This time, however, the subject matter concerned life in a remote fishing village on the south shore of the St Lawrence River. The film shows the daily routine of fishing there, providing both factual description and lyrical documentary. *Movie Makers* named it one of the ten best amateur films of 1935, and called it:

> A cinematic study of the highest order, with impeccable and often very striking photography, showing the primitive ways of men and women who live from the sea ... This picture is a restrained work of art that depicts the austere beauty of toil. Repairing boats and nets, catching and cleaning the cod, salting and storing the fish for market and the fishermen leaving for home are the raw material from which this black and white production draws its rugged and satisfying beauty.[13]

As this description suggests, the film frames non-fictional material in aestheticized ways, and indeed *Fishers*'s opening title describes it as a "documentary film." In sequences that recall John Grierson's *Drifters* (1929), the film presents the activities of the fishing life in lyrical and rhythmic terms, such as the casting and reeling in of the fishing lines. The movement of the water and texture of the rocky terrain provide visually striking compositions and backgrounds.

The film also echoes (if not directly emulates) Robert Flaherty's *Man of Aran* (1934). Flaherty's influence is particularly notable in the film's final sequence, which shows one fisherman carrying oars across a rocky terrain. Shot from several different angles and distances, this sequence situates the fisherman in his milieu and shows his craggy features against those of the rocky landscape and the sky (see figure 3.7). In 1934, *Movie Makers* referred to Flaherty as "a dean of amateurs" in the subtitle of an article he penned about the filming of *Man of Aran*. Though primarily technical in nature, this article linked issues of technology – and particularly the use of telephoto lenses – with a quasi-ethnographic impulse to capture images of people with all traces of their self-consciousness eliminated.[14] The same issue of *Movie Makers* also contained a column praising various aspects of Flaherty's film, and particularly its "plot": "Straightforward and unaffected, this presentation of the labor of the Aran Islanders could serve as a guide as to the best manner of treating similar, natural native life. Explorers and other producers of stories of

3.7. This sequence situates the fisherman in his milieu and shows his craggy features against those of the rocky landscape and the sky.

native existence *in situ* can study profitably this leaf from Mr Flaherty's book of accomplishments."[15] Some amateurs, including Thatcher, appear to have followed this advice and used films like *Man of Aran* as a model for their own travel films. Even before he made this film, *Toronto Daily Star* arts critic Augustus Bridle cited Flaherty as an important influence on Thatcher's previous works (especially Flaherty's city symphony film *24-Dollar Island*, which Thatcher probably only read about).[16] Indeed, what is striking about Thatcher's films is their well-executed adherence to these existing film conventions: not fiction film conventions, but conventions of the nascent independent art-documentary cinema. His films also reinforce the centrality of Flaherty's role as the most-recognized independent filmmaker of the era, and one whose films exerted a powerful influence on the emergence of film art, especially in Canada.

THE TORONTO AMATEUR MOVIE CLUB

During the 1930s, Thatcher's primary film community was the burgeoning international amateur film culture which included contests sponsored by Hollywood's *American Cinematographer* and New York's Amateur Cinema League. Closer to home, Thatcher was instrumental in founding the TAMC, which held its inaugural meeting at the Royal York Hotel on 12 December 1934. According to one report, 200 people attended this meeting. The organizers "had learned that there were three hundred owners of cine equipment in the City of Toronto and suburbs, and felt that there were great possibilities for an amateur movie club in Toronto."[17] The first film screened was Thatcher's *Mighty Niagara*, a fact that not only points to Thatcher's reputation among amateurs but also recalls the origins of commercial film exhibition in Canada, which some four decades prior had presented similar footage of the Falls. Several other films were also shown, including some from the ACL's library of award-winning amateur films and two sound-film productions loaned by the Associated Screen News.[18]

The TAMC was founded to support local amateur filmmakers and enthusiasts and was originally divided into two sections, one to deal with "cine" (cinematography) or technical issues, the other to produce and screen amateur "photoplays." Thatcher was the first vice president of the club and participated in its activities in a variety of ways, including writing its first group film production and organizing demonstrations of film equipment by local dealers. By 1937, when its official membership had reached ninety-one people, the club was leasing its own quarters, which satisfied at least some of the following needs: "a club room available for use at all times – an editing bench – storage facilities for unedited films – titling tables – dark-room – developing tanks and racks – photographic books – bridge table for a quiet game of bridge – social evenings such as dances and movie evenings of some outstanding pictures – office space and editorial offices for which we are sadly in need – and a permanent address."[19] Thatcher's own award-winning films predated these facilities, but they did support other amateurs' filmmaking activities and the growth of the amateur film community in Toronto.

The TAMC's newsletter, *Shots and Angles*, reveals multiple facets of amateur filmmaking work during this period. The club's activities focused primarily on three subjects: the technical improvement of films, the production and presentation of members' travel films, and the production, as a group, of short fiction films. But even if these activities suggest distinctly middlebrow attitudes toward filmmaking, the amateur moviemaker's relationship to art could sometimes be more complex. For example, editorials and short articles in *Shots and Angles* occasionally commented on the creative challenges of amateur filmmaking, as in this one from a 1937 issue:

> Our minds conceive beauty. There are certain forms of beauty in chaos. The blues and the warm browns of our earth can form beauty, or one can take the tumbled-down shacks in some of the older quarters of any of our cities and be amazed at the colours that form combinations to delight artists and cinematographers, who can compose and realize these many forms of beauty ... With our amazingly fine new colour film a person could continually find beauty in projections.[20]

The editorial continues with a discussion about the relationship between beauty and ugliness in urban scenes and then concludes by reprinting a poem by Group of Seven painter Lawren Harris called "A Note of Colour." It calls on painter-poet Harris for a way of describing the creative composition of urban milieu, in ways that also resonate with Thatcher's city symphony *Another Day*. Though Thatcher's film was black and white, both of these instances present the artist-filmmaker observing and framing imagery that is not traditionally beautiful subject matter and presenting it in a way that makes viewers see it anew.

In a similar vein, another article in *Shots and Angles* foregrounds the role of an individual filmmaker's creative intervention in producing a film that was completely individual or personal: "It is indeed, one of the strongest lures of our hobby that a man can stamp his personality on his film so definitely and vitally that it is, in effect, a picture of his own mind – his own thoughts – and his own reactions to the place and circumstances he sets out to depict."[21] Understood in this way, amateur non-fiction filmmaking was not just an act of reproducing the visible world, but also included the possibility of filtering, perhaps even modernizing, our vision of both familiar spaces like the city, and also more exotic destinations like Niagara Falls and Grande Anse. Both Thatcher's films and these *Shots and Angles* articles reflect an effort to interpret and adapt ideas about contemporary art-making to local amateur, that is to say vernacular, filmmaking circumstances.

Apart from the TAMC's activities, Toronto was not a city with any significant independent or art film culture during the 1930s. As early as 1926, critics in Toronto had bemoaned the absence of a film society or "little theatre" where films that catered to more serious and sophisticated tastes could be presented. They pleaded for a venue to show artistic works like *The Cabinet of Dr. Caligari* and *Ballet Mécanique*, which were otherwise only read about in Toronto.[22] In 1935, Bridle renewed this call for a small theatre for art films, arguing that artistic and serious films came to Toronto too infrequently because the theatre chains did not believe they would be profitable enough.[23] The decade that is bookended by these two calls marked a period of flourishing international art cinema, but in Toronto the challenging works of Eisenstein, Murnau, and Leger, among many others, were known almost entirely second hand, via print accounts and the individual reports from people who travelled abroad. Thatcher's films, and other works of amateur or non-commercial nature, found their only exhibition venues among clubs like the TAMC or other groups of specialized audiences. While Thatcher's films were lauded abroad, the absence of a "little" specialized theatre for non-commercial films in Toronto meant they found only a very narrow audience in the film-maker's hometown.

In the absence of a robust art-film culture, Flaherty's films were repeatedly held up as exemplars of independent and artistic filmmaking in Toronto's press (as they were by the ACL). Fuelling Flaherty's stature in Toronto even further was his status as a native son: a former pupil of Upper Canada College whose early photography and film efforts had been supported and encouraged by Bridle. In several articles, Bridle recalls the early and non-theatrical presentations of Flaherty's films in Toronto, first of his early footage of the Inuit in 1914 (predating his 1922 *Nanook of the North*), and then the later private presentation of *Moana* at Toronto's Arts and Letters Club, prior to the film's censorship in Ontario.[24] When Flaherty's *Man of Aran* arrived in Toronto in January 1935, it was with much critical fanfare. In his review, Bridle describes *Aran* as, "so great an original sensation in pictography that new words rush to be born to describe it."[25] Bridle remarks on the "matter-of-fact sublimity" of Flaherty's camerawork and claims he is "the world's greatest outpost cameraman – from Toronto." If not exactly a box-office hit, the film played for several months in Toronto theatres.[26]

Given his prominence in Toronto and the relative paucity of a more robust film "art world," it is perhaps not surprising that Thatcher's films so clearly recall Flaherty's. But this resemblance should not be understood as a shortcoming, so much as his vernacular reworking of prominent film styles. Indeed, what the ACL and Toronto critics alike so often held up as significant about Flaherty was the way his attention to camera composition and narration elevated non-fictional materials above the status of mere snapshots. In a 1934 *Toronto Daily Star* profile of Thatcher and his award-winning films, Bridle praises the amateur's style in these terms, and notes his films' debt to Flaherty. Commenting on *Mighty Niagara* and *Another Day*, Bridle remarks, "Both these films are examples of camera-thinking and storycraft as distinct from snapshot values."[27] For Flaherty, and the amateurs who emulated his approach to filmmaking, the cinema's most important quality was its revelatory capacity; in the hands of filmmakers who were patient, careful observers the cinema had the capacity to record and transform the documentary materials of everyday life.

CONCLUSION

In this chapter, I have examined a filmmaker whose amateur work during the 1930s made important but unrecognized contributions to Canadian film history. During this decade, Leslie Thatcher received international attention and even acclaim for his amateur works. His prize-winning amateur films screened around North America and Europe during the 1930s and belonged to a "first wave" of North American amateur filmmaking: works that staked a claim to the film's role as a new modern art form. Some of Thatcher's significance emerges from the films themselves, which are vivid and complex documents of travel and everyday life. They transposed and adapted visual strategies from more famous travelogue, experimental, and ethnographic films of the day, and in this sense suggest the vernacular reworking of these forms by Canadian amateurs. But Thatcher's significance also resides in the case he presents for considering the context of film art at a particular moment: a young filmmaker struggling against somewhat inhospitable circumstances, that is to say, a city without much in the way of a robust film "art world" to support his work. Of course, the question of making Canada hospitable for the production, circulation, and appreciation of film is one that continues to perplex scholars and policymakers alike.

By the end of the 1930s, Thatcher appeared to be moving toward the production of industrial and sponsored films. The last of his films to be recognized in amateur circles was a film that bridged amateur and industrial filmmaking, *Techniques and Principles of Spinal Anaesthesia with Nupercaine*, which was named one of *Movie Makers*' ten best for 1939 in the "special class" of films that were made for financial gain.[28] Thatcher continued to be involved with film production after the 1930s, making two short films with the NFB in the early 1940s and establishing his own company, Thatcher Film Productions, around the same time. From 1939 until the end of the 1960s, this company produced a range of non-theatrical, industrial, and television films, but it is not clear whether filmmaking was Thatcher's main source of income or just a semi-professional (which is to say, semi-amateur) sideline.[29] In shifting from amateur activities to industrial or sponsored production, Thatcher was not alone; Budge Crawley followed a similar path, receiving numerous amateur filmmaking awards in the 1930s before establishing his successful Crawley Films production company after World War II. How many other Canadians followed this trajectory from amateur to commercial filmmaker? In tracing the complex pathways between independent and industrial filmmaking, as well as creative and documentary production, in Canadian film history there is still much work to be done. By the time the history of Canadian cinema was starting to be written several decades later, Thatcher's contribution to Canadian film was nearly forgotten.

LESLIE THATCHER FILMOGRAPHY

This preliminary listing of films by Leslie Thatcher illustrates his trajectory from amateur to industrial filmmaker (via the NFB) and provides a starting point for further research. Extant films are marked with an asterisk.

**Mighty Niagara* (1933)
**Another Day* (1934)
**Fishers of Grande Anse* (1935)
In Old Quebec (c. 1937)
Murder at Midnight (c. 1937 – TAMC Club Film directed by Thatcher)
Techniques and Principles of Spinal Anaesthesia with Nupercaine (1939)
From Cartier to Confederation (1941 – NFB – photographed by Thatcher)
Flight of the Dragon (1942 – NFB)
** The Story of Ingram and Bell* (c. 1944)

Thatcher Film Productions ca. 1939–1951[30]

The Key to Better Living (Frigidaire Products of Canada Ltd)
Crowning Achievement (Frigidaire Products of Canada Ltd)
Save that Pig (Canada Packers Ltd)
California Shoe Production (Bata Shoe Company, Ltd)
**The Quality of Mercy* (The Salvation Army of Canada)

More Thatcher Film/TV Productions ca. 1940–67[31]

The Living World
All Hail the Premier
He Who Would Valiant Be
Career Girl
Dr. H. Radar – Interview
Stagier – Interview
I Was a Stranger
The Impossible Bargain
Ornamental Iron
Music and Message
Choose You This Day (Salvation Army – colour series)

NOTES

1 Seth Feldman and Joyce Nelson, eds., *Canadian Film Reader* (Toronto: Peter Martin Associates, 1977), 48. The author would like to thank Josephine Black and the Toronto Film and Video Club for providing access to the club's films and documents; Paul S. Moore for helping track down some information about Thatcher; and Anthony Kinik for sharing his research on city symphony films.

2 Varrick Frissell's *The Viking* is a significant exception, as were the "quota quickies" produced in British Columbia – both examples of American-produced films in Canada.

3 These films first came to my attention via a list of the Amateur Cinema League's Ten Best Winners assembled and published by Alan Kattelle in 2003; see Alan D. Kattelle, "The Amateur Cinema League and Its Films," *Film History* 15, no. 2 (2003): 238–51. I was able to track down Thatcher's extant films in the library of the Toronto Film and Video Club, the descendant of the club Thatcher helped found in the 1930s. Local amateur movie clubs survive in dwindling numbers today, but still represent fascinating and neglected areas of motion picture activity.

4 Miriam Hansen, "The Mass Production of the Senses: Classical Cinema as Vernacular Modernism," in *Reinventing Film Studies*, ed. Christine Gledhill and Linda Williams (London: Oxford University Press, 2000), 332–50.

5 Founded in 1926, the ACL was a New York-based international organization that promoted the rise of amateur filmmaking and culture in many ways, including holding competitions and publishing *Movie Makers* magazine; Thatcher was a member of the ACL as early as 1934.

6 Fifth Census of Canada, 1911, retrieved from Library and Archives Canada, "Census of Canada, 1911," accessed 3 June 2014, http://www.bac-lac.gc.ca/eng/census/1911/pages/1911.aspx.

7 Holmes and FitzPatrick were two well-known travelogue personalities whose short films were widely seen as a regular part of commercial movie exhibitions during the 1920s and '30s. For more about the history of travelogues see Jeffrey Ruoff, ed., *Virtual Voyages: Cinema and Travel* (Durham, NC: Duke University Press, 2006).

8 "8 mm. Picture Ranks High in 1933 Competition," *American Cinematographer*, December 1933, 342. During the 1930s, *American Cinematographer* catered to an amateur readership by publishing a monthly section devoted to amateur issues, and by holding annual movie competitions for most of the decade.
9 Tom Gunning, "'The Whole World within Reach': Travel Images without Borders," in *Virtual Voyages*, ed. Jeffrey Ruoff (Durham, NC: Duke University Press, 2006), 37.
10 Anthony Kinik, "City of Contrasts: *Rhapsody in Two Languages* and the Politics of Modernity" (paper presented at FSAC 2009).
11 "The Ten Best," *Movie Makers*, December 1934, 513.
12 Harry Alan Potamkin, "The Montage Film: Europe's Contribution to the Art of Editing," *Movie Makers*, February 1930, 89.
13 "The Ten Best for 1935," *Movie Makers*, December 1935, 515 and 550.
14 Robert Flaherty, "Filming Real People: The Dean of Amateurs Tells How He Made His *Man of Aran*," *Movie Makers*, December 1934, 516.
15 "Critical Focusing – *Man of Aran*," *Movie Makers*, December 1934, 517.
16 Augustus Bridle, "Leslie Thatcher's Hobby is Rewarded," *Toronto Daily Star*, 22 December 1934, 8.
17 Betty Peterson, *The Toronto Movie Club: Its First Fifty Years, 1934–1984* (Toronto: pamphlet, nd. [1984]): 1.
18 Ibid., 1–2.
19 Cliff Shorney, "Club Rooms – Pro and Con," *Shots and Angles*, November 1936, 2.
20 "Editor's Note," *Shots and Angles*, May 1937, 1. The "new" colour film referred to here is likely Kodachrome film, introduced for 16 mm in 1935 and 8 mm in 1936. Kodachrome succeeded the less successful Kodacolor process (which had been available since 1928) and was widely used by TAMC members.
21 "An Editorial by the Club President," *Shots and Angles*, November 1937, 1.
22 Celluloid, "Needed, A Little Theatre for Film Connoisseurs," *Toronto Daily Star*, October 1926, 8.
23 Augustus Bridle, "High-Quality Films Flop at Box-Office," *Toronto Daily Star*, 15 June 1935, 8. In 1936, Bridle reported that the Royal Ontario Museum was developing plans to screen less-mainstream fare on a regular basis, but it is unclear if this ever came to fruition; Augustus Bridle, "Films Intensely National Waiting to Cross Borders" *Toronto Daily Star*, 28 March 1936, 9.
24 "Waves 500 ft. High Seen in New Film," *Toronto Daily Star*, 12 May 1934; and Augustus Bridle, "Censor Has Banned Film which Artists Acclaim as Wonderful Picture," *Toronto Daily Star*, 4 February 1926, 1 and 35.
25 Augustus Bridle, "'Man of Aran' Saga of Epic Proportions," *Toronto Daily Star*, 19 January 1935, 8.
26 Bridle, "High Quality," 8.
27 Augustus Bridle, "Leslie Thatcher's Hobby is Rewarded," *Toronto Daily Star*, 22 December 1934, 8.
28 Between 1936 and 1947, the ACL's annual "Ten Best" contest included awards for sponsored films, a decision that complicates our understanding of amateur work as non-remunerative. Thatcher's *Techniques* appears to be lost, but the award citation describes the film as follows: "Imagine, if you can, a subject which would be harder to present in motion pictures than the effects of a spinal anaesthetic ... Because most of the action takes place within the body, it

was necessary to do some real thinking before a suitable motion picture presentation could be worked out ... A considerable use of X-rays served to show clearly just how the hypodermic needle should be handled, while well photographed diagrams and models aid the film's clarity ... The picture is a study in straightforward exposition and, as such, it should serve its sponsors admirably. It is to be noted that Mr Thatcher showed admirable restraint in his brief shots of operations. While sufficient for the medical man, they are not too long or gruesome for a lay audience." "The Ten Best and the Maxim Memorial Award," *Movie Makers*, December 1939, 633–4.

29 *Business Screen,* February 1951; and *Business Screen Annual*, 1967, 188.

30 *Business Screen*, March–April 1951, 56.

31 *Business Screen Annual*, March 1967, 188.

4 "MENTAL PROPHYLAXIS"
CRAWLEY FILMS, MCGRAW-HILL EDUCATIONAL FILMS, AND ORPHAN CINEMA

Scott MacKenzie

For Bill O'Farrell

MY RESEARCH ON Crawley Films began with one of many visits with the late Bill O'Farrell, who was chief of film preservation at the National Archives of Canada for many years. Bill was incredibly generous in allowing scholars and researchers access to the archive's holdings, making great swathes of uncatalogued and otherwise orphaned material available for consultation. Bill was especially proud of the Crawley Films collection, as his father, Bill O'Farrell, Sr, had worked there for many years, starting as a truck driver and eventually becoming vice president. One of the many impressive aspects of this collection are the complete production files for a majority of the films produced by Crawley, including the educational films that the company made for New York publisher McGraw-Hill. Bill posted the following account of this aspect of the collection on www.archive.org:

> After production was completed, McGraw-Hill did unfortunately acquire the original elements for all their Crawley productions, and years later they all were discarded, lost, destroyed – whatever term you wish to use. Unlike most sponsored business film companies that wasn't the case for the majority of the Crawley films. Over 30,000 cans are stored at the Library and Archives Canada, along with a large collection of production files and stills. Many of these can only be seen on site by appointment. Amazingly, the actual production files regarding the Crawley-made McGraw-Hill films do exist. They include internal company memos, production data, scripts and revisions, budgetary data, animation and titling requests, telegrams and mail between Ottawa and New York, the

> whole range of production data, inside the studio and its relationship with the sponsor. It's exceedingly rare that such files have been saved anywhere for these types of films.[1]

In this chapter, I draw on the production files Bill made available to me on one such visit, detailing the rich possibilities for research on educational and "mental hygiene" films afforded by the archive's preservation of Crawley's production files. Bill was an orphan film archivist before there was an orphan cinema movement; his commitment to marginal, industrial, amateur, and ephemeral film was *pur et dur*. For these reasons, this chapter is dedicated to him, memorializing his commitment to the as-of-yet unwritten history of unknown Canadian cinemas.[2]

MENTAL HYGIENE: ORIGINS AND EDUCATIONAL REFORMS

In this chapter, I consider a group of mental hygiene films in the Health for Effective Living series produced in the 1950s for McGraw-Hill by the Canadian production house Crawley Films, along with scripts and the correspondence between the firms. In particular, I focus on the production file of one film, *Should You Drink?* (1958), as a case study. These documents shed light on the at times perverse conceptualisation of the role played by both the family and also education in then-contemporary North American culture, allowing one to examine the behind-the-scenes drive toward middle-class conformity undertaken in post-World War II educational films.

To situate the importance of Crawley's educational films, I first consider the central role played by the concept of mental hygiene in North American education in the late 1940s and early 1950s. While the educational uses of the cinema date back to Thomas Edison's earliest productions, a specific genre of educational film emerged after the war. Drawing heavily on the mode of address and propagandistic underpinnings found in war-time training documentaries, mental hygiene films grew out of a series of debates arising around the restructuring of primary and secondary education to not only include traditional forms of knowledge (readin', writin', 'rithmetic) central to the educational process, but to also inculcate ideas of sociability, conformity, and citizenship. Classic educational films such as *Shy Guy* (Coronet, 1947), *Dating: Do's and Don'ts* (Coronet, 1949), *A Date with Your Family* (Simmell-Meservey, 1950), *Personal Hygiene for Boys* (Coronet, 1952), and *Gang Boy* (Sid Davis, 1954) all function as attempts to introduce – and I am tempted to say inflict – notions of conformity onto the children and adolescents of middle-class America. Because of the overbearing presence of these precepts in the philosophy of mental hygiene, many of the films now associated with the movement seem quite obviously both naive and reactionary. Nevertheless, it is instructive to note that the first producers of this brand of educational cinema were very much concerned with educational reform – albeit a kind of reform that proselytized a Stepford Wives-like conformity among adolescents – and thought of themselves as progressives.

The mental hygiene film movement emerged at a time when both the left and right wings of the American political spectrum were obsessed with educational reform. These concerns manifested themselves in a myriad of approaches and platforms, all devoted to reimagining education and the psychology of childhood and adolescence. Indeed, the key mental hygiene films emerged at the same time as Benjamin Spock's first edition of *Baby and Child Care* in 1946, an influential text that championed a progressive, nontraditional approach to child rearing, turning away from behaviourist practices and instead drawing on the then-current insights offered by psychoanalytic practice.[3] Spock's methodological shift, however, was at odds with what the mental hygienists considered "progressive." Their progressive tendencies were greatly offset by their generalized belief in the positive role that conformity played as the backbone not only to education but also to social acceptability. Writing on the educational ethos of the time, Danny Gregory notes:

> Schoolchildren would be taught useful things: how to dress, how to fit in with each other, how to stay healthy, how to be workers ... The deeply anti-intellectual mood of the times translated into suspicion of abstraction and anything not patently "useful" ... This radical approach had a highly conservative goal: to mold children to fit into existing slots, under the guise of self-actualization. For much of the 1940s and 1950s, this was the main thrust of public education in America, instilling the same bland values in all of us.[4]

The mental hygiene movement found its way into educational films in 1946 with the release of George Blake's film about the socially acceptable ways for a proper young girl to comport herself at a party, entitled *You and Your Family* (B.K. Films, 1946).[5] The term "mental hygiene" itself has a much longer history. The concept emerged in 1908, when Clifford W. Beers, a recovering psychiatric patient, wrote *A Mind that Found Itself*, an account based on his experiences of how he felt the treatment of the "insane" could be improved and how "insanity" itself could be prevented through mental hygiene.[6] Beers's book was a success, and the general theory of mental hygiene developed quite quickly, leading to the founding of the National Committee for Mental Hygiene in 1909. However, it was only during the 1930s that the notion of mental hygiene gained any kind of truly popular currency. Its influence expanded greatly during the Depression, and by the mid-1930s mental hygiene principles appeared in education textbooks. For instance, in his 1935 textbook *Educational Psychology*, William A. Kelly summarizes mental hygiene in the following manner:

> Mental hygiene may be described as sanitary engineering in the field of psychology. The purpose of mental hygiene is to prevent mental disorders; to acquire habits of healthful activity, both physical and mental. Mental hygiene is mental prophylaxis. This means the scope of mental hygiene is the preventions of all the conditions which bring about maladjustment ... It has for its purpose the development of wholesome, hygienic habits, attitudes, and interests that constitute a normal integrated personality. The chief aim is normality. An individual is considered to be normal when he is able to adjust himself to his environment; when he is capable of performing a significant task; when he possesses the ability to get along peaceably in the social groups in which he is a member; when he knows and observes the moral law; when he seeks to achieve the end for which he was created. Integration signifies the coördination of the powers of the intellect, of will and of emotions into a unit. The chief characteristic of an integrated personality is self-control.[7]

The rise of this kind of "mental prophylaxis" must be understood against the backdrop of the Great Depression and World War II. In many ways, it was a genuine, albeit paranoid, response to the social and political instability of the previous twenty years. Parents were concerned about the lives that their children had already experienced. As Ken Smith notes:

> The kids in American schools in 1946 had never known prosperity or peace. Twelve years of economic privation had been followed by five years of domestic upheaval during the bloodiest war in human history. Adults remembered what had happened to American children after World War I. That conflict produced – or at least was popularly believed to have produced – the Lost Generation of the 1920s, young people who viewed the world through sceptical eyes, who abandoned traditional values and responsibility for shallow, hedonistic pleasures.[8]

America was striving not only to produce "well-adjusted" kids, but also ones who would broadly share all the same attitudes and dispositions and who would value social acceptance over individuality. This American take on eugenics was meant to lead not only to social acceptability, but also to a productive, non-disruptive labour force.

In *The Lonely Crowd*, an influential study of the post-war American psyche, David Riesman illustrates why mental hygiene was gaining prominence in American schools at the time. Its publication in 1950 introduced a series of terms that can be seen as the backbone of the psychology and educational philosophy underlying the mental hygiene film. Riesman introduces the term "other-directed," and describes it in the following manner:

> What is common to all the other-directed people is that their contemporaries are the source of direction for the individual – either those known to him or those with whom he is indirectly acquainted, through friends and through the mass media. This source is of course "internalized" in the sense that dependence on it for guidance in life is implanted early. The goals towards which the other-directed person strives shift with that guidance: it is only the process of striving itself and the process of paying close attention to the signals from others that remain unaltered through life.[9]

Riesman's other-directed individual, postulated as ascendant in America, is precisely the kind of child mental hygiene films were attempting to produce: children and adolescents who were "well-socialized" through an overall desire to fit-in by conforming to a middle-class projection of what was and was not socially acceptable. Unlike the propagandistic "hammer" of the documentary, conceptualized as a positive national and social force during the war years by everyone from John Grierson to Joseph Goebbels, mental hygiene worked by engendering fear not of a threat from outside to the self and one's own personal (capitalistic, consumptive) needs, but of the noticeable presence of difference within one's own culture. One was no longer fighting for ideological ideals formulated around the political structure of the nation-state; one was now fighting for sublimation, which in due time became the new ideological ideal in the United States, as is evident with McCarthyism, HUAC, and the Kefauver Commission. And, in terms of the mental hygiene educational film, Crawley Films played a key role in this development.

FILMS INTO UNIFORM

Between 1945 and 1960, there were approximately 3,000 mental hygiene films produced in North America, an average of 200 per year (in contrast, each of the Big Five Hollywood studios produced on average twenty-eight films, or 140 in total, per year between 1943 and 1949). Almost all of them were produced by independent production companies on the margins of the film industry in cities like San Francisco, Chicago, and Ottawa. It is easy to generalize and claim that these films, made by small-timers who wanted to enter the film business by any means necessary, only paid lip service to new formulations of "progressive education" and that it is precisely for these reasons that the films – which, under the guise of social conformity, explored subjects from sex to drugs to dating to driver safety – were as stilted and wooden as they were. Indeed, many of these films are both formally and ideologically atrocious when examined from a contemporary perspective. Yet it is easy to mistake ideological dogma for simple-minded filmmaking. While these films may not have single-handedly reprogrammed the socially unsociable youth of the 1950s, the debates that surrounded their production were more complex than they might first appear. Indeed, the production and the reception of these films ought to be reconsidered for at least two reasons: because of the prevalence of discourses about social conformity that pervaded both academic and popular writing at the time, and because the ubiquity of the films themselves points toward their importance. As Robert Eberwein notes, by 1950, "20,471 or 84 percent of all public high schools had 27,257 projectors." By 1954, it was estimated in one report that the number was closer to 100,000.[10] Similar statistics can be found for Canada. In the 10

December 1956 edition of *Crawley Commentary*, the in-house newsletter for Crawley Films, Graeme Fraser notes: "We find 4,500 16 mm projectors in Canadian schools, plus 4,000 filmstrip projectors. Available are over 40,000 16 mm prints (over a fifth in colour) and 20,000 filmstrips. Advertisers and associations will be interested to know that the provinces now report 827 sponsored motion pictures. A total of 7,331 schools obtain films and the annual number of school screenings is estimated to be in the excess of 60,000."[11] This illustrates that films were more widely screened in schools than in movie houses and points to the ways in which the mental hygiene film, and educational films in general, permeated contemporary North American media (sub)consciousness. (Incidentally, it also may begin to explain why the effects of these films live on as a kind of mass-mediated unconscious in *avant-garde* and found-footage film.)[12]

ALCOHOL AND ELIXIRS

Between 1950 and 1962, Crawley Films produced forty-five films for McGraw-Hill's Text-Film Department, the majority between 1955 and 1958. Most of these films, with titles such as *Discipline during Adolescence* (1958), *How Much Affection?* (1958), *Social Acceptability* (1958) and *Should You Drink?* (1958), quite obviously address coming of age and conformity.[13] And despite Ken Smith's claim that "by the late 1950s Crawley films had developed a distinct depressing quality,"[14] most of the McGraw-Hill films are fairly level-headed, given the kind of hyperbole and shock tactics that were often deployed in other mental hygiene films produced by outfits such as Centron, Coronet, and Sid Davis.

The Health for Effective Living series consisted of five films: *Quacks and Nostrums* (1958), *Choosing a Doctor* (1958), *Community Health Is up to You* (1958), *Making Life Adjustments* (1958), and *Should You Drink?* (1958). *Quacks and Nostrums* is probably the best known of these films today (and the only that is readily available; it can be seen online at the Prelinger Archive site) and is a good introduction to the series. It tells the story of a mother going to see a healer named Aluka Ka-humana, who sells her a herbal tea, or nostrum. Her son, doubtful of this "medicine," goes on a quest to learn about quacks (and to use what he finds as research for a term paper). Along the way, he finds out about other quackery claims such as the need for people to realign themselves to magnetic North through devices sold through the mail. Talking to doctors, the US Postal Service and the Food and Drug Administration, he discovers that many people "cured" by quacks are not really sick in the first place, while others feel better temporarily through the placebo effect, but become far worse later. This proves to be the case when his mother has a gallbladder attack, and eventually Aluka Ka-humana is arrested. Alternative medicine functions in a similar manner to the Communist threat in the narrative structure of *Quacks and Nostrums*, working as the foreign "other" (as can be discerned by the quack's name) that needs to be ostracized to reaffirm middle-class conformity.

Quacks and Nostrums and the other films in the Health for Effective Living series are in many ways prototypical mental hygiene films. Yet, the series's production files tell a story that goes beyond the seemingly simplistic narrative of these films, and offers an account of the thought processes that went into developing characters and the roles they play in perpetuating an image of social conformity. To illustrate this claim, I wish to examine the script development and pre-production processes that took place between Crawley Films and McGraw-Hill, focussing on one film provisionally entitled *Alcohol*, that became, after a long and arduous process, *Should You Drink?* By examining the Crawley files, it is apparent that there were quite a few tensions between Crawley and McGraw-Hill over what kind of "tone" the film should take. These tensions point to the problems in constructing "normality" as a means of social conformity through cinematic representation.

The correspondence between Crawley and McGraw-Hill in the late 1950s illustrates quite vividly the previously unknown and rarely, if ever, considered debates that went into making educational films at the time. The genesis of *Alcohol* illustrates these tensions quite well. The film tells the story of Jerry, who may or may not have a drinking problem, of his friends, who all drink to various degrees, and of his fiancée Julie, who has to put up with everyone and decide whether or not marrying Jerry is a good idea. A serious question arises from the debates surrounding the production of the film: how does one set up an identificatory process between the audience and the protagonist and provide the protagonist with a set of problems that the audience wants to see him overcome, without making the character so damaged by his social unacceptability that he alienates the viewer and disrupts the identificatory process, therefore eliminating the possibility of the viewer shifting toward the social conformity deemed as central to good citizenship?

Should You Drink? began more as an instance of shock cinema than as a social adjustment film. In a 15 July 1957 letter to Donald Carter,

Crawley's director of production, Alan Kellock, the production manager of the Text-Film department of McGraw-Hill, writes:

> We would open with a shocker sequence. First we would see a human derelict of the skidrow type, disheveled and dirty, sprawled out cold on a stoop or in the gutter. The narrator would comment on how some lives are completely wasted and useless – just existing from day to day. We would then cut to a shot of a lovely young child of about two years old, toddling about or playing on a rocking horse. The narrator would comment that once upon a time this derelict was like this and that he could have amounted to something.[15]

This voice-of-God/doom narration continues as the derelict is taken to the drunk tank, where the narrator postulates that alcoholism is a waste of human resources. This leads to the question of what causes alcoholic dereliction and a tautological answer Kellock proffered: the bottle. The bottle is both the problem and the incorrect answer to Jerry's problems; or, put another way, an individual's power of self-control, and not society, is responsible for one's problems, no matter what their origin. The proposed narration then becomes a bit hyperbolic, even for a mental hygiene film. As the camera dollies in on an empty bottle of whiskey, "The narrator asks whether this is the monster of our civilization, the constant plague, the devil's ready active agent."[16] From this shot, Kellock argues, the film would then fade into the main narrative. *Should You Drink?* was not made in this manner, and Crawley's scriptwriter Carl Schubert did not follow these suggestions. This led to a series of problems between Crawley and McGraw-Hill once the first draft of the script came in.

On 3 October 1957, Kellock, not followed by Crawley, responded to the script in a letter in the following manner:

> There is an inconsistency between the way we visually develop the character of Jerry and the extent in the mind of his fiancee about his irresponsibility and the tendency to drink. He is also severely criticized by his friends behind his back, and again this criticism does not seem justified by the way we develop Jerry's character. It is possible that part of this weakness is inherent in the script but we feel, and believe [director] George Gorman agrees, that most of the weakness stems from the way we visualize Jerry on the screen.[17]

Kellock obviously believed that the conceptualisation of Jerry on-screen – his actions and behaviours – as of yet did not justify the concerns of those around him; he wanted the actions to be more extreme. The character of Jerry was then developed in this direction. Following on from these epistolary interventions, Gorman reported to scriptwriter Schubert the following about his conversations with McGraw-Hill's production manager on 20 November 1957. This time the characterisation of Jerry has swung too far toward being an alcoholic basket case:

> [Kellock] thinks the general structure is all right but feels more work has to be done on it before it can be considered ready.
> He has two specific comments to make. The first deals with Jerry, the alcoholic. He feels he is now a case for psychiatry and as such he is too far gone for discussion by the intended audience. He feels, and I am inclined to agree, that Julie becomes rather silly in wasting her time with him. Al feels that Jerry has to be toned down a bit. I think this can be done, don't you? The other thing concerns the dialogue during the party. He feels it is a little stiff and stilted and not the type of chatter that results from having a few sociable drinks before dinner. Perhaps "stiff" and "stilted" are the wrong words – "dull" is more applicable.[18]

As the problems could not be easily resolved, others were consulted. Kellock wrote to Gorman on 4 February 1958 to convince him that the "suggestions" script consultant Stephen Lewis offered improved the film and its message. Kellock writes that Lewis felt that the film:

> Suffered from too much emphasis on the problem of alcoholism as a disease because of the attention we were giving to Jerry as an out-and-out alcoholic. There was no question but that Jerry in the previous script needed psychiatric help and he was probably too far gone for anyone to even consider the possibility of his marrying Julie. Steve has attempted to shift this emphasis back, so that Jerry is somewhere between a moderate drinker and an alcoholic, and some argument can still be made for the two of them to get married.
> I think you will agree that Steve's suggested revision actually could streamline and simplify the presentation.[19]

One begins to see the underlying tension guiding the production of the film and its need to fit in with the period's dominant notion of mental hygiene. While Gorman and Crawley thought they were producing a film about alcoholism – which would make sense, as the main character was portrayed as an alcoholic – McGraw-Hill was actually making a film that only used alcoholism to elucidate the ways in which social acceptability is the cornerstone of proper socialization, which leads to the real payoff of the film: not sobriety, but marriage. Kellock and Lewis could thus argue that a film called *Should You Drink?* focuses too much on alcoholism. Nevertheless, Gorman did not agree with the streamlining of the presentation of the effects of alcohol; responding to McGraw-Hill's comments offered by Lewis, Gorman granted that Lewis's changes made Jerry "less of a psychiatric case," but he nevertheless wrote the following to Kellock on 20 February 1958:

> The last half of the party scene from the time-lapse as outlined by Stephen Lewis does not ring true to me. I am rather inclined to think that Jerry is just what the party needed and that everyone would not be annoyed with him. After all, they have been taking on a little steam themselves. And unless we give him something to do, like spilling a drink on his hostess' dress or on Julie's which, as a result of the reaction from the other guests, would make him feel repentant I don't see how, without cause, we can expect him to throw off the effects of the liquor for a moment and then assume them again.[20]

As production hit its crisis point, and arguments became not only conceptual but also fiscal – much like *Apocalypse Now!* (1979), the script's problems were not solved before shooting began – Kellock approached Budge Crawley himself to solve the outstanding issues. Kellock begins his letter by stating: "I am sorry that so many troublesome differences seem to have grown up to interfere with our working relationship, and I trust all possible points of confusion and irritation may soon be cleared up." Nevertheless, Kellock does think "it is quite important for us to see the interlock of this revised film before we proceed with final editing of the negative." Kellock goes on to describe a whole series of checks and balances he wants to have put in place so that McGraw-Hill can ensure it is getting what it wants in the film and not what Crawley thinks it needs, but ends his letter on a pleasant note, stating, "shortly after our phone conversation, your complimentary copy of the new Columbia record of Canadian Folk Songs arrived. I was delighted to receive it as our family has received many hours of enjoyment playing the record which you sent us last year made by the William McCauley Choir."[21]

Eventually, *Should You Drink?* was released, with Jerry portrayed equally as an outsider (the real disease in the time of other-directed individuals) and as an alcoholic. But the battles over the production of the film continued almost to the moment it came out. These tensions point to not only differences in terms of film style or concerns over who should foot the bill to reshoot key scenes (a cost that, after much haggling, McGraw-Hill covered), but also the inherent problem of making mental hygiene films. In order to promote conformity, educational firms and film producers needed to devise ways to show so-called deviant behaviour in a negative light, but leave enough space for the audience to identify with the deviant characters, allowing for the possibility that these characters, if they became self-controlling and morally strong, could function as the spectator's avatar. The ideological self-controlling aspect of the mental hygiene movement was far from progressive; instead, it was an attempt to impose Foucauldian models of self-regulation on children and adolescents as they came in to their adult subjectivity. Because of this, mental hygiene films – and many other kinds of educational films – should not be understood, ideologically speaking, as so much ideologically motivated propaganda for middle America. Instead, they should be seen as constructing – under the guise of education – a fear-based, and quite paranoid, model of subject positioning that alleviates mainstream American culture from social problems and instead places the onus of socialization on the often confused and contrary individual. The fact that these films were so pervasive in the United States during the 1940s and 1950s often elides the fact that many of the key mental hygiene films were produced in Canada. In a country such as Canada, where the "marginal" forms of filmmaking (documentary, animation) often dominate production because of the proximity of the United States, it is ironic that a generation of children and adolescents saw the Canadian Crawley Films in order to learn how to be well-integrated, socially productive Americans.

NOTES

1 Bill O'Farrell, "Quacks and Nostrums," accessed 29 May 2011, www.archive.org/details/quacksan1959.

2 One of O'Farrell's unfinished projects was a book he was co-editing with Christopher Faulkner entitled *Canada's Unknown Cinemas*, which he began working on in 1996. I am unsure where the incomplete manuscript is, but having seen it years ago I can attest to the fact that it unearthed a plethora of new research and films from the margins of Canada's cinematic history.

3 Benjamin Spock, *The Common Sense Book of Baby and Child Care* (New York: Duell, Sloan and Pearce, 1946). The influence of this book cannot be understated; it has gone through eight editions and been in print continuously for the last seven decades.

4 Danny Gregory, *Change Your Underwear Twice a Week: Lessons from the Golden Age of Classroom Filmstrips* (New York: Artisan, 2004), 46–7.

5 Ken Smith, *Mental Hygiene: Classroom Films 1945–1970* (New York: Blast Books, 1999): 15.

6 Clifford W. Beers, *A Mind that Found Itself* (New York: Doubleday, 1908).

7 William A. Kelly, *Educational Psychology* (New York: The Bruce Publishing Co, 1935), 435.

8 Smith, *Mental Hygiene*, 18.

9 David Riesman, *The Lonely Crowd: A Study in the Changing American Character* abridged. (New Haven: Yale University Press, 1989), 21.

10 Robert Eberwein, *Sex Ed: Film, Video and the Framework of Desire* (New Brunswick, NJ: Rutgers University Press, 1999), 117.

11 Graeme Fraser, "Audio-Visual Education in Canada," *Crawley Commentary*, 10 December 1956, 1.

12 For more on this phenomena and a consideration of how the formal components of the educational film have transmogrified into avant-garde practices, see Scott MacKenzie, "Flowers in the Dustbin: Termite Culture and Detritus Cinema," *Cinéaction* 47 (1998): 24–9.

13 Crawley's did not only make sponsored films for adolescents: one of its most inspired "conformity" sponsored films was *Winter in Blunderland* (Canada, 1949), produced for Molson Breweries, about the threat of poor and drunk drivers. Directed by and starring George Gorman, the film is a comical, Canadian prescient pastiche of many underground cinema tropes, foreshadowing Kenneth Anger's *Puce Moment* (US, 1949), *Scorpio Rising* (US, 1964), and *Kustom Kar Kommandos* (US, 1965) morphed with the early films of the Kuchar Brothers, and ending with a proto-Brechtian breaking of the fourth wall by the actor/director, all in the service of a message in good road etiquette. It also foreshadows the Canadian industrial film pastiche *Springtime in Greenland* (John Paizs, Canada, 1981).

14 Smith, *Mental Hygiene*, 78.

15 Alan Kellock, letter to Donald Carter, 15 July 1957, Crawley files #1,226, National Archives of Canada.

16 Ibid.

17 Alan Kellock, letter to Graeme Fraser, 3 October 1957, Crawley files #1,226, National Archives of Canada.

18 George Gorman, memo to Carl Schubert, 20 November 1957, Crawley files #1,226, National Archives of Canada.

19 Alan Kellock, letter to George Gorman, 4 February 1958, Crawley files #1,226, National Archives of Canada.

20 George Gorman, letter to Alan Kellock, 20 February 1958, Crawley files #1,226, National Archives of Canada.

21 Alan Kellock, letter to Budge Crawley, 19 December 1958, Crawley files #1,226, National Archives of Canada.

5 A THRILL EVERY MINUTE!
TRAVEL-ADVENTURE FILM LECTURES IN THE POST-WAR ERA

Liz Czach

IN THE FALL OF 1958, the Toronto Anglers and Hunters Association announced its upcoming film lecture series. The 1958–59 Global Adventure all-colour film lecture round-up promised five travel-adventure films that would be presented during the October to April season. Screening in Toronto's art-deco Eaton Auditorium, a non-theatrical venue with a 1,264 person capacity, the film lecture series included Sir Hubert Wilkins's *Off to the Arctic* (c. 1958), which included sequences of Eskimo life; Howard Shelley's *Hunter's Moon* (c. 1956), which depicted a Northern Ontario moose hunt; Murl Deusing's wildlife film *Adventure in Africa* (c. 1955), which featured exotic animals; Lowell Thomas Jr's *Flight to Adventure* (c. 1955), which showed the pygmies of the Equatorial Rain Forest, the Dead Sea, and pyramids; and finally, *Headless Valley* (c. 1957), a film made by the Calgary-based couple Melvin and Ethel Ross, which recounted a two-month canoe trip into the Nahanni Valley in the Northwest Territories.[1] In many respects, this series is unremarkable, as similar film lectures took place across North America on college, university, and high-school campuses as well as in civic clubs, museums, community centres, town halls, and other venues. In big cities as well as small towns, audiences large and small gathered to hear filmmakers narrate presentations of travel, outdoor adventure, or nature films that they themselves had shot. Notably, however, three of the five films in the Toronto Anglers and Hunters Association's film lecture series featured Canadian subject matter, attesting to the enduring popularity of Canada as a film lecture topic despite the dominance of American lecturers in the travel film field. In what follows, I will undertake a preliminary excavation of post-war travel film lecturing, promotion, and exhibition practices in Canada and the United States, while also paying attention to the national context of film lectures and the degree to which Canadian filmmakers and images of Canada circulated. I will turn occasionally to the career of travel film lecturers Melvin and Ethel Ross as a way to focus my discussion.[2] Moreover, I will illustrate the degree to which production and exhibition practices established in the silent era persisted and flourished in the post-war period.

Film scholarship on travel lectures of the pre-cinematic and silent film eras has been vital in reconstructing film lecture practices and norms that were established during this period. The origins of the film lecture have been traced to pre-cinematic antecedents in the illustrated travel lecture. One of the of the best known travel lecturers was American John L. Stoddard (1850–1931), who toured widely from the 1870s until 1897, presenting his lantern slide shows over 3,000 times to an estimated four million people.[3] Stoddard distinguished himself from other illustrated lecturers by presenting countries that he had visited himself, establishing the first-person perspective that would become one of the defining and enduring features of the travel lecture. Lyman H. Howe (1856–1923) and Burton Holmes (1870–1958), for example, both followed Stoddard's lead and narrated their presentations as travellers who had visited the foreign locations they presented. Howe and Holmes also introduced films into their presentations, and Holmes claimed to be the first showman to illustrate his lectures with films.[4] These presentations firmly established, for generations to come, audience expectations of the travel lecturer's "authenticity" as someone who speaks from first-hand knowledge and with expertise. Indeed, post-war travel film lecturers continued the tradition of narrating films that they themselves had filmed.

Much of the scholarship on travel lectures in the silent era suggests, or implies, that the phenomenon was short-lived and confined primarily to the silent period. Rick Altman hypothesizes that the travel film accompanied by a lecturer slowly became obsolete as films increasingly became standalone products. Explanatory intertitles supposedly eliminated the need for a lecturer and the films became industrial products removed from their roots as "homemade films about foreign places and events [that] had provided itinerant lecturers with personalized props for their programs."[5] The industrialization of filmmaking with the arrival of the studio system did, no doubt, alter production practices. As Altman also points out, standalone commercial travelogues proliferated, first with intertitles and then with a soundtrack.[6] These industrially produced travelogues did not render film lectures obsolete, but rather pushed them to the margins of mainstream filmmaking, and "homemade films about foreign places and events" continued to be produced and exhibited. Indeed, advances in film technology, such as the introduction of 16 mm in 1923 and the increasing affordability of film production, meant that growing numbers of filmmakers could enter the film lecture field. In the post-war period this was particularly pronounced, and as Charles Musser notes: "The wide diffusion of the 16 mm format, which reduced costs and made projection in nontheatrical settings much easier, after World War II revitalized the practice of traveling exhibition."[7] As travelogues became more industrialized, independent filmmakers forged an alternate path continuing the tradition of producing films that would screen at non-theatrical exhibition sites accompanied by a live lecture, films that Musser suggests "might be described as polished home movies."[8] The availability of 16 mm production equipment enabled the production of film lectures to grow exponentially, and Jeffrey Ruoff has traced the practice of film lecturing well into the late twentieth century.[9]

It is tempting to characterize the films that populated the film lecture field as mere amateur efforts, particularly since the travelogue has long been a staple of amateur film production. For example, a cursory glance of films that placed in the Amateur Cinema League (ACL) list of the "ten best winners in the 1930s" indicates that travel topics such as Herman Danz's *Havana* (1930), Stephen F. Voorhees's *Italy* (1931), and John V. Hansen's *Venice* (1934) were popular.[10] Seeming to further collapse the distinction between amateurs and film lecturers is the fact that some filmmakers affiliated with the ACL also worked the travel lecture circuit. For example, Stan Midgley's film *Yosemite on Two Wheels* placed on the ACL top ten list in 1947, and his work later appeared on the film lecture circuit in the 1950s and 1960s with his film *Northwest Adventures*, among other titles. Amateur filmmakers and film lecturers thus shared a pursuit of making "polished" films and both sought aesthetic complexity while operating outside of industrialized production and exhibition circuits. However, film lecturing offered the potential of earning one's livelihood as an independent film producer and exhibitor, which led to a highly competitive and professional environment.

Professional film lecturers made a living at their filmmaking, but their films were produced outside of the studio system and exhibited in nontraditional venues, often leaving little trace. Reconstructing the world of the post-war film lecture circuit is a daunting task. Film lectures are a fundamentally ephemeral practice, as they are accompanied by an irreproducible live oral commentary. Some films survive in archives but often lack documentation of their exhibition practices, narrations, or other supporting materials. Recreating the milieu of post-war film lecturing requires piecing together the productions of individual filmmakers and their presentations, delving into the histories of exhibition sites and booking agencies, and probing the collections of museums, universities, and archives in search of films, while also turning to back issues of the lecture industry's publication, *Program: The Magazine of the Platform World*, published between 1934 and the early 1980s, for further clues. My preliminary investigation of post-war film lecture practices in this chapter is primarily based on two archival collections: the Eaton Auditorium files, held at the Archives of Ontario, provide a glimpse into the workings of a non-theatrical exhibition venue; and the extensive Melvin and Ethel Ross collection at the Provincial Archives of Alberta aids in recovering some of the material conditions of the production and exhibition of film lectures through the practice of one filmmaking couple. The collection contains all of the Rosses' films as well extensive paper documents including the typed scripts of the oral commentaries that accompanied them. Additionally, Melvin wrote two memoirs of his and Ethel's filmmaking adventures: the first, *The Long Road South*, was published in 1968 and chronicles their adventures driving through South America; the other, *Cine Vagabonds*, an unpublished and undated manuscript, details how they entered travel filmmaking and acquired the skills and acumen to become professional travel film lecturers. These materials, in addition to the reviews of their films, letters from fans, announcement posters, and other print matter, helps flesh out the material conditions of their travel film lecturing from production to exhibition.

Despite existing on the margins of industrial film production, film lectures were not a marginal practice. In 1975, when film lecturing was on the decline due to pressure from television and other entertainment options, there were still an estimated 1,000 ongoing travel lecture series and over 500 professional travel lecturers.[11] To get a sense of how popular film lecturing was before the mid-1970s, one need only look at an exhibition venue such as the Eaton Auditorium in downtown Toronto; this large capacity, non-theatrical venue played host to three ongoing film lecture series at mid-century.[12] Of these, the most explicitly travel themed was the long-running World Adventure Tours, which began in 1947 and continued for forty-one years until 1988 (travel film lecture promoter

Estelle Craig moved the series to Ryerson Theatre after the Eaton Auditorium closed in 1977).[13] Two other long-running series, the Audubon Screen Tours (1943–77) and the aforementioned Toronto Anglers and Hunters Association's Global Adventure film series (1943–60), regularly presented film lectures that dealt with nature themes and outdoor or wilderness adventures, respectively. Scholars have widely attributed the appeal of illustrated travel lectures in the pre-cinematic and silent eras to the manner in which they offered a form of "armchair travel," transporting the viewer to exotic locales without the inconvenience or expense of actual physical travel. In the late nineteenth and early twentieth century, many audience members had very limited time, resources, and means to travel, and thus film provided a convenient and exciting means to visit foreign places in the world; places they would most likely never see in person. By the mid-twentieth century, however, the opportunities for travel by the middle and even working classes had expanded considerably. Car travel had grown in popularity and jet travel had become not only widely available but also increasingly affordable.[14] These developments were undoubtedly a partial response to the pent-up demand for travel unleashed after years of wartime restrictions. However, the increased accessibility of travel did not diminish the appeal of travel films, but rather created new audiences. As Craig points out, these presentations appealed to three kinds of audiences: "The Planners, who do preliminary homework on the countries they plan to visit; The Brushuppers, who have seen the countries depicted but come back to nudge each other ecstatically: 'Oh, do you remember that?': The Armchair Travelers who know they won't see the country by any other means."[15] For the Brushuppers, the screening would not only be a means to rekindle memories of past travels, but a way to compare the lecturer's impressions against their own. For example, the theatre manager's report for a screening of Karl Robinson's *China Journey* at the Eaton Auditorium in 1948 notes: "Speaker very good. Pictures good, but people who knew China felt pictures shown were not true to China."[16] The travel lecturer of the post-war era needed to appeal to a broad spectrum of viewers, from the uninitiated to the seasoned traveller.

Success on the film lecture circuit required mastering not only cinematographic skills, but also required a commanding presence and the ability to construct a compelling story arc to sustain the audience's attention for the length of a feature film. A 1959 *Globe Magazine* article cites Craig as estimating, "it takes five years of time and patience, a backing of $15,000 and much professional skill to qualify. To be a good photographer is not enough. It requires facility as a speaker and a definite personality, for the comments of the film man substitute for a soundtrack."[17] When approached by aspirant filmmakers about how to break into the travel lecture field, Craig was gently discouraging, as they often failed to recognize the difference between a vacation home movie made for private enjoyment and a travel film with broader appeal. Furthermore, would-be film lecturers had to contend with a competitive field and one that was driven to a large degree by well-known personalities. These personalities could be lecturers who achieved status through their filmmaking or well-known personages who turned to travel film lecturing to capitalize on their celebrity. For example, filmmaker Lowell Thomas Jr, son of Lowell Thomas of *Lawrence of Arabia* fame, was easy to promote based on his father's fame and name. As one promotional poster read, "You and your family will now be able to say, 'We saw and heard Lowell Thomas, Jr.' Famous son of a famous father, is the modern Gulliver, covering with giant steps the fascinating areas of the world's surface." Meanwhile, filmmakers like Don Cooper made their reputations as film lecturers. When the University of Iowa presented his film *A Lumberjack's Bold Adventure* in its 1960–61 Color-Adventure Film lecture series, it advertised him as "destined to stardom in the film-lecture field." Indeed, Cooper did become a fixture on the film lecture circuit, producing over twelve films that he toured with regularly for decades and illustrating how the circuit created its own personalities and celebrities.

Personality and celebrity driven, the film lecture circuit in the post-war era was difficult to break into, as the aspiring film lecturers Melvin and Ethel Ross would discover. In the fall of 1952, the pair attended a film screening in the Banff area where the evening's entertainment featured a travel film of a South Seas yacht voyage with the filmmaker narrating a live commentary. Although intrigued with the presentation, the Rosses, who were making a living building and selling homes in the Calgary area, initially dismissed serious thoughts about taking up film lecturing, reasoning that they knew little about either yachting or filmmaking. Over the next year they saw three more film lectures on Tibet, India, and Mexico, but as Melvin would later recount in his unpublished manuscript *Cine Vagabonds*, it was decidedly that first travel lecture that struck him and Ethel with a case of "movietis."[18] Eventually, they purchased a 16 mm camera, taught themselves filmmaking, and began to make travel films. Breaking into the film lecture field, Melvin and Ethel had to compete against established lecturers and known celebrities. They began to tour in the mid-1950s with their first short films, *Calgary Stampede, Indian Stampede,* and *Oil Well Fire,* which they shot in and around Calgary. Their initial ventures into exhibition were on a relatively small scale. Reflecting on their naiveté, Mel notes, "Truly we were babes in the woods in our knowledge of the lecture field ... We just drove into a town, booked the hall, nailed up our posters and drove on. Nothing could have been simpler ... Why hadn't we heard about this lecture field earlier?"[19] Yet, the simplicity of this mode of exhibition quickly proved difficult to sustain. Arranging screenings in this manner necessitated an advance booking trip, which meant covering the same ground twice: once to arrange a screening and once for the actual presentation. This process worked well for small-town bookings within driving range, but once they set their sights on larger cities, such as Calgary, and bigger audiences, the Rosses ran into a stumbling block. As Mel writes: "Our idyllic interlude ended. Now towns were larger, halls were booked far in advance, and hall rents had jumped to between $20 and $50 per night. In these larger centers one was also expected to be sponsored by some local service organization on a percentage split, and these organizations only held meetings once or twice a month."[20]

Increasingly aware of the complexity of non-theatrical exhibition, the Rosses sought out an agent but were turned down on the grounds that they were not nationally known celebrities. The majority of film lecturers, however, were represented by agents and booking agencies. A 1951 survey published in the American bulletin of the National Association of Secondary School Principals indicates that schools used as many as forty different organizations to procure lecturers, including film lecturers, for assemblies. Programs were booked "from agencies especially geared for educational service. Some had utilized the offerings of nearby colleges or the lecture bureaus of state university extension services. Others had taken advantage of the services of informal education centers such as museums. Several, usually in conjunction with a civic group, had obtained programs, particularly evening performances, from agencies booking only nationally known artists and public personalities. A small number of schools had secured programs from free-lance agents."[21] Among the better-known managers, agents, and agencies representing film lecturers were

Harold R. Peat, Inc, W. Colston Leigh, Inc, National Lecture Bureau, Associated Platform Artists, and the Redpath Bureau. Innumerable film lecturers did their own promotion and booking, but the agent/manager system permitted lecturers to devote energies to their filmmaking rather than to securing bookings. Agency representation could also work as a form of quality control for programming organizations; since films were narrated live and filmmakers provided their own prints, series organizers and other sponsoring groups had to rely on their relationships with agents to ensure audience-pleasing lecturers, as they could rarely pre-screen material. For example, Toronto-based World Adventure Tours programmer Craig notes that the relationship of trust she built with a New York-based agent was critical to the success of her long-running series.[22]

The scope of the post-war film lecture circuit was extensive, both in terms of sponsoring groups and venues. Lecturers routinely criss-crossed the United States and Canada to present films underscoring the transnational nature of this exhibition practice. A brief summary of locations and organizations that hosted the Rosses' films give us a sense of how far and wide filmmakers would travel to present. Initially the Rosses screened their short films in smaller venues such as churches and community centres within easy driving distance of their home in Calgary. As they moved into feature length productions, they set their sights on larger venues and cities. Without an agent, they went on the road to make contacts across western and central United States. They contacted Canadian and American sponsoring organizations and venues, managing to secure a respectable list of screenings. At an early stage, Melvin sent out inquiries that he considered a form of advertising campaign since he did not expect to get any actual bookings until they were better known. To his surprise, the Toronto Anglers and Hunters Association 1958–59 adventure lecture series, as noted in the introduction, included *Headless Valley*. Established series such as this were the bread and butter of the travel lecture circuit. Filmmakers were generally paid well, screenings took place in large venues, and if the event went well there was the potential for future dates when the filmmakers might return with new films. For the Rosses, successful presentations helped garner references from the University of California and the University of Colorado that, in lieu of an agent, assisted in securing further dates. The Rosses presented their films at such ongoing travel lecture films series as the Shorewood Travel and Adventure Series in Milwaukee, Linde World Travelogues in Phoenix, and the Adventure Film Series at the University of California, Berkley, and the University of Iowa. Organizations that sponsored screenings included, among others, the Los Angeles Nature Club, the Iowa Mountaineers, Canadian Union College, Madison College, South Missionary College, Santa Monica City College, and the outdoor clubs of Vancouver, Oshawa, and San Diego. In sum, records indicate that they travelled as far as Edmonton to the north, Phoenix to the south, Vancouver to the west, and Oshawa to the east, proving just how far filmmakers would travel to present their films, as well as demonstrating the wide range of venues and organizations hosting film lectures.

The range of non-theatrical venues in which the Rosses presented their films also illustrates how easily film lecturers moved across the Canada-US border presenting their films to audiences in both countries. The Canadian and American non-theatrical lecture circuit was intertwined in a manner reminiscent of theatrical feature film distribution and, like its mainstream counterpart, American films and filmmakers dominated. The Rosses, based in Canada, were an exception to the American dominance of the lecture field, although Melvin's Minnesotan birth was often included in promotional material in a tone that assured American audiences that his perspective would not be too foreign. American organizations sponsoring a Melvin Ross film lecture may have stressed his birthplace, but Melvin himself was interested in developing and supporting a film lecture culture within Canada. In a letter dated 12 September 1962, Melvin wrote to the Eaton Auditorium management inquiring about "Canadian filmers" with "good programs" that he might book into a travel film series he was initiating for the following spring. He explains: "While I do receive 'Program magazine' and have a large list of American film-lecturers to choose from, I am hoping to make this series primarily available to the Canadian film-lecturer."[23] Aware of the preponderance of American film lecturers, Melvin was interested in supporting and promoting a Canadian roster of filmmakers.

The films of Melvin and Ethel Ross cover both Canadian and international destinations. They completed six films, including *Dinosaur Badlands* (1955); *Alberta: Home on the Range* (1955–56); *Headless Valley* (1957); *Pan-American Highway* (1961); *Europe* (1963); and *Quebec* (1967). In 2009, the Provincial Archives of Alberta released a two-DVD set containing *Headless Valley* and *Pan-American Highway* with a soundtrack of Melvin's narration as it would have been presented with the films. Given the ephemeral nature of the live commentary or lecture that accompanied such films, this DVD is one of the rare instances that approximates this otherwise largely undocumented practice. Of course, a narration recorded for a DVD cannot replicate the live experience in an exhibition context, and the shaky voiced narration of an aged Melvin, who was in his early nineties when it was recorded, stands in stark contrast to the film's depiction of a robust couple in their forties. Nonetheless, the DVD provides a glimpse, even if partial, into the practice of presenting a film lecture.

Headless Valley was undoubtedly the Rosses' most popular film. It screened in a wide variety of venues, from high-school gyms to large auditoriums, and was sponsored by innumerable outdoor and sportsmen's organizations, including the aforementioned Toronto Anglers and Hunters Association. The work fits comfortably in the long tradition of outdoor adventurer films as it recounts the Rosses' two-month canoe trip into the Nahanni river valley, one of the most remote and rugged regions of the Northwest Territories. As with most successful film lectures, *Headless Valley* relies on a compelling narrative arc of suspense and intrigue interspersed with moments of comic relief. It starts quaintly enough, with a medium shot of the Rosses sitting in their living room perusing newspaper clippings of stories associated with Headless Valley. A series of close-ups on the articles they are reading is coupled with Melvin's narration explaining the contradictory myths about Headless Valley: on the one hand, it is a dangerous destination where no fewer than thirty people, mostly prospectors and trappers, have ventured in never to return; while on the other hand, these tales are discounted as superstitious myths. This prologue quickly establishes the adventure theme of their trip – they are daring to head into dangerous and possibly life-threatening territory to determine whether the stories of Headless Valley are fact or fiction.

Following this brief prologue, an animated hand-drawn map, a staple of the travel lecture film, illustrates the path of their proposed trip, indicating how far the Nahanni river valley system is from the American border while stressing that it is within 300 miles of the Arctic circle and providing visual support to how northerly and remote the destination is. The film's narrative trajectory follows the Rosses as they work their way from populated areas into the more isolated and untamed wilderness. Sequences depict them loading up with 800 pounds of supplies in Fort Nelson, then spending a night in Fort Liard with a final stop at another

South Nahanni trading post before leaving these last traces of "civilization" behind. Animated maps punctuate these sequences to illustrate the progress our intrepid voyageurs are making. The longest portion of the film is the middle section that recounts the trials of making it upstream through various river valleys to Nahanni's majestic falls. As Melvin tells us, their small canoe is equipped with a 7.5 hp engine, but they have been repeatedly told that no one has made the trip with an engine with less than 10 hp. This, along with the limitation on how many supplies they can take, suggests the difficulties they will face. They encounter obstacles from fierce rapids that quickly deplete their gas reserves, as well as rocky waters that repeatedly break their steering pins and propeller. They portage when the rapids are impassable and when possible track the boat to conserve on gas, although the steep cliffs of the valleys make this difficult and they almost lose all their possessions when the towrope breaks and the canoe comes perilously close to slipping away. This almost catastrophic accident is not depicted but rather recounted by Melvin on the soundtrack since the filmed sequences are carefully staged. For example, shots as they travel by canoe show Melvin in the back of the canoe from Ethel's vantage point in the front or vice versa as they swap roles as camera operator. When Ethel and Melvin are shown together, they are obviously shot from a tripod using a timer, and Melvin even shows the device he ingeniously concocted from an alarm clock and fishing wire to permit such filming. Impressively, some of the tripod sequences feature the principles of analytical editing, that is, Melvin and Ethel are shown in an establishing shot with subsequent shots moving closer to medium shots and close-ups. The variation on shot distance and shot length keeps the film well paced and doesn't exhibit the static "nothing happens" long shots and long takes that are often associated with "boring" amateur films and home movies.

The Rosses' tale of tackling the inhospitable Nahanni Valley terrain is punctuated with lighter moments that provide moments of comic relief. In one instance Melvin is playfully pushed into a shallow pool of water that Ethel has deemed to cold too swim in. A similar incident shows Melvin bathing in a canoe full of water he has warmed in the sun when Ethel enters with a large container of cold water and douses him. The film also depicts more mundane domestic moments, such as Ethel cooking meals or Melvin shaving, and these scenes underplay the trip's status as a life-threatening wilderness adventure. In fact, Melvin recounts a number of times what an ideal vacation spot the Nahanni Valley would be if it were a little more accessible and thus blurs the line between threatening wilderness adventure and relatively safe vacation.

The film's climax is undoubtedly when the Rosses arrive at the spectacular Nahanni falls, which we are told are 316 feet high in comparison to Niagara's 150 feet and rival the Victoria Falls in Zambia at 330 feet.[24] The narrative has been building to this moment and now that the Rosses have reached their destination at just a little past midway through the film, the story's emphasis slightly shifts. At this point, the Rosses stow their gear and hike into the backcountry with only their packs. The threat has shifted from the perils of traversing the treacherous rivers to the lure of the backcountry that beckons them to continue further and further into the bush. They must resist the seduction of exploring the next mountain ridge or just one more cavern. As they try to battle this "call of the wild," they find what appear to be cave paintings as well as gold. Neither of these discoveries can be verified, since the gold is swept away by a swift current when Melvin is crossing a river and the caves can't be accurately pinpointed on a map, since they are, quite literally, investigating uncharted territory. An earlier sequence showed Ethel with a map trying to locate where they were only to find a blank, uncharted section. After a few days hiking the backcountry, the Rosses return to their remaining provisions and canoe, and quickly make their way back south with the current now in their favour. When they do ultimately run out gas they only need to paddle a few remaining miles to the first outpost, and have made their way back to "civilization" safe and sound.

Headless Valley can be situated within the tradition of actualities and travel films that depict Canada not as a modernized urban nation, but as an untamed wilderness. From the silent era through to post-war iterations of the lecture film, Canada is represented as an expansive and untapped north: a country rich in natural resources and unpopulated except for animals and the occasional Aboriginal person. The success of *Headless Valley* must also be, in part, attributed to the manner in which it productively interweaves traits of the three dominant genres of the post-war film lecture: the nature film, the adventure film, and the travel film. To clarify, the nature film focuses on the specificities of flora, fauna, and so forth; the adventure film features intrepid explorers travelling into rough terrain, often featuring hunting and fishing, and sometimes an expeditionary aspect under the guise of scientific research; and finally, travel films present voyages to exotic locales. These genres could be discrete, but films like *Headless Valley* blended these different approaches to representing Canada – an enduringly popular destination. Below, I offer a brief overview of some film lectures that demonstrate these varied approaches to representing Canada.

The film lectures that were organized under the auspices of the Audubon Screen Tours, launched in 1943, focused on animal and plant life. These presentations brought the National Audubon Society's message of conservation to new audiences in dozens of cities across North America, with prominent nature photographers, naturalists, and scientists as presenters. For example, Bert Harwell, chief naturalist at California's Yosemite National Park for eleven years through the 1930s and 1940s, appeared as part of the Audubon Screen Tours at the Eaton Auditorium in 1949. His film *Canada West* was sponsored by the Royal Canadian Institute and the Toronto Field Naturalists and attended by 1,182 people. The film was "made in the wilds of western Canada, shows many close-up views of birds and mammals." In keeping with the Audubon Society's history of cataloguing birds, the promotional material highlights Harwell's "extraordinary ability in imitating the songs of birds."[25] Here the emphasis is on animal preservation and appreciation, and not on animals as the target of sport. Harwell returned to Toronto a decade later in 1959 to cover the other half of the country with his film lecture *Canada East*. Another prominent naturalist presenting with Audubon Screen Tours was the Canadian-born Arthur Twomey, the curator of ornithology at the Carnegie Museum of Natural History in Pittsburgh, who presented naturalist film lectures about his fieldwork in Canada, among other topics.

In contrast to the conservationist approach evident in many of the Audubon Screen Tours nature films, the outdoorsman adventurer film, another popular film lecture genre, prominently featured hunting, trapping, and fishing. Groups such as the Toronto Anglers and Hunters Association frequently hosted this type of film lecture, and it screened *A Hunter's Moon*, by Michigan native Howard Shelley, featuring a Northern Ontario moose hunt that combines "the gorgeous beauty of autumn – a panorama of colour – with unusual and seldom seem wildlife episodes of hunting and trapping during a Hunter's Moon."[26] Big game hunting was primarily linked to the African Safari film, but was, as *Hunter's Moon* makes evident, also the purpose of many Canadian hunting trip films. For example, Mr T.A. Mellon funded a Carnegie Museum of Natural History big game hunting expedition to the Canadian Rockies in August 1945 that resulted in a number of films, including *Alberta's Timberline Trophies* and *Trophies from the Timberline.*

The third prominent genre of film lecture on the post-war circuit was the travel film, which presented a trip, with the most popular films transporting viewers to exotic or inaccessible locales. Canada was represented in a range of films, such as those dealing with specific provinces such as Dick Bird's *Newfoundland* (c. 1950) made on the occasion of Newfoundland and Labrador joining the confederation, and the Rosses' *Quebec* (c. 1967), one of a number of Quebec-themed film lectures made around the time of Expo 67. Broader regions were covered in films such as *Acadian Reflections* (Robert E. Fultz, c. 1974) and *Western Canada* (Robert Friars, c. 1952), while the whole country was tackled in *Canada* (Laura Boulton, c. 1946), *Profile of Canada* (Willis Butler, c. 1962), and *Canadian Holiday* (Don Cooper, c. 1967). These titles give a sampling of the wide range of possible approaches to Canada as seen in the travel film lecture, but undoubtedly one of the most popular tactics was to focus on Canada as a northern destination with an emphasis on the Arctic. While many established American film lecturers featured an Arctic adventure in their repertoires of titles, there was at least one filmmaker, David Jarden, and one filmmaking couple, Betty and Lewis Rasmussen, who focused exclusively on Canadian destinations with an emphasis on Aboriginal life and the north.

Jarden, from Wyncote, Pennsylvania, is credited with no fewer than eighteen canoe trips into Northern Ontario from which resulted several films, including *North to Hudson Bay*, *Lost in Cree Country*, and *Ojibway Country*. Promotional material for an April 1958 screening of the *Ojibway Country* states:

> *Ojibway Country*, an unusual film, portrays a canoe trip that David Jarden took with an Indian family deep in the wilderness territory of Northern Ontario. You will see them carry heavy loads over the portage trails, snare 30 pound fish, set out fish nets, cook delicious bannocks, make baskets out of birch bark and moccasins from moose hide. You will race huge bull moose across the rivers in canoes and stalk them along the shore. You will delight in seeing Jarden and his Ojibway guide pull in trout, pickerel, northern

> picke [*sic*] and sturgeon which, with moose meat, provided them with most of their food.[27]

Positioned as a tale of adventure, the film's description suggests an ethnographically inflected approach that presents native life as pre-modern. *Ojibway County* promises "a look into the life of Ojibway Indian much as it was in primitive times" and to demonstrate that Aboriginal ways "ha[ve] changed little for centuries."[28] Unfortunately, I have been unable to locate any of Jarden's films, leaving the promotional descriptions as the only extant trace of their content.

The inheritance of the ethnographic expedition film, by way of the popular mainstream feature films of Robert Flaherty and Edward Curtis, is equally apparent in the films of Betty and Lewis Rasmussen from Racine, Wisconsin. Promotional material describes the Rasmussens as "explorers, lecturers, photographers" as well as "hunters and modern explorers" whose filmmaking career during the late 1940s and into the 1950s was devoted exclusively to Canadian subject matter. Their film lectures, *The Great Mackenzie*, *Arctic Journey*, *James Bay Country*, *Arctic Holiday*, *Prairies to the Mountains*, *North of South*, *Canada: Coast to Coast*, *Newfoundland*, *Packsacks and Portages*, *Canoe Country*, and *Land of Nanna-Bouoju*, covered an area from the Rockies to Newfoundland and up to the Arctic Circle. A brochure from Redpath Bureau, the Rasmussens' booking agency, claims: "Years of travel, work and study among the peoples of the Canadian Arctic and sub-Artic [*sic*] regions have enabled the Rasmussens to produce travel and adventure programs of the highest caliber."[29] The Rasmussens not only gathered images for their film lectures, but also collected native art and handicrafts on their travels. These material objects, along with several surviving films, are housed at the Kenosha Public Museum in Kenosha, Wisconsin.[30] There are no audio recordings or scripts of the narration for the films, but shot sequence lists with cursory notes are included with some of the surviving films. For example, the museum collection includes a typed list of the sequences and the order in which they appear in *Arctic Holiday* along with brief descriptions. Using this list and the surviving colour-reversal 16 mm print, I will briefly describe *Arctic Holiday* to provide a sense, albeit fragmentary, of this film lecture's content and structure.

A one-page flyer for *Arctic Holiday* (see figure 5.1) stresses the care and time taken to complete the film, claims it was two years in the making,

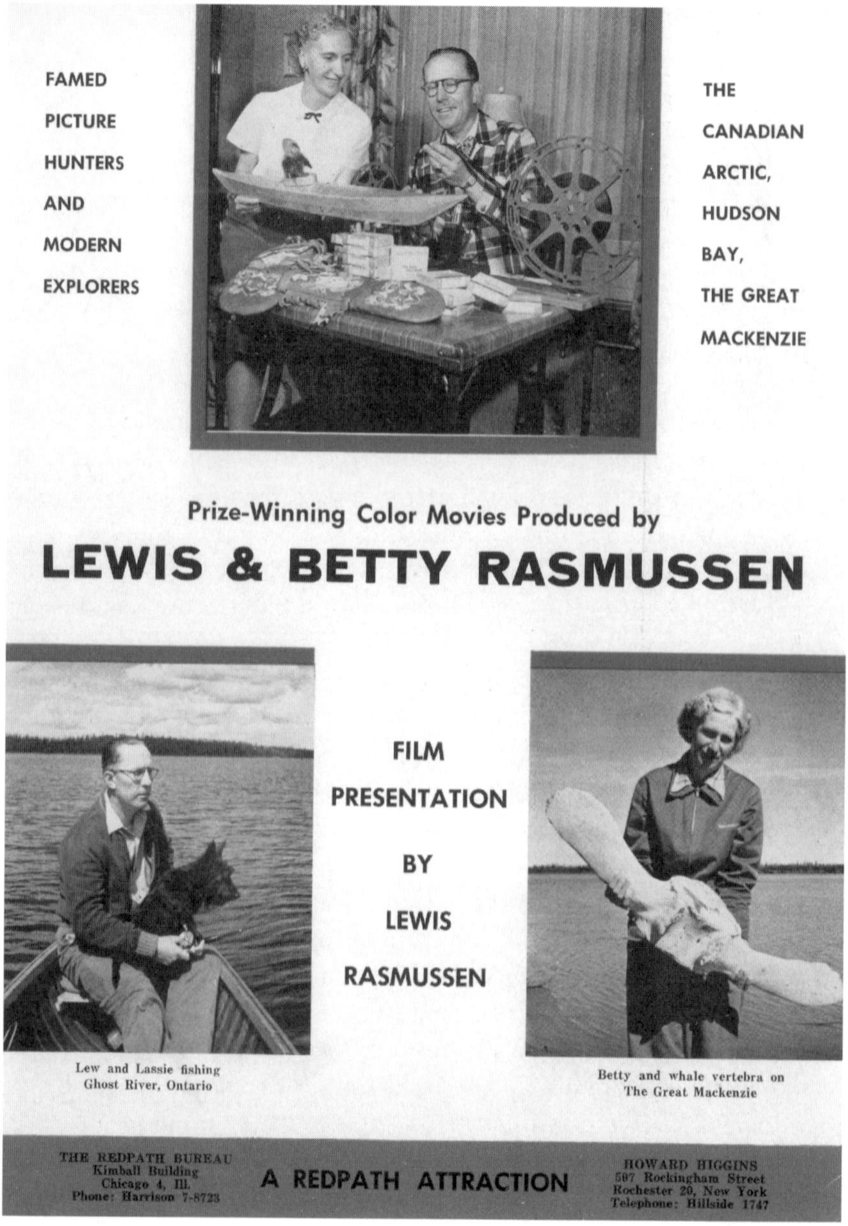

5.1 A flyer advertising Betty and Lewis Rasmussen, film lecturers from Racine, Wisconsin. Represented by the Redpath Bureau, the Rasmussens made a series of Canadian-themed film lectures, mostly about the North and the Arctic, in the 1940s and 1950s, including *Arctic Holiday*.

and says it was "produced, and is narrated, by two people who know the Far North ... who understand the Eskimo and his way of life."[31] Similar claims of authority, despite filmmakers' lack of formal credentials in anthropology or ethnology, were a staple of film lecture promotion, but *Arctic Holiday* appears to focus on representing Indigenous culture. For example, the film's title could be easily read by Southern non-Indigenous audiences as a reference to the Rasmussen's holiday in the north, whereas the notes and the film make it evident that the title refers to the Inuit community's summer respite from the long, cold, dark winter months. The shift in focus from the white filmmakers' perspective to that of the Inuit is worth noting, and *Arctic Holiday* does include many sequences of native life, customs, and rituals that display a degree of intimacy evident in frequent close-ups and longer sequences that engage with its subjects. As the promotional flyer further claims: "*Arctic Holiday* comes to you packed with drama and pathos ... with the warmth of arctic sunshine ... with the excitement of the hunt in the world's largest migration of animals, the Caribou ... with intense human interest amidst a tribe of primitive peoples many of whom are far superior, intellectually, than white man." The latter part of this description rather contradictorily reinforces the notion of the Inuit as "primitive" while simultaneously exalting their potential for intellectual superiority. The film uneasily balances the need to replicate the racist discourse of seeking out the Indigenous other, given audience expectations and the fundamental centrality of this convention to representations of the Arctic, on the one hand, while representing the Rasmussens' experience of mid-twentieth century Inuit life as decidedly modern on the other hand. Unfortunately, without the complete narration, the scope of this tension is impossible to tease out fully.

Arctic Holiday begins with various shots of Churchill, Manitoba, the starting point of the Rasmussens' trip north. There are shots of ice floes in Hudson Bay (even though it is the tenth of July), lemmings at work, the Prince of Wales Fort, and weather balloons being released from a weather station. This is followed by images of muskeg, the limits of northern tree line, and various flowers and birds. This succession of shots demonstrates that *Arctic Holiday* draws on the conventions of the travel, adventure, and nature film lectures with its depiction of historic sites, scientific inquiry, and plant and animal life. The Churchill section ends with the Rasmussens boarding the Arctic supply schooner MS Fort Severn and heading north to the community of Eskimo Point (now Arviat). Upon arrival, scenes of sled dogs and panning shots of the landscape, shrubs, and people erecting tupiks (tents) establish the location. The lecture notes indicate that an explanation of the "origin of these 'nomads' of the northlands" accompanies a sequence of close-ups of "Eskimo faces." At this point, the film introduces a running gag – the recurring difficulty Betty experiences getting into deerskin clothing. This ongoing joke reverses the prominent humorous motif of populist ethnographic films in which the Indigenous subject, untutored in Western ways, fumbles with modern amenities, as in this instance the bumbling white explorer struggles with native ways.[32]

The bulk of *Arctic Holiday* depicts Inuit life in Eskimo Point over the course of the summer of 1947. Inuit men are shown unloading the supply schooner, doing odd jobs, and fishing and hunting, while women are shown preparing skins, constructing clothing, and making tea and meals. *Arctic Holiday* relies on the common narrative convention of Arctic films, that of the "daily struggle for survival," stressing the relentless search for food and fuel via scenes that depict the collection of wood shavings and brush for fuel, a family eating bannock because, as the lecture notes claim, there are no caribou left and fishing for char is the only available food source until the caribou return from the north. Yet, *Arctic Holiday* does not attempt to present a pre-contact idyll and instead depicts the "Eskimo" as enmeshed with southern culture, from early scenes of unloading the shipping schooner to images of the southern white missionary to women using a Singer sewing machine alongside their traditional ulu. Although it is difficult to accurately piece together *Arctic Holiday*'s narrative, there seems to be little to suggest that it engages in a "vanishing natives" project of "salvage ethnography" and is more interesting in straightforwardly representing Eskimo Point as it exists in the contemporary moment. Thus, at least in this key way, it departs from many ethnographic and travel-adventure films about Aboriginal peoples in the Arctic.

In closing, films such as *Headless Valley* and *Arctic Holiday* demonstrate the enduring appeal of Canada, particularly the North and Aboriginal peoples, as a destination for adventure and travel film lecturers long into the post-war period. The coming of sound did not end the practice of film lecturing, nor did the increased accessibility of travel in the years after the World War II-era decrease the appeal of travel- or adventure-themed film lectures. On the contrary, the practice of film lecturing proliferated in part through the availability, affordability, and accessibility of 16 mm filmmaking equipment, and became an extremely popular form of entertainment from large metropolises to small towns. All across Canada and the United States, audiences gathered to hear filmmakers narrate their films of travel, adventure, and wildlife. Rarely discussed in film history, this preliminary foray into the practice of post-war film lectures suggests further exploration of this phenomenon is warranted to expand our knowledge of non-mainstream and non-theatrical film practices. Moreover, paying attention to the national contexts of lecturers and their films sheds light not only on the enduring appeal of Canada as a film topic, but also on how Canada is represented in the popular imaginary to Canadian and foreign audiences alike.

NOTES

1 Filmmakers often lectured with a film for several seasons as well as frequently repurposed material for several different films, and so it is difficult to pinpoint the exact year of production. Throughout this chapter, I indicate the approximate year the film was first presented, based on my estimates from available records (newspaper listings, posters, archival records, etc.).

2 For roughly two decades, the Rosses toured the film lecture circuit across North America with their films *Dinosaur Badlands* (1955), *Alberta* (1955–56), *Headless Valley*, (1957), *Europe* (1963), *Quebec* (1967), and *Pan-American Highway* (1961), which recorded their drive from Calgary to the tip of South America.

3 X. Theodore Barber, "The Roots of Travel Cinema: John L. Stoddard, E. Burton Holmes and the Nineteenth-Century Illustrated Travel Lecture," *Film History* 5, no. 1 (1993): 70.

4 See Charles Musser and Carol Nelson, *High Class Moving Pictures: Lyman H. Howe and the Forgotten Era of Traveling Exhibition, 1880–1920* (Princeton, NJ: Princeton University Press, 1991); Alison Griffiths, "'To the World the World We Show': Early Travelogues as Filmed Ethnography," *Film History* 11, no. 3 (1999): 282–307; Jennifer Lynn Peterson, "Travelogues and Early Nonfiction Film," in *American Cinema's Transitional Era: Audiences, Institutions, Practices*, ed. Charlie Keil and Shelley Stamp (Berkeley: University of California Press, 2004), 191–213; Jennifer Peterson, "Travelogues," *Encyclopedia of Early Cinema*, ed. Richard Abel (New York: Routledge, 2005): 641–2; Jennifer Peterson, *Education in the School of Dreams: Travelogues and Early Nonfiction Film* (Durham, NC: Duke University Press, 2013); and Rick Altman, *Silent Film Sound* (New York: Columbia University Press, 2004).

5 Rick Altman, "From Lecturer's Prop to Industrial Product: The Early History of Travel Films," in *Virtual Voyages: Travel and Cinema*, ed. Jeffery Ruoff (Duke University Press, 2006), 76.

6 For example, the travelogue was a common subject for studio-produced shorts. Most notably, MGM produced the Traveltalks series of short sound travelogues hosted by James Fitzpatrick, known as the "Voice of the Globe,"

which screened theatrically from the early 1930s until the mid-1950s. Leonard Maltin notes, "the 1950s and 1960s saw an increase in the number of sponsored travelogues shown in theatres." Leonard Maltin, *The Great Movie Shorts: Those Wonderful One- and Two-Reelers of the Thirties and Forties* (New York: Bonanza Books, 1972), 208.

7 Musser and Nelson, *High-Class Moving Pictures*, 276.

8 Ibid.

9 See Jeffrey Ruoff, "Show and Tell: The 16mm Travel Lecture Film," in *Virtual Voyages: Cinema and Travel*, ed. Jeffrey Ruoff (Durham, NC: Duke University Press, 2006); and Jeffrey Ruoff, "Around the World in Eighty Minutes: The Travel Lecture Film," *Visual Anthropology* 15, no. 1 (2002): 91–114. Ruoff's essays cover up to the late 1990s but ongoing series continue at various locations, including the Kenosha Public Museum, the Washington University in St Louis (celebrating its 116th travel lecture series in 2013–14), and Seattle's World Cavalcade (the sixty-seventh season in 2013–14).

10 Alan D. Kattelle, "The Amateur Cinema League and Its Films," *Film History* 15, no. 2 (2003): 244.

11 Lois Kuter, "Take Me to Paradise – The Travel Film and the Real World," *Saying Cheese: Studies in Folklore and Visual Communication* (Folklore Forum: A Communication for Students of Folklore and Bibliographic Series, 1975), 63.

12 For more on activities in the Eaton Auditorium, see the F229-134 through F229-140 holdings at the Archives of Ontario.

13 For more on Craig's involvement with World Adventure Tours, see her autobiography *Under the Circumstances: How to Meet Celebrities without Leaving Home* (Bloomington, IN: Author House, 2005).

14 See Susan Sessions Rugh, *Are We There Yet? The Golden Age of American Family Vacations* (University Press of Kansas, 2008); and Orvar Löfgren, *On Holiday: A History of Vacationing* (Berkeley: University of California Press, 1999).

15 Kay Kritzwiser, "She Helps Bring the World to Your Armchair," *Globe Magazine*, 24 October 1959, 7.

16 Archives of Ontario, F229-134, container B415210.

17 Kritzwiser, "She Helps Bring the World," 7.

18 Melvin Ross, "Cine Vagabonds" (unpublished manuscript, no date), Provincial Archives of Alberta, PR2004.0122/6.

19 Ibid., 44.

20 Ibid., 45.

21 Nellie Z. Thompson, "Arranging Those Assembly Programs," *NASSP Bulletin* 35, no. 180 (October 1951): 65.

22 Interview with the author, 24 June 2011.

23 Handwritten in pencil at the bottom of the letter is: Dick Bird, Bill Lang, Paul Provencher. All of these Canadians had presented film lectures at the auditorium.

24 The figures noted in the film are somewhat inaccurate: Niagara Falls is 167 feet tall, Victoria Falls is 360 feet, and the Virginia Falls in the Nahanni is 295 feet.

25 The description of the film is from the *Bulletin,* Field Museum of Natural History (Chicago, IL) 22, no. 4 (April 1951): 2.

26 Poster for the Toronto Anglers and Hunters Association's Great 1958–1959 Global Adventure all-colour film-lecture round up. Provincial Archives of Alberta, ACC.PR2004.122 1.7 Folder 1.

27 Flyer for Toronto Anglers and Hunters Association's 1952-1953 lecture series. Archives of Ontario F229-134, container B226363.

28 *Bulletin,* Field Museum of Natural History (Chicago, IL) 37, no. 3 (March 1996): 8.

29 For examples of the Redpath Bureau's Rasmussen promotional flyers, see the Traveling Culture-Circuit Chautauqua in the twentieth century digital archives of the Iowa Digital Library at the University of Iowa Libraries, accessed 15 June 2012, http://digital.lib.uiowa.edu/cdm/landingpage/collectin/tco.

30 The films housed at the Kenosha Public Museum are *Arctic Journey, The Great Mackenzie, North of South,* and *Arctic Holiday.*

31 *Arctic Holiday* photocopied flyer, courtesy Kenosha Public Museum.

32 One of the best-known examples of the conceit that Indigenous people do not understand Western technology is the gramophone scene in Robert Flaherty's *Nanook of the North* (1922). For a longer discussion of this scene and film, see Fatimah Tobing Rony's *The Third Eye: Race, Cinema and Ethnographic Spectacle* (Durham, NC: Duke University Press, 1996), 99–249.

6 "VERSIONS, REVISIONS, AND ADAPTATIONS"
FILM PRODUCTION IN TWO LANGUAGES AT THE NATIONAL FILM BOARD

Christine York

IN 2008, FOR the first time, the National Film Board (NFB) set out a policy on version production requiring that all audiovisual works produced or co-produced after 1 April 2005 be made available in both French and English. In the case of animated films, a voice-over version would have to be produced, and in the case of documentary films, a subtitled version at minimum.[1] Today, any DVD released by the NFB includes a version in the other official language as an option. But it wasn't always this way. Since the establishment of the NFB in 1939, each studio decided whether or not to produce a version in a second language depending on the interest in the film and its distribution potential. And when studios made second-language versions, they did not simply add subtitles or dubbing as an option to a DVD menu, but created the versioned film as an entity on its own. Over the past seven decades, language versions produced at the NFB have employed a wide range of techniques depending on the time period, the production personnel involved, and the genre, whether animation, fiction, experimental film, or documentary. In many cases, these techniques allowed viewers to experience the film without reference to the original, as all visual and verbal signs of the original language were effaced. Whereas today version production aims to overcome the language barrier and provide access to the original work, in the early decades of the NFB versions were a way to create films that would blend in alongside those already circulating in the target language.

From the late 1940s to the early 1960s, several version-making methods existed simultaneously as the traditional narration-dependent documentary was called into question by the emergence of the direct-cinema aesthetic and the advent of television in Canada. The previously dominant method, in which the narration was translated and a new rendering substituted for the original one, became inadequate as documentary conventions changed and other voices found their way onto the soundtrack.

Furthermore, the increased production of dramatic short films, partly in response to the demand for television programming, created a need to translate dialogue. As a result, the range of translation methods expanded to include techniques from feature filmmaking like subtitling, dubbing, and adaptation. Covering both documentary and fiction films, in this chapter I will identify and describe the main translation methods, and then consider the extent to which version making afforded an opportunity to transform and recontextualize the originals and position the resulting films as new products that would connect with new audiences. From this perspective, version production is not incidental to the history of the NFB, but a defining characteristic; indeed, what sets the NFB apart from similar but shorter lived state-sponsored filmmaking institutions, like the Australian National Film Board and Deutsche Film-Aktiengesellschaft of post-war Germany, is that it has long produced film in two languages, mainly for domestic audiences – and that it has translated those films, again for domestic audiences. Yet despite the substantial number of publications on the NFB that have covered numerous aspects of the institution and its output,[2] very little has been written about the versions; instead, English and French production are seen as two separate threads of filmmaking history. Here, I am concerned with the intertwining of those threads.

NARRATION-LED DOCUMENTARY AND THE OPPORTUNITY FOR INTERVENTION

In the propaganda films the NFB produced during World War II, archival footage from disparate sources was held together by voice-over narration, which strung the images into a single storyline and established a consistent perspective on the events shown. Using direct address to the viewer, the narration adopted a tone of authority and presented a structured argument, often in the form of a solution to a problem or a call to action. The "voice of God" model of narration, with its booming male voice from an unidentified off-screen source, served to "interpret or explain images that might otherwise, in a multitude of ways, remain incoherent."[3] Such was the dominance of narration that the visuals of the "World in Action" newsreels were described as simply illustrations of the commentary.[4] After the war, the compilation documentary gave way to films made with original footage, but narration continued to "carry the weight of the argument."[5] The potential for imposing a new interpretation on audiences by altering the narration is high, as Chris Marker memorably illustrates in a scene of *Letter from Siberia* (1958) in which the same footage of Soviet workers building a road is shown three times with different narrations, first extolling the benefits of the communist system, then decrying the miserable conditions, and lastly describing the scene in ostensibly neutral terms. That potential for interpretation was exploited in the English-to-French versions of narration-led documentaries of the late 1940s and 1950s.

Before the arrival of television in Canada in 1952, the vast majority of the total film output in French was composed of versions of English-language films, with a few exceptions like Vincent Paquette's *La cité de Notre-Dame* (1942), on Montreal's tercentennial. The NFB administration was not particularly concerned about the high percentage of versions compared to original productions; in fact, film commissioner Ross McLean commented in 1948 that versions were preferable to original French productions because they cost less and amounted to the same thing.[6] The most influential figure in French version production was Jacques Bobet, a Frenchman hired by the NFB in 1947 who went on to a distinguished career as writer, producer, director, and executive producer of numerous films. He supervised the production of hundreds of French versions, using a straightforward process: "It was very easy at the time because the films consisted only of visuals and off-camera commentary. I just translated the commentary, moved the music slightly, and it worked. We made five hundred versions like that."[7] He approached translation with a sense of freedom and opportunity, not hesitating to change details in the narration; indeed, his comments suggest that he took more pride in creating a poetic text than in respecting the content and style of the original. For example, *Underwater Round-up* (1949), a three-minute vignette in the newsreel series *Eye Witness/Coup d'oeil*, portrays lobster fishing in New Brunswick through close-up shots of lobsters and images of fishermen at work. The narration concludes: "New Brunswick lobsters go out full of vim and vigour. In a matter of hours from the time they leave their icy Atlantic water, they're on the table in famous restaurants, about 30 million pounds of them a year. That's quite an underwater round-up!" In a 1984 text, Jacques Bobet recalls how this narration was translated:

> Finalement notre rêve s'accomplit: nous avons écrit en vers libres tout un texte sur l'élevage du homard. L'envoi, je m'en souviens, était touchant:
>
> Et voici le sort
> Pathétique
> Des homards du Nouveau-Brinswouique [*sic*].
> Ils ont vécu et ils sont morts
> Pour les restaurants d'Amérique.
>
> Nous n'avons jamais eu d'échos de telles prouesses stylistiques. Nous n'en avions pas besoin. Notre bonne conscience nous suffisait.[8]

In his view, then, translating the prose of the original narration into rhyming free verse is a stylistic accomplishment; the fact that the narration differs markedly from the original – and that a key statistic has been omitted – is of no concern.

Bobet's intervention in the text went beyond style: in some cases, he added references to French Canadians or Quebec as a way of orienting the version toward the target culture. Nowhere is this more apparent than in *Paul Tomkowicz: Nettoyeur d'aiguillages*, his version of *Paul Tomkowicz: Street-Railway Switchman* (Roman Kroitor, 1954). The original is clearly situated in Winnipeg and follows an aging Polish immigrant through a night of work in the winter cold as he sweeps the ice and snow from streetcar rail-switches. The narration is unconventional in that it is spoken in the first person, based on a recording of Tomkowicz's own words. Yet the French version refers to him in the third person and moves the action from Winnipeg to Ottawa: "Un tramway qui doit tourner à gauche ne doit pas tourner à droite. À gauche, c'est Ottawa, l'Ontario, la langue anglaise. À droite, ce sont les ponts, la ville de Hull, la province de Québec. On va à droite ou on va à gauche."[9] Only years later, when Richard Hancox interviewed him in 2000 while researching an article on the film, did director Roman Kroitor realize the narration had been changed.[10] The specifics of the central character's identity are pushed aside by the elimination of references to his memories of the horrors of war in Europe and his reflections on a lonely life in Winnipeg. Instead, the French narration reinterprets the images as raw material – like the visuals of the wartime compilation films – and recontextualizes the film as a new product for Quebec audiences.

DIRECT CINEMA'S REFUSAL OF NARRATION

In the late 1950s, a new aesthetic emerged that called into question some of the tenets of the traditional Griersonian documentary – including the use of narration to set out a consistent point of view and provide coherence to the images. Based on their philosophy, drawn from Henri Cartier-Bresson's *The Decisive Moment* (1952), that the significance of an ordinary moment can be recognized and captured on film by a photojournalist or documentarian, filmmakers in Unit B created a television series called *Candid Eye* that took advantage of the NFB's new hand-held 16 mm cameras to film everyday events with minimal intervention. These experiments were further explored by *l'équipe française*, an informal grouping of francophone filmmakers whose short films include some of the most celebrated works of the NFB's "golden age."[11] The direct-cinema aesthetic modernized documentary shooting by favouring small, polyvalent crews, synchronized sound recording, and wide-angle lenses that obliged the cameraman to move into the thick of the action, and by rejecting the use of scripts and detailed shooting plans. Yet while the French originals innovated by rejecting narration altogether or using "found sound" as a substitute, the English versions of many of these films reverted to the traditional model of the narration-led documentary (see figure 6.1).

One such film is *La lutte* (1961), directed by Claude Fournier, Michel Brault, Claude Jutra, and Marcel Carrière, which presents an evening of professional wrestling at the Montreal Forum. Influenced by an encounter with Roland Barthes, who had written about wrestling (known in France as "le catch") in *Mythologies*, the directors film it as a spectacle of good and evil along the lines of classical theatre: the main bout pits world champion Édouard Carpentier – smiling and clean-shaven, French-speaking, described by the sportscaster as "a fine physical specimen of manhood" – and teammate Dominic DeNucci against a pair known as the Fabulous Kangaroos, composed of Al Costello and Ivan Kalmikoff – a bearded, snarling "Russian" who rails against the referee in English – along with their flamboyant manager Red Berry. Shot by five cameramen who capture the action from all angles, the film cuts between the men grappling on stage and the audience – including many women – shrieking in delight and apprehension. The original soundtrack contains dialogue, ambient sound, and music; film critics were quick to point out the absence of narration. Writing in *Objectif* in October 1961, Jacques Lamoureux states, "Cela est quasiment incroyable: croyez-le ou non, mais ce film, réalisé par

6.1 Whereas *La lutte* featured only the sportscaster's play by play, *Wrestling* was made more conventional by the addition of narration.

l'ONF ne comporte pas de commentaire!"[12] But to say there is no narration is not entirely accurate: for about ten minutes of the film's twenty-eight, we hear play-by-play commentary by Michel Normandin, a well-known sportscaster who covered not only the weekly wrestling shows but also baseball and Montreal Canadiens hockey games. The filmmakers obtained the commentary by asking Normandin to come in to the studio and improvise while watching the edited fight sequence.[13] Similarly, for the English version, *Wrestling*, press agent Norman Olson was hired to record the play-by-play commentary in the NFB studios.[14] However, the English film also has several paragraphs of narration, voiced by Stanley Jackson, who wrote and read so many narrations he is sometimes called the official voice of the NFB.[15] As the film opens over wrestlers training, he comments, "Tony Lanza's school in Montreal. In the daytime, the pupils have ordinary jobs. At night, they pursue dreams of glory." Later, over shots of excited audience members caught up in the action, the narrator wonders, "Why do they come? A lady who is perhaps too squeamish to pluck a chicken certainly hasn't come to enjoy a display of naked brutality. She has come to see a hero in action." The English version does not allow the event to simply unfold before the viewer's eyes and ears, but adds a level of mediation. Although it provides no essential details, the narration offers a note of reassuring familiarity to viewers already challenged by the film's unconventional subject matter and structure, and brings the English version into line with original productions of the same language and time period.

THE NEW CHALLENGE OF FICTION FILMMAKING

While documentary – whether the traditional narration-led style or direct cinema – continued to account for the majority of films produced at the NFB, another approach came to the forefront starting in the post-war period. It involved the use of dramatization or re-enactment and featured performances by actors – professional or non-professional – playing carefully scripted roles. In one of few studies to focus on these post-war social dramas, Peter Morris notes that they draw on the vocabulary of both fiction and documentary: "They make the same claim to social truth or social reality as does the documentary, yet do so within a fictionalized format."[16] Inspired by Italian neo-realism, the films were for the most part shot on location rather than in studio. Following the convention of classical documentary, they tended to make use of narration to provide links and explanations and guide viewers through the film; narration was nonetheless secondary to the dialogue, which occurred during the events themselves and drove the story forward.

As reliance on narration diminished, the established method for version making – substituting a translation for the original narration – could no longer suffice as a means to account for all the verbal information in the film. The NFB would try out several new methods. In a few cases, off-camera narration remained the vehicle for translation, but was extended to cover the dialogue as well, in a manner similar to voice-over. More frequently, methods from feature filmmaking were put into practice. The impact of these techniques varied: while dubbing and adaptation resulted in films that could be received without recognition of their status as language versions, subtitling – used for the first time at the NFB during this period – clearly signalled the films' original context.

Narration/Voice-over Hybrid

This method bears some similarity to voice-over, presently used in documentaries broadcast on television, in which a voice reading a translation is heard simultaneously over that of a person giving an interview or conversing on camera. Convention has it that the original voice is heard for a few seconds before the volume is lowered and the new voice inserted; the translated text is usually shorter so that the original voice can be heard again for a few seconds at the end of each segment.[17] However, whereas now a number of voice actors play the various participants in the original film, in the method used at the NFB in the 1950s and early 1960s a single voice actor would play all the roles, in addition to serving as the narrator.

Les aboiteaux/The Dikes (Roger Blais, script by Léonard Forest, 1955) follows this hybrid method. Set in Acadie, where for centuries dikes or *aboiteaux* have been built to prevent farmlands flooding when the water level in the Bay of Fundy rises, the story centres around an elderly dike-keeper who warns the local farmers that their dikes are ill maintained. When the autumn rains cause a breach in a dike, the men must work around the clock to save the village. Help comes from the Maritime Marshlands Reclamation Administration, a government program that used modern engineering techniques to reclaim and protect tidal farmland. The original French film uses a range of narrative techniques, starting with a full-screen intertitle just after the opening credits that sets the scene and followed by a fragment of off-camera narration by Placide, the dike-keeper: "Ils m'avons choisi [he uses an Acadian verb construction] pour voir aux aboiteaux. Ils m'avons choisi pour voir aux levées. Ils m'écouteront pas quand je dis que ça ira mieux de les réparer. Il sera trop tard bientôt, il sera trop tard."[18] The rest of the film contains dialogue – strikingly wooden dialogue between uncomfortable-seeming performers. Morris suggests that the stiff and unnatural dialogue often found in the social dramas signified that the characters were "real" people, not professional actors who would have a more "natural" delivery.[19]

By contrast, the English version has a single voice from start to finish: an actor playing the role of Placide. The information contained in the intertitle becomes the opening sentences of the first-person narration; Placide goes on to introduce himself and to quote the other characters ("But the marsh, I said, would you give it back to the river, then? It is not my marsh, he said"). The re-edited English version has been shortened from twenty-two minutes to ten and a secondary theme eliminated – the idea that Placide is considered too old to be useful until the community finally recognizes his knowledge of tides and currents. Having a single voice read both narration and voice-over emphasizes the role of the main character at the expense of all others. Nonetheless, unlike the documentaries previously discussed, the film is clearly positioned as a version and the Acadian setting is maintained through the characters' names, Placide's accented voice, and the audible background voices speaking French.

Dubbing

In dubbing, translated dialogue is synchronized to actors' lip movements to create the illusion they are speaking in another language. As in subtitling, the other channels of information – the pro-filmic image and the non-verbal elements of the soundtrack – are left unchanged. Dubbing is invariably more expensive than subtitling due to the cost of preparing the synchronized translation and working with specialized voice actors, and it was infrequently used at the NFB prior to the production of feature-length fictions. Nonetheless, in a few of the social dramas produced during the 1950s, dubbing was the central method for creating the version – but not the only method, as these films tended to be presented by a narrator or on-screen host who would introduce a character grappling with a problem like alcoholism or life after prison and place the events within a larger context.

The dubbed dialogue of these social dramas tends to remain very similar to the original, yet differences abound in the translated narration – just as the versions of narration-led documentaries sometimes differed considerably. *The Son/Le fils* (Julian Biggs, 1952) tells the story of a young man in rural Ontario who works on the family farm for low pay; unable to become independent enough to marry, he resents being kept under his father's thumb. The conflict is resolved when the father and son sign an arrangement to share ownership of the farm, ensuring it will stay in the family for another generation. The opening and closing narration in the English original is attributed to an inhabitant of the village. Over images of a man pumping water and a woman hanging out the laundry, he introduces his neighbours: "There's Fred Hayward. He does a bit of carpentry. And Mrs Flaherty. She does a bit of housekeeping and an awful lot of gossiping." By contrast, the French narration is in the third person and dispenses with any reference to the villagers; instead, it repeats platitudes about the uneventful village life. Over these same images, the narrator comments, "Et les jours sont scindés par les gestes domestiques. Et les semaines par le linge blanc qui sèche."[20] Again, the French narration omits some of the content and treats the images as raw material, open to interpretation. The tendency of the French version producers to adapt original films for French audiences is maintained – not through dubbing, but through changes to the narration.

Double Shooting and Adapting Television Programs

The arrival of television in 1952, with the launch of CBFT Montréal and CBLT Toronto, had a major impact on production at the NFB. CBFT, initially bilingual, began to broadcast exclusively in French in 1954 when its English-language sister station CBMT was launched, leading to the establishment of two separate networks. In order to supply the broadcasters with material, the NFB had to adjust to producing programs quickly, on a low budget, and to a standardized length, as well as to delivering them on a weekly basis. The sheer number of programs is remarkable: in 1954–55, for example, 117 films for television were produced in English and French, of which sixty-five were originals and fifty-two were revisions.[21] To achieve this high level of production, additional staff were hired, units dedicated to television production were formed, and the NFB resorted to a mix of original films, versions, and "revisions" – the name given to films that had already been released but were re-edited or updated to make them suitable for broadcast. While the result was an eclectic mix of formats and styles, such a hectic pace of production could not have been maintained without versions, adaptations, and revisions.

Adaptations came into prominence at this time, and like the multilanguage version of the early talkie era were produced through double shooting. The introduction of sound in the late 1920s created a predicament for the film industry, which suddenly had to consider the translation of dialogue to enable foreign distribution.[22] Hollywood studios hit upon the idea of shooting the same film in various languages by using a single set and script with different directors and casts. MGM preferred to import actors and directors to Hollywood, while Paramount, Warner Brothers, and other majors built studios in Europe. Features were shot around the clock in up to fourteen languages; at their peak between 1931 and 1932, multi-language versions represented 70 per cent of foreign-language production, with the remaining percentage shared between subtitling and dubbing.[23] But in 1932, the method was abandoned as inefficient, aesthetically unsatisfying, and financially disastrous.[24] Nonetheless, it has remained in use in Canada, both at the NFB and in the private sector, as when the NFB teamed up with Ciné St-Henri in 1982 to simultaneously shoot *Bonheur d'occasion* and *The Tin Flute*.[25]

Within this category, production varied greatly. In some cases, films in two languages were produced separately and shared only the story. *Le retour* (Bernard Devlin, 1956) and *Raw Material* (Julian Biggs, 1955) are based on a script by George Salverson, a dramatization of the John Howard Society's work helping ex-convicts reintegrate into society. *Raw Material* starts with a scripted interview between host Fred Davis and a caseworker – actually actor William Needles – and continues with dramatized scenes shot in Toronto and at the Kingston Penitentiary. *Le retour* also starts with an interview, between Gil LaRoche and a French actor playing the caseworker, before moving on to dramatization. It was shot in Montreal, with prison sequences shot at the Saint-Vincent-de-Paul jail, and refers to the work of another agency, the Société d'orientation et de réhabilitation sociale. The English film was broadcast in December 1955 as the opening film in the series titled Perspective, while the French film showed in April 1956 as part of Passe-Partout.[26]

At the other end of the spectrum, sometimes both films were made simultaneously. *Les suspects* (1956) and *The Suspects* (1957) were shot on the same set and have the same director (Bernard Devlin), camera operator, and sound recordist; one of the actors, Henri Poulin, plays the police chief in both films. A young couple is picked up by the police for loitering and interrogated by an investigating detective, who tries to browbeat a confession out of them until the police chief intervenes. Written by Fernand Dansereau, the films are intended to show "something of the problems faced by ordinary policemen in their ordinary work, in the hope that it will encourage public understanding and responsibility for the men who maintain the law."[27] The French film was broadcast on 27 January 1957, and the English one aired only two weeks later.[28] Double shooting was a way to produce television programs in two languages that would be received by both audiences as original works, not versions.

Subtitling

Although subtitling can be traced back to the very beginning of the talkie era with the screening of a subtitled version of *The Jazz Singer* (1927) in France in January 1929, the method was associated with the dialogue of fiction films rather than the narration of documentary. Given that NFB documentaries had long favoured narration as the central expository device in both originals and versions, dating right back to the wartime newsreels, subtitles were virtually absent from NFB films before the 1960s. When technological developments opened up the possibility of shooting sync sound with 16 mm film, other voices became part of the soundtrack in documentaries and created a need for different methods of translation, like the ones examined above and eventually, subtitles.[29] But as early as 1952, long before subtitling became widespread at the NFB, there was one film – a fiction – that chose this method of versioning: *L'homme aux oiseaux* (Bernard Devlin and Jean Palardy, 1952) (see figure 6.2).

Original French production accounted for only a small number of films in the NFB's early decades, as the bulk of French-language output consisted of versions. By the release of the 1951 Report of the Royal Commission on National Development in the Arts, Letters and Sciences, chaired by Vincent Massey, as little as 2 per cent of the total number of films shot at the NFB were originally in French[30] – leading the commission to recommend that more films be produced for French-speaking Canadians on contemporary subjects.[31] One such project was the adaptation of a short story by Roger Lemelin, who had achieved literary success with *Les Plouffe*. The story of a dreamer who loses his job, *L'homme aux oiseaux* was an unusual project in that it was a drama with actors and a sizeable budget. Producer Don Mulholland, worried that such an expensive undertaking would have a limited audience, considered an English version even before shooting began. He described the proposed structure to film commissioner Arthur Irwin in a 1950 memo: "As you will see the commentary for the film will be in English, but the dialogue will be in French, for the obvious reason that the people who live in

6.2 *The Bird Fancier* was one of the first NFB films to be translated through subtitles instead of voice-over.

Quebec speak French." The "folksy" commentator would explain what the people are saying: "Cleverly handled, this could be quite effective."[32] Although Irwin continued to question the film's budget, it was shot the following summer and released theatrically in Quebec. It went on to win a Canadian Film Award and become a significant vehicle of Quebec culture.

Instead of being versioned through the usual methods, the film was released with subtitles under the title *The Bird Fancier.* This was due to the intervention of scriptwriter Lemelin, who did not want to repeat the experience he'd had with the English version of *Les Plouffe.* In a memo to producer Guy Glover dated 28 March 1952, Lemelin explains, "The film deals with local color where the ungrammatical dialogue and its intonations is in harmony with the characters. I am positive that the dubbers would massacre this accent, this casual and nonchalant French-Canadian tone, and in my opinion it would be a mistake to dub the film into English."[33] Unlike the narration-led documentaries, which could be versioned and released without being immediately recognizable as originally made in another language, *The Bird Fancier* was clearly positioned as a French-Canadian film in translation. The subtitled version maintained the voices, and it was obviously set in Quebec City: the opening narration, the scene with a tour guide who points out several landmarks, and the many identifiable shooting locations give the city itself a role (today, the NFB website description reads in part: "The film is also a memorable portrait of Québec, the 'Grande Dame' of Canadian cities"). Subtitles made the original accessible to English-Canadian audiences without altering its status as a French-Canadian folk tale.

CONCLUSION

The pivotal period between the late 1940s and early 1960s represented a moment of experimentation in audiovisual translation, during which many methods were used to produce alternate language versions of films. These versions were a boon to the NFB in that they helped the institution meet its broadcast commitments when it ventured into television production, and allowed it to list a higher number of productions in its annual reports – particularly during the years when the level of original French production was extremely low. That situation would gradually change in the years leading to the establishment of separate French and English production streams in 1964, following sustained pressure by Quebec filmmakers, administrators, and media.[34] Whereas film scholars like Pierre

Véronneau and Yves Lever trace the emergence of modern Quebec cinema by considering original productions,[35] I have shown that we need to consider French versions as well, as they demonstrate an awareness of the specificity of Quebec audiences and provide clues to the themes that would later come to the forefront of Quebec cinema. Constituting the majority of French-language output in this period, the versions are characterized by an effacement of evidence of the original language. By contrast, the English versions of certain fiction films, like *Les aboiteaux/The Dikes* and *L'homme aux oiseaux/The Bird Fancier*, foreshadowed the currently dominant approach by allowing audiences to be constantly aware of the films' French origins.

This research further points to a way that translation analysis can contribute to film and documentary studies. By observing the changes in meaning that occur in the movement from one language to another, it is easier to get a clearer sense of the contribution of various elements – speech, other aspects of the soundtrack (music, sound effects), image, text on-screen – to the construction of meaning in the film as a whole. As speech in documentary already represents an interplay between the voices of narrator, participants, and filmmaker, the addition of a translator's voice adds a layer of complexity. Given the importance of the NFB to the history of French and English culture in Canada, the study of these various voices has much to contribute to our understanding of the intertwined threads that link these cultures.

FILMOGRAPHY

Biggs, Julian. *Raw Material.* National Film Board, 1955, 30 min. / Devlin, Bernard. *Le retour.* National Film Board, 1956, 30 min.

Biggs, Julian. *The Son.* National Film Board, 1952, 26 min. / Biggs, Julian. *Le fils.* National Film Board, 1952, 25 min.

Blais, Roger. *Les aboiteaux.* 1955, 22 min. / Blais, Roger. *The Dikes.* 1955, 10 min.

Devlin, Bernard, and Jean Palardy. *L'homme aux oiseaux.* National Film Board, 1952, 29 min. / Devlin, Bernard, and Jean Palardy. *The Bird Fancier.* National Film Board, 1955, 30 min.

Devlin, Bernard. *Les suspects.* National Film Board, 1956, 30 min. / Devlin, Bernard. *Les Suspects.* National Film Board, 1957, 30 min.

Founier, Claude. *Bonheur d'occasion/The Tin Flute.* Ciné St-Henri and the National Film Board, 1983, 123 min.

Fournier, Claude, Fournier, Michel Brault, Claude Jutra, and Marcel Carrière. *La lutte/Wrestling.* National Film Board, 1961, 27 min.

Kroitor, Roman. *Paul Tomkowicz: Street-Railway Switchman/Paul Tomkowicz: Nettoyeur d'aiguillages.* National Film Board, 1954, 9 min.

La famille Plouffe. Based on the novel by Roger Lemelin, broadcast on Radio-Canada from 1953 to 1959.

Macartney-Filgate, Terence, Stanley Jackson, and Wolf Koenig. *The Days before Christmas.* National Film Board, 1958, 29 min. / Macartney-Filgate, Terence, Stanley Jackson, Wolf Koenig, and Georges Dufaux. *Bientôt Noël.* National Film Board, 1959, 29 min.

Marker, Chris. *Lettre de Sibérie/Letter from Siberia.* National Film Board, 1957, 62 min.

Paquette, Vincent. *La cité de Notre-Dame.* National Film Board, 1942, 28 min.

Underwater Round-up, "Eye Witness No. 15," National Film Board, 1949, 3 min. / *Rassemblement sous-marin*, "Coup d'œil no. 15," National Film Board, 1949, 3 min.

NOTES

1 "Politique sur les versions de l'ONF," National Film Board, 30 May 2008.

2 The past ten years have seen the publication of no fewer than five book-length studies on the NFB in English and French: Caroline Zéau, *L'Office national du film et le cinéma canadien (1939–2003): Éloge de la frugalité* (Brussels: Peter Lang Publishing, 2006); Zoë Druick, *Projecting Canada: Government Policy and Documentary Film at the National Film Board* (Montreal: McGill-Queen's University Press, 2007); Marion Froger, *Le cinema à l'épreuve de la communauté: Le cinema francophone de l'Office national du film 1960–1985* (Montréal: Les Presses de l'Université de Montréal, 2009); Gail Vanstone, Toronto; Sumach *D is for Daring: The Women behind the Films of Studio D* (2007); and T. Waugh, M.B. Baker, and E. Winton, eds., *Challenge for Change: Activist Documentary at the National Film Board of Canada* (Montreal: McGill-Queen's University Press, 2010).

3 Stella Bruzzi, *New Documentary* (New York: Routledge, 2006), 63.

4 "The World in Action," *Documentary News Letter,* May 1942, 72.

5 Peter Morris, "After Grierson: The National Film Board 1945–1953," in *Take Two: A Tribute to Film in Canada,* ed. Seth Feldman (Toronto: Irwin Publishing, 1984), 184.

6 Pierre Véronneau, *Résistance et affirmation: La production francophone à l'ONF – 1939–1964* (Montreal: Cinémathèque québécoise, 1987), 19.

7 Unless otherwise indicated, all translations are by the author. Jacques Bobet, "Survol Historique – Interview by Richard Gay," in *Les 50 ans de l'ONF* (Montréal: Les Éditions Saint-Martin; Les Entreprises Radio-Canada, 1989), 26. "C'était très facile à cette époque-là parce que les films n'étaient que visuels avec des commentaires hors champ. Alors je traduisais les commentaires, je déplaçais légèrement la musique, et ça allait. On a fait cinq cents versions comme ça."

8 Jacques Bobet, "Les racines cachées," in *La production française à l'ONF: 25 ans en perspectives*, ed. Carol Faucher (Montréal: Cinémathèque québécoise, 1984), 15. "Finally, we realized our dream: we wrote a whole text on lobster farming in free verse. As I recall, the envoi was quite touching:

And this
Is the sorry fate
Of the lobsters of New Brunswick
They lived and they died
For the restaurants of America.

We never got any feedback on these feats of style. But we didn't need any: our own clear conscience was enough." Bobet's recollection of the narration, thirty-five years later in 1984, is not quite accurate. The recorded version is as follows: "Et voici la très triste histoire des homards du Nouveau-Brunswick. Ils sont partis de l'Atlantique où leur vie était sans histoire. Ils ont vécu et ils sont morts, sans amertume et sans remords. Ils ont gagné l'éternité pour le bien de l'humanité."

9 "A streetcar that must turn left must not turn to the right. To the left is Ottawa, Ontario, the English language. To the right: the bridges, the city of Hull, the province of Quebec. One turns right or one turns left."

10 Richard Hancox, "Geography and Myth in *Paul Tomkowicz*: Coordinates of National Identity," in *Candid Eyes: Essays on Canadian Documentaries*, ed. J. Leach and J. Sloniowski (Toronto: University of Toronto Press, 2003), 16.

11 Gary Evans covers the classics of the *équipe française* in a chapter called "The Golden Years, Part II," and Caroline Zéau includes them in a section called "L'âge d'or de la production à l'ONF." Gary Evans, *In the National Interest: A Chronicle of the National Film Board of Canada from 1949 to 1989* (Toronto: University of Toronto Press, 1991); Zéau, *L'Office national du film et le cinéma canadien (1939–2003)*.

12 "It's quite incredible: believe it or not, this NFB film has no narration."

13 Vincent Bouchard, *Pour un cinéma léger et synchrone! Invention d'un dispositif à l'Office national du film à Montréal* (Villeneuve d'Ascq: Presses Universitaires du Septentrion, 2012), 100.

14 NFB production files.

15 G. Marsolais, *L'Aventure du cinéma direct revisitée: Histoire, esthétique, méthodes, tendances, textes des cinéastes, repères chronologiques, glossaire, index* (Laval, Quebec: 400 coups, 1997), 85.

16 Morris, "After Grierson," 185.

17 Díaz Cintas and Orero, quoted in Anna Matamala, "Teaching Voice-over: A Practical Approach," in *The Didactics of Audiovisual Translation*, ed. Jorge Diaz Cintas (Philadelphia, PA: John Benjamins, 2008), 117.

18 "They chose me to watch over the dikes. They chose me to watch over the levees. They won't listen to me when I say it'd be best to repair them. It'll be too late soon, too late."
19 Morris, "After Grierson," 189.
20 "And the days are broken up by domestic tasks. And the weeks by white laundry on the line."
21 NFB Annual Report, 1954–55.
22 Abé Mark Nornes, *Cinema Babel: Translating Global Cinema* (Minneapolis: University of Minnesota Press, 2007), 124–5.
23 Ibid., 139–40.
24 Ginette Vincendeau, "Hollywood Babel: The Multiple Language Version," *Screen* 29, no. 2 (1988): 25.
25 Leila Basen, "Translating the Reality," *Cinema Canada* (July 1982): 25–6.
26 NFB production files and Albert Ohayon, NFB English Film Collection analyst, email to the author, 6 June 2011.
27 Quoted from the film's opening titles.
28 NFB production files and Albert Ohayon, email to the author, 6 June 2011.
29 Among the few documentaries to use no narration prior to the direct-cinema period are Pierre Petel's *Au Parc Lafontaine* (1947), a six-minute sketch of the Montreal park set to an original song, and Colin Low's *Corral* (1954), an eleven-minute story of a cowboy breaking a wild horse whose soundtrack contains only guitar music composed for the film.
30 Véronneau, *Résistance et affirmation,* 19, and "Early Activities of the Francophone Group at the National Film Board," in *A Celebration of Canada's Arts, 1930–1970,* ed. G.B. Carruthers and G. Lazarevich (Toronto: Canadian Scholars' Press, 1996), 167–8.
31 *Report,* 312–13.
32 Quoted in Véronneau, *Résistance et affirmation,* 21.
33 Production file of *L'homme aux oiseaux* and Albert Ohayon, email to the author, 30 May 2011.
34 Véronneau, "De la féodalité à la fronde, de 1939 à 1964," in *La production française à l'ONF: 25 ans en perspectives,* ed. Carol Faucher (Montréal: Cinémathèque québécoise, 1984), 9–10.
35 Véronneau, *Résistance et affirmation;* Y. Lever, *Le cinéma de la Révolution tranquille: De* Panoramique *à* Valérie (Montréal: Institut québécois du cinéma, 1991).

7 BREAKING NEW GROUND
CANADA'S FIRST FOUND-FOOTAGE FILMS

William C. Wees

IN THE SECOND half of the 1960s, Canadian experimental filmmakers discovered the creative possibilities of working with film footage that had already been used in other contexts or set aside or left – figuratively or literally – on the cutting-room floor.[1] The Canadian pioneers in what is commonly known today as *found-footage film* or *recycled cinema* were Charles Gagnon, Arthur Lipsett, Jack Chambers, Joyce Wieland, and Betty Ferguson.[2] Since the sixties, Canadian found-footage films have proliferated thanks to, among others, David Rimmer, Al Razutis, Peter Lipskis, Bruce Elder, Jean-Claude Bustros, Mike Hoolboom, Richard Kerr, and Gerda Cammaer. In this chapter, however, I will focus on films by Canada's first generation of found-footage filmmakers: Wieland and Ferguson's *Barbara's Blindness* (1965), Wieland's *Handtinting* (1967–68), Lipsett's *A Trip down Memory Lane* (1965), Gagnon's *The Eighth Day/Le huitième jour* (1967), and Chambers's *The Hart of London* (1968–70). A critical analysis of these films offers an opportunity to rediscover the subjects, formal techniques, sources, and circumstances of production of five films that broke the ground for recycled cinema in Canada.

Within the Canadian context, these films from the second half of the 1960s may have seemed like unique explorations in a new, unnamed film genre. Or, for anyone who had read Jay Leyda's *Films Beget Films: A Study of the Compilation Film*, published in 1964, they might have seemed like a subgenre of the compilation film, which, in Leyda's words, "*begins* on the cutting table," with film footage that "originated at some time in the past."[3] For Leyda, compilation films belonged in the tradition of the documentary; consequently, experimental filmmakers' unorthodox re-editing of stock shots, selections from newsreels, and a diverse array of other pre-existing film footage goes unrecognized in *Films Beget Films*. But the history of experimental film includes found-footage films as early as

Guido Seeber's *Kipho* (1925), Henri Storck's *L'Histoire du soldat inconnu* (1932), Dziga Vertov's *Three Songs of Lenin* (1934), Len Lye's *Rainbow Dance* (1936) and *Trade Tattoo* (1937), Joseph Cornell's *Rose Hobart* (1939), and a number of other films Cornell made in the 1940s and 1950s. In France, Isidore Isou's *Traité de bave et d'éternité* (1951), a number of films by Maurice Lemaître, and Guy Debord's *Sur le passage de quelques personnes á travers une assez courte unité de temps* (1959) and *Critique de la séparation* (1961) include varying amounts of found footage. (Debord's best-known film with found footage, *La Société du spectacle,* did not appear until 1973.) Closer to home and more likely to be known by the first Canadian found-footage filmmakers were the early work of the Americans Bruce Conner and Stan Vanderbeek. Conner's *A Movie* (1958) is probably the best-known and most frequently screened of all found-footage films – or "collage films," as they were usually called at the time. Along with *A Movie,* Conner's *Cosmic Ray* (1961) and Vanderbeek's *Newsreel of Dreams* No. 1 and No. 2 (1962) and *Breathdeath* (1964) joined a growing body of extremely diverse films that by the late 1960s were frequently screened under the banner of underground film and attracted substantial audiences to venues devoted to new, experimental work in the film medium.[4]

Comparable developments were taking place in Canada, though they were somewhat later, on a smaller scale, and with American and European films sharing the stage with works by Canadians such as Michael Snow's *New York Eye and Ear Control* (1964) and *Wavelength* (1967); Wieland's *Water Sark* (1966), *1933* and *Sailboat* (both 1967), and *Reason over Passion* (1968–69); Keewatin Dewdney's *Maltese Cross Movement* (1967); and Rimmer's *Migration* (1969). Predominantly young audiences attended screenings in colleges and universities as well as small, often makeshift screening spaces in art galleries, lofts, and apartments. At the time, the films suited the social, political, and aesthetic preferences and practices of the 1960s "counter-culture."

As I will show, Lipsett's and Gagnon's found-footage films had quite different origins – and for the most part different audiences – from the films of Wieland, Ferguson, and Chambers. Nevertheless, all five not only belonged to the Canadian and international movement of avant-garde/experimental/underground film of the 1960s, but continue to hold interest as demonstrations of the expressive potential of found footage when it falls into the hands of dedicated film artists.

"SOMETHING THAT MADE US GO CRAZY": *BARBARA'S BLINDNESS*

Shortly after Joyce Wieland and her then-husband Michael Snow moved from Toronto to New York in 1962, Wieland met Betty Ferguson, who was working there as a film editor. They became good friends – a friendship that lasted until Wieland's death in 1998 – and decided to make a film together using footage that Ferguson had accumulated from various sources and originally intended to use as filler while editing other people's films.[5] According to Ferguson, her principal contribution to the project was the found footage she brought to the editing table, while Wieland generally made decisions about the juxtaposition of shots.[6]

The principal source for *Barbara's Blindness* is an educational film, narrated by a male voice-over, about a blind girl's first impressions of the visual world after an operation has restored her sight.[7] "We started out with a dull film about a little blind girl named Mary," Wieland said, "and ended up with something that made us go crazy."[8] There was, however, method in their madness. The intention behind the original film was to encourage young people to pay attention to and more fully appreciate the world around them – albeit a very limited, bucolic world of flowers, butterflies, ducklings, chickens, sheep, horses, waterfalls, and the like. By simply reproducing clips from the source film, Wieland and Ferguson expose its shallow sentimentality, but by also using numerous clips from other films to interrupt the original narrative, they accomplish much more than that. While it is evident Wieland and Ferguson had fun juxtaposing footage of the original film with incongruous clips from their heterogeneous collection of other found sources, they also used those clips to play a game of perception by repeatedly interrupting the original film's narrative unity and challenging its uplifting message about discovering the ordinary wonders of a springtime world.

A few examples must suffice to illustrate Wieland and Ferguson's editing strategies. Mary, who sits in a sunlit garden with her eyes still covered with a large dressing wrapped around her head, kisses her doll. Cut to Valentino in Arabian garb kissing a young woman. Accompanying another shot of Mary and her doll, the narrator informs us that although she is still living in a world of darkness, she thinks, "there are lots of good things in my world too." Cut to a partially unwrapped mummy turning and lurching toward the camera. Cut to a very brief shot of a girl whose head is jerking forward and backward as if she is being violently shaken. Cut to Mary still holding her doll. A shot of roses with the narrator exclaiming,

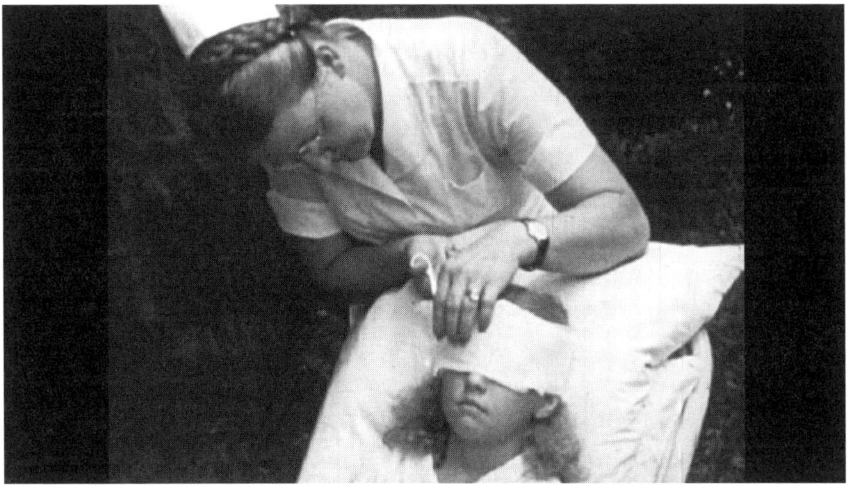

7.1 In a few moments Mary will see the world for the first time, thanks to the miracle of modern medicine.

"their fragrance was heavenly," is followed by a cut to a 1920s flapper with a long cigarette in her hand coyly looking into the camera as she exhales a cloud of smoke. With another shot of a rose, the narrator says Mary thinks its odour "is like summertime." Cut to an overhead shot of the expanding mushroom cloud of a nuclear explosion. When a nurse starts cutting through the dressing covering Mary's eyes there is a cut to a grimacing African witchdoctor in heavy beads and feathered headdress dancing with his arms spread apart. Cut to the nurse continuing to remove the dressing (see figure 7.1). Cut to a shorter shot of the dancing witchdoctor. Then, as the nurse finishes removing the dressing, the narrator tells us what she says: "Mary, open your eyes."

There follows a very rapid montage of approximately fifty fragments of found footage occupying about ninety seconds of film time with a shot of a couple of sunflowers between most – but not all – clips of other found footage. A few direct juxtapositions of images include: an explosion at the edge of an ice floe – sunflowers – two Eskimo children who dance together – sunflowers – a walrus with huge tusks – a female wrestler picks up her opponent, drops her to the mat, and jumps on top of her – sunflowers – a curvaceous young woman in tight shorts strikes a pin-up girl pose in front of an American flag – sunflowers – a motorcyclist races around a curve in the road, hits a rock, and flies through the air – a time-lapse image of a sunflower slowly opening – Buster Keaton (in *Cops* [1922]) lights his cigarette with the lit fuse of a bomb – a nuclear explosion – a melting snowman. Near the end of the montage sequence, the narrator of the original film says, "And so what had been make-believe became real," followed by more time-lapse shots of flowers opening – negative footage of a fashion model – a time-lapse close-up of a rose opening – an upside-down close-up in reverse motion of a man un-inserting a hotdog into his mouth – and another rose opening, followed by a shot of Mary running in a meadow, anxious "to see all that she had dreamed about."

Interrupting Mary's exploration of her newly visible world of trees, flowers, farm animals, and a pond with water lilies are shots of, among other things, elephants, hippos, giraffes, a zombie-like male figure staring menacingly into the camera, and, in a grimly comic metaphor for Mary's emergence from the dark world of blindness, a zombie-woman in a ragged dress and caked with dirt slowly emerges from soil loosened by a passing tractor and staggers along a road with her face lifted to the sun (see figure 7.2). When she wades into a stream and immerses her face in the water the film cuts to Mary arriving at the edge of a large pond followed by a cut to a man struggling in choppy seas to save a drowning girl (the same one who was being violently shaken earlier in the film).[9] A few intervening shots of Mary at the edge of the pond are followed by shots of a baby in diapers swimming under water, intercut with shots of crocodiles sliding into the water as if they were going after the baby. As the film ends the girl saved from the stormy sea rushes up to her rescuer on the deck of a ship. Their tearful embrace, intercut with time-lapse close-ups of roses opening, is accompanied by the soaring final measures of generic happy-ending movie music – the orchestral equivalent of the final words of the narrator in the film about Mary: "Thus Mary's story ends as all good stories should end. She lived happily ever after. But my story and your story may not begin until that day when we really open our eyes and truly see the wonderful world around us: the land of real belief."

Between truly see and "the wonderful world around us," Wieland and Ferguson add their last bit of found footage: a grotesque, vampire-like monster turning toward the camera. This moment is the filmmakers' final reminder that to truly see involves far more than Mary and the viewers of her story are allowed to view. Throughout *Barbara's Blindness,* the inserted fragments of found footage not only fracture the coherent narrative of the original film, but subvert its underlying assumption that we live in a

7.2 A zombie woman emerges from the ground in a grotesque parody of Mary's emergence from blindness.

safe and sane, stable, and comprehensible world, and all we have to do is open our eyes to appreciate it. Wieland and Ferguson's montage of found footage wryly suggests otherwise.

"IT WAS A POEM": *HANDTINTING*

The satiric, deconstructive spirit that pervades *Barbara's Blindness* is nowhere to be found in Wieland's *Handtinting*, made two years later and without Ferguson's participation.[10] At least four factors account for that change in tone and intention: the source of the film's images, the content of those images, the way they are optically manipulated and edited, and the absence of sound to accompany them. Overarching all of these factors is the desire to create an aesthetically satisfying unity out of fragments of found footage, to produce, in Wieland's words, "mystery and rhythm and some repetitive portraits of some beautiful faces." It is in that context that she calls *Handtinting* a "poem."[11]

The original footage had nothing to do with poetry. It was intended for a documentary about a Job Corps retraining centre run by the Xerox Corporation for poor, undereducated, and mostly black women in their

7.3 Young women enjoying themselves at a Job Corps retraining centre. The original black and white footage is tinted magenta in Weiland's film.

late teens or early twenties. Apparently Xerox was unhappy with some of the film's content and it was never released. However, Wieland was one of the camera operators for the project, and as she explains, "I took some of my own outs from the film – some of which were genuine old-fashioned cutaways, and which I felt very strongly about, and began to make *Handtinting*."[12] Despite the depressing conditions for the trainees at the centre, as Wieland saw them – "what they were offered in the way of education was humiliating to me, some rooms with typewriters, and a machine that spoke to them as they typed"[13] – there are no shots of rooms with typewriters or women learning to type. What we see instead are young women dancing, laughing, and unselfconsciously socializing, or wearing bathing suits and caps as they prepare to go swimming or participate in a swimming lesson (see figure 7.3). Interspersed are a few shots of one or more of them quietly watching the dancing or staring pensively into space.[14] In a memorable moment, a slightly chubby black woman throws up her arms, then plants them on her hips in a pose for the camera

7.4 Besides embodying the playful camaraderie of the young women at the retraining centre, this pose suggests a momentary liberation from the straitened circumstances of the women's everyday lives.

before doubling over in laughter (see figure 7.4). The mood of the film, in other words, suggests nothing of the dreary training for a (probably poorly paid) job. It is much lighter, more positive and upbeat, due in part to the frequent shots of the young women laughing and dancing to music playing on a jukebox visible in the background of one shot.

Equally important are the editing rhythms and other devices Wieland employs to transform prosaic footage into cinematic poetry. Although most of the clips are short and frequently end before a movement or gesture is completed, Wieland's editing completes the uncompleted movements and gestures by integrating them in the rhythmic flow of images that unifies the film as a whole and produces a dynamic and sympathetic group portrait of the young women at the retraining centre. Like dance movements, many shots are repeated several times or looped or reversed or flipped so that a left-to-right movement becomes a right-to left movement. Very brief passages of black and coloured leader separate many of the shots, and the original black and white film is dyed in tints of magenta, green, blue, sepia, and orange, with the footage "often streaked and uneven as if tie-dyed."[15] Some of the leader and a few shots are punctured with small holes that produce their own dancing rhythms when the film is projected. There are also quiet, contemplative pauses when the camera lingers in close-up on, as Wieland says, "some beautiful faces." Throughout, the absence of a soundtrack allows viewers to respond to the rhythms of the editing and the movement – or lack of movement – within individual clips. Recognizing the intense interplay between the original footage and her manipulation of it, Wieland says, "the editing and the so-called subject matter are equal. You can look at the editing or you can look at the girls."[16]

While "editing" in this case must be understood to include all of the ways Wieland reworked and added to the original footage, one does not have to choose between looking at the editing or looking at the subject matter. As Lauren Rabinowitz writes, "emphasis on the materials does not devalue or undermine the representational expressiveness that the images of the black girls' faces and bodies render, resulting in a formal and pictorial political statement."[17] Along the same lines, Kass Banning argues, "While the 'materialist' techniques of the film work against and undermine the transparency of the image and the possibility of situating the latter in an immediate relation to a profilmic 'real,' the image maintains both a discursive and a referential value."[18] Today, the film's political and discursive dimensions may not seem as significant as they did when *Handtinting* first appeared – three years after the passage of the Civil Rights Act of 1964, the creation of the Job Corps as part of the Equal Opportunity Act passed in the same year, and, perhaps most importantly, the resurgence of feminism in the 1960s. Worth remembering, too, is that working with found footage and employing materialist techniques were vanguard tactics that have become all too familiar since the '60s. Nevertheless, Wieland's command of her material allowed her to produce a politically inflected and aesthetically rich "poem" as fresh today as it was when it first appeared.

"OUR NEW AWARENESSES": *A TRIP DOWN MEMORY LANE*

Making films at the National Film Board of Canada gave Arthur Lipsett access to a much larger body of found footage than was available to Wieland and Ferguson when they made *Barbara's Blindness.* Lipsett was able to draw on footage and sound tracks from the NFB's own films (including out-takes and other discarded visual and sound material), as well as stock shots, newsreels, and other footage he could purchase from film libraries and archives with funds the NFB provided. The technical facilities available to him at the NFB also meant that the production values of Lipsett's films surpass, by a considerable degree, those of *Barbara's Blindness* and *Handtinting*.[19]

A Trip down Memory Lane begins with shots of a beauty queen contest accompanied by the insistent beating of military drums. The heavy drum beat gives way to wavering music in a minor key from the soundtrack of a travelogue about India as a procession of marching and mounted troops in ceremonial finery passes among throngs of spectators. An elephant with the maharajah ensconced in a howdah on its back lumbers to the centre of the crowded scene as the narrator exclaims, "with a final superb touch of spectacle the ruler arrives." Cut to a medium close-up of a pale-faced adolescent boy in the open cockpit of a small airplane. Well-wishers shake his hand and the plane takes off. Cut to a dapper man, hat in hand, striding toward a large public building, mounting part-way up the stairs, and turning to look at the camera while Bing Crosby backed by a ragtime band sings, "Louisiana, Louisiana, I've been sad, I've been sad / Louisiana, Louisiana, now I'm glad, boy I'm glad." The song continues over shots of a young girl in an elaborate headdress and costume standing on top of a hot air balloon that takes off and sails over city streets with the tiny figure of the girl still visible on top. Cut to a man wearing a waiter's outfit and carrying a tray of food as he inches his way along a girder at the top of a tall building under construction. Several workers standing and sitting on another girder shout encouragement. As one worker stands up to meet the "waiter," the film cuts to two men lifting a third man into the cockpit of a small glider. They push the glider off a high bluff, and it immediately crashes on the rocks below. The pilot is helped up the steep slope and waves to indicate that he is okay. Cut to an old-fashioned, silent film intertitle: "It was a nice job while it lasted."

The glider's crash ends what is, in effect, the film's prologue, as the image literally brings down to earth the preceding references to flights and heights. In addition to the literal heights, there are the metaphorical heights attained by a beauty queen on her throne and a maharajah atop an elephant. Through Lipsett's editing, the maharajah is replaced as "ruler" by a kid whose airplane lifts him into the sky as he, metaphorically, leaves behind the old, tradition-bound cultures of the East. At another

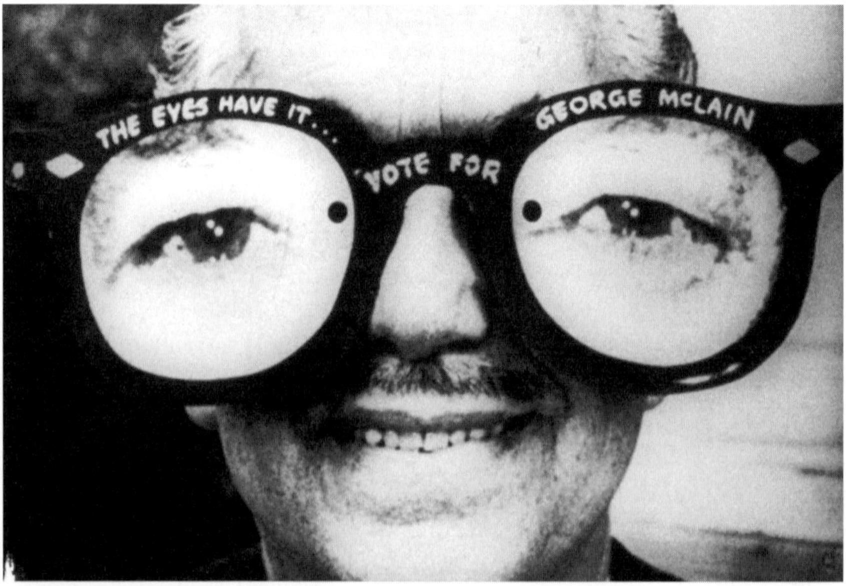

7.5 In his film's next-to-last image, Lipsett sums up his view of the shallow and stupidly comic character of twentieth century Western culture.

level of reference, the film clips form a procession of their own with beautiful women in swimsuits and marching colonial troops leading the parade and the intertitle gag – "it was a nice job while it lasted" – bringing up the rear. As the film continues, the chronology of the archival footage moves forward from the 1920s and 1930s to the war years and into the 1950s, and the predominant thematic content references science, politics, religion, and war. Footage that evokes World War II – battleships, soldiers, a Japanese man with radiation burns – is mixed with footage of laboratory experiments, a Catholic priest in ceremonial finery conducting an outdoor service, scenes of everyday life, and images of iconic public figures such as John D. Rockefeller, Benito Mussolini, Emperor Hirohito, Pope Pius XII, Dwight D. Eisenhower, Harry Truman, Konrad Adenauer, and Richard Nixon. Next, a sword swallower performs for a crowd in a city square, followed by the last two shots of the film: a photograph of a man wearing large fake eyeglasses with hugely magnified eyes behind the lenses and a photograph of the sad-eyed, deeply lined face of Albert Einstein, who seems to be contemplating the sorry state of the world (see figures 7.5 and 7.6).

7.6 The film ends with a photograph of Einstein seemingly contemplating the sorry state of the world depicted in the rest of the film.

Taking "a trip down memory lane" is a familiar conceit of compilation films that do little more than exploit the sounds and images of earlier times for their comic or historical or nostalgic value. In *A Trip down Memory Lane*, however, the comedy tends to be dark and disquieting, and any chance for nostalgia is undercut by the ironic juxtapositions of the film's montage. Moreover, as the film's subtitle, "Additional Material for a Time-Capsule," suggests, Lipsett envisioned his film as a cinematic equivalent of the documents, images, and objects that are placed in time capsules to provide future generations with material evidence of how people lived and what they thought at a particular time and place in the past. In some notes he prepared for Donald Brittain, the film's producer, Lipsett writes, "What are the forces that have shaped, and are shaping, our new awarenesses; and what are our new responsibilities?"[20] This suggests that Lipsett's trip down memory lane was designed to collect audiovisual evidence of those "forces" and preserve them in a cinematic time capsule, with disjunctive, allusive montage serving as a model of the new awarenesses that are needed for contemporary society to recognize and accept the new responsibilities history has imposed on it. Although it is composed primarily of sounds and images from the past, the film's sound-image collage is, in itself, an example of the new kind of awareness Lipsett regarded as essential to understanding and acting responsibly in the present.

"WAR HAS NEVER STOPPED": *THE EIGHTH DAY/LE HUITTIÈME JOUR*

Charles Gagnon made *The Eighth Day/Le huitiéme jour* for the ecumenical Christian Pavilion at Montreal's Expo 67.[21] While the building was designed by Montreal architects Roger D'Astous and Jean-Paul Pothier, its interior design and multimedia presentations were Gagnon's responsibility.[22] The film's first life, in other words, was as a component of a multimedia environment that included "photographs displayed, illuminated, and projected on modular structures" accompanied by avant-garde music by various twentieth century composers and "recorded interviews, industrial noise, and corporeal sounds such as [an] amplified heartbeat, as well as live sounds channelled from outside of the pavilion into the exhibition rooms."[23] The Christian Pavilion was one of several at Expo 67 that called upon "new awarenesses" to be fully appreciated.

With the aid of a film researcher in New York, Gagnon was able to locate and purchase the archival footage he needed for his film. For photographic images he drew upon the photo library of the US Defence Department and the NFB, and he hired a professional photographer in Montreal "to take pictures of piles around Montreal: automobiles, graveyards, hardware stores, foodstores."[24] In many cases he re-filmed the photographs, as well as photos and ads cut out of magazines, and frequently cropped them to emphasize particular details or "animated" them with a zoom lens. Although *The Eighth Day* was his first film and independently produced, its production values equal those of the NFB-produced *A Trip down Memory Lane*. And like Lipsett's film it was aimed at a large, general audience, rather than a small, elite audience knowledgeable about and appreciative of experimental/avant-garde film. It was projected in a separate, small theatre in the basement of the pavilion, but was conceived as an integral part of the multimedia, McLuhanesque environment of the pavilion as a whole. Nevertheless, it can stand on its own as an early example of an experimental found-footage film designed to illustrate and implicitly denounce the social, political, and economic forces that lead inevitably to the organized violence of war.[25] As Gagnon puts it, "While working on the film, I came to realize that the strongest thing about violence and the most abstract thing about violence is its sequential nature, that war has never stopped, and that it is just the leading of one conflict into another. I could keep this film going on forever."[26] *The Eighth Day* not only provides innumerable illustrations of that violence but conveys a sense of its irresistible momentum through the rhythm of Gagnon's montage of archival footage and photographs.

The film begins innocently enough – or so it seems – with a time-lapse shot of a misty sunrise over a broad expanse of water accompanied by the haunting sound of "Japanese *shakuhachi* flute music."[27] A gull glides high over head, and water advances and recedes peacefully on a deserted beach. The tranquil mood is shattered by the sounds and images of a beach packed with people in bathing suits, a skyrocket exploding, and crowds at a Coney-Island-style amusement park where patrons ride the merry-go-round and slam into each other in bumper-cars – immediately followed by old footage of two cars crashing head-on. Already, Gagnon has introduced the primary and secondary concerns of the film: violence (exploding skyrocket, bumping, crashing cars) and the programmed conformism of modern mass society (crowds on the beach and at the amusement park). The latter is augmented with shots of highways and city streets jammed with traffic, lines of uniformed drum majorettes marching in tight formation, and crowds in department stores, at lunch counters, in city streets, and descending on escalators (a modernist trope also exploited by Lipsett in *21–84* [1964] and American experimental filmmaker Standish Lauder in *Necrology* [1967–70]). The violence continues in shots of a a bull knocking down a matador, boxers mauling each other (both shots intercut with cheering crowds), Laurel and Hardy punching and kicking each other, racing car accidents with pieces of a car flying through the air, and stunt drivers crashing a motorcycle through a flaming wall and flipping a speeding car on its side. The opening sequence comes to an end with shots of Buster Keaton (in *Cops*) chased by a hoard of policemen (interrupted by one shot of a cavalry charge – the first direct reference to the violence of war). It serves as the film's prologue, and from that point on, as in *A Trip down Memory Lane*, the film proceeds chronologically.

The footage Gagnon selected to represent the period from the beginning of World War I to the end of World War II is not notably different from what one would expect to see in a conventional compilation docu-

7.7 As the film nears its end, a dandelion's full head of seeds suggests the continuance of the natural order of fertility and the renewal of life.

mentary of the sort Leyda examines in *Films Beget Films*. What distinguishes Gagnon's treatment of the footage is the tighter, quicker rhythms of his editing and the absence of an explanatory voice-over to accompany a montage that includes the funeral of the Austrian Archduke Franz Ferdinand, German officers in spiked helmets on parade, cannons firing, troops in trenches and charging across open ground, falling back under heavy gunfire, and entangled in barbed wire, a torpedoed ship rolling over, dead bodies of soldiers in muddy trenches, soldiers and civilians celebrating the armistice, leaders of the Western world congregating to sign the Treaty of Versailles, and a victory parade down a wide city boulevard – at which point Gagnon breaks out of compilation film conventions by inserting more footage from *Cops*. The cops pursuing Keaton push their way into a police station, after which Keaton emerges dressed as a cop, locks the door to the station, throws the key in a trash can, and brushes his hands in a gesture that says, "That's the end of *that*!" and walks away.

7.8 Gagnon brings his film to a pessimistic conclusion with a negative image of a dandelion's full head of seeds, suggesting it has been burned black by the nuclear explosion in the immediately preceding shot.

But, of course, it is *not* the end of violence. After a moment of silence and a black screen, the film continues with a speeded-up extract from Leporello's "catalogue aria" from *Don Giovanni* accompanying shots of Mussolini declaiming from his palace balcony and Hitler speaking into a microphone, followed by more shots of Mussolini and a violently gesticulating Hitler whose downward gesture is synched with the end of the aria. There follow shots of book burning, Nazi rallies, Italy's invasion of Ethiopia, the Spanish Civil War, and many shots of tanks charging, artillery firing, the bombing of Pearl Harbor, soldiers charging across fields, battleships firing banks of guns, and planes exploding in mid-air. The already rapid pace of the editing accelerates even more in a very fast montage of photos of bombs falling and exploding and fighting on the ground and at sea, ending with photos of surrendering German soldiers. Contributing to the intensity of the sequence are quick zooms in on details of many of the photographs. The pace slows down with horrific photographs of emaciated corpses that American troops found when they entered the Nazi death camps, though Gagnon continues to zoom in on some of the photos to drive home the horror of what they show. The mood suddenly changes with newsreel footage of crowds in London celebrating the end of the war in Europe, which is interrupted by a silent nuclear explosion and an aerial view of the desolate wasteland of destroyed Hiroshima. The upbeat mood returns with crowds in Times Square celebrating the end of the war in the Pacific.

From that point on the principal emphasis is not on the ongoing violence of war but on the frenetic pace of life in North America from the end of World War II to the years immediately preceding the opening of Expo 67. There are a few found-footage clips (Fidel Castro preparing to give a speech, Jack Ruby shooting Lee Harvey Oswald in the Dallas police station, a Buddhist monk's self immolation), but the vast majority of images are photographs and magazine ads that Gagnon frequently crops or "animates" and juxtaposes in bursts of montage accompanied by insistently pulsating music that suggests – to this viewer – a dangerously rapid heartbeat. A complete shot list would include several hundred images, but to mention a few more: throngs of pedestrians and shoppers; magazine ads for lipstick; rows of Barbie dolls in boxes; several photos of John F. Kennedy, including a frame from the Zapruder footage of his assassination; exotic dancers; a skimpily dressed woman fronting a rock band' a *Playboy*-style nude; stacks of consumer goods including cooking utensils, mousetraps, and hammers; and finally, junk yards filled with the discarded and obsolete detritus of a consumer society. Following a photograph of a row of junked cars piled on top of each other, the film arrives at its apocalyptic conclusion: a time-lapse shot of a dandelion opening to reveal a full, round head of white, fluffy seeds, a flash of white and a reverberating roar accompanying the emerging image of the rising, white mushroom cloud of a nuclear explosion, a negative image of the dandelion closing without releasing its seeds (see figures 7.7 and 7.8). The soft, white disk of the rising sun at the beginning of the film is echoed in both the round white heads of the dandelion and the mushroom cloud. With the final negative image turning white into black and metaphorically withdrawing the promise of renewed growth, Gagnon implicitly suggests that with the ever-present threat of a nuclear confrontation between the United States and the Soviet Union, he could not, in fact, "keep this film going on forever." "Forever" would end with a nuclear holocaust.

"YOU MUST BE VERY CAREFUL": *THE HART OF LONDON*

At eighty minutes, Jack Chambers's *The Hart of London* is by far the longest of the five films discussed here. It also comes closest to being a personal statement, despite the fact that more than half of it is composed of footage from 16 mm newsreels shot in and around London, Ontario, in the 1950s, which Chambers acquired from the archives of the local television station, and anonymous snapshots that he collected by placing an advertisement in the local newspaper.[28] Together, they provide what Bart Testa describes as "a community chronicle, an archive of memories ... as authorless as they are artless."[29] The remainder of the film's footage was shot by Chambers himself and has very much the feel of home movies. For that reason it can be regarded as the most "personal" material in the film, but through montage and special optical effects, Chambers brings the found footage and photographs into a unified personal vision of what Bruce Elder describes as "the struggle of consciousness for a sense of place."[30]

The "place," in the most immediate geographical sense of the word, is London, Ontario, where Chambers was born and spent most of his life. In a more figurative sense, place is anywhere one "belongs," where one can feel "at home." In this broader sense, place is an intersection of time (past and present) and space (the locale, in the sense of the local). It is also an intersection of the subjective and the social, the individual and the communal. This, I suggest, is what *The Hart of London* is about, and this is why the archival footage and the photos provided by members of the community are so important. They document the past, from somewhere in the late nineteenth century to approximately the time the film was made, and because they are anonymous records of people, places, and events in and around London, they convey a sense of communal experience. In Chambers's film, they represent a collective memory in which the filmmaker tries to find his own, individual place, which is represented quite literally in Chambers's integration of his own original footage with the found footage and photographs that constitute the rest of the film's imagery.

While the archival images and old photographs may represent the collective memory, they are not necessarily trustworthy records of actuality, past or present. Like memory, they are selective, and their images have no fixed and innate meaning. As Alan Sekula puts it, "not only are pictures

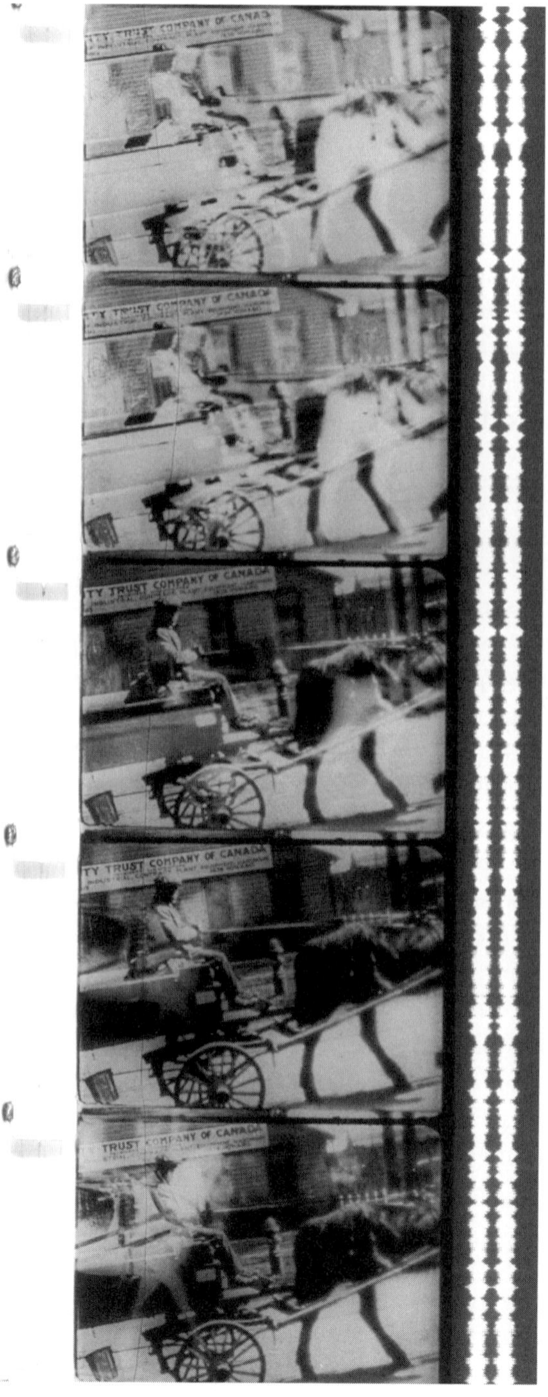

7.9 One of many archival images manipulated by Chambers to represent the fragile and insubstantial – yet still present – memories of the past.

in archives often *literally* for sale, but their meanings are up for grabs."[31] And over a long enough period they fade and decompose. Chambers recreates memory's counterpart of these processes by using overexposure, superimposition, and a mix of positive and negative images. These effects dominate the first half of *The Hart of London*, in which Chambers evokes the poignancy of a past that is literally fading away or slipping in and out of memory with glimmering, ephemeral images that merge with other equally fleeting and insubstantial images. This often beautiful and haunting palimpsest of grey and white images is more than a post-structuralist assertion of the instability of signifier and signified – it is also a poetic rendering of individual and collective memory immersed in the ambiguity, insubstantiality, and impermanence of documentary records of historical reality (see figure 7.9).

If *The Hart of London* is about "place" – spatial and temporal, physical and mental, individual and communal, past and present – then my emphasis on the ambiguity and insubstantiality of images in memory and in archives might seem to imply that Chambers's film suggests no such place exits. Taken as a whole, however, the film seems to imply that there is no lasting, permanent place where everything comes together and the questing consciousness can come to rest. Instead, place is like Heraclitus's river, a permanent flow, always present and always changing with no fixed place one can step into more than once. This Heraclitian flow is evoked at the end of the film, in a kind of coda composed of repeated pans along a river and up into the sky. The flow is also suggested in other river imagery in the film, the most ironic being newsreel footage of a man – a Polar Bear Club type – swimming across a narrow river in mid-winter. There is also the frequent sound of flowing water on the soundtrack in the central section of the film (introduced by footage of a man spraying water for an outdoor skating rink), and to my ears the sound during the first part of the film is an electronic simulation of waves crashing on a beach.

Images and the sound of water are not the only elements of the film to suggest the permanent flux of existence. The constant merging of images through superimposition and montage, does as well, along with many images that taken together allude to the flow of life from birth to death: shots of fetuses, an infant emerging from the womb, younger and older children, adults, and an elderly couple at what looks like a wedding anniversary attended by three generations of offspring. Death is ritualistically embodied in the slaughter of two sheep, which is followed

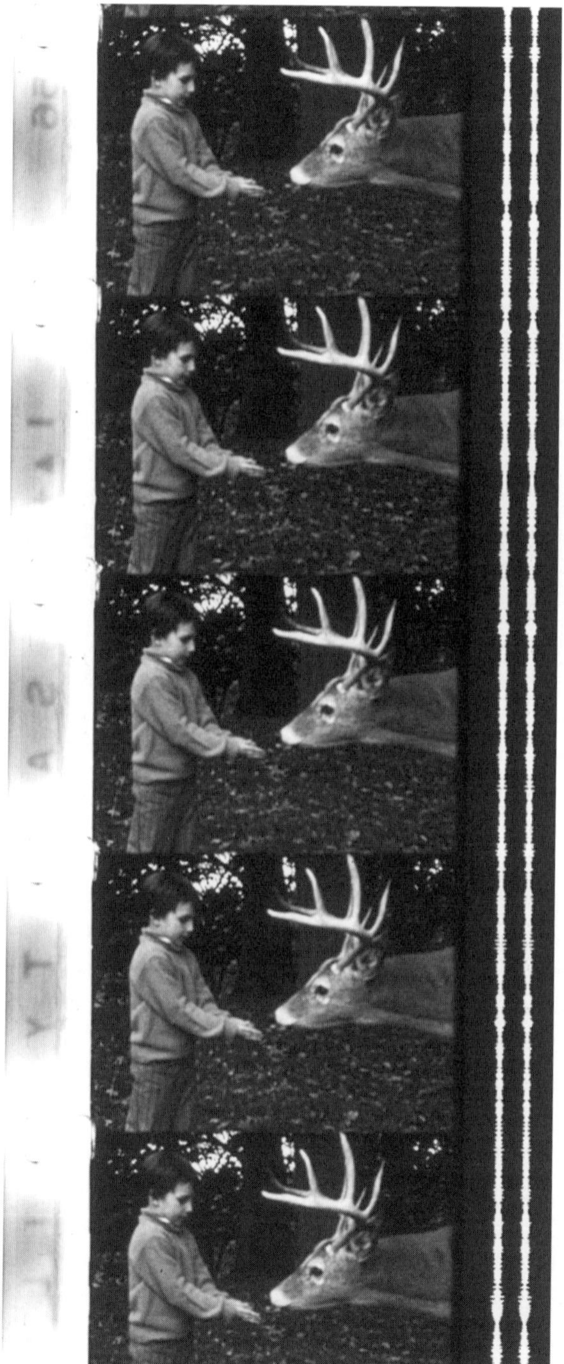

7.10 Chambers's home movie footage of one of his sons feeding a deer brings the film into the present while alluding to the past in which newsreel footage showed a deer leaping over fences in the backyards of London, Ontario.

immediately by Chambers's footage of the birth of one of his children. Chambers's montage also alludes to the past-destroying "progress" of modern society with, for example, archival footage of old, obsolete locomotives and old water towers being pulled down or blown up. What was once essential is now obsolete. Nothing is permanent, except change.

But in change there is still continuity – the Heraclitian stream flows on, but it is still the same stream. Preceding the coda referred to above, Chambers inserts his own home movie footage of his two young sons gingerly feeding some small deer on a green hillside (see figure 7.10). The soundtrack features what sounds like high-speed traffic on a nearby highway mixed with the voices of the boys' parents cautioning their children not to move too quickly and frighten the deer. "You must be very careful," the mother whispers. That cautionary phrase repeats nearly a dozen times as the film comes to an end. We hear it for the last time in the coda, as the camera makes one last pan up the river and into a reddening sky.

The home movie footage of the boys and the deer recalls the film's opening: a deer darting across a field and leaping over backyard fences, presumably on the outskirts of London. In subsequent footage it is unclear if this hart of London is killed or only tranquillized in order to return it to its natural habitat. What *is* clear is that it is "out of place" in London – or in a slightly different reading, it is, in fact, London's wild hart/heart disturbing the town's orderly domesticity. The opening and closing sequences of the film exemplify the overarching theme of the film: that place is a geographic, temporal, and psychological site of change within continuity. What was, still is – but different. The opening sequence is of the past; the closing sequence is of the present, and the presence of the filmmaker's children implies a future (one that Chambers would only live a few more years to observe before leukemia ended his life at the age of forty-seven).

Without necessarily endorsing Stan Brakhage's praise of Chambers's film as "one of the greatest films ever made,"[32] I assert that of the films discussed here, *The Hart of London* most movingly demonstrates what a filmmaker working with found footage can accomplish by rigorously adhering to the aesthetic and ethical imperative to "be very careful."

The release of *The Hart of London* in 1970 capped a half-decade of Canadian experimental filmmakers' exploration of the aesthetic, political, and personally expressive possibilities offered by recycling found footage. With his combination of home movies, local television footage, and photographs provided by fellow citizens of London, Ontario, Chambers created the most "personal" exploitation of the otherwise unrecognized significance of the found footage he was able to collect for his film. For Wieland, the out-takes and cut-aways of an unreleased film provided the raw material for a cinematic poem/dance/celebration of the efforts of young women to negotiate the social and economic constraints imposed on underprivileged women – especially African American women – in the 1960s. With a banal educational film and an array of other found footage, Wieland and Ferguson created a combination of humour and critique that would become a popular manoeuver among many film-makers working with found footage – including Lipsett and Gagnon, though both invested their films with a sharper and more overtly political critique of the modern world. Both also drew upon and at the same time subverted the well-establish form of the compilation film, which is, after all, where the practice of recycling film footage began. "We can start with the premise," Leyda writes, "that anything that has been put on film can be employed a second time – usually with more force than the first time, depending on the artist who shapes the second employment."[33] The films discussed here show what can happen when that "second deployment" escapes the enclosed pastures of compilation documentaries for the open range of experimental/avant-garde/underground film.

NOTES

1 Strictly speaking, found footage was used much earlier in the wartime compilation films of the National Film Board of Canada, but in intention and execution those films fall outside the generally recognized perimeters of experimental filmmaking. For more on the history, theory, and practice of found-footage filmmaking, see Yann Beauvais, *Found Footage/Films retrouvés* (Paris: Galerie nationale du Jeu de Paume, 1995); James Peterson, *Dreams of Chaos, Visions of Order: Understanding the American Avant-Garde Cinema* (Detroit: Wayne State University Press, 1994), 145–77; Patrik Sjöberg, *The World in Pieces: A Study of the Compilation Film* (Stockholm: Aura förlag, 2001); and William C. Wees, *Recycled Images: The Art and Politics of Found-Footage Films* (New York: Anthology Film Archives, 1993).

2 Betty Ferguson, an American who subsequently moved to Canada and became a Canadian citizen, also made three found-footage films of her own: *The Telephone Film* (1972), *The Airplane Film* (1973), and *Kisses* (1976).

3 Jay Leyda, *Films Beget Films: A Study of the Compilation Film* (New York: Hill and Wang, 1964), 9.

4 *Underground film* disappeared from the lexicon of experimental/avant-garde film in the early 1970s, but the kinds of films it was intended to describe

(including found-footage films) continue to appear to the present day – though increasingly in digital rather than film formats.

5 Filler or slug is scrap film used by film editors to temporarily "hold a place" in a film for footage that will be added later in the editing process.

6 Information about Wieland and Ferguson's friendship and collaboration on the production of *Barbara's Blindness* comes from a telephone conversation with Betty Ferguson on 21 December 2010.

7 Betty Ferguson and Joyce Wieland, *Barbara's Blindness*, 1965, 17 min., b&w, sound, 16 mm, distributed by the Canadian Filmmakers Distribution Centre (CFMDC) and the New York Filmmakers' Cooperative, also available in *The Complete Works of Joyce Wieland*, vol. 1, DVD, CFMDC, 2011.

8 Quoted in *Filmmakers' Cooperative Catalogue*, no. 7 (New York: Filmmakers' Cooperative, 1989), 490.

9 The man and girl are Horst Buchholz and Hayley Mills in the 1959 feature film *Tiger Bay*. My thanks to Blaine Allan for identifying the source of this footage.

10 Joyce Wieland, *Handtinting*, 1967–68, 5:30 min., colour, silent, 16 mm, distributed by CFMDC and the New York Filmmakers' Cooperative, also available in *The Complete Works of Joyce Wieland*, vol. 2, DVD, CFMDC, 2011.

11 Kay Armatage, "Kay Armatage Interviews Joyce Wieland," in *The Films of Joyce Wieland*, ed. Katherine Elder (Toronto: Cinematheque Ontario, 1999), 154.

12 Ibid., 154.

13 Ibid., 153–4.

14 While most of the women in the film are black, a few are white – a fact that frequently goes unmentioned in descriptions of the film.

15 Regina Cornwell, "The Films of Joyce Wieland," in *The Films of Joyce Wieland*, ed. Katherine Elder (Toronto: Cinematheque Ontario, 1999), 53. Wieland used fabric dyes to apply colour to the film.

16 Armatage, "Kay Armatage Interviews Joyce Wieland," 154.

17 Lauren Rabinovitz, "The Development of Feminist Strategies in the Experimental Films of Joyce Wieland," in *The Films of Joyce Wieland*, ed. Katherine Elder (Toronto: Cinematheque Ontario, 1999), 110.

18 Kass Banning, "Textual Excess in Joyce Wieland's *Handtinting*," in *The Films of Joyce Wieland*, ed. Katherine Elder (Toronto: Cinematheque Ontario, 1999), 131.

19 Arthur Lipsett, *A Trip down Memory Lane*, 1965, 12:30 min., b&w, sound, 16 mm, distributed on DVD by the National Film Board of Canada. Lipsett made a second found-footage film, *Fluxes* (1967), before he resigned from the NFB in 1970. The following discussion of Lipsett's film is a condensed and somewhat revised extract from William C. Wees, "From Compilation to Collage: The Found-Footage Films of Arthur Lipsett," *Canadian Journal of Film Studies* 16, no. 2 (2007): 2–22.

20 Arthur Lipsett, "Notes and Proposals," *Canadian Journal of Film Studies* 7, no. 1 (1998): 56.

21 Charles Gagnon, *The Eighth Day/Le huitième jour*, 1967, 14 min. b&w, sound, 16 mm, distributed by CFMDC and in *Charles Gagnon: 4 Films*, DVD, Spectral Media, 2010.

22 For information about the Christian Pavilion and the controversies it produced, see Monika Kin Gagnon, "The Christian Pavilion at Expo 67: Notes

from Charles Gagnon's Archive," in *Expo 67: Not Just a Souvenir*, ed. Rhona Richman Kenneally and Johanne Sloan (Toronto: University of Toronto Press, 2010), 142–62.

23 Ibid., 152.

24 Danielle Corbeil, "Charles Gagnon, Painter, Filmmaker, 35 Years Old, Lives in Montréal" (from a taped interview recorded by Danielle Corbeil), *Artscanada* 27, no. 2 (April 1970): 40; reprinted in Monika Kin Gagnon, ed., *Charles Gagnon: 4 Films* (Spectral Media, 2010, booklet accompanying the DVD), 33.

25 Corbeil, "Charles Gagnon, Painter, Filmmaker, 35 Years Old, Lives in Montréal," 39. Probably the earliest found-footage film made with similar intentions is *L'Histoire du soldat inconnu* (1932) by the Belgian filmmaker Henri Storck. While it is unlikely that Gagnon saw Storck's film, he would have had the opportunity to see Bruce Conner's *A Movie* (1958) and Arthur Lipsett's *Very Nice, Very Nice* (1961) and *A Trip down Memory Lane* – films that share some of the same techniques and cultural-political critiques found in *The Eighth Day*.

26 Corbeil, "Charles Gagnon, Painter, Filmmaker, 35 Years Old, Lives in Montréal," 39, and Gagnon, *Charles Gagnon: 4 Films*, 33.

27 Gagnon, "The Christian Pavilion at Expo 67," 154.

28 *The Hart of London*, 1968–70, 79 min., b&w and colour, sound, 16 mm, distributed by CFMDC.

29 Bart Testa, "Chamber's Epic: *The Hart of London*, History's Protagonist," in *The Films of Jack Chambers*, ed. Katherine Elder (Toronto: Cinematheque Ontario, 2002), 147.

30 R. Bruce Elder, *Image and Identity: Reflections on Canadian Film and Culture* (Waterloo: Wilfred Laurier University Press, 1989), 382.

31 Allan Sekula, "Reading an Archive," in *Blasted Allegories: An Anthology of Contemporary Artists*, ed. Brian Wallis (Cambridge, MA: MIT Press, 1987), 116.

32 Stan Brakhage, "*The Hart of London*: A Document of the City," in *The Films of Jack Chambers*, ed. Katherine Elder (Toronto: Cinematheque Ontario, 2002), 123.

33 Leyda, *Films Beget Films*, 131.

8 UNFINISHED FILMS AND POSTHUMOUS CINEMA

CHARLES GAGNON'S *R69* AND JOYCE WIELAND'S *WENDY AND JOYCE*

Monika Kin Gagnon

R69 IS AN UNFINISHED 16 mm film that my late father, Charles Gagnon, began in 1969. *Wendy and Joyce* is a 16 mm film that Canadian artist Joyce Wieland started in 1967 but never completed. These unfinished films unite these artists. Yet there is more that connects Gagnon and Wieland: the duration of their artistic careers, as both started producing art in the 1950s and died five years apart; their distinctive multidisciplinarity; and the late 1960s' artistic conjuncture of urban Canada all offer further consonance. Their films' unfinished potential generates what I call *posthumous cinema*, which I offer as a working concept. By this, I am not looking to establish a new genre or subcategory of cinema whose primary characteristics would be that its films are unfinished. Rather, in this chapter I mobilize the concept of the *posthumous* to understand the ontology of unfinished films (and the archives supporting them), as well as to lay bare the complexity of filmmaking processes. At their most basic, are unfinished films truly films? While they are materially composed *of* film, can unedited images exposed on celluloid, raw exposed footage, and their surrounding ephemera (notes, storyboards, interviews) be considered films? I propose that the concept of posthumous cinema brings attention to their unfinished nature, while productively operationalizing them. Animating the film elements from both Wieland and Gagnon's unfinished films brings out historian Carolyn Steedman's sense that "*nothing happens to this stuff, in the Archive*" especially acutely; as she continues, "as stuff, it just sits there until it is read, and used, and narrativised."[1] To transpose Steedman's comments to the particularities of film archives, her statement of how "stuff ... just sits there until it is read, and used, and narrativised" would change to how film "stuff" just sits there until it is (at least) projected and viewed. The need to physically manipulate and project film means that access to original, often fragile films is complicated by the imperatives of film archives that would restrict this handling in the interest of maximizing material preservation of the artefacts themselves. Posthumous cinema, I will demonstrate, is this animation of unfinished film elements after the filmmakers' deaths: it encourages the use, examination, viewing, and analysis of archived film fragments and ephemera that would otherwise "just sit there" in refrigerated vaults. It brings them to projected life. My aspirations in this chapter are to underline the importance of film archives at a moment when their specialization is being undermined and moratoriums are being placed on collections, and to explore the rich potentialities of unfinished films by offering concrete practices and forms of creative archival animation devised from them.

The term *posthumous* originated in 1668 to describe a book publication subsequent to an author's death. Posthumous cinema thereby involves unfinished films that are conditionally completed after a filmmaker's death. In this chapter, I consider the archives of Gagnon and Wieland's unfinished films, both housed at the Cinémathèque québécoise in Montreal, as well as the necessarily provisional "texts" of these unfinished films, as forms of posthumous cinema – that is, as unfinished film fragments that are studied after the filmmakers' deaths. I affirm the importance of archives for producing meaning that goes beyond completed films alone and expand the viewership of unfinished, archived films. I further offer a compelling pathway toward exploring film archives in the specifically digital context. Unfinished films function as objects of analysis, while the working concepts of *posthumous collaboration* and *posthumous cinema* function to open up the cultures of (experimental) production and the future viewership of seemingly dormant film and other media-based archives. In other words, digital media formats can creatively activate seemingly inactive analogue film archives, which are frequently anchored to prohibitive technological processes of projection, and other conditions of access including physical handling, that may contravene the imperatives of archival preservation.

The recent surge of scholarly interest in the changing ontologies of traditional archives and film archives with the advent of digital media offers a propitious framework for such an exploration. Several fruitful concepts engaging the transformative role of media in relation to archiving are theoretical frames that inform my preliminary exploration of these two unfinished experimental films. José van Dijck's concept of mediated memories attributes transformations of human memory to the proliferation and ubiquity of digital photography and video, and thereby points to the material specificities of film and its digital versions. New media theorist Wendy Hui Kyong Chun's inversion of Mary Ann Doane's imbrication of film as historical artefact and its indexical moment as historical event is especially apposite here, as Chun argues that artefact and event "are separated in digital media, and it is this separation that grounds computer media as such."[2] Chun's theorizing of digital media as "enduring ephemeral" effectively captures the aspirations and limits of digital archives ("digital media is not always there," she writes), and signals the already unstable and constantly changing qualities of any archive.

TWO UNFINISHED FILMS

In this framework, Gagnon and Wieland's unfinished films and archives are considered posthumously for their generative capacities to think about the specificity of film archives, their migration to digital formats, and the implications of creative forms of archiving for cultural memory. *R69* began shooting in 1969, the fourth and last film Charles Gagnon made, as the focus of his practice shifted more intensively to painting and photography for the rest of his career. He had mentioned *R69* several times in the two years before his death in 2003, and with increased frequency after his long-time friend, the late Quebec painter Yves Gaucher, died only a few years earlier in 2000. *R69* is named after a lively red painting by Gaucher (see figure 8.1). According to his wife, Germaine Gaucher, who still has the painting, the title refers to a paint catalogue number, the vibrant red #69 that he used to create this work.

Part of the historical interest of *R69* is that sections of the footage show Gaucher as he prepares and paints this canvas in his studio – one floor of the large building on St-Paul Ouest in Old Montreal, which he shared with fellow artists Gagnon and Jean McEwen from the 1960s until 1984 – offering an intimate glimpse into his working space (see figure 8.2). *R69*'s conjuring of Gaucher's painting moves us imaginatively and literally through the creation of this canvas in the artist's studio. As in the opening scenes of Gagnon's earlier film, *The Sound of Space* (1970), the artist's studio is a site rich for exploration, where contemplation and creative labour occur, also offering historical insights into the techniques and everyday working environments of these painters. The film then follows Gaucher's painting to its first showing in the exhibition *Grands formats* (or large formats) at the Musée d'art contemporain de Montréal in

8.1 Yves Gaucher with the finished painting *R69* in his studio, 1969.

8.2 Yves Gaucher's studio, prepping canvas for *R69.*

8.3 Yves Gaucher interviewed in front of his painting, *R69* (1969), by Klaus Fuchs, at the opening of *Grands formats* at the Musée d'art contemporain de Montréal, 1970.

January 1970, where Gagnon and his then-student Klaus Fuchs interview Gaucher, McEwen, and fellow artists Henry Saxe, Guido Molinari, Claude Tousignant, and Jacques Hurtubise as they stand in front of their artworks and speak wryly about the status of art, painting, and culture in Quebec and Canada (see figure 8.3).

What triggers posthumous (self-)appointments? My posthumous engagement and "finishing" of *R69 [unfinished/inachevé]* began with the discovery of three storage boxes that my father had left behind in his studio after his death.[3] It is unlikely that I would have been involved with *R69* had my father been alive (most obviously, he might have completed the film himself; less evident are other interpersonal factors). Yet my sense of posthumous collaboration with him was palpable over the five years I worked with his archives, giving way to what I named posthumous cinema, an activity in the outer limits of unfinished films. The first image I saw from the original rough assembly footage of *R69* was of my father, decades younger and strangely alive, peering directly into his Bolex camera lens (see figure 8.4). I was rattled by his visage staring directly at me. But, if his opening self-portrait startled me, hearing my father's voice was even more unsettling. In addition to the fifty-five-minute, 2,000-foot rough picture assembly he had left behind, he had gathered almost

8.4 Charles Gagnon checking the camera.

four hours of sound that had been recorded on quarter-inch audiotape and on magnetic film (to cut sound to picture). Among these elements were recordings he had done with a portable Nagra tape recorder while standing in a field out in Ayer's Cliff, Quebec, where my family and I spent our summers on an old farm, and where my father had a studio where many of his paintings were made from 1968 onward. It was clear that the audiotape was fragile; I could even detect disintegration. I had it transferred to a DAT disk, then converted into MP3s for my iPod. His voice transported me to a field he described as Ayer's Cliff, and it was as if I was there and he was alive again, standing before me with a microphone. Because of the crickets that follow on the soundtrack, I imagine it to be night-time. But some footage that shows him walking through a field with a camera and a mike boom, his full shadow from the bright sun appearing in the grass and wildflowers, syncs perfectly with some sound recordings. If his image startled me, his voice took my breath away, and still does every time I hear his distinct intonations and timbre, the unmistakable grain that seems so present, life-like, and embodied.

In writing about the history of sound technologies, from the telegraph through the microphone, telephone, phonograph, and radio, John Durham Peters claims that sound technologies mark the most radical of all sensory reorganizations in modernity: "Except for echoes, hearing disembodied voices has, for most of the history of our species, been the preserve of poets and the mad. The phonograph was one of several sound technologies to democratize this experience, and as with most things democratic, the oracular edges have worn off with use. The phonograph presented a human voice without a human body. The human soul, the breath, had taken up residence in a machine."[4]

It is from this experience of mediated disembodiment that *R69* became a posthumous collaboration: contending with those unfinished bits and pieces of my father's filmic things, making sense of them, and reordering this constellation of intertextual significations in a way that would resonate with his aesthetic sensibility and the historical context in which the unfinished film originated. If we have come to forget the strangeness of disengaging the voice from the body, as Peters suggests, the departure of an intimate to *l'au delà* imbues material traces with a heightened sense of value and meaning, generating connections between material objects and memory. There is an acute spectral quality to encountering unfinished films, including the anxious sense of the dead presiding over your every move. But this spectral effect is further evoked by the fragmentary and partial nature of materials and suggests an active mind in creative experimentation.[5] Peters describes how modern media complicate the boundaries of communication between the living and the dead when he writes:

> The two key existential facts about modern media are these: the ease with which the living may mingle with the communicable traces of the dead, and the difficulty of distinguishing communication at a distance from communication with the dead. The same phantasms of the living that are "communicated" to far-off destinations in telecommunications can be captured for playback in recording media. The key difference is that a dialogue can be conducted over distance, but a dialogue with the dead is quite another matter. As communicators the dead are a particularly enigmatic bunch.[6]

Engaging with a dead person's belongings (my father's, no less), and exploring the textures of a unique form of communication and communion (with its strange sort of mourning, which still eludes my comprehension), introduces emotionally charged and affective registers to how cultural and media history get written. The advantages I had of complete archival access were undercut by the layers and layers of personal history that seemed to imbue *all* his film elements with importance, making for an intriguing, if sometimes vexing, configuration of archaeological homage-research. In the case of *R69*, determining how to discern what was relevant and how to sift through these found materials was an affective, intellectual, and scholarly challenge.

A welcome antidote to this was my serendipitous encounter with Canadian artist Joyce Wieland's unfinished film, *Wendy and Joyce*, which she began in 1967 and never completed. Considered together, Gagnon and Wieland's films were collaborations by artists with (artist) friends, were unfinished at the artists' deaths, and permit, albeit in distinctive ways, an active exploration of alternative modes of animating film archives. As unfinished films, Gagnon's *R69* and Wieland's *Wendy and Joyce* are productively illuminated by the concept of posthumous cinema in that they require a range of considerations to fully engage them. This reveals more of the working processes of two Canadian artists who made experimental films as parts of their wider multidisciplinary practices. This is perhaps the most compelling aspect of unfinished films: encountering film fragments that are in the midst of an engaged and vibrant creative process of making to which we become engaged as witness-observers.

Wieland's complete filmic archives were donated to the Cinémathèque québécoise following her death in 1998. With her film distributor, the Canadian Filmmakers Distribution of Canada (CFMDC), a DVD compilation entitled *The Complete Works of Joyce Wieland* was produced in 2011 that brings together sixteen shorts and two feature films that Wieland produced in her lifetime. As an unfinished film, *Wendy and Joyce* is not among these eighteen films, but a rough assembly and some disparate film and sound elements labelled "Wendy and Joyce" are housed at the Cinémathèque, while her paper-based notes and sound elements are held in the Clara Thomas Archives and Special Collections at York University. *Wendy and Joyce* was a collaboration Wieland commenced with her friend film critic Wendy Michener in 1967 – the same year that Wieland began another collaboration with filmmaker Hollis Frampton, *A and B in Ontario*, which she did go on to complete after his death in 1984. In her biography of Wieland, *Artist on Fire*, Jane Lind writes: "Joyce wanted to develop her stored material for a film she and her dear friend, Wendy Michener had begun. Wendy, at age thirty-five, had died of an embolism on New Year's

Day in 1969. The disparate film footage and photographs required total concentration – something that Joyce did not seem to have, and she made no progress. She was also unable to get the funding she needed. 'Wendy and Joyce' was never completed."[7]

To engage some symmetry, the first images I saw from *Wendy and Joyce* are what I deduce from Wieland's notes to be film footage that Wieland shot shortly after her friend Michener died on 1 January 1969. As Wieland's notes reveal, this black-and-white footage shows "Wendy's husband and children at breakfast, in silent pain after Wendy's premature death."[8] If the first scene I encountered from *R69* was the eerie presence of my father's face and his voice, *Wendy and Joyce*'s breakfast scene is marked by a silent soundtrack and Michener's eerie absence from a domestic scene in which she would likely have ordinarily been at the centre: her young daughter, Caitlin, who appears to be six or seven years old, lightheartedly aware of Wieland's camera as she eats a bowl of cornflakes as her infant brother sits watching from his highchair. They play a bit, and she then dresses and dances for the camera in her white tights and tartan skirt. Michener's husband, Les Lawrence, presides over the familial scene in his pyjamas, sitting later with Caitlin on his lap, chatting with her as he smokes a cigarette.[9] Michener's absence commences Wieland's fifty-five-minute rough assembly, loosely compiled sequences and scenes that were to eventually make up her (their) film.

While filming for *Wendy and Joyce* had begun in 1967, Michener's sudden death in 1969 clearly foreclosed any further possibility of direct collaboration between her and Wieland. Yet Wieland returned briefly to the project when she was re-editing and completing several other unfinished films with the assistance of her niece, filmmaker Su Rynard, and with financial support from an Ontario Arts Council grant in the mid-1980s. *A and B in Ontario, Birds at Sunrise* (1972–86), and *Peggy's Blue Skylight* (1964) were completed during this period. And although Wieland's notes had included it with these other films that were slated to be completed, *Wendy and Joyce* remained unfinished. Rynard recalls viewing some of the footage of *Wendy and Joyce* with Wieland at this time, but also recollects that the material was too unshaped and less complete than the other films Wieland edited to completion during this later period; she also recalled that Wieland had expressed sadness upon seeing images of Michener.[10] In the Cinémathèque archives, footage designated as "Wendy and Joyce" consists of original archival 16 mm film elements that were initially inaccessible for viewing as they were stored in their climate-controlled vaults for preservation. In addition to these original archival film elements, there are video transfers of Michener's family's home movie archives over several generations from 1938 to 1958 (given her father's status as politician and sitting governor general from 1967 to 1974, these "home movies" include highly public international events). There are dozens of quarter-inch sound tapes that are labelled as Wendy Michener's radio interviews for the CBC with numerous filmmakers including Pier Pasolini and Satyajit Ray, among many others; as well, there are several tapes described as conversations between Wieland and Michener. Permission from the Cinémathèque and York University to digitize and access Wieland's *Wendy and Joyce* film elements enabled my preliminary exploration. Along with paper archives from the Joyce Wieland fonds at York University, I discovered more exact information about the contents of these elements and Wieland's plans for her film. Her grant application to the Ontario Arts Council (of which there is a handwritten version, as well as multiple copies typed onto the A-Grant form) concisely identifies portions of the film fragments, such as the breakfast scene, which could subsequently be supplemented and comprehended in more detail:

> Wendy Michener was one of Canada's most respected film critics when she died in 1969, leaving a husband and two small children. She was the daughter of then Governor General Roland Michener and the impeccably gracious Mrs. Michener.
>
> Wendy and I were friends, and this film is about us. We were two young women interested in making art, making food, making friends, and making films.
>
> The footage that exists now consists of about 2000' of 16 mm reversal, shot in turns by Wendy and me. It includes an episode in winter at Wendy's parents official residence (the two of us skating on a large outdoor rink, Wendy with her parents inside, and Wendy with photographs of her parents); Wendy and Joyce preparing and eating food; fragments of a film that we were making together (a book in the snow, a dog, a car shot through a window); Joyce preparing for an exhibition at the Vancouver Art Gallery (sewing a quilt on the train, dusting and touching paintings and assemblages

8.5 Image of Wendy Michener (holding a Bolex film camera) and Joyce Wieland (with her back to camera), on a train between Toronto and Vancouver in the late 1960s.

> in the gallery, and mingling at the vernissage); Joyce shooting parts of REASON OVER PASSION on the return train; and finally Wendy's husband and children at breakfast, in silent pain after Wendy's premature death. Our friendship develops as we film each other.[11]

A still photograph from the York archives, which appears in Wieland's rough assembly, documents Wieland and Michener on a train and captures their film-shooting process as they both cradle Bolex cameras pointed toward each other (see figure 8.5). Lind's description seems to further the photographer's scene: "In January [1967], Joyce had a retrospective at the Vancouver Art Gallery and decided to travel west by train, accompanied by Wendy Michener and Rose Richardson. She took her camera, and filmed hours and hours of footage of the train window to capture the winter landscape as they went."[12] Lind then quotes Wieland:

> [I] got on the train with the Bolexes and tape machine, and as soon as we got past Lake of the Woods the snow started, and it was the most idyllic, exquisite trip I think I've ever taken in my entire life. As soon as we came to the Prairies, it was just this vast glacial

> winter and then into British Columbia where the trees were heavily laden with snow and I photographed every day all day from the train window. I used every possible combination of the camera, fooling around with exposures, using different film stocks, different camera speeds.[13]

POSTHUMOUS RECIPROCITIES

Death swirls around these two projects in captivating ways. While death is inherent to their unfinished quality (in the sense that the filmmakers did not complete these films before their deaths), it also pervades the subjects and relations within the films themselves. For Gagnon, filmmaking seemed to be a way of negotiating the passing of friends, and perhaps in *R69*'s *vernissage*-event of *Grands formats*, as artists mingle with patrons at the museum with their cocktails and cigarettes in hand, the passing of a historical and cultural moment. As Gagnon himself intimated in an interview, his 1970 film *Pierre Mercure (1927–1966)* followed the celebrated young composer Mercure's sudden death in a car crash, and Gagnon's sense of wanting to respond by creating images: "The film on [Pierre] Mercure is the one I consider the most personal and the most interesting. I believe that I made it as much for him as for me; I felt I owed him something, and the film is a kind of homage to Mercure, an homage which came and joined itself to my realization of what life was, what death was."[14] Perhaps for similar reasons he had wanted to return to and complete *R69* after Yves Gaucher's death. For Gagnon, then, filmmaking could be considered to be a kind of posthumous collaboration enabling the animation of traces, remnants, and remains: a (re)animation of relations with recently deceased friends.

For Wieland, it seems that Hollis Frampton's death in 1984 spurred interest in the completion of their earlier, uncompleted film and she would enter into the last phases of post-production editing *A and B in Ontario*, which could be analogously described as a form of posthumous collaboration with Frampton. Lind describes:

> Joyce had black-and-white footage for a film she and her close friend Hollis Frampton had shot in the summer of 1967, chasing each other with their cameras, beginning at Wendy Michener's home in the Casa Loma area of Toronto and ending at Ward's Island. They didn't complete it before Frampton died of lung cancer in the spring of 1984 at the age of forty-eight, just when the Albright-

> Knox Gallery in Buffalo, New York, was mounting a major traveling retrospective of his work. Considering the importance of this film, the Albright-Knox wanted to see *A and B in Ontario* completed.[15]

That the completed film so actively represents a form of hide-and-seek between the filmmakers and their cameras must have been an eerie experience to edit and complete so soon after Frampton's death, as the shots quite literally alternate portraits of Wieland and Frampton.[16] Both filmmakers react and respond to the presence of the other's camera, so the main points of view alternate between collaborators, much like *Wendy and Joyce*'s shots have a similar symmetry and reciprocity between Wieland and Michener. Wieland's willingness to revisit *Wendy and Joyce* in the 1980s, the same period she describes in her grant application, expresses another anticipated form of posthumous collaboration, this time between Wieland and Michener, which would regrettably go unrealized. Yet, we learn about *Wendy and Joyce*'s latent potential by engaging the completed *A and B in Ontario*, which captures playfulness, collaborative irreverence, and creative friendship. (Additionally, one sound tape in the Wieland fonds' "Wendy and Joyce" files is a seven-minute audio recording of a short sequence from *Daisies* (1966), Czechoslovakian filmmaker Věra Chytilová's controversial, wildly experimental film about two mischievous young women, which lends speculative insight into Wieland's influences for her own film, especially its "collage" techniques, special effects, and camera tricks.)[17]

Elsewhere, I refer to posthumous collaboration as a way of recognizing the affective relationships and connections between people and the material filmic traces of unfinished films.[18] Any posthumous ordering of these traces, fragments, and idea-evocations diverge inevitably from an artist's intentions, alternately expanding their creative texts into the present and future through a relation of care and engagement that animates, rather than merely classifies and preserves, archival materials through archival protocols. This transforms archival collections (especially moving image artefacts), into active, living, and communicative processes. Posthumous cinema is, inherently, a posthumous collaboration of sorts, a form of communication with a filmmaker across their filmic and extra-filmic elements. It acknowledges the multifaceted nature of the filmmaking process, in that it recognizes the extended and clearly defined phases of production (planning, shooting film, and recording sound) and post-production (picture and sound editing, distribution, screening/reception) required

8.6 Yves Gaucher mixing paints for *R69* in his studio, 1969.

to initiate, create, and complete a film. In highlighting the various phases of the filmmaking process, it situates unfinished films in the preliminary phases of planning and initial production (film shooting and recording); it recognizes that any notion of a final, fixed filmic "text" is, in some sense, waylaid or deferred. Posthumous cinema is thereby less a definable genre with identifiable typologies and characteristics than an exploration that permits, as heuristic devices do, a productive process of searching and discovery. As there is no definitive film text that exists in its entirety, we remain playfully suspended in the realm of the extra-cinematic: film and sound fragments, notes, anecdotes, speculations, idea-evocations, and aspirations. These film and sound fragments, illuminated by paper notes in these archives or archives-in-progress, spur speculations based on these filmmakers prior films, the overlaps between them, and the supplementary information that can palpably emerge out of the engagement with existing archival and other extant materials. Posthumous cinema highlights the multifaceted and overlapping relationships – aesthetic, affective, archival, ethical, institutional, and technical – that are activated when unfinished films are engaged. My interest in this chapter is on the interrelations of the first three: the archival material's aesthetic qualities and how these signify and are imbued with affect.[19]

Conventional archives are historically those affiliated with established institutional organizations and structures, which caretake the documentation of past activities, the archive is a place where artefacts, traces, and fragments of the past (usually in an original and written form) are deposited, then catalogued and indexed.[20] Film and media archives involve ever more complex issues concerning the very nature of archives as their ontological premises of originality and authenticity come under challenge and as volumes of digital data exponentially increase their very content.[21] At a practical level, the *R69* project I undertook simply aimed to digitize the cinematic materials and assemble them in some manner that would make them accessible and comprehensible to an interested viewership.[22] In the case of *Wendy and Joyce*, digitization of the film's dormant archival elements permitted access and viewing, which were otherwise restricted by the institution assigned to safeguard them.[23] The migration (of sorts) from the original film and audio elements to digital formats transforms its material and essential or ontological properties. In Chun's formulation, migration from the historical artefact to the digital ephemeral transforms its very temporality and its futures.

CINEMATIC DIALOGICS

Peters's suggestion, cited earlier, about communication with the dead is apposite when working with the unfinished films of the deceased and offers the challenge of how to formulate and conceptualize collaboration across these realms. In the context of art theory, Charles Green teases out a notion of a "third hand" in the working processes of some performance artists, which is generative to thinking about the multifaceted dimensions of collaboration in such projects. Of performance artists Marina Abramovic and Ulay, Green writes: "The energy exchange during their performances created, both artists thought, a third, independent existence."[24] And artists Komar and Melamid describe their artistic partnership in this way: "We invented that third person, the third artist, but we never specifically named that third artist."[25] This sense of a third party emerging through a working process is apposite in posthumous collaboration where "doppelgängers, phantoms and spectralized bodies" evoke a kind of complicity and exchange across the (filmic) thresholds of the living and the dead.

In the case of *R69*, I might speak of third *hands*. Following my retrieval of the boxes of film, the next person to engage materially in this negotiation with my late father and the anxious forces of a third hand was film editor Mary Stephen, whom I met around the time of my father's death and who knew him in the 1970s as a film teacher. Accustomed as a film editor to picking up on the imprint and shaping that the director has placed upon the film (her previous work includes long-standing contributions as editor to the films of French filmmaker Eric Rohmer as well as her own films), Stephen entered into a kind of communion with the *R69* material. The existent manipulations and expectations of *R69* were already present for her, and depended upon her specialized abilities as an editor to finesse and, in a sense, usher to completion. The state of the cinematic fragments held an inner logic, one that bespoke a cinematic specificity. My father's rough picture assembly, which edited extended scenes together in a particular sequence with tape-edits, was the point of departure in a conversation. Although the possibility of a verbal dialogue was curtailed, communication through the film medium itself seemed to be taking place.[26]

In this case, if the encounter with fragments and "ruins" characteristic of posthumous cinema constructs a dialogue between the living editor and the dead filmmaker regarding what to do with what remains, the third hand is the haunting spectral subject of that negotiation. It is a third subject in two ways: it seems to direct the film to completion, but it is also a subject of the experience of watching the film. The negotiation between the "finished" film and its archive becomes an extra layer of the aesthetics and ethics of posthumous cinema. One clear instance of this was changing the original decision to *reconstruct* Gagnon's initial picture assembly using the undamaged pristine master footage. Such a reconstruction meant the disappearance of those traces of my father's seeming presence in his own original picture assembly, which included scratches and dust on the film, tape edit marks, and transitions, such as film sprockets and full light exposures that he had chosen to retain between reel changes. Eliminating these traces seemed like a blatant, violent excision of his presence that had not only aesthetic implications, but also ethical dimensions. And so, the final assembly on the DVD is from his original: slightly faded, scratches, dust, and all.

In encountering *Wendy and Joyce*, Wieland's notes and archival finding aids indicated that there was a work print of approximately 2,000 feet (about fifty-five minutes). Again, the scratching and wearing of her film footage give evidence of Wieland's handling and editing, introducing an aesthetic dimension that signifies the artist's embodied presence that gave a preliminary shape to the otherwise disparate elements classified as *Wendy and Joyce*. In this instance, aligning Wieland's notes with the available film and sound elements offers insight into her intentions for the text's (future) production.

Wieland's undated handwritten notes for a grant completion report refreshed the status of *Wendy and Joyce* in the following way: "At this point, the original footage from 'Wendy and Joyce' has been rejuvenated, a work print made and a rough cut completed." She continues:

> Interesting film footage, photographs and sound material has been newly "discovered" with the assistance of Wendy' [*sic*] husband Les Lawrence.
>
> This material includes a 60's newsreel film of the Michner [*sic*] family at a formal meeting in India with Madame Ghandi and then Prime Minister Nehru, as well as film footage of a television interview at the time of my show at the Vancouver Art Gallery in 1968. Sound "discoveries" include early audiotape interviews between Wendy Michner [*sic*], film critic, and Indian film director Satyajit Ray, and between Wendy Michner [*sic*] and Italian director Fellini. Also discovered are early audiotape dialogues between myself and Hollis Frampton, and American experimental directors Mike and George Kucher [*sic*].
>
> Sound will be a key element in "Wendy and Joyce." As in "Birds at Sunrise" and "A and B in Ontario," *no sound was recorded at the time of filming* [my italics].
>
> In "Wendy and Joyce" a complex collage/narrative will have to be created, especially taking into consideration the newly discovered material. In order to do this I will utilize the skills of a script writer to ensure that the fragments of audio recordings, dialogues, letters and memoirs are assembled in a manner that provides a loose, informative, yet poetic narrative for cinema. Image/text will also be used.
>
> A great deal of work has already gone into "Wendy and Joyce". The new material will add yet another important element into the life of Wendy Michner [*sic*]. I plan to have the film "Wendy and Joyce" completed for the AGO screening in April 1987.[27]

As the possibilities created by digital migration and copies have increased availability, access, and circulation, the practical and conceptual challenges of creating dynamic approaches to archives and archiving, especially of moving images, have flourished, but also brought attendant problems. Media archaeologist Wolfgang Ernst observes, "when the talk is about maximized computer memory capacities, this discourse still continues an old occidental obsession that culture depends on storage (historic architectures, libraries, museums). My media analysis tells me that the future cultural emphasis will be rather on permanent transfer, not storage (without undoing storage, though). There is already an implosion of storage mania into processual data flows, a different economy of the archive as dynamic agency 'online.'"[28] What is the meaning of the "permanent transfer" Ernst predicts, and its implications for unfinished analogue films? Considering the current drive to digitize archives and place them online (even more accelerated and extensive now than when Ernst observed this phenomena ten years ago), film-specific historical antecedents to similar cultural moments of transition for archives are instructive. Paula Amad's concept of the *counter archive* concisely captures how in early twentieth century France, the indexical capacities of film for visual and temporal documentation were anticipated to replace the very *raison d'être* of the traditional, document-based archive; yet in spite of these aspirations, the cohabitation of various media in the archive would be its future. Similarly, for the unfinished *R69* and *Wendy and Joyce*, examining film or audio artefacts, and/or their digital transfers when possible, supplemented by paper archives – storyboards, notes, grant applications – all yield unique posthumous forms of meaning and insight into these film fragments, these artists' practices, and their creative aspirations.

ACKNOWLEDGMENTS

My thanks to Gerda Cammaer for initially suggesting to me that Joyce Wieland had an unfinished film, and to Su Rynard for pointing to me to the Cinémathèque québécoise and Clara Thomas Archives and Special Collections. I am grateful to Jean Gagnon, director of collections at the Cinémathèque québécoise, for facilitating access to Wieland's "Wendy and Joyce," and Anna St Onge at the York Archives for her specialized insights and support. Kenza Oumlil provided cogent research assistance, while Scott Toguri McFarlane and Chantal Nadeau provided cogent editorial comments. My thanks to SSHRC for generous research funding of this investigation and writing.

FILMOGRAPHY

Chytilová, Věra. *Daisies.* 1966.
Gagnon, Charles. *Charles Gagnon: 4 Films.* 2009.
Gagnon, Charles. *Pierre Mercure 1927–1966.* 1970.
Gagnon, Charles. *R69 (unfinished/inachevé).* 1969–.
Gagnon, Charles. *Sound of Space.* 1968.
Gagnon, Monika Kin. *Archiving R69.* 2011.
Wieland, Joyce. *Birds at Sunrise.* 1972–86.
Wieland, Joyce. *Peggy's Blue Skylight.* 1964.
Wieland, Joyce. *Reason over Passion/La raison avant la passion.* 1967–69.
Wieland, Joyce. *The Complete Works of Joyce Wieland.* 2011.
Wieland, Joyce, and Hollis Frampton. *A and B in Ontario.* 1984.

NOTES

1 Carolyn Steedman, *Dust: The Archive and Cultural History* (New Brunswick, NJ: Rutgers University Press, 2002), 68.

2 Wendy Hui Kyong Chun, "The Enduring Ephemeral, or the Future is a Memory," *Critical Inquiry* 35 (Autumn 2008): 160. Chun is referring to Mary Ann Doane's *The Emergence of Cinematic Time: Modernity, Contingency, the Archive* (Cambridge, MA: Harvard University Press, 2002), and her discussions on page 223.

3 This chapter draws in part from my earlier essay, "Posthumous Cinema: On Archiving *R69*," which appears in the DVD collection *Charles Gagnon: 4 Films* (Spectral Films, 2009). The DVD centres on the unedited 16 mm film footage of *R69* and reproduces the three other experimental films Gagnon created in the 1960s. Charles Gagnon is well-known in Quebec and Canada for his paintings, photographs, and films, and an illustrious exhibition career spanning forty-five years until his death in 2003. His work is included in museum collections across Canada, he had two major retrospectives during his lifetime, and he has garnered several awards.

4 John Durham Peters, *Speaking into the Air: A History of the Idea of Communication* (Chicago: University of Chicago Press, 1999), 161. Jeffrey Sconce's *Haunted Media: Electronic Presence from Telegraphy to Television* (Durham, NC: Duke University Press, 2000) similarly undertakes a cultural history of media technology and cultural practice of speaking to the dead.

5 The film program, *The Unfinished Film*, at the Gladstone Gallery in New York from 24 June to 27 July 2011, included thirty-eight films and a short catalogue edited by programmer Thomas Beard. The films demonstrated the fragmented, creative nature in progress in the works of filmmakers such as Andy Warhol (*Batman/Dracula*) and Maya Deren (and her unfinished collaboration with Marcel Duchamp from 1943, *Witch's Cradle*), as well as a week-long focus on sections of Hollis Frampton's epic, *Magellan*. Thirty minutes of unedited film footage from Theresa Hak Kyung Cha's unrealized film, *White Dust from Mongolia*, was also premiered, and is the focus of my current research; see

my "Communicating the Intermedia Archive: The Theresa Hak Kyung Collection," at http://dnaanthology.com/anvc/dna/index.

6 Peters, *Speaking into the Air*, 149.

7 Jane Lind, *Joyce Wieland: Artist on Fire* (Toronto: James Lorimer and Company, 2001), 276.

8 Joyce Wieland fonds, accession 1993-003 / 002 (13), York University Libraries, Clara Thomas Archives and Special Collections.

9 Cigarette smoking is a notable feature in many 1960s films, denoting the social acceptability of smoking liberally in private and public spaces, even in the museums whose opening *vernissages* appear in both unfinished films.

10 Su Rynard, telephone interview with the author, 15 June 2011.

11 Joyce Wieland fonds, accession 1993-003 / 002 (13), York University Libraries, Clara Thomas Archives and Special Collections.

12 Lind, *Joyce Wieland: Artist on Fire*, 168.

13 Wieland quoted in Lind, *Joyce Wieland: Artist on Fire*, 168.

14 Charles Gagnon, "Témoignage," *Ovo-Photo* (French edition), June 1974, 4, 27. My translation. (The English edition of this magazine contains an abridged translation of the interview, but does not include this particular excerpt.) It is also worth noting here that Mercure was to have collaborated on the music and sound design for the Christian Pavilion at Expo 67 for which Gagnon did the interior design, including the making of the found-footage film, *The Eighth Day* (1967); see C. Gagnon's reproduced notes in M.K. Gagnon, *Charles Gagnon: 4 Films*.

15 Lind, *Joyce Wieland: Artist on Fire*, 275–6. Of this same period, Lauren Rabinowitz writes in *Points of Resistance*: "[Wieland's] renewed enthusiasm for filmmaking began when Hollis Frampton died of cancer in the spring of 1984 and his widow asked Wieland to complete a film Frampton and Wieland had begun together in 1967. *A and B in Ontario* (1984) is a kind of playful hide-and-seek between the two filmmakers in which they use cameras and their individual fields of vision to 'tag' and capture each other" (219).

16 Hollis Frampton and Joyce Wieland's interview, "I Don't Even Know about the Second Stanza," discusses the shooting of their film (in *The Films of Joyce Wieland*, ed. Kathryn Elder [Toronto: Cinematheque Ontario, 1999], 161–81). See also, R. Bruce Elder's perceptive "Notes after a Conversation between Hollis and Joyce" in the same collection, 183–93.

17 The original quarter-inch recording consists of seven minutes of audio of musical selections, snippets of dialogue and sound effects, labelled "'Daisies,' originally from Optical June '87/'Wendy & Joyce' Vera Kitlova."

On comparison between the film and Wieland's tape, the recording appears to be the soundtrack from Věra Chytilová's 1966 film *Sedmikrásky* [*Daisies*], and is further labelled as having been recorded by sound engineer David Bennell in 1987. The film is a lively, satirical slapstick comedy highlighting the antics of two young women. This was considered a key film in the Czech New Wave movement, was originally banned and director Chytilová was forbidden to work until 1975. Claire Clouzot's untitled review of *Daisies* in *Film Quarterly* 21, no. 3 (Spring 1968): 35–7, and Katarina Soukup's "Banquet of Profanities: Food and Subversion in Vera Chytilova's *Daisies*," in *Tessera* 24 (Summer 1998): 38–52, are effectively evocative of the original film, and thereby, for my purposes, its suggestiveness for Wieland. My thanks to York archivist Anna St Onge for suggesting Chytilová as Wieland's inspirational source.

18 Gagnon, "Posthumous Collaboration," 10–15.

19 The capacity to now digitize archives and circulate them in multiple forms, combined with the limitations and provisions of copyright ownership, are two major forces reconfiguring archives and issues of access, and their subsequent impact on shaping memory and history; these issues are beyond the scope of this chapter to explore in detail. Yet, it is worth noting that ownership and copyright issues underlay initial access to these materials, which has seemingly extended into increasingly obscure facets of material ownership, proprietary access, and licensing that had ethical and institutional implications. In the case of *R69*, a copyright lawyer I consulted advised that I have my mother transfer ownership and copyright of my father's films, which she did, in order for me to have legal propriety on licensing requirements; it is also worth noting that I acquired licenses to reproduce the paintings in the background of each of the artist interviews, in addition to the actual releases with the artists (or their descendants) for the interviews themselves. One facet of the ethical undercurrents of posthumous cinema involves authorial intention and collaborative authorship, making for a rich set of questions when challenged by the particularities and ease of circulation of digital media archives. The borders of my father's artistic authorship became sufficiently clear as choices about what to include and exclude, as well as how to present them became apparent, while my own interests in exploring alternative modes of communicating the media archive began to emerge.

20 For descriptions of conventional archives, see Carolyn Steedman, *Dust*; Michael Hill, *Archival Strategies and Techniques* (Thousand Oaks, CA: Sage, 1993); and Mike Featherstone's concise "Archive," *Theory, Culture and Society* 23 (2–3) (2006).

21 See José Van Dijck, *Mediated Memories in the Digital Age* (Stanford: Stanford University Press, 2007), Caroline Frick, *Saving Cinema: The Politics of Preservation* (New York: Oxford University Press, 2011), especially "The Plurality of Preservation," and Martin Hand, "Lost in Translation: Authenticity and the Ontology of the Archive," in *Making Digital Cultures: Access, Interactivity, and Authenticity* (Burlington, VT: Ashgate, 2008).

22 The *R69* project eventually culminated in two digital film-based "versions" that used the original film footage: a conventional DVD *Charles Gagnon: 4 Films* (2009), which in addition to the linear, rough assembly of *R69* includes three of his earlier experimental films from the 1960s; and an interactive Korsakow-film, *Archiving R69* (2011), in which I have nestled the archival footage within an exploratory process using database cinema that randomizes the order of film, sound, and paper elements. *Archiving R69* is accessible for viewing at www.ArchivingR69.ca.

23 The film elements labelled "Wendy and Joyce" were initially unavailable for viewing or listening in their original 16 mm or reel-to-reel audiotape formats (following the paradoxical preservation imperatives of film archives).

I initiated and underwrote the digitization process and expense, subsequent to institutional permission from the Cinémathèque Québecoise, which holds copyright of Wieland's film archives. I am permitted research access and presentation in educational and scholarly contexts based on our agreement. Digitized film elements of *Wendy and Joyce*, ancillary sound materials, and text documents are now available and accessible to other researchers on the website of the Cinémathèque's website (http://collections.cinematheque.qc.ca/dossiers/joyce-wieland/wendy-and-joyce) as part of *Joyce Wieland's Unfinished Films*, two multimedia dossiers curated by myself and Vanessa Meyer for the Cinémathèque. Posthumous cinema in relation to *Wendy and Joyce* involves simply viewing and describing the existing transferred elements, but not handling the elements themselves, nor completing them as a film in any cinematic form, as it did for *R69*.

24 Charles Green, *The Third Hand: Collaboration in Art from Conceptualism to Postmodernism* (Minneapolis: University of Minnesota Press, 2001), 181.

25 Ibid., 179.

26 Stephen herself speaks directly to this in her short piece, "December Steps: Notes on Archiving *R69*," in *Charles Gagnon: 4 Films*.

27 Joyce Wieland fonds, ibid.

28 Geert Lovink, "Interview with Wolfgang Ernst: Archive Rumblings," February 2003, http://laudanum.net/geert/files/1060043851 (republished in Wolfgang Ernst, *Digital Memory and the Archive* ([Minneapolis: University of Minnesota Press, 2013, 193–203]).

9 *TIGER CHILD*

IMAX AND DONALD BRITTAIN TIMES NINE

Seth Feldman

FEW FILMS APPEAR to be so deliberately ephemeral as Donald Brittain's 1970 short, *Tiger Child.* Produced by Roman Kroitor and Graeme Ferguson in their capacity as co-founders of the IMAX Corporation (then known as Multiscreen), the film was designed for a technology being invented as it was shot. The prototype IMAX camera was, according to its producers' estimate, able to provide only about 5 per cent of the images in the film – the rest were shot with conventional 70 mm cameras turned on their sides and 35 mm motion-picture cameras.[1] There was, until very shortly before *Tiger Child*'s completion, no projector on which to show it in its intended format.

Although Multiscreen intended to provide permanent venues for its large format films, *Tiger Child* was designed specifically for the Fuji Pavilion at Expo 70. That inflatable structure was meant to function only for the 183 days of the Expo, 15 March to 13 September 1970, and was listed on the English-language program as the Air Dome to invoke a sense of its tenacious structure. As the pavilion's producer, Hiroshi Kawazoe, describes it: "The building is air and the program inside is air. This is the age of air."[2]

Multiscreen had no plans for *Tiger Child*'s distribution after Osaka as it had no idea if anyone would adopt its new technology. As a result, the film screened in the Fuji Pavilion was less archived than it was simply kept by the company. Its out-takes and other original production materials were destroyed. When the first permanent IMAX theatre was opened at Toronto's Ontario Place in 1971, the premiere screening was another film, Graeme Ferguson's *North of Superior. Tiger Child* was rarely seen until a new print was struck for the company's fortieth anniversary celebration in 2007. It has been shown only sporadically since.[3]

Even as a document relating to IMAX's history, the film has its limitations. It was not exactly the first film Multiscreen produced, a distinction that goes to a training film by Roman Kroitor for the Canadian military before the development of IMAX technology. Nor is it indicative of the kinds of IMAX films that became familiar to audiences as the company and its technology matured. *Tiger Child*'s editing of up to nine simultaneously viewed images within the frame celebrates less the founding of IMAX than it does the impulse behind it: the films of Expo 67 and the 1964 New York World's Fair. After *Tiger Child*, IMAX's interest in multiscreen productions gave way to the production of more conventionally framed and edited documentaries. The company's signature became its technological ability to produce a single image filling the viewer's entire field of vision. Making IMAX versions of conventional feature films, while a much later development, moved the company yet further from its multiscreen (or Multiscreen) origins.

Another aspect of *Tiger Child*'s ephemeral nature is its subject matter. Far more than most Expo films, Brittain conceived it as a commentary on the specific social ills of the period in which it was made. It was a time capsule of the concerns of 1970 and the cumulative unease they produced. Brittain's subject matter not only ran counter to the Osaka Expo theme of "Progress and Harmony for Mankind," but also (as I will discuss below) spoke to the use of specific factual information within Expo films and documentary as a whole.

Despite its timeliness, little was written about *Tiger Child* during the run of the Osaka Expo. The small number of publications that mention the film concentrate on its technical aspects and on the difficulties of undertaking a complex Canadian-Japanese co-production.[4] This may well be because it was generally seen in an incomplete and random fashion, as was the designers of both the film and the pavilion in which it was screened intended. In addition, while the Osaka Expo was a hugely popular event in Asia, it attracted only a fraction of the North American and European interest enjoyed by Expo 67. Nor was the Fuji Pavilion seen as an entirely successful attraction. Japanese audiences responded with some confusion to what they found there – to the point where a sign was posted outside the pavilion entrance assuring viewers that they need not worry about finding their experience somewhat incomprehensible.

Despite this tepid response, the minimal literature concerning it and irregular exposure of the film today, *Tiger Child* survives as something considerably more than an historical curiosity. It is a work that reminds us of how a given film is more than its diegesis or the stylistic means of producing that diegesis – rather, it is a narrative that encompasses the broader material means of its production as well as its distribution, exhibition, preservation, study, and reception. As a result, the entity in question is both individualized (with as many perceptions of it as there are individuals aware of its being) and continually in flux. *Tiger Child* has been and continues to be seen far less than most films. Yet it is like any film in the sense that the object in question is a compendium of what appears on the screen and our understandings of everything else having to do with it. For this reason, the *Tiger Child* I will be looking at here consists as much of production, exhibition, and the difficulty of accessing the film as it does of the film itself as text. I will then try to discover how the two versions of *Tiger Child* – the film as it was exhibited in 1970 as part of a multimedia event and the version available today – may work together.

PRODUCTION

Tiger Child can trace its origins directly to two multiscreen films at Expo 67: the Labyrinth Pavilion created by Roman Kroitor, Colin Low, and Hugh O'Connor, and Graeme Ferguson's film, *Polar Life*, screened at the Man the Explorer Pavilion. Chamber One of Labyrinth used two wide-ratio screens, one placed lengthwise along the floor and the other vertically on its side. Viewers watched the film from two sets of four balconies arrayed on either side of the "L" shaped screening area. Images on the two screens played off one another but could also play against each other. A father looked down from the vertical screen at his infant on the horizontal screen. Alternatively, shots in a nightclub on the vertical screen were juxtaposed with an astronomer's view of the stars at night.

In Labyrinth's Chamber Three, an architecturally more conventional theatre, the frame was composed of five wide aspect screens: three placed next to each other across the centre of the frame with the other two stacked above and below the centre screen. In the editing of this five-screen film, Tom Daley pioneered some of the intricate means of intercutting between screens that would be used again in the nine screens of *Tiger Child*. He found, for instance, that he could vary the juxtaposition of shots in ways that drew the viewer's attention to the desired meaning. When, for example, several screens were visible simultaneously, Daly determined that the content of each screen would have to be left on longer than would be the case with a conventional shot in order to have an equivalent impact. However, if a screen remained visible for substantially more time than the screens around it, it would drain attention from the other screens. The screen in the centre would always be taken as the key image upon which other screens would comment. A screen at the bottom of the frame would appear closer than shots on the top.[5]

In Daly's stylistics of multiscreen, one of the most important elements would be a consideration of comparative shot distance within the screens (e.g., close-ups, long shots, etc.). If there were a clear progression in movement or theme between two screens, audiences would anticipate its continuation in a third screen. The audience could be set up for this progression, and then shocked by a break in it. Another element in multiscreen editing involved changing the number and arrangement of screens available within the frame. Throughout the film, there are instances when fewer than five screens appear, the absent screens serving to vary the cruciform format and underline the content of the screens that remain.

If Labyrinth provided an editing technique for projecting the multiscreen film in Osaka, *Polar Life* was a model for presenting it. Its venue, the Man the Explorer Pavilion, placed viewers in four revolving theatres from which they could see only two or three of the pavilion's eleven screens at any given time. These twin movements – the projection of the film and the trajectory of the audience's viewing of it – maximized the visual fluidity of the experience. Rather than simply have a film presented to them, individual viewers were obliged to select their own film from an infinite variety of possibilities.

The Labyrinth films and *Polar Life* were also a link between *Tiger Child* and a larger heritage of producing this sort of interaction between viewers and large screen projected images. That heritage goes back at least as far as the Cinéorama at the 1900 *Exposition Universelle* in Paris, which used ten synchronized 70 mm projectors to provide the illusion of a panoramic airship tour of Paris.[6] Yet as popular as these and the other multiscreen productions were, it was clear from the beginning that they could have little future beyond the fairs themselves. The temporary pavilions had to be built not only to accommodate the mechanics of moving the audience about but also the complicated banks of projectors often required to produce an immersive image. Even when such venues were constructed outside of Expos, they tended to be one of a kind. While this began to change with Hollywood's wide screen theatrical formats in the 1950s, the conventional feature films shown hardly reflected the ambition of earlier experiments or the potential of the large screen to present multiscreen images.

Kroitor and Ferguson sought to address the problem of making ambitious multiscreen and immersive format films available beyond these single venues. They, and *Polar Life* co-producer Robert Kerr, formed Multiscreen in September 1967, in order to build a system to project films in a large screen immersive format using a single projector. A second instrument of the new technology was a camera that would allow for filming of high quality images large enough to fill the immersive screens, themselves large enough to dominate each viewer's field of vision. The frame they chose would be the equivalent of three 70 mm images turned on their sides, producing a vertical 7:10 ratio screen.

Kroitor, Ferguson, and Kerr saw the proposed film, with its million-dollar budget, as Multiscreen's opportunity to develop their company's technology. It was initiated shortly after Expo 67 when the Fuji Bank, then part of a consortium of thirty-six companies known as the Fuyo Group (now known as the Mizuho Bank), asked Multiscreen to design a film that would be the centerpiece of its pavilion at the Osaka Expo. The project, encompassing the film and the pavilion, was to be headed by Hiroshi Kawazoe, an entrepreneur and impresario with ties to the Japanese royal family. In a 1969 *New York Times* interview, Kawazoe, who was simultaneously producing a Japanese version of the musical *Hair*, described 2,000 viewers being simultaneously transported through a twenty-minute show presenting "a symphony of art, music, film, lights, a poem symphonique."[7]

From the outset, Kawazoe intended the film to be a Canadian-Japanese co-production. A Japanese company, Asuka Productions, was hired to work with Multiscreen in order to facilitate post-production in Japan. Kroitor was paired with a co-producer, Kiichi Ichikawa, who had been producer of, among other films, *Woman in the Dunes* (Hiroshi Teshigahara, 1964). Teiji Ito, a music composer, assembled the still photographs used inside the pavilion.

The music used in the film was composed by Toshiro Mayuzumi, a student of Western experimental music with a particular interest in *musique concrète*. He later worked with a hybrid of Western experimental and traditional Japanese styles composing a variety of orchestral pieces as well as operas and ballet. By 1970, he was also known for his prolific writing of film scores for Japanese and foreign features, including John Huston's *Reflections in a Golden Eye* (1967). Mayuzumi was known in Japan for an erotic right-wing militarism similar to that of Yukio Mishima.[8]

Yutaka Murata, the architect of the Fuji Pavilion, planned it around the nineteen-by-thirteen-metre vertical screen on which the new film would be shown. It was a surface far larger than those at Labyrinth –

although the height and width of the pavilion (forty and fifty-one metres respectively) would have dwarfed the huge screen. Filling that screen with an image of acceptable density would require an image that would be the equivalent of three adjacent 70 mm frames turned on their sides. William Shaw, then the head engineer at CCM Sports, agreed to supervise design of the equipment. To accomplish this, Multiscreen licensed a Rolling Loop projection mechanism from an Australian inventor, Ronald Jones. Shaw and Ferguson would build the projector using that mechanism. At the same time, Shaw ordered a custom-built camera from a Norwegian engineer, Jan Jacobsen, who had extensive experience with large screen equipment design.

Kroitor hired Donald Brittain to direct the film, "simply because he was a very good filmmaker, and it was likely he would do something interesting."[9] Although Brittain had written commentaries for the Expo 67 film *We Are Young* and for the two films in the Labyrinth pavilion, he was not an obvious choice to direct a non-narrated, intensely visual multi-screen production. He was among the most literary of the pantheon of Canadian documentary filmmakers to emerge in the 1950s and 1960s – and hence was among the most dependent on language. By the time Brittain directed *Tiger Child*, his signature had become the ironic twist in exquisitely composed voice-over narrations, which he read with a trademark droll delivery.

Brittain also came to *Tiger Child* with a track record for grappling with large and often difficult subjects. His first major film was the thirteen-part series *Canada at War* (1962). Working at the National Film Board, he achieved an international reputation with *Fields of Sacrifice* (1964), on Canadian war cemeteries, and *Memorandum* (1965), on the Holocaust. A former journalist, Brittain had the ability to establish a rapport with those he interviewed and wished to study at length. This served him well in three mid-1960s biographical documentaries: *Bethune* (1964), *Ladies and Gentleman… Mr. Leonard Cohen* (1965), and *Never a Backward Step* (1966) on media magnate Roy Thomson. Later in his career he integrated dramatic scenes into his documentaries, most memorably in his docudrama hybrid, *Canada's Sweetheart: The Saga of Hal C. Banks* (1985).

Tiger Child's large budget allowed Brittain and his cinematographer, Georges Dufaux, to shoot at locations around the world: African deserts, snowy prairies, an Alpine ski race, Asian villages, and a British cathedral, among others. They carted with them Jacobsen's often dysfunctional camera, which Brittain describes as being "the size of a refrigerator."[10]

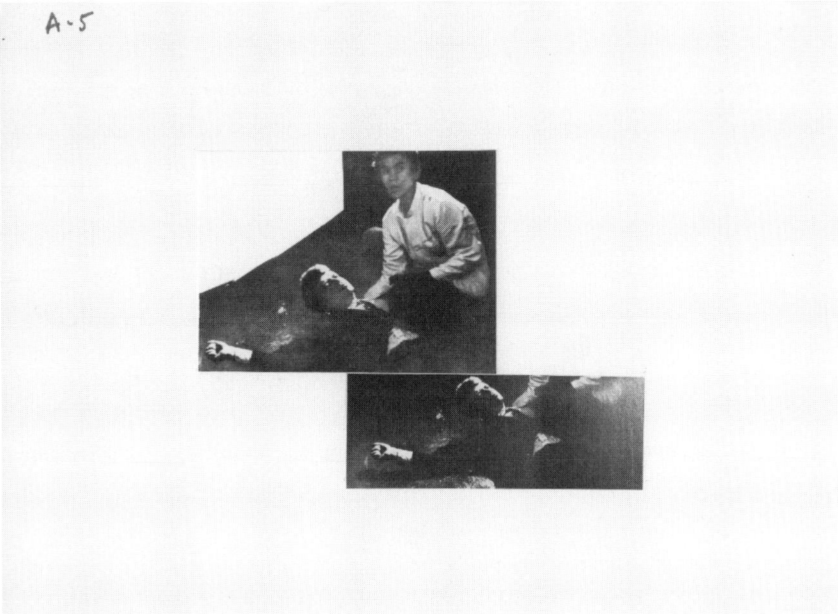

9.1 One of Colin Low's arrangements of irregularly shaped multiple screens within the frame.

Colin Low, who had worked closely for two decades with Kroitor and Daly at the NFB's Unit B, was hired as visual designer. Low had collaborated with Kroitor and Daly in the design of the Labyrinth Pavilion, used his experience with Labyrinth's multiscreen productions to storyboard Brittain's footage as a multiscreen production. His *Tiger Child* drawings are of two types. In one set, Low envisions the placement of Brittain's footage, including the single images shot using the IMAX prototype camera; footage shot by three attached 70 mm cameras turned on their sides; and a great deal of 35 mm footage to be used in the construction of the nine-screen collages. In the other set, Low imagines using creating clusters of the 35 mm images connected as single images, irregularly shaped mini-frames within the larger format (see figure 9.1).

While many of Low's 160 sketches are similar to the arrangement of screens in the finished film, the creation of these mini-frames was simply too difficult to achieve using the editing equipment at the filmmakers' disposal. That equipment was a five-projector custom-built device contributed by Asuka Productions. While the rushes ran through the projectors, editing assistants manipulated mirrors to position the screens within the larger frame. The work was painstakingly complex and made more arduous by the language barrier between the Canadian director and the Japanese editors.

While the film was being edited, Shaw, working in a McMaster University laboratory, was finding it difficult to build a working projector from Jones's rolling loop design. A backup plan had been devised that would allow the film to be projected by three 70 mm projectors turned on their sides – exactly the kind of cumbersome system that Multiscreen had set out to replace. As the editing progressed, a decision had to be made as to whether the nine-screen imagery would be printed on one roll of film, as intended if the projector worked, or on three rolls of film, one for each of the three projectors in the backup plan. Deadlines came and went. Shortly after the last absolute deadline passed, the projector finally worked and the film was duly printed on a single roll. That was the format in which it was screened at Osaka.[11]

Tiger Child exists today as two films. The film as seen by audiences in Osaka (what I am going to call its "originally perceived mode") can only be approximated through technical descriptions and anecdotal evidence. The seventeenth-minute film in its entirety as projected during the IMAX fortieth anniversary screenings (what I will call its "linear mode") allows for more detailed discussion. Ultimately, these two tiger children are siblings that arrive at similar conclusions through these two differing modes.

ORIGINALLY PERCEIVED MODE

During the summer of 1970, visitors to the Fuji Pavilion entered Murata's nine-story yellow and orange structure made of inflated tubes bent into an inverted "U" shape and tapered at both ends. A two-story cube housing the projection system protruded from one end of the structure. The interior of the pavilion was covered with slides projected on the inside of the inflated tubes. Almost as soon as they entered the pavilion, visitors walked up an incline and stepped onto a slowly moving doughnut-shaped turntable, which was elevated above an exhibition floor. It was while standing on the turntable that they approached, passed in front of, and moved away from the giant screen on which *Tiger Child* was projected.

Visitors entered the pavilion and rode the turntable continuously, often filling the pavilion's 2,000-person capacity. The projection of the film was also intended to be continuous. However, because a loop cabinet capable of handling the IMAX format film was not available, each screening required a break in order to rewind the reel. During that time, a slide show created by the Japanese photographer Teiji Ito was projected onto the screen. That slide show – which Kroitor remembered as being a series of mandala patterns – has not been preserved. As had been the case with *Polar Life*, the net result was a film individual audience members perceived as having an infinite variety of beginnings, middles, and ends.

The degree of immersion in the image also changed as viewers rode the turntable. Upon entering the pavilion, the screen could be viewed as part of the overall pavilion design, part of the total multi-image display that incorporated the slides. As the turntable brought the spectators closer to it, the film not only filled the field of vision but also became the primary environment through which the audience passed. The effect produced was a kind of spatial crescendo that involved not simply the nature of the images and sounds projected, but also the play of proximity itself upon the viewers' senses. Put another way, the conventional narrative strategy of having the readers or viewers enter, observe, and leave a film on a conceptual level was here realized as a physical act.

In historical context, the pavilion's exhibition strategy may, like other Expo films, be seen in the context of the development of installations as an art form. Consequently, Brittain's film could be regarded as one element of the installation. An alternative to this slightly anachronistic perspective would be to see the film's presentation as a reminder that all films are part of distinct screening environments, which are less frequently acknowledged in the discussion about them. A conventional movie theatre is an installation designed with specific intent and the product of a long architectural history. This was to be made especially clear in the decade after *Tiger Child*, with the rise of multiplex screening environments, and in the decade following that, with the growth in home screening options.

LINEAR MODE

While *Tiger Child*'s screening in its original venue can only be imagined today – and its near infinite number of possible permutations is decidedly less accessible – it is possible to look at the film itself in the linear mode in which it exists today. Seen in that mode, a coherent structure is readily discernible through a progression of sequences, each composed of similar images pointing to a single theme. Taken together, these sequences produce a set of movements:

1 Conception, pregnancy, children at play (a couple making love in a field, a pregnant woman, happy couples, Asian children painting, choir boys, African and Asian children, European children watching a puppet show)
2 Adults at play (men flying giant kites, racing skulls, African dancers, a ski race, polka dancers, adults at an amusement park)
3 The end of innocence (alienated people, busy city streets, shooting victims, a facial contortionist, a young man being chased by police intercut with shots from a slaughterhouse)
4 Stabs at redemption (Buddhist monks, people helping thalidomide children)
5 The scope of human work and experience (congested, polluted urban landscapes, sub-Saharan Africans and Bedouins living traditional lifestyles, cowboys herding cattle, a stunt driver flipping a car)
6 Descent into the modern wasteland (a taxidermist, a cobra, a stripper, the Berlin Wall, sick children in African hospital, a Ku Klux Klan rally, violent demonstrations, a blind man amid the wreckage).

This breakdown of the film's movements is far from inclusive or definitive. It also does not do justice to the intricate editing within the six movements and the transitions between them. In a general sense, though, the use of distinct sequences within broader movements is readily apparent, in a way that is more than simply a matter of related content within each sequence. Unique visual configurations of the nine screens frequently introduce or identify sequences, which often entails going to either a single image that fills the entire frame (the thalidomide/ Buddhist monks sequence) or to a pattern composed of vertical images (vertical left and vertical right of jail cells in the prison sequence). Sequences frequently transition using a multiscreen dissolve, in which screens begin to show images from the upcoming sequence during the current one.

The construction of these individual sequences through the editing of multiple screens is the product of a rich but finite palette. There are instances in the film when a single image fills the entire screen, creating something akin to IMAX as it is generally viewed today. In one example, a woman who appears to be pregnant stands in front of a curtained picture

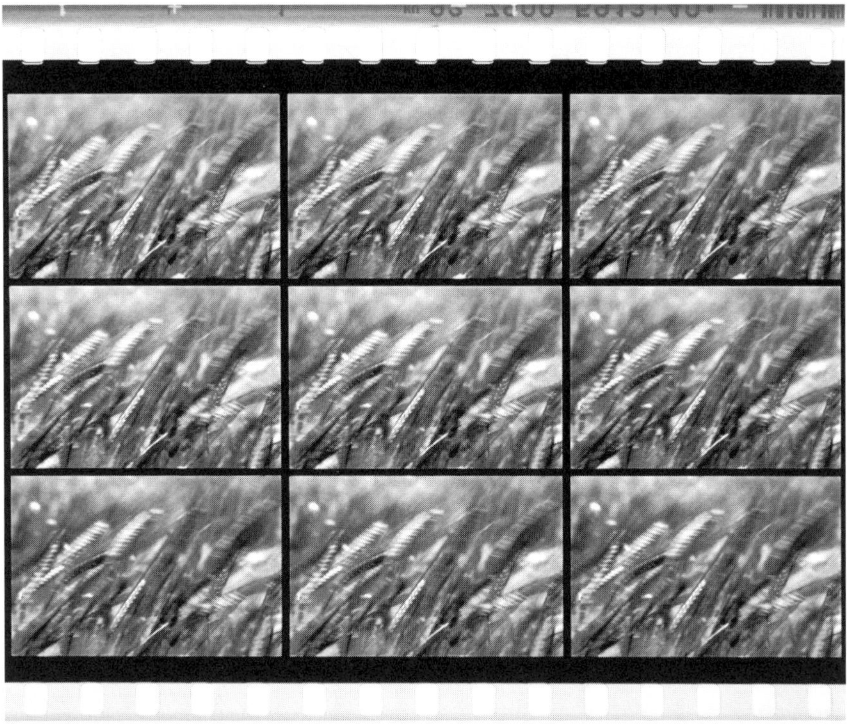

9.2 The nine-screen compositional palette.

window. Other instances of the use of full frame include the close-up of the pregnant woman's abdomen; a close-up of a barking dog; and a turntable revolving to reveal two Japanese musicians in traditional costume.

There is one instance in the film when the full screen is used to project nearly identical images in each of the nine multiscreens it contains. It comes at the beginning of the linear version of the film when all nine screens display stalks of wheat waving in the wind. The nine-shot display connotes the extent of the wheat field. At the same time, it establishes the nine-screen compositional palette (see figure 9.2).

More frequently, three vertical 70 mm images fill the screen. These screen left, right, and centre vertical images appear either individually or in combinations with one or both of the two other vertical compositions (see figure 9.3). This composition also benefits from an introductory image, the full-screen shot of the pregnant woman in front of the curtains mentioned above. The shot is revealed to be not a single image but rather

9.3 The three part vertical composition found throughout *Tiger Child*. In this case, what appears to be a single image is revealed to be three separate frames.

a three-part composition as the left hand vertical is replaced by an entirely different image while the camera zooms in on the right. The vertical compositions work well to accentuate images such as those of a giraffe or cars in a traffic jam. The frequently used combinations of these vertical compositions are even more telling: vertical compositions of choir boys running toward and away from camera on the left and right sides of the screen; vertical compositions of two sumo wrestlers on the left and right sides of the screen; vertical left and vertical right of slaughtered cows in slaughterhouse and vertical centre of a stripper on stage; vertical left and vertical right of Buddhist monks praying and vertical centre of a Thalidomide child.

The most common use of the multiscreen format in *Tiger Child* is to produce montages of the nine single screens that juxtapose the images being projected within each. Any number of screens and combinations of the nine screens could be used. In most instances, two or more of the screens would contain thematically related images. This relationship could be formed around a dramatic unity of time, space, and action linking the screens; for example, three frames with the identical shot of a desert road taken through the windshield of a vehicle driving down it; a puppet show and the young children watching it; or individual frames showing blowing snow, some of which are replaced by shots of cowboys riding in a snowy landscape. Or the frames could be arranged to produce an intellectual montage. In one instance, we see an indication of a person's growing realization of his hopeless position in a manner not terribly different from the way in which Sergei Eisenstein uses intercut shots of a massacre of workers and butchers in a slaughterhouse his film, *Strike* (1924). The *Tiger Child* variant shows: the centre left frame containing a mid-shot of young man standing against wooden fence; the centre frame showing a machine forcing open the jaws of slaughtered animal head; and the centre right frame containing a close-up of the same man in centre left pressed against the same wooden fence. A similar use of intellectual montage takes place during the Ku Klux Klan sequence (see figure 9.4).

Although individual screens may last longer than corresponding shots in a conventional film (as per Daly's technique), the reconfigurations of the nine screens take place quickly. Not only do viewers not know what will be in the next shot within a screen, but we can only guess what the next configuration within the entire viewing space will be. To illustrate, the film's relatively straightforward ski race sequence shows the following:

1 A full-screen long shot of a ski-racer in a red suit taken from behind at the starting gate of the course
2 The top left, top right, and centre screens contain medium-shots of a different ski racer in a black suit pushing off from a starting gate. Those shots simultaneously zoom out to long shots as the three skiers start their runs.
3 A vertical combination of the three centre screens shows a single long shot of the run down a ski hill as seen from ski racer's point of view
4 Vertical combinations of the three right and three left hand screens show identical long shots of the skier in black racing down a slalom
   i To which is added a vertical combination of the three centre screens showing a different shot of the racer on the slalom

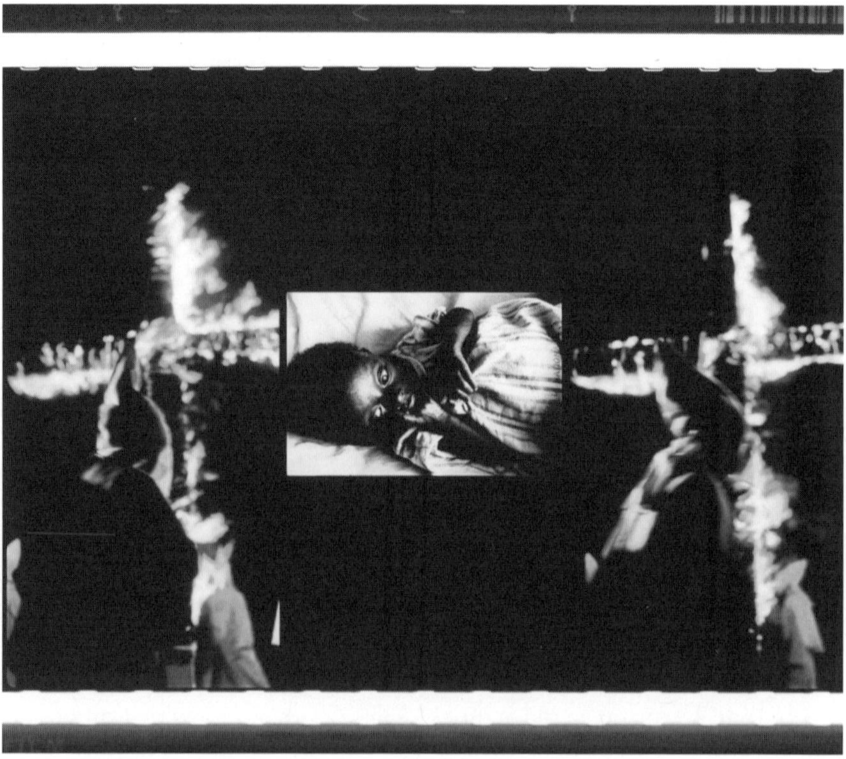

9.4 Intellectual montage within the frame during the Ku Klux Klan sequence.

course that ends with him departing from the shot at the bottom of the hill

ii At which point the right vertical and left vertical combination shots cut to a continuation of the point of view shot seen in the third shot

5 The centre left, centre, centre right, and bottom centre screens each present different long shots of the different skiers racing through the slalom course toward the camera

6 The top right, centre, and bottom left screens present long shots of other skiers going downhill on course

7 A full screen long shot of a skier reaching bottom of course and coming to halt

8 The centre screen presents a close-up of the skier's face

i To which are added shots in the top centre, centre left, and centre right screens of crowds at the bottom of the hill

ii These shots are replaced by close-ups of hands playing musical instruments in the centre left, centre right, and bottom centre screens

iii In the centre screen, the skier's face fades out, i.e., there is a multi-screen "crossfade" into the next sequence.[12]

The editors worked in tandem with Toshiro Mayuzumi's score to both suture the transitions from the various screen configurations and complement the images' association with modernist stream of consciousness. Within the sequences, synchronized sounds from the filmed locations counterpoint the more elaborate levels of abstraction created by the multiscreen patterns. The use of these sounds reminds the audience that what we see are not only compositional elements but also representations of a real world – just as adding music to the mix asserts that there is a larger theme to be taken from the multiplicity of individual images. In the childhood sequence, for example, the mix begins with an emphasis on location sounds of children playing, the boys' choir, and the shouts of excited boys running. It then adds purely musical elements as the sequence works its way to the more abstract montage of children at play around the world. The net effect is to base the indexical nature of the music commentary in the wild location sound. Conversely, this use of sound suggests that the location recording demands commentary through the composed (in much the same way that the visual images elicit commentary through their potential for editing).

Location (though rarely synchronized) sound also works as a catalyst to enhance the impact of individual shots and sequences. During the sequence of the Ku Klux Klan rally, a voice says, "I want you to understand why you're here." The nonsense song sung by a facial contortionist is a recurring element in the long-running third sequence depicting the end of innocence and descent into violence.

The closest *Tiger Child* comes to a voice-over are the two instances in which Gordon Lightfoot sings. His song "Softly" comes at the beginning of the (linear) film over shots of a couple making love in a field. Its lyrics correspond directly to the images, and Lightfoot, who is seen singing the centre frame, appears to be serenading the couple. It is the only instance in the film in which an individual is depicted in sync for a relatively extended period.

Lightfoot is not seen when he sings "Leaves of Grass" (which is unrelated to the Walt Whitman poem of the same name). The song comes a bit more than halfway through the film, shortly after one of its most meditative sequences. The sounds of a Buddhist chant play over images of Buddhist monks crosscut with Thalidomide children. The Buddhist chant then dissolves into Lightfoot's singing. The song's lyrics compare the futility of violent death to the leaves of grass that provide fertilizer for the eternally growing grass. Life, damaged and futile as it may be, goes on.[13]

The placement of "Leaves of Grass" would, of course, be far more purposeful for an English speaking audience than it would be for the Japanese viewers who comprised the majority of the Fuji Pavilion's visitors. With this consideration in mind, I return to the question of the film's meaning.

DISCUSSION: CIRCLING THE LINEAR

For most viewers in Osaka, *Tiger Child* produced a continual tension between disorientation and reorientation. The product of the film's venue and editing – by the viewer's physical placement and through the use of multiscreen configurations – is a convergence of montage effects that compresses the viewer's perception of cinematic time. It takes more and more rapid work than is typically the case in order to extract meaning. At very least, the film foregrounded technique. For many Osaka viewers, the experience of seeing *Tiger Child* in its pavilion would take precedence over their more familiar experiences with cinema. They were, in fact, encouraged to accept a certain amount of dissonance. Without consulting the filmmakers, the pavilion's managers placed a sign near the entrance telling visitors that they were about to see a challenging, non-narrative work.[14]

Even if, as that notice indicates, the film was seen by some as a sensory overload, then it at least succeeded in evoking a consideration of what "overload" or "sensory" mean. For those experiencing something other than sensory overload, there were other possibilities. Three of *Tiger Child*'s principal creators have testified as to what the film was meant to impart to viewers. In July 1968, Brittain was asked to write a treatment in order to address the sponsor's growing curiosity as to what was actually being done. He wrote in part:

> Man has been thrown in to a Global Village, and yet he is alienated from his surroundings. He is a lonely, loveless creature in a crowd, unable to either comprehend the technological explosion in which he lives, or to contemplate the eternal beauties of the Earth. With many forces of chaos and violence at work in the world, the only counter-force with sufficient energy to restore human equilibrium, is the force of compassionate love, a form of love which rejoices in the diversity and individuality of all things on earth, while recognizing that there is a single human bond.[15]

In an interview published in the *New York Times* in 1969, Hiroshi Kawazoe says, "Our theme is the 21st century, unimonde, globalism."[16] In Roman Kroitor's evaluation of the film, written during our correspondence for the preparation of this article, he states simply that *Tiger Child* "does not have a linear story. Think of it as a free form visual meditation of what it is to be in the world."[17]

Both statements point to the genre of the Expo film in its offering of a universal perspective a generic world or, to use the title of the work that influences so much of this post-war Expo humanism, a Family of Man. For Brittain, it appears, the presumed ideology of Edward Steichen's 1955 photographic exhibition, stressing the kinship of the many disparate people photographed, had worn out its welcome.[18]

The Family of Man model was also losing its credibility by virtue of a changing perception of documentary practice. What had once been accepted as a dominant style of documentary – a montage of silent images organized into a thesis by voice-over narration and music – had been transcended by the more intimate and presumably less manipulative direct cinema of the time. As Robert Fulford writes in his condemnation of the Labyrinth films at Expo 67: "Here is man's journey through life depicted in brilliantly cinematic terms. But the subject is once again Man (a creature not deeply interesting), as opposed to *a* man (who can be deeply interesting). What some of us hoped would be a major work of art turns out, instead, to be only a magnificent exhibition film."[19]

Fulford's complaint echoes as well a deeper question in documentary theory regarding the specificity of documentary subjects – an argument that goes back at least as far as the Soviet formalist critics of the 1920s.[20] The question is whether generic subject matter is consistent with its self-proclaimed opposite, the film of fact. For those who believe it is not, names, specific locations, dates, and times are posited as essential in order to lend credibility to what is being presented.

Brittain appears cognizant of this challenge in an attempt to avoid making "only a magnificent exhibition film." He responds by taking a middle ground between the specific and the generic. There are, among the many generic images, attempts at specificity. *Tiger Child* depicts, for instance, familiar landmarks such as the Wailing Wall in Jerusalem, Stonehenge, and the Berlin Wall. Some, like the "white haired couple," appear at various points in the film. Others, like the Thalidomide child, the bent over African with the walking stick, and the facial contortionist, dominate their sequences. And of course there is Gordon Lightfoot, the only face in the film to whom a name can be easily put, as well as the film's only character heard (singing) in sync. To the Canadians he was a "name" that needed no introduction. To the Japanese, we can only assume he appeared to be someone who, at least to Canadians, had a self-evident identity.

In sum, Brittain creates in *Tiger Child* a distinction between the unnamed and the anonymous. The individual people we meet appear to offer unique narratives – even if we only catch a glimpse of those narratives as the fast-paced film flies by. Their *typage* is refocused as an *entré* into their lives. This is particularly true of the "fictional" characters, i.e., those obviously acting for Brittain's camera: the couple making love, the young woman suffering from some form of urban alienation, the young man being pursued by police, and the sniper and his victims. Fictional though they may be, we are passing by poignant scenes from a larger drama, passing by like an audience on a doughnut-shaped turntable.

Brittain creates a sense of a "generic" 1970 milieu rising to meet the specifics of that historical moment. The film captures the era's rise in group-consciousness reflected in social movements and other bonding within demographics. Individuals strove to define themselves through gender, ethnicity, and political movements, taking on the fashions and grooming habits of their respective tribes.

Yet, as Kroitor notes, there is also a process of subjective meditation in *Tiger Child* that counters the invocation of collective consciousness. Ideally, that subjectivity would be the individual reactions of all its viewers. Each one could come to their personal conclusions. Failing that, *Tiger Child* is certainly Brittain's meditation. In its linear mode, the film appears

9.5 The "tiger child" juxtaposed with a desert landscape.

to be carefully structured around an exposition of ideas that might even be called an argument about the state of the world. Brittain's statement to the sponsors, despite the circumstances under which he wrote it, is a more than valid description of what we see and hear.

In discussions of the film, both Brittain and Kroitor provide explanations of *Tiger Child*'s title, perhaps a clue as to how we should read the film as a whole. As Brittain commented after the film's release: "In each man is the fierce heart of the tiger and the sweet soul of the child. Together they constitute the Human Spirit and this film is a proclamation of that spirit"[21] (see figure 9.5). Kroitor's more practical explanation nevertheless points to the same intended theme. He recalled that the phrase was originally used in reference to the armless Thalidomide child being lifted into the swimming pool. This was later called the "Tiger Child Shot." Eventually, the phrase seemed an appropriate way to describe the film as a whole.[22]

This stated theme is not terribly different from the characters Brittain had depicted to that point, particularly in his three biographic films. Each – Norman Bethune, Leonard Cohen, and Roy Thompson – are imbued with the "fierce heart of the tiger."[23] Yet in all three cases, there is also something vulnerable and hence attractive about the subjects. Bethune, an idealist with a flawed personal life, dies tragically far from home. Cohen is an abandoned man reduced to singing of his abandonment. Thompson, for all his wealth and crudeness, is in his more candid moments more like a child playing with a gigantic toy.

The abjectly dark tone of so much of *Tiger Child* should also be contextualized. Between the Summer of Love – and of Expo – in 1967 and the opening of the Osaka Expo in 1970, there were, among other violent and depressing events: the assassinations of Martin Luther King and Robert Kennedy; the Tet Offensive and My Lai massacre in Vietnam; the "events" of 1968 in France; the Russian invasion of Czechoslovakia; the massacre of protesters during the Mexico City Olympics; the Cultural Revolution in China; massive confrontational protests in Japan over the building of Norita Airport; and an escalation of FLQ violence.

The exception proving the rule was the moon landing of 1969. *Tiger Child* is devoid of the iconic rocket lift-offs and images of astronauts seen in the films of Expo 67. This was in contrast to the most popular exhibit at the Osaka Expo, the newly collected moon rocks at the United States pavilion. In Brittain's world, though, space exploration had changed nothing back on Earth. The absence of this imagery reflects a reconsideration of the "space race," exemplified in Kubrick's *2001: A Space Odyssey* (1968). That film shifted the iconography of space exploration from technological triumphalism to a sterile extension of corporate branding and governmentality whose most beneficial purpose was to facilitate an alien intervention.

Also changed since Expo 67 was the understanding of the role of youth. In Expo 67 films, young people were a happier lot. Clean-cut post-adolescents in Francis Thompson and Alexander Hammid's *We Are Young* struggled with nothing more arduous than the boredom of an entry-level office job. In the following years, though, films began to depict youth in a state of conflict with a far less benevolent social order, such as Mike Nichols's *The Graduate* (1967), Dennis Hopper's *Easy Rider* (1969), Godard's *Le Gai savoir* (1969), Robert Kramer's *Ice* (1970), and Peter Watkins's *Punishment Park* (1971).

Much of this context is clearly visible in *Tiger Child*. Police pursue a young man across rooftops, a young woman walks through landscapes in shell-shocked meditation, and protesters battle police amid clouds of tear gas. As Allison Whitney writes, the dark tone of *Tiger Child* is epitomized in the sequence depicting Thalidomide children:

> This sequence is an explication of our problematic engagement with technology: the pharmaceutical scandal of Thalidomide, and the heart-rending grotesquerie of babies trying to move their twisted limbs are glaring criticisms of technological hubris. The power of these images is augmented by their presentation in an IMAX format because of its position in the history of technological art, the ways its functions as a medium for addressing humans' relationships with technology, as well as the World's Fair notion of progress.[24]

The net effect, as Whitney sees it, is "a critique of the ideology inherent in the World's Fair film and World's Fairs themselves."[25] And yet even within this critique, there is a moderation to *Tiger Child*'s bleakness. Love is depicted not only in the rather sheepishly framed shots of non-simulated sex being performed by Brittain's actors, but also in the images of the elderly couple and the caregivers working with Thalidomide children. The filmmaker appears to have genuine affection for the ordinary people of the planet. In opposition to the depiction of "exotic" peoples in many world's fair films, *Tiger Child* generates an inclusive affection. We can love the broken people as well as the beautiful people in their various cultures.

In its linear mode as well, *Tiger Child* offers a circularity of sorts, a yin/yang between the misery it depicts and the hope it offers. Its sequences move from depictions of innocence, to the end of innocence, to persistence in the face of challenge, to life affronted by yet more horrors. Viewers in the Fuji Pavilion would have then been led back to innocence. Were they to enter at any point during the film they would, at very least, have perceived one or more of these transitions. Approaching *Tiger Child* in the middle or toward the end of a given sequence would, as the viewing progressed, give way to an idea of structure or, as Kroitor points out, a sense of meditation, i.e., coming to an understanding or acceptance of what was once seen as transient.

There is even a duality to the linear film's last image, which is of a blind man who has been led through the wreckage caused by a violent

9.6 The blind man amid the rioting.

demonstration (see figure 9.6). One reading would be that humanity is blind to the destruction its conflicts have caused. But the film leaves us with the idea that at least it can keep on walking – or, as it were, riding its turntable.

Tiger Child's place in the development of IMAX also made it pivotal in the long history of film – and, for that matter, pre-film spectacle. IMAX's goal of finding permanent venues for large format Expo films was not dissimilar to the impulse after the Great Exhibition of 1851 to make permanent the experience and the role of that event. Victorian entrepreneurs opened a second, permanent Crystal Palace in 1854 hoping to sustain the original's scope, ideology, and pedagogical intent. Their efforts failed, and long before it closed the second Crystal Palace had taken on a number of far less exalted functions.[26]

IMAX became a cinematic reprise of the Crystal Palace. It has produced and continues to produce a line of Expo-tone short documentaries largely constructed around the experience of being immersed in the large format screen. The many IMAX scientific, historical, and travel films that circulate through the world's museums harken back to the "cinema of attractions," films that thrive on the visual pleasures of their innovative imagery. But like the second Crystal Palace, IMAX today is sustained less by activities associated with its original purpose than by a more conventional role in the entertainment industry. It is an adjunct to the Hollywood studios, whose blockbuster films, ever since *Matrix Revolution* (2002), are now routinely released as IMAX and IMAX 3D versions in first-run theatres.

This attempted move to a sustainable Expo cinema demonstrates a difference between film as spectacle and film as ritual. Expos are designed as spectacle and hence to be ephemeral. They must be attended during the summer allotted to them. That attendance often requires a pilgrimage to a distant location that entails expense and discomfort (e.g., the long queues). Charles Acland sees this as a particularly Canadian trait, an "expo-mentality," that results from the exclusion of Canadian cinema from mainstream exhibition venues.[27] That mentality worked well with the increasingly complex pedagogical and sociological (as opposed to theatrical) practices generated by the National Film Board's evolving documentary agenda.

Expos and World's Fairs also frame themselves in relation to one another. They serve as a perceptual equivalent of the Olympics, the promise of a break in the quotidian relations between peoples to celebrate higher callings. It is no surprise then that much of the material in Expo productions reflects this celebratory mode. But, as we learned in an examination of the Olympics, there are no breaks in the quotidian relations of peoples, their ideologies, and economic imperatives. *Tiger Child*'s virtue in that regard is not its discontinuity with previous practices, but rather that it pointed through its new technology and unique venue toward a more nuanced documentary depiction of the world beyond.

NOTES

1 Author's conversation with Roman Kroitor, 5 March 2012, and email from Graeme Ferguson, 31 March, 2012. See also Brian Nolan, *Donald Brittain – Man of Film* (DigiWire: 2004), 152.

2 Mel Gussow, "Fair (Osaka) and Hair (Tokyo) Keep Producer Busy," *New York Times*. 9 October 1969, http://query.nytimes.com/mem/archive/pdf?res=f30f10fc345f127a93cba9178bd95f4d8685f9.

3 For the sole purpose of this article, IMAX was kind enough to shoot an off-screen DVD. There are at present no plans to digitize the film for commercial DVD release.

4 This includes Japanese sources, surveyed for the writing of this article by Masaki Kondo during the summer of 2011.
5 Daly's own description of the editing of Chamber Three may be found in Donald Theall's unpublished report, "McGill University Study of Audio-Visual and Multi-Media Aspects in Selected National and Theme Buildings at Expo 67: Prepared for the National Film Board," section VIII. Two items in this section are entitled "Tom Daly on the Editing Techniques on *Labyrinth*" and "Interview with Tom Daly on the Editing Techniques on *Labyrinth*."
6 The early evolution of widescreen and multiscreen formats in the contexts of World's Fairs has been most recently discussed in: Lauren Rabinovitz, *Electric Dreamland: Amusement Parks, Movies, and American Modernity* (New York: Columbia University Press, 2012).
7 Gussow, "Fair (Osaka) and Hair (Tokyo) Keep Producer Busy."
8 A detailed discussion of Mayuzumi's ideology and its relation to his compositional techniques may be found in: Steve Nuss, "Music from the Right: The Politics of Toshiro Mayuzumi's *Essay for String Orchestra*," in *Locating East Asia in Western Art Music*, ed. Yayo Uno Everett and Frederick Lau (Middletown, CT: Wesleyan University Press, 2004), 85–118.
9 Email from Roman Kroitor to the author, 26 January 2011.
10 Nolan, *Donald Brittain – Man of Film*, 149. Graeme Ferguson remembers it as being "more like the size of a block of ice." (Email to the author, 31 March 2012).
11 Most of these details of the production of *Tiger Child* come from Roman Kroitor's remarks at IMAX's fortieth anniversary celebration (13 September 2007), which he entitled, "The Beginnings of IMAX and the Making of Tiger Child in 300 Seconds." The projector invented for *Tiger Child* was installed in the Cinesphere at Ontario Place in Toronto in 1971. With some modifications, it was in continuous use there for nearly forty years.
12 I have prepared a shot list for *Tiger Child* that is available upon request.
13 Gordon Lightfoot, "Leaves of Grass" Sunday Concert album (United Artists, 1969).
14 Telephone conversation with Roman Kroitor, 5 March 2012.
15 My thanks to Graeme Ferguson for providing a copy of Brittain's document. A slightly different statement by Brittain appears in Nolan, *Donald Brittain – Man of Film*, 159.
16 Gussow, "Fair (Osaka) and Hair (Tokyo) Keep Producer Busy."
17 Email from Roman Kroitor to the author, 24 February 2011.
18 Steichen's original exhibition was not nearly so naïve as the variations of it that were used as international good will gestures by the US government. In the original show at the Museum of Modern Art in New York there are, as there are in *Tiger Child*, a number of oppressed or marginalized people. That show ended with a large image of a nuclear explosion – the only colour image Steichen allowed.
19 Marshall Delaney, "Film Technique at Expo '67," *Saturday Night* (July 1967), 33.
20 See, for instance, Elizabeth Arnold Papazian, *Manufacturing Truth: The Documentary Movement in Early Soviet Culture* (DeKalb: Northern Illinois University Press, 2009).
21 Nolan, *Donald Brittain – Man of Film*, 159.
22 Telephone conversation with Roman Kroitor, 5 March 2012.
23 Nolan, *Donald Brittain – Man of Film*, 151.

24 Alison Whitney, "Labyrinth: Cinema, Myth and Nation at Expo 67," (unpublished MA thesis, McGill University, 1999), 106, http://digitool.library.mcgill.ca/r/?func=dbin-jump-full&object_id=21278&local_base=gen01-mcg02. Thalidomide, a tranquilizer, was approved for use in October 1957. It was accepted as causing birth defects in late 1961 and was withdrawn from markets worldwide (Canada was the last country to do so). The damage done to tens of thousands of children was the subject of a widely syndicated series of articles that first appeared in 1968 in the *Sunday Times* of London.

25 Whitney, "Labyrinth," 105.

26 A concise discussion of the second Crystal Palace may be found in Jim Secord, "Monsters at the Crystal Palace," in *Models: The Third Dimension of Science*, ed. S. de Chadarevian and N. Hopwood (Stanford: Stanford University Press, 2004), 138–69.

27 Charles R. Acland, *Movies, Multiplexes and Global Culture* (Durham, NC: Duke University Press, 2003), 193.

10 EPHEMERAL GODARD
VIDEO, HISTORY, AND QUEBEC

Jerry White

WHAT REMAINS OF the adventures of Jean-Luc Godard in Quebec is "ephemeral." But one of the assumptions bringing the chapters in this book together is that "ephemeral" is by no means the same thing as "unimportant" or "mere curiosity," and so it is with Godard and Quebec. In this chapter, I will both tell the story of Godard's significant trips to Quebec[1] – a trip to Abitibi in 1968 and a series of lectures at Concordia University in 1978 – and also explain how the pieces of video that remain – which are either so fragile as to be illegible or housed at Concordia University's media centre and not meant for circulation – anticipate and help to explain key periods in his career. I will try to illustrate the degree to which the Abitibi trip synchs up with *Le Gai savoir* (1969) and the French television series *Six fois deux: Sur et sous la communication* (1976), and the ways in which these Concordia lectures anticipate both the concerns and the aesthetic of his massive video series, *Histoire(s) du cinéma* (1988–98). Neither Abitibi nor Concordia figures very centrally in most critical discussions of Godard and, as I will show, when his time in Quebec comes up at all the discussion tends toward the brief or dismissive. This relates to the ephemeral quality of the work; the degree to which the images Godard created or facilitated in Quebec are either hard to access or simply non-existent, and so nobody should expect them to be all that central to a discussion of his work overall.

The situation is slowly changing, led by the relative availability of one memento of the Concordia lectures, Godard's 1980 book *Introduction à une véritable histoire du cinéma*, which, as I will discuss below, was based on lectures Godard gave at Concordia. This book is long out of print, although is available in many university libraries. In 2014, Montreal publisher Caboose issued a massive translation of this book, one that added considerable material left out of the French edition (the translator Timothy Barnard pored over the videotapes of Godard's lectures and re-inserted lacunae as well as questions from the interlocutor Serge Losique and the audience). The volume also includes Michael Witt's introductory essay, "Archaeology of *Histoire(s) du cinema*," a fantastic source of information about Godard's time at Concordia. Witt emphasizes the importance of montage in Godard's conception of film history, and argues that he is influenced on that matter by Henri Langlois and André Malraux. Witt writes that Malraux's studies of art history "not only deployed a highly lyrical style of writing, but also explored the creative and critical potential of the juxtaposition of images, of the passage to and fro between reproductions of whole works and details, and of shifting image-texts relationships on the page."[2] The publication of this edition is a watershed in Godard scholarship for sure, but a transcription of the lectures tells only part of the story of Godard's time in Quebec. A big part of what separates the Godard of the French New Wave from the later, more politically engaged – and, some would say, more gnomic – Godard is the latter's embrace of video, an embrace that made a very different kind of cinematic palette available. He dabs at that palette in his 1960s and '70s ephemera, and in Quebec one gets the sense of him making some serious if tentative studies for the later work.

This should not come as a surprise, for Godard's interest in Quebec is long-standing. He first references this interest in the very long interview he gave to Jacques Bontemps, Jean-Louis Comolli, Michel Delahaye, and Jean Narboni of the *Cahiers du cinéma* in 1967 (it was published in no. 194), titled "Lutter sur deux fronts," in which he states:

> The Canadian cinema is interesting as an example. The National Film Board is an impressive film factory, more so than Hollywood today. It's a great set-up. But what's the pay-off? Zero. There's nothing to see for it. The films just aren't coming out. What Daniel Johnson ought to do is nationalize all the cinemas in Quebec. But he won't do it. The best he's capable of is seeing that de Gaulle gets a welcome in the metro screens. So, over there as well, cinema is subject to a special brand of imperialism, just like everywhere else.[3]

This evinces familiarity with Quebec politics. Godard knew not only of de Gaulle's 1967 visit to Montreal (where he famously shouted "Vive le Québec libre!" as he addressed a crowd from city hall), but also about Daniel Johnson, at that time the premier of Quebec as a member of the

Union Nationale, a more-or-less nationalist party[4] with a generally conservative social policy and a generally classical-liberal approach to economic policy (hence the reluctance to nationalize Quebec's cinemas). Godard is also keenly aware of and impressed by the work of the National Film Board of Canada (NFB), as well as of the fact that few Canadians actually get to see very many of its extraordinary films. Godard gave this interview in the same year that he shot *Le Gai savoir*, which is important as a sort of transitional work, positioned between the New Wave Godard of the 1960s and the later, more political and essayistic Godard of the 1970s onward. Colin MacCabe also makes this case, writing, "In its concern to understand the language of cinema by taking it back to its component parts, and in its funding and subsequent rejection by television, *Le Gai savoir* can be taken as a model for all the subsequent Dziga Vertov group films."[5] At one point, the screen goes black and Léaud says, "Here, the image is missing. The English-Canadian police gouged out the eyes of the cameraman who was filming the faces and landscapes of Free Quebec."

Thus it is strange to encounter the indifference to, and occasional hostility toward, questions about Quebec evident in Godard's March 1977 visit to Montreal. He came as part of a retrospective of his work organized by Serge Losique, founder of the Montreal World Film Festival and at that time also director of the Conservatoire d'art cinématographique de Montréal, which Witt describes as "a film archive and reparatory cinema under the auspices of the university [Concordia], which was housed in a university building in downtown Montreal (1455 Boulvard de Maisonneuve Ouest) until the university, during a period of budget cuts, closed it down in 1998."[6] Today Concordia has videos of the Q&A sessions from this retrospective grouped with the tapes of Godard's 1978 lectures. In the first of these Q&A sessions, an unseen questioner (who Losique identifies as "un professeur du cinéma" – it is Thomas Waugh) asks why Godard has agreed to a retrospective that includes films he does not like anymore, and also asks what his goal is in making this intervention in the cultural and political life of Quebec. Godard hems and haws about how he was invited and is just coming along as part of a course he will do on film and television history. Losique takes the microphone at that point and scolds Waugh for not knowing that it was he and not Godard who chose the films, and then says, "Pour la second partie de votre question, c'est complètement stupide."[7] Later on, someone asks Godard about his experience with community television in the Lac

St-Jean area. Godard tries to correct the questioner and fumbles for the name Rouyn-Noranda, which is actually where he visited and recalls that the trip to Abitibi to participate in community television never came to much, the attempt to bring video cameras down to a strike culminating with a big snowball fight. No doubt that the audience members had no idea that Godard had once sung the praises of the NFB, criticized Daniel Johnson, and, in one of his most experimental films, invoked the troubles of those who wanted to film the faces and landscapes of Québec libre.

ABITIBI

> Canadians are exiles too; they just don't know it. That's where their problems come from, and so, maybe especially Quebec, they're not at all exiles from Europe in my opinion, they're exiles from America. I myself being an exile from France.
>
> Jean-Luc Godard, *Introduction à une véritable histoire du cinéma*[8]

Although I would categorically reject this dismissal of Godard's Canadian experience, I have to admit that this is how a lot of people remember his voyage to *les trente arpents*. Richard Brody, in his biography *Everything Is Cinema: The Working Life of Jean-Luc Godard*, recalls that Godard had really liked the Canadian landscape and that he was friendly with Quebec producer Claude Nedjar. Nedjar had a scheme to bring Godard to Rouyn-Noranda, in the western Quebec region known as Abitibi, to get him to collaborate with a group of leftist filmmakers who wanted to use video cameras to document a strike. Brody summarizes the experience this way:

> Nedjar, who had a connection with media executives in Rouyn-Noranda in rural Quebec, proposed an ambitious scheme: that Godard put together a ten-part television series there in collaboration with a group of leftist filmmakers ... The ten-part project was to begin with documentary material: Godard intended to film discussions with local workers and students and to develop a fiction film from that research. Working with a group of politically active videomakers from the area, Godard recorded a large amount of video footage, but according to [Godard's then-wife] Anne Wiazemsky, he was unclear about what he wanted to do ... Godard quickly lost interest in the project and told her simply "we're going home." It

> was a fittingly inconclusive end to a year of frenzied, unfocused activity, which was only to escalate.[9]

The year Brody refers to is 1968; Godard was in Abitibi in December. That was the year of the famed May strikes in Paris, in which Godard had been actively involved. But it was also the year that Godard travelled to the United States to collaborate with D.A. Pennebaker on a film about revolutionary sentiments in the United States, which was to be titled *One A.M.* or *One American Movie.* Godard abandoned that work, although Pennebaker eventually edited a version called *One P.M.* (1972), sometimes known as *One Pennebaker Movie.*

Michel Larouche, in a 1989 article called "Godard et les Québécois" tells this story of Godard in Abitibi differently than Brody does; he somewhat sarcastically indicates that Godard was not there for very long, but also gives a detailed sense of the complex local situation:

> 1968 was "The Godard Affair," as we call it in Quebec ... For about three weeks, four television broadcasts were completed (of a half-hour for the first three and one hour for the last one), and they were very low-quality, the staff technicians having refused to help (the recordings made by a recorder weren't transferred, but were simply re-filmed to be broadcast, and this produced a practically illegible image). For this reason, and for obvious ideological reasons, the project was very controversial and provoked violent reactions in the community. As for Godard, he only stayed three days.[10]

Pierre David describes the experience of the broadcasts along these lines as well, and recalls in Julie Perron's 1998 NFB film *Mai en décembre: Godard en Abitibi* how in rural Quebec, the status of a professional television technician was as prestigious as that of a notary or a lawyer, and an iconoclast like Godard proposing experiments such as filming someone on the toilet was, to them, a sacrilege.[11] Just as sacrilegious, really, was Godard's budding Brechtianism. During an interview with the local television station CKRN, he moved behind the camera and started talking to the operator, saying that he had just as much of a right to participate in the discussion, and pointing out that even if he questioned the operator directly he would not answer. A desire to move fluidly between the spaces in front of and behind the camera was the essence of the self-conscious cinema that Godard had been trying to develop though the 1960s, and that interest in "behind the camera" would also become important for the films and television series he produced with Anne-Marie Miéville a few years later. Explaining the genesis of Godard and Miéville's 1976 television series *Six foix deux: Sur et sous la communication*, Michael Witt writes: "In a sense, this series could be considered to be a partial realisation of a project Godard had been working on since 1968, tentatively entitled *Communications.* This was supposed to be a group film of 24 hours, which would examine various means of communications (you can see more of this in the events documented in Julie Perron's film *Mai en décembre: Godard en Abitibi*, which is in part a detailed piece of research on this ongoing project)."[12] There can be little doubt that this Quebec experience greatly influenced Godard's thinking on communication and set the stage for his work with Miéville; it was also a preview of the limitations he would face. For while Nedjar's suggestion that Godard, in Brody's retelling, "put together a ten-part television series there in collaboration with a group of leftist filmmakers" sounds like a blueprint for *Six fois deux: Sur et sous la communication*, the unexpected response of the local technicians – the local petty bourgeoisie, essentially – and the degree to which that response was discouraging were also shades of things to come. Neither of the series that Godard and Miéville made for French television (they finished the six-part *France tour détour deux enfants* in 1979) enjoyed much support from the broadcaster or much success in terms of viewership (however sophisticated at the level of both ideology and form they may have been).

Those French television series are hard to see these days, but they are available (English-dubbed or -subtitled versions are distributed by New Yorks Electronic Arts Intermix); not so, really, with the audiovisual fruits of Godard's trip to Abitibi. The four broadcasts about the strike were directed not by Godard but by members of the group of filmmakers from Abitibi, Alain Laury and Pierre David specifically. Larouche lays each of them out in some detail, and suggests that some formal tics (such as shots of film reels) might have been influenced by Godard's films.[13] The CKRN broadcast in which Godard tries to engage the operator in a discussion exists only as a reconstruction in Perron's film *Mai en décembre*; she uses the soundtrack and still photos to give a sense of it, as the video had deteriorated to the point of illegibility. The traces of Godard's presence in Abitibi have not exactly vanished, but they have come perilously close to doing so. What does remain, however ephemeral, gives a sense of how Godard was at the end of the 1960s, as he tried to come to grips with the ways that television was transforming cinematic aesthetics. This process began with the 1967 filming of *Le Gai savoir* (1969), a work influenced in equal parts by Brechtian theatre and Eisensteinian montage, made for and then rejected by French television and shot almost entirely on a darkened sound stage. It continued in North America. The first North American instalment was *One A.M.*, which as Brody recalls was commissioned in New York as part of WNET's "Public Broadcasting Laboratory," the television station's experimental program that Brody calls "the precursor to PBS."[14] The second instalment was the effort in Abitibi, which engaged labour activists, cutting-edge video equipment, and conventional chat shows, all very close to the kind of television he was trying to create throughout the 1970s as part of his Sonimage production company (which he called an "atelier" or workshop), based first in Grenoble, France, and later in Rolle, Switzerland. This culminated in the aforementioned series for French television (*Six fois deux: Sur et sous la communication*, in addition to 1979's *France tour détour deux enfants*, which was less explicitly engaged with communication), works that, however unsuccessful in terms of viewership, were remarkably ambitious and that remain a key part of Godard's corpus. The efforts in Abitibi, however ephemeral their outcomes, are a key part of this narrative.

HISTOIRES

> "Vous êtes les fabricants de mon histoire."
> Jean-Luc Godard[15]

The completion of Godard's massive video series *Histoire(s) du cinema* (1988–98) saw the publication of a large number of assessments, in both English and French, that argued for the series as a culmination of Godard's entire career, a career defined in equal parts by film criticism and filmmaking. Most of these assessments mentioned the series' genesis in Godard's 1980 book *Introduction à une véritable histoire du cinéma*, and a few mention that book's genesis in Montreal. Witt's introduction to the Screen's "Godard Dossier" of 1999 is a good example:

> *Histoire(s) du cinéma* represents the realization and culmination of a project cherished and nurtured for almost three decades: that of thinking film history through images and sounds. As early as the

> beginning of the 1970s Godard proposed an image/text collage scenario for a project on the history of cinema to Italian television (RAI). In 1978 the project reappeared, this time at the Montreal Film School (the Conservatoire d'Art Cinématographique), where Godard – at the invitation of Serge Losique, and following in the steps of Henri Langlois – delivered a series of lectures (or *voyages*, as Godard called them) on cinema history. Rather than delivering lectures, Godard proposed a form of historical cinematic montage, whereby the projection of one of his own films, together with a range of other films, would provide the basis for reflection on cinema history and his place within it. These lectures, partially transcribed and published in France in 1980 as *Introduction à une véritable histoire du cinéma*, were never intended as an end in themselves, but rather as the "scenario" for a series of films on cinema history. Although this project failed to materialize in this form, we are now seeing its fulfillment through video in *Histoire(s) du cinéma.*[16]

After the aforementioned retrospective that Losique organized in 1977, Godard visited Montreal four times in 1978 to give these classes: in April, May, June, and October. At the end of the October classes, Losique told the assembled group that the next meetings would be at the beginning of December, and even cracked that the journalists in the audience would no doubt write that down. But no further lectures materialized. Godard hints at one reason for this in his brief introduction to *Introduction à une véritable histoire du cinéma*; he recalls there that the original deal had been for the Conservatoire to share with Sonimage a sum of $10,000 per chapter (which seems to mean each lecture), but, "then everything came to a halt, as Losique had financial difficulties and was writing Sonimage rubber checks and then none at all. But just the same, he was bold enough to break new ground, and *nobody's perfect.*"[17]

Part of the innovation here was the way in which Godard used fragments of films to explain the evolution both of film history and his own filmmaking. Montage was always a key component of Godard's cinematic practice, and he organized these Concordia sessions as a series of fragments. Witt recalls that after some experimenting with the formatting, "he and Losique settled on a method: screening individual reels of three to five films in the morning, followed by one of his own in its entirety in the afternoon. Thus the morning session acquired 'a kind of montage quality,' as Godard put it, in which he sought to create 'a connecting thread, like a film, a musical theme.'"[18] These classroom sessions were recorded on video, and while the sound frequently becomes unbalanced or disappears altogether (questioners are sometimes audible, sometimes not), the videos as a whole are a fascinating record of Godard thinking through the problems of film history aloud. These were thus not really "lectures" at all, and the word "course" does not really capture what seems to be going on here. What these videos document is a sustained effort – an *essai*, to put it in a nicely ambiguous French way – in film history and artistic self-interrogation. Losique's impeccable connections in the international cinematheque world gave Godard freedom to show 35 mm prints of a wide variety of films, and he frequently marvels at Losique's ability to get material in (the first lecture opens with Godard saying, "I don't know how Serge does it but you ask him for a print of a film and there it is.").[19] But the only films Godard showed in their entirety were his own. As he moves through the project, the montage he is building becomes more ambitious and complex: in the first session he focuses on *Fallen Angel* and *A bout de souffle*, in the third session he pairs five films, and in each of the last two he pairs four different films with one of his own (the last session is devoted to Godard's *Les Carabiniers* along with *The Lost Patrol*, *Alexander Nevsky*, *Rome Open City*, and *The Green Berets*). And that sense of unpredictable, complex combination really is what constitutes the daring innovation that Godard alludes to in his half-hearted absolution of Losique's financial sins: this is pedagogy, and history, as montage.

These tapes, though, suggest that what seemed really daring at the time was the attempt to conduct sustained, precise research into film history, with the hopes of finding something genuinely new. Losique says as much when he introduces the first of these classroom sessions on 14 April; he alludes vaguely to problems he was having with the administration, and states adamantly that they are doing research, that they are trying to discover the real history of cinema, and that it will be a long process. Godard explains the project that way, too, and reproduces his explanation in the text of *Introduction à une véritable histoire du cinéma*: "If there is nothing there, well, you look elsewhere. Exactly like scientists in a laboratory. But this laboratory does not exist. The only research taking place is in pharmaceuticals and a little bit in medicine, or scientific research, or in universities, but this research is closely connected to the military system. There you find a little research, they give you the tools.

In film, there is none."[20] The idea of archival research was not somehow new or daring, but what Godard and Losique were trying to present as new was the effort to look for the *real* history, *une véritable histoire.* They knew what they wanted, even if they did not know quite what it looked liked, and if they failed to find it, they would just look in other places – an approach that does not sound like historical research as it is generally conducted (or was being conducted in the 1970s). It does not sound much like scientific research either, although Godard's analogy with pharmacy is instructive. It is like they were looking for a cure for some sort of disease, some antidote to the sickness that was gripping film history: the sickness of nationalism, of aesthetic blindness, of chronological myopia. This cocktail of films – *M* with *Le Petit Soldat,* mixed a few days later with a combination of *Man with a Movie Camera, The Bad and the Beautiful, La Nuit Américaine,* and *Le Mépris* – seemed to offer a way to look at film history that did not privilege generic categories (experimental documentary can coexist with commercial narratives), national identities (Soviet films can illuminate American ones, and together they can illuminate French ones), or a chronological history (Weimer Germany said a lot about a film made during and more or less about France's Algerian war).

Again, the key concept for understanding Godard's approach to cinema is montage, the key intellectual strategy the creation of meaning through combination. That approach is the aesthetic of *Histoire(s) du cinéma,* the analytical strategy of *Introduction à une véritable histoire du cinéma,* and the ethic of Godard's courses at Concordia. Like the line that runs through Abitibi and toward *Six fois deux,* a line defined by an interest in communication as a fundamental political and existential problem, there is a line that runs through Concordia straight on to *Histoire(s) du cinéma,* a line defined by a desire to find a new way to think about cinema and history together. The videos of these classes held by Concordia's media centre have the air of ephemerality about them, although that may overstate the case. Barnard's "Note on the Text" of *Introduction to a True History of Cinema and Television* notes that he worked off "consultation copies" and used originals only when trying to improve on the sound quality. He summarizes the condition of the original tapes by saying, "the sound and image were recorded onto sixty-minute reels of half-inch black-and-white 3M Scotch videotape, a brand which luckily is not prone to the kind of degradation of magnetic tape known as sticky shed syndrome."[21] The material, then, is not as ephemeral as other cinematic objects under discussion in this book, although it is hardly easily available (it does not circulate off of the Concordia campus). But like the images and sounds pieced together by Perron's *Mai en décembre*, these Montreal sessions are crucial pieces of the Godard puzzle and offer key insights into fundamental principals of some of his most important work.

CONCLUSION

I am utterly at a loss as to why Losique found the question about Godard intervening in Quebec's cultural and political life so stupid. Godard was aware of Quebec – its culture and politics – and had shown a far more serious interest in the place than any of his French New Wave colleagues. Furthermore, 1977 was the year that he did work in Mozambique, a small country that, as he remarks in *Introduction à une véritable histoire du cinéma*, was dependent on South Africa for much of its electricity. That work in Mozambique comes up quite a bit in *Introduction*, and Godard's desire to talk about it should give some sense of the degree to which he was interested, in the 1970s, in getting out of the metropolis and into more marginalized regions. In the 1970s, he left Paris for Grenoble before finally settling in the Swiss town of Rolle. He made a film about Portugal, 1976's *Comment ça va?* He spoke of his desire to create a kind of television, a kind of communication, that was not dependent on the colonizing metropolis for its efficacy. Quebec in the 1960s and '70s – defined as it was by furious debates about language, regionalism, federation, and sovereignty, and home to a cinema that was always implicated in such debates – seems like an entirely logical place for him to gravitate toward. These ephemeral bits of cinema – these broadcasts rebuilt from stills and audio tapes, these grainy and sometimes inaudible videos – are the most powerful checks against Godard's own tendency to downplay the logic of this connection, to say nothing of that of grouchy interlocutors.

NOTES

1 I will leave aside his trips to Montreal's World Film Festival or Festival du nouveau cinéma to appear with films.

2 Michael Witt, "Archaeology of *Histoire(s) du cinéma*," in Jean-Luc Godard, *Introduction to A True History of Cinema and Television*, trans. Timothy Barnard (Montreal: Caboose, 2014), xxiii.

3 Jean Bontemps, Jean-Louis Comolli, Michel Delahaye, and Jean Narboni, "Struggling on Two Fronts," trans. Diana Mathias, in *Cahiers du Cinéma: The 1960s, New Wave, New Cinema, Reevaluating Hollywood*, ed. Jim Hillier (Cambridge, MA: Harvard University Press, 1992), 294.

4 Johnson famously chafed against Ottawa, and the Union Nationale's 1966 campaign slogan was "Égalité ou indépenance." He was also the premier during de Gaulle's 1967 visit to Quebec.

5 Colin MacCabe, *Godard: A Portrait of the Artist at Seventy* (London: Faber, 2003), 204.

6 Witt, "Archaeology of *Histoire(s) du cinéma*," xxvii.

7 One of the joys of Barnard's edition of Godard's *Introduction* is his recovery of a heated exchange during the actual Concordia lectures between Godard, Losique, and a very aggressive audience member who seems to be something of a nationalist. At one point he says, seemingly to Losique, although it's a little hard to tell, "you're stupid and an idiot and a fascist. And Concordia University is an English university, Mr. Godard. That's your mistake." When the audience member mentions the Parti Québécois, Losique says he'll throw him out, threatens to call security, and says, "you'll answer to the courts for the word fascist." He shortly mellows on the last issue there, though, saying, "No, stop. That's not an insult. Why is fascist an insult? [*Inaudible.*] Because you said it as an insult. If you had called him a Catholic he wouldn't have gotten upset. [*Laughter.*]." See Jean-Luc Godard, *Introduction to A True History*, 51–6.

8 Jean-Luc Godard, *Introduction à une véritable histoire du cinéma* (Paris: Albatros, 1980), 54. My translation.

9 Richard Brody, *Everything Is Cinema: The Working Life of Jean-Luc Godard* (New York: Metropolitan, 2008), 343–4.

10 Michel Larcouche, "Godard et les Québécois," *CinémAction* 52 (1989): 150. My translation.

11 Julie Perron, *Mai en décembre: Godard en Abitibi* (Montreal: National Film Board of Canada, 2000), video.

12 Michel Witt, "Paroles non-éternelles," in *Jean-Luc Godard: Documents*, ed. Nocole Brenez et al. (Paris: Centre Georges Pompidou, 2006), 260. My translation.

13 Larcouche, "Godard et les Québécois," 12.

14 Brody, *Everything Is Cinema*, 342.

15 Godard, *Introduction à une véritable histoire du cinéma*, 203.

16 Michael Witt, "Introduction. Jean-Luc Godard: *Histoire(s) du cinéma*," *Screen* 40, no. 3 (Fall 1999): 304.

17 Godard, *Introduction to A True History*, xi. Original in Godard, *Introduction à une véritable histoire du cinéma*, 15. "Nobody's perfect" is in English in the original.

18 Witt, "Archaeology of *Histoire(s) du cinéma*," xxxv.

19 Godard, *Introduction to A True History*, 7. Original in Godard, *Introduction à une véritable histoire du cinéma*, 21.

20 Godard, *Introduction to A True History*, 9. Original in Godard, *Introduction à une véritable histoire du cinéma*, 23.

21 Timothy Barnard, "A Note on the Text," in Godard, *Introduction to a True History*, lxxvii.

11 OUT HERE

FEELING BAD, FEELING GAY IN MICHEL AUDY'S *LUC OU LA PART DES CHOSES* AND *CREVER À VINGT ANS*

Micky Storey and Jason B. Crawford

FORMING PART OF a larger trend that runs through contemporary Anglo-American queer studies, Ann Cvetkovich is concerned with examining queer affect – the complex of feelings and emotions that arise from a uniquely queer experience of the world – and the role it might play in constructing archives that may be drawn on in the creation of alternative public histories and cultures. Her focus on depression – or what she, in typically personal and less clinical terms, refers to as "feeling bad" – is particularly relevant in the present context, for the two films of Michel Audy we discuss in this chapter are about such feelings, and especially how they lead us to do the things we do, however inexplicable, dangerous, or traumatic they may be.[1]

In this chapter, we employ Cvetkovich's notion of the archive of feelings as way to think about the ephemeral nature of two gay films from Québécois auteur Michel Audy. Cvetkovich's concept of the archive of feelings is made of both actually existing material objects, traditionally collected in institutional and community archives, and the invisible, emotion-based feelings that come from one's experience. She includes ephemera in the archive of feelings as well: memories, photographs, and objects that seem to have no official purposes for institutional research. She notes that trauma – or, feeling bad – often unsettles the traditional concepts of the archives because, as she writes, "trauma can be unspeakable and unrepresentable and because it is marked by forgetting and dissociation, it often seems to leave behind no records at all."[2] Linking the experiences of trauma with gay and lesbian cultures, Cvetkovich highlights that memory is both a historical resource and a resource for political resistance to "official histories" that would seek to erase or alternately rewrite the stories of gays and lesbians.[3] The archives of feelings thus exists as both material and immaterial cultural artefacts, including ephemera, as records of gay and lesbian experiences.[4]

Here, we are thinking of these gay films not only as archives of feeling, but also as gay archives. These two films depict and evoke a range of emotions about gay life in non-urban Quebec, a significant contribution to the corpus of gay film in Canada, particularly given the metro-central (i.e., Montreal-Toronto-Vancouver) nature of most gay film in Canada.[5] The feelings archived in these films document gay sensibilities around coming out, sex work, loneliness, friendship, and teen suicide. In a time when school bullying and teen suicide dominate public debates and government policy formation around queer youth and bullying, Audy's films constitute both a historical record of how these issues have been presented in the recent past and also a key through which we may access these feelings through the art of moving images. Given the marginal place of these films in circulation networks, we discuss the material and aesthetic quality of their decay through transferral from film to video to digital copy and mine these disintegrations for their haptic and emotional affect. Finally, we conclude that while the ephemeral nature of these two French-language films is due to a variety a factors – language and culture, funding and distribution politics, and sexual politics – we urge the resuscitation of both these films that can inspire us to rethink the role of gay and queer film in public discourse and politics.

The tongue-in-cheek "out here" in the title of this chapter is a reference to the setting for nearly all of Audy's films. While Trois-Rivières is no Charlevoix or Chibougamou, it is decidedly non-urban and feels rural despite its medium-sized population. More importantly for our purposes, these films depict the local accent and way of life in Quebec outside of the province's two metropoles. Situated geographically between Montreal and Quebec City, Trois-Rivières is best known for its Forges du Saint-Maurice, the birthplace of the Canadian iron industry, and also as the "poetry capital" of Quebec. It is fitting, then, that Audy's characters are from the working class strata, his actors are non-professional *Trifluviens,* and his stories are rooted in his poetic landscapes.

Michel Audy was born in 1947 near Trois-Rivières in the village of Grand-Mère and studied cinematography at the National Film Board (NFB)/Office national du film (ONF) from 1969 to 1971. In the 1970s and 1980s, Audy worked at the CEGEP de Trois-Rivières as a specialist in teaching technologies and has been a filmmaker and independent producer since 1968. He has made over thirty short films and eleven feature-length films, of which the two most widely known are *Luc ou la part des choses*

(1982) and *Crever à vingt ans* (1984). While not the only gay Québécois filmmaker to focus on stories from the hinterlands, Audy offers a window into another way of thinking about gay life in Quebec. While many queer youth from outside Quebec City or Montreal continue to gravitate toward the relative anonymity of those urban centres and their associated gay cultures, Audy's main characters are decidedly rooted in Trois-Rivières. The emotional pull of the non-urban, both capturing and captivating his characters, is characteristic of Audy's corpus of films and subjects his audiences to the feelings of being marginal within the marginal landscape of Trois-Rivières. These two works by Audy offer an archive of feelings of gay youth in a particular place and time, and demonstrate how his gay films are like a record of the human condition. The current physical condition of these films also produces feelings and sensations, and these emotional experiences make up the centre of our critical discussion of these two important gay Canadian films.

LUC OU LA PART DES CHOSES (1982)

> Another corpus of films and videos assumes the nonurban as the place of here and now, the site of the self, rather than of the other, anchored in the everyday texture of rural or small-town life without the normalizing urban referent.[6]

> Attachment *to* places can be thought of as attachment *through* places to the people, events and ideas one has built one's life around. Places become synecdoche for people, family, memories, security and cultural values.[7]

Probably the most widely seen of Michel Audy's film corpus is his remarkably stark, emotionally effervescent, and socially instructive film, *Luc ou la part des choses* (Luc, or his share of things). Even though this film could be framed as representative of Audy's work, the unique circumstances surrounding its production, its author's intentions, and its funding source relegate *Luc* to a particular genre of ephemeral film: the didactic melodrama. This nomenclature might lead one to analyse it solely based on its pedagogical merits or its relationship to other educational fiction films. To do so, however, would be to obscure its singularly most important value: a document of gay life woven inseparably into the visual landscape of Trois-Rivières. The film, as these authors viewed it, is accessible primarily as a transfer from film to video to DVD. These transformations have left the currently viewable version of *Luc* grainy, fuzzy, and at times inaudible. All the same, and perhaps because of these distortions, it is visually affecting and its subject, given the recent social and media focus on the bullying of queer youth, makes it a candidate for reinsertion into popular discourse. In the following discussion of *Luc*, we highlight both its merits as a fictional representation of really lived everyday situations of many gay youth situated within an affect-producing visual landscape and its representation of gay life *dans les régions* in early 1980s Quebec that stands as both a visually and politically significant film.[8]

Luc ou la part des choses tells the story of a young *Trifluvien* who quits school to work as an auto mechanic.[9] Luc spends his free time building a sailboat with his friend François and drinking in the local *taverne*. It is in the *taverne* that he, along with François and their gay friend Louis, takes notice of a particular *motard* – a bearish biker man who, in turn, takes note of Luc. On one occasion, Luc, who has a particular interest in motorcycles, takes up the *motard*'s offer for a ride with him that brings them to a flooded quarry where the two skinny dip in the summer sun and where Luc has his first gay sexual experience. Shortly after this encounter, word spreads about Luc and the *motard* and Luc is gay bashed by local drunkards. After coming out to his mother, father, and girlfriend – all of whom fail to fully support him – Luc attempts suicide by ingesting a vial of prescription pills. Sitting alone at the kitchen table and drowsy, Louis, who happens to stop by for a visit, saves Luc from near death. After a period of depression and a move to Montreal, Luc finds solace and encouragement – not from his family, but from his life-long friend François, who counsels him on self-esteem and offers him unconditional support.

As a project funded by the Quebec Ministry of Education, Audy spent a year researching social work intervention and counselling techniques as well as interviewing young gay men about their experiences.[10] The result is a charming yet brutal depiction of the realities many gay youth face as they discover their sexualities, come out – or are outed – and figure out how they are going to live their lives. Despite its original intention as an instructional film for college social work students, *Luc* continues to work as a portrait of the everyday life of young people's struggles with homosexuality, offers helpful examples of both positive and negative reactions, and ends with a balanced, supportive, open-minded approach to sexual identity. As a pedagogical tool it is also a political intervention in the struggle to make society more fair and just for those who differ from dominant sexual norms. As a narrative feature, the film pulls us into a site, a place, a landscape not unlike many other places outside Canada's urban centres.

Tom Waugh describes the landscape of Trois-Rivières in *Luc* as a "town of lyrical, hazy roofscapes, the kind of pretty little place that gay people can't wait to get away from, though director Michel Audy views it with great affection."[11] However, the roofscape scenes of Trois-Rivières, appearing no less than five times in the film, suggest that the rooftop space is a special place for Luc and for the audience. It is on the rooftop that Luc shares his thoughts and feelings with François and discovers a naked Louis having sex with a beautiful young man. It is on the rooftop that Audy also offers some of the most affecting images of Trois-Rivières. These images help us identify with Luc's situation, reflecting his loneliness, and characterize the emotion, colour, and texture of the story. The moments *sur le toit* offer Luc private instances of reflection and escape and are a kind of third space – a place apart from home or work, a place for sex (as Luc discovers), a place for secrets. With an almost watercolour brilliance, Audy creates both the actual *toit* and the landscape of Trois-Rivières as third spaces, that is, neither small village nor Montreal, neither the busy street, nor the isolation of the bedroom. Caught between, neither here nor there, up here – a third space – Luc contemplates his reality and his future, and tries to grab hold of his own life. The director's fine hand brings us here to the rooftop with Luc, who takes us up *sur le toit* to see Trois-Rivières, creating an affect, a feeling of loneliness but also of desire – the desire to understand one's own reality. Through Audy's roofscapes, and through the feelings the visual landscape of the film produces, the audience can come to identify with the character's experience. It is just as important to think of the (first) intended audience of Luc, the *Trifluvien* and *Trifluvienne* college students who could have easily recognized their city in the film, its landmarks and streets. The ways that viewers come to identify with the story of *Luc* is arguably as important as the options for dealing with homosexuality that Audy's film offers. Viewers can identify with Luc and become sensitized to the difficulties of coming out, but also see a beautiful document of Audy's own gay sensibility through his portrayal of Trois-Rivières as a third space within Quebec. The marginality of *Luc* in the corpus of Québécois and Canadian queer film belies both its contemporary message and its artistic value. The technical flaws of the film's soundscape and the difficulty of fully grasping the dialogue at times ultimately create an affective pull that evokes a certain emotionscape. *Luc* was filmed by a mixed team of experienced and neophyte technicians and artists, and so it often has a "dirty" sound. This means that during some scenes, the background noise of trucks and cars driving by drowns out the actors' voices.[12] The combination of limited funding for editing or remixing the sound along with the decay due to transfers from film to video to digital video creates another aesthetic layer for audiences of *Luc* in its current form. The dirty sound occurs at inopportune moments, which frustrates viewers – we really do want to hear the details of the conversation between Luc and his girlfriend once he has come out to her. However, the strain to understand the actors in the film can metaphorically represent Luc's own straining to understand himself in relation to his newly claimed identity. This film's materiality – the images and sounds – and immateriality – its emotions – work to evoke Luc's own desperation, embodied in the story and expressed in the often grainy and dirty sounds of the film. As Cvetkovich notes elsewhere:

> The archive of feelings is both material and immaterial, at once incorporating objects that might not ordinarily be considered archival and at the same time resisting documentation because sex and feelings are too personal or too ephemeral to leave records. For this reason and others, the archive of feelings lives not just in museums, libraries, and other institutions, but in other more personal and intimate spaces and also, very significantly, within cultural genres.[13]

The currently accessible version of *Luc*, with all its technical flaws, is an archive of the feelings of coming out in a small community. Aesthetically – and the current state of the film's decay may be considered as part of this – we can understand the film as expressing a constellation of feelings associated with coming out. The landscapes of the film situate us in a particular time and place while the soundscapes of the film convey a kind of yearning for understanding, desire for connection, and the difficulties to fully understand what is going on in one's life. The lack of an English version adds another layer to the films ephemerality.

The inaccessibility of an English version of *Luc* is a result of the low priority given to English-language versioning by the previous (and current) funding structures of the Canadian film industry.[14] This adds yet another level to *Luc*'s ephemeral qualities. As a consequence, and given the pedagogical intent of this film, the discourse about coming out and Audy's depiction of the ways that different people in Luc's life respond – both negatively and positively – to his coming out are lost on all but a francophone audience. Various persistent cultural effects of the "two solitudes" in Canada marginalized this important film. Despite the problems of accessibility and material decay, *Luc* still gains social importance in these times when gay youth suicide is back in the news (on which more below). This aesthetically appealing Trois-Rivières film remains ephemeral due to its existence on bad DVD copies or deteriorating film prints and videotapes, waiting to be resuscitated and made part of the current wider public discourse about this topic.

CREVER À VINGT ANS (1984)

> Forged around sexuality and intimacy, and hence forms of privacy and invisibility ... gay and lesbian cultures often leave ephemeral and unusual traces. In the absence of institutionalised documentation or in opposition to official histories, memory becomes a valuable historical resource and ephemeral personal collections of objects stand alongside the documents of the dominant culture in order to offer alternative modes of knowledge.[15]

Audy's second feature, *Crever à vingt ans* (Done for at twenty), also evokes Cvetkovich's work,[16] both because of the film's state of dilapidation and because of its powerfully prescient content. While we would like to concentrate on the content of the film, on its exploration of the effects of feeling bad, most of our attention here will be devoted to the form in which we first came to experience the film, drawing on some of Laura U. Marks's theoretical writings as a point of departure.

A researcher googling Audy's name will find very few traces of this elusive author, either in French or in English, besides some negligible biographical details and a small entry in Thomas Waugh's otherwise encyclopaedic study of Canadian queer cinemas.[17] Though, at least initially, this dearth of information was frustrating, it soon became a source of excitement: we had to take a trip to the archive. Regrettably, the Cinémathèque québécoise, a site that, to all intents and purposes, is rich in Quebec's cinematic culture and history, has only one 16 mm film available to watch by Audy and it is a poor-quality video recording. Entitled *Jean-François-Xavier de...* (1969), the film is an extended and, at times, disjointed meditation on adolescence, family relations, religion, and death, which certainly has some correlation with his later work but which is simultaneously removed from it, especially stylistically. Later, we managed at some cost to acquire his two main features from the deep freeze (a term that, for us, illustrates well this filmmaker's undeserved passage into relative obscurity). *Corps et âme* (1971) and *La Maison qui empêche de voir la ville* (1974) are structured around more conventional narratives of loss, guilt, trauma, mental illness, unrequited male-male longing, mourning, and death. The black-and-white prints were gloriously well-preserved (surely another sign of their neglect) and the experience of watching them in the plush comfort of the cinémathèque's movie theatre was very moving. We were ready for more.

Reading Waugh's book further, we found that two films were still missing from Audy's corpus and that these were the ones that seemed most interesting, both because they received direct funding from the Quebec Ministry of Education and because they were widely distributed in the province.[18] After contacting Audy, we finally received DVD copies of the original video recordings. It is to these recordings and, more specifically, *Crever* that we now turn. Before proceeding, though, we will take a moment to look at the film more closely, especially since very little is known about it.

Like all of Audy's work, *Crever* is set in Trois-Rivières, his long-standing place of residence and the provincial town he has stubbornly held on to since the beginning of his career. The film is an archetypal melodrama, in the best sense of the word, following the story of two young, down-and-out friends, Claude and François. Struggling to make ends meet, they turn to selling their bodies in the local bar, drinking excessively and taking drugs to get through their hustler existence. When Claude meets a wealthy client willing to look after his needs, François is left alone, desperately in love with his partner. After François is sexually assaulted in the woods toward the end of the film, he decides to commit suicide, dying alone. In the final sequence, Claude returns to their apartment to find François lying dead on the bed they used to share.

Watching *Crever* is not the most cinematic of experiences. The image is either grainy or entirely distorted, the titling is amateurish, and the soundtrack is poorly recorded and sometimes non-existent. While its diminished audiovisual coherence initially proved frustrating, We were easily drawn into the film, particularly because of the prescience of its subject matter.[19] Indeed, its state of deformation and disrepair quickly becomes emotionally affecting, inviting great pathos, because it both highlights the film's precariously ephemeral status and also underscores the (almost lost) tragedy of its main events. At times, the total breakdown of the image and sound makes the experience of the film entirely different.

In "Loving a Disappearing Image," Laura U. Marks considers the similarly diminished quality of video art films from the 1990s[20] and the effects this poor quality might have on viewers' experience of watching, whereby a tactile or haptic visuality replaces a traditionally optical or cognitive mode of viewing. As part of this shift in spectatorship, she notices the correspondences that exist between the diminished quality of the medium, its relation to the videos' aesthetics, and the fact that these works also deal with the loss of coherence of human bodies through their physical and psychic suffering. In short, she explores how dying images of dying bodies might affect our experience of cinema at the level of the senses, and, more generally, how a sense of proximity, intimacy, and even contact with the dying image might change how we deal with death altogether.

Like Cvetkovich, Marks distances herself from Lacanian psychoanalytical discourses that in the past have dominated the discipline of queer and film studies. As such, instead of aligning our confrontation with alterity – with the Other's perishing body, in this case – as tantamount to self-destruction, Marks demonstrates how all the videos here "appeal to a look of love and loss."[21] The effectiveness of this look hinges upon video's relation with the real or, rather, its capacity to provide the viewer with an indexical, yet always fragile, relation to reality, for, "to love a disappearing image one must trust that the image is real in the first place; that is, that it establishes an indexical link between the long-ago objects recorded by a camera and the present-day spectator. We mourn the passing of the young lovers/actors because we are sure they existed."[22] As mentioned above, the dialectical relationship between past and present she emphasizes here is nonetheless ephemeral, which, because of its threat of disappearance, forces us to grasp hold of it and to engage with it more thoughtfully. Indeed, the disappearing image, more than any other type of image, she suggests, "invites a kind of compassion and open-ended love that can also be a way to engage with people and with death."[23] This is what was happening in our initial experience of viewing Audy's film, especially because of recent events concerning teen suicide and the way in which such high-profile news items are so quickly forgotten.

Although Audy's film is not formally experimental and does not concern itself with diseased bodies, as Marks's examples do, its bodies are nevertheless in a state of anguish, whether this is self-inflicted, at the hands of the johns who lust after them, or down to the locals who despise and abuse them. For instance, witnessing the rape sequence in Audy's film was an emotionally wrenching moment, particularly given how distorted and disorientating the image was in this section of the recording. Let us take a closer look.

Toward the end of the film when François gets into the car of what he thinks is another one of his clients, it suddenly jolts forward at high speed, cruising off into the distance. The film then cuts to the woods outside of the town where the same car is parked up in the bushes. François is bundled out of the car by two large men. At this moment, the shot becomes shaky and difficult to decipher, as if we were watching some sort of experimental documentary or amateur video, an aesthetic that arguably lends the film a greater degree of "authenticity," bringing us closer to the action. The camera then cuts to a confusing close-up of all three of their clothed bodies, grazing over François's back and their fumbling hands, until it becomes difficult to make out where one body ends and the other begins. Finally, in the confusion the camera comes to focus on François's face, fixed in a blurred rictus of extreme pain and humiliation – his mouth open, his eyes seemingly watering – as the hands of his aggressors run hungrily over his back and hair, gripping hold of his T-shirt before they both come to finish the act.

Throughout this sequence the image is distorted, blurred, and, at times, illegible, which enhances its affective impact, appealing once again to what Marks labels a "haptic" or tactile look. In particular, the close proximity of François's pained face, combined paradoxically with his state of indecipherable distance as it is dispersed in close-up across the screen, invites, to borrow Marks's words, a "look that uses the eye like an organ of touch."[24] This tactile look is not about exposing the abject trauma of rape or about anticipating his tragic suicide, as a conventionally optical look and psychoanalytical reading might infer, but rather is about loving a believable image whose coherence (in the video's materiality) and whose dignity (diegetically) is literally disappearing before our eyes, while at the same time attempting to commit to memory an image of the more complete, loving self witnessed earlier in the film.

To return to Cvetkovich, then, at this moment of profound tenderness, the formal quality of the film – in addition to the melodramatic diegesis – becomes a separate, complementary archive of feelings, which appeals to a sense of mourning, of loving, and of loss through a close, almost tactile, identification with the disintegrating image of his dying body. Additionally, in successfully appealing to our emotions in such a way, the trauma present in Audy's film, instead of being pushed to the peripheries of trauma culture, could function in a way to catalyse the creation of further and much deeper cultural archives and political communities devoted to raising awareness around the problem of teen suicide among queer adolescents.

The issue has, moreover, entered the forefront of political debate in Ontario and Quebec, where the suicides took place. The Liberal-backed Bill 13 has been adopted in Ontario; in Quebec anti-bullying legislation came into law in June 2012 where the provincial government began a high-profile advertising campaign.[25] A plethora of visual material has appeared on video streaming and social network websites, commemorating the lives of queer teens and attempting to raise awareness about homophobic bullying and its link to suicide. Major news channels in Canada have also joined the fray, as have Canadian celebrities and grassroots activists as part of the It Gets Better Canada campaign and the more irreverent FCKH8 project. Reading this, it would seem that the problem of queer teen suicide is beginning to be resolved in Canada or, at least, that the right kind of progress is being made. However, as has happened with well-meaning public campaigns in the past, this recent proliferation of concern could fizzle away just as quickly as it came to prominence. Without wishing to downplay or discredit the considerable efforts politicians, celebrities, and parents are making, we must remember – as Audy's film attests – that queer teen suicide is not a new issue and, crucially, that the vast digital archive of the Internet is arguably even more delicately ephemeral than Audy's film as it changes everyday according to its users' oscillating whims.

The prescience of his work is where we see most value in Audy's proto-queer film corpus and, furthermore, why we argue his work deserves proper exhibition and archival preservation before it falls into complete disrepair. All of his films are important in their documentation of gay life of the recent past in provincial Quebec at a time when homosexuality was a moral and religious crime, but more significantly, their distorted images, especially in *Crever*, speak to the present in a powerful and emotionally enriching way, so much so that, to borrow Cvetkovich's words, they could offer, as much through their formal qualities as through their content, "alternative modes of knowledge" about the past, present and, even, future lives of the gay population in Quebec.[26]

CONCLUSION

While we do not wish to belabour the challenges of ephemerality in general, we have demonstrated that the reality that creative and politically necessary gay films such as Audy's end up as culturally ephemeral is a problem. What is more, the authors have also been responsible for producing what will inevitably become an ephemeral video. In November 2011, along with two other young filmmakers and cultural theorists, we set out for Trois-Rivières to interview Michel Audy and film his oral history for research purposes. We digitally filmed and edited two days of interview and discussion, which we will deposit at Concordia University and the Cinémathèque québécoise in Montreal. We hope those researching gay film in Canada and Quebec will use this document. However, the funding to translate the entire six-hour interview does not exist, and so, in effect, we have produced a document – an archive of gay feelings – that is accessible only to those who understand Québécois French and who can gain access to these two institutions. On the one hand, it is reasonably acceptable to us that our filmed oral history of Audy has ended up as an ephemeral research document. On the other hand, what is vitally important to us is that Audy's films breathe new life into current political discussions on youth suicide, youth sexuality, and non-urban gay realities. Audy's films remain ephemeral and marginal and their reinsertion into the public sphere through exhibition remains the central problem in need of political and cultural intervention.

FILMOGRAPHY

Audy, Michel. *Luc ou la part des choses*, 1982, 90 min., 16 mm.
Audy, Michel. *Crever à vingt ans*, 1984, 74 min., 3/4" video.

NOTES

1 Ann Cvetkovich, *An Archive of Feelings: Trauma, Sexuality, and Lesbian Public Cultures* (Durham, NC: Duke University Press, 2003), 2.
2 Ibid., 7.
3 Ibid., 8.

4 We consciously use both "gay" and "queer" here. However, we use gay to refer to characters and experiences in Audy's films themselves because "queer" only emerged in Quebec as an activist concept predominantly amongst Anglophones in the 1990s in Montreal. We use "queer" to refer to contemporary interpretations and experiences – both in politics and culture and in reading Audy's films in the present moment. Irène Demczuk and Frank W. Remiggi, *Sortir de l'ombre. Histoires des communautés lesbienne et gaie de Montréal* (Montreal: VLB Editeur 1998), 390–2. Our use of "homosexuality" or "homosexual" reflects its wide use in both French and English in Quebec.

5 See Thomas Waugh, *Romance of Transgression in Canada: Queering Sexualities, Nations, Cinemas* (Montreal: McGill-Queen's University Press, 2006), 12–13, 77–80.

6 Waugh, *Romance of Transgression in Canada*, 101.

7 Nancy Duncan and James Duncan, "Doing Landscape Interpretation," in *Sage Handbook of Qualitative Geography*, ed. Dydia DeLyser, Aitken Stuart, Linda McDowell, Steve Herbert, and Mike Crang (London: Sage Publications Limited, 2009), 243. Emphasis in the original.

8 "In the regions." This shorthand phrase is used in Quebec to refer to those areas of the province outside of the Montreal and Quebec City urban areas. Despite this description, Trois-Rivières had, in 1981 (the time of the filming of *Luc*), a population of 111,453 – statistics for 2011 show its population at 130, 407, placing in the mid-size city category. La Ville de Trois-Rivières, "Population de a la Ville de Trois-Rivieres," accessed 18 April 2012, http://laville.v3r.net/docs_upload/documents/langue1/renseignements_/population_de_trois-rivieres_en_2011.pdf.

9 *Trifluvien* is the demonym for a resident of Trois-Rivières. A *taverne* is bar and restaurant in Quebec. From 1937 to 1981, women were not allowed to enter these spaces (see Francois Drouin and Yves Lille, "La taverne Québécoise: Histoire d'un commerce en voie de disparution," *Cap-Aux-Diamants: La revue d'histoire du Québec* 1, no. 2 [1985]: 32–4). A *motard* is the colloquial term for a person who drives a motorcycle, a biker.

10 Christian Bordeleau, "Les Bons Coups," *Sortie: Le Journal Gai* 1 (October 1982): 35.

11 Waugh, *Romance of Transgression in Canada*, 137.

12 Audy 2011. Filmed in 16 mm, *Luc* is already limited in comparison with what our ears are used to with 35 mm, in addition to the inevitable loss of quality of sound due to transfer from 16 mm to VHS at the time. Michel Audy, interview with Alain Ayotte, Jason B. Crawford, Dominic Poliquin, and Micky Storey (Trois-Rivières, Quebec: 25–6 November 2011).

13 Cvetkovich, *An Archive of Feelings*, 112.

14 For example, many essential films by such recognized auteurs as Anne Claire Poirier, Maurice Bulbulian, and Gilles Groulx remain unavailable in English. An example of the impracticality of current funding structures for such films as *Luc* and *Crever* is Telefilm Canada's requirement that films must have a contract for theatrical release in order to be eligible for versioning funds. Telefilm Canada, "Telefilm Versioning Assistance Program Guidelines," 4, accessed 11 June 2012, http://www.telefilm.ca/files/fonds_prog/versioning-assistance-program-guidelines.pdf.

15 Cvetkovich, *An Archive of Feelings*, 8.
16 Cvetkovich, *An Archive of Feelings.*
17 Waugh, *Romance of Transgression in Canada*, 363.
18 Ibid.
19 Just a few weeks before we watched the film, a fifteen-year-old gay teenager took his own life in Ottawa, which was followed soon after by the suicide of a fifteen-year-old lesbian teenager in Quebec.
20 These works are *Twilight Psalm II: Walking Distance* (1999) by Phil Soloman; *Frank's Cock* (1994) and *Letters from Home* (1996) by Mike Hoolboom; *The Hundred Videos* (1992–96) and *Everybody Loves Nothing* (1997) by Steve Reinke; *De Profundis* (1996) by Lawrence Brose; and *The Color of Love* (1994) by Peggy Ahwesh.
21 Laura Marks, "Loving a Disappearing Image," *Cinémas: Revue d'Études Cinématographiques* 8, no. 1–2 (1997): 94.
22 Ibid., 98.
23 Ibid., 100.
24 Ibid., 104.
25 Ontario's Bill 13 received royal assent on 19 June 2012. In Quebec, the bill known as Loi 56 was adopted by the National Assembly on 12 June 2012 and received royal assent on 15 June 2012. Legislative Assembly of Ontario, "Bill 13, Accepting Schools Act, 2012," http://www.ontla.on.ca/web/bills/bills_detail.do?locale=en&billid=2549&detailpage=bills_detail_status; Assembly Nationale du Quebec, "Projet de loi n°56: Loi visant à prévenir et à combattre l'intimidation et la violence à l'école," http://www.assnat.qc.ca/fr/travaux-parlementaires/projets-loi/projet-loi-56-39-2.html.
26 Cvetkovich, *An Archive of Feelings*, 8.

12 AGAINST EPHEMERALITY
THE CBC'S ARCHIVAL TURN, 1989–96

Jennifer VanderBurgh

EPHEMERALITY IS OFTEN a question of value. That which is valued tends to be saved, while everything else is left to entropy, deterioration, and other forms of degradation and loss. In ascribing value to objects, archives take steps to conserve what would otherwise disappear. But since understandings of value are discursive and changeable, what factors determine whether objects are archived? How, in practice, do potential artefacts go from being ephemeral to being considered worthy of archiving?

One story of value's relationship to ephemerality is illustrated in the archival trajectory of the Canadian Broadcasting Corporation's (CBC) broadcast content in the early 1990s. Following a series of aggressive funding cuts and changes to Canadian cultural policy that mandated cultural institutions become more market-driven, the CBC stepped up its custodial interest in preserving and archiving its broadcast content.[1] Cultural and industrial values had long been a source of tension between the CBC's archives and its broadcasting operations that, at times, threatened the preservation of broadcast content. Under conditions of rising market pressure, though, preserving broadcasting content made sense within both heritage and market discourses, both of which CBC management could use strategically to justify its existence.

The early 1990s was a period of collaboration in which inter- and intra-institutional tensions around management of broadcasting content appeared momentarily aligned by a common anxiety about magnetic tape, the CBC's exclusive storage medium. According to CBC documents, despite the fact that all of its post-film era TV content was housed on magnetic formats, as of 1992 no uniform policies yet existed for handling, managing, storing, and archiving magnetic media.[2] With digital formats on the horizon, and with upward of fifty formats of magnetic media moving toward obsolescence, cooperation around magnetic media preservation was motivated during this period around a common concern about the survival of content across the CBC's broadcasting, archival, production, and engineering constituencies. Arguably, cooperation was the key intervention against content's ephemerality, brought about, in part, by the impending obsolescence of its storage medium.

In demonstrating how these new alignments and understandings of broadcast content's value resulted in steps against ephemerality, in this chapter I first outline problems with collecting, archiving, and accessing broadcasting content that became apparent in this period of archival housekeeping. In what follows, I use CBC documents and a series of conversations with Ernest J. Dick, the CBC's corporate archivist from 1989 to 1996, to identify the problems thought to pose a threat to collecting, archiving, and accessing broadcast content at that time. I then outline some proposed steps undertaken as solutions. Finally, by way of conclusion, I offer an assessment as to whether – a quarter century on and well into the digital transition – these gestures have had long-term success and for whom.

PROBLEMS IDENTIFIED

In this section, I identify key challenges for collecting, archiving, and organizing CBC broadcasting content to which interventions in the 1990s were responding. While many of the issues were presented in documents as rhetorically entangled sets of perennial and pragmatic concerns, recurring themes do emerge: broadcasting's inherent ephemerality; competing philosophical differences between public and broadcasting archives; and insufficient standardization of methods and criteria used to index material for accessibility. Additionally, magnetic media's format specificities were considered to have attendant issues for dealing with content and were seen to have led to ad hoc stockpiling practices and debates about the politics of heritage discourses. In what follows, I present each of these issues in turn.

Broadcasting's inherent ephemerality is named in CBC documents of the period as a concern and as an obstacle to effectively collecting and archiving content. As Dick contended at the time, "the ephemeral and transitory nature of broadcasting contributes to its non-permanent, non-archival character."[3] Broadcasting's inherent non-materiality – as a phenomenon that literally arrives via the air – was considered to exacerbate its elusive nature for the CBC's archival and collection projects. One report, seeking to develop a systematic "archival acquisition strategy," notes, for example, that broadcasting "is simultaneously ubiquitous and ephermeral [*sic*] ... [I]mages and sounds are seen and heard ad nauseam [*sic*] and yet the broadcasting signal is fundamentally intangible."[4] Developing archival strategies for broadcasting content were, therefore, understood to be fundamentally challenged by broadcasting's ephemerality.

Ephemerality, in this context, is understood to be a quality of the broadcasting signal, which tends only to be noticed or cared about when the value ascribed to its content changes – for instance, in retroactive attempts to archive content for which no recordings were kept.[5] While concern for broadcasting's ephemerality as loss is especially acute and observable in such cases, this concern arguably applies to all of broadcasting's content, because while master tapes were kept of CBC shows, recordings were rarely made of its actual broadcasts. Efforts to preserve broadcasting content are, therefore, perennially challenged by ambiguity about what the *artefact* of broadcast content is.[6] This raises questions, such as whether it is enough for archives to keep master recordings of programs or whether tapes with production elements should also be saved. Should recordings be made of a show's broadcast – how a program appeared to viewers – and if so, which broadcast and in which region? While the question of what constitutes broadcasting content is still an ongoing concern for archives and collections, it was especially relevant at the CBC during the 1990s, considering the urgency presented by the cumbersome nature of magnetic media recordings and, as the process of migrating material to digital formats began, the need to develop criteria to triage the transfer of over a half-century's worth of broadcasting content.

Determining priorities for collecting and archiving broadcast content during this period was complicated by the fact that the CBC did not have complete control of its archives. As a Crown corporation, the CBC had long-standing arrangements with Public Archives of Canada (which became National Archives Canada [NAC] in 1987 and Library and Archives Canada [LAC] in 2004) to share responsibility for its holdings. Over the years, transfers of CBC records, both administrative and audiovisual, meant that PAC/NAC (herein referred to as NAC) effectively functioned as a warehouse and a broadcasting archive for the CBC. According to one report by the CBC's Engineering Operations Department, between 1984 and 1990, the "CBC deposited an average of 25,900 hours of audiovisual records per year" at NAC. Through its off-site record centres, the National Archive functioned as an extension of the broadcaster insofar as it provided storage and duplication services and transfer master tapes.[7] This arrangement meant that neither the CBC nor NAC had complete autonomy over the CBC's materials and, importantly, over the methods with which they were collected or managed. Since NAC functioned as the CBC's broadcast archive, the CBC was beholden to NAC's resource allocation. This meant that the CBC could not independently determine archival priorities or even intervene in pragmatic matters such as deciding tape format for housing broadcasting content. From NAC's perspective, the arrangement to "receive records created by CBC" fundamentally challenged the archive's "custody of medium of record," a principle that presumed autonomy of NAC collections.[8] Under this unusual arrangement, NAC was accountable to the CBC in direct contravention of one of its governing principles. This meant that custodial responsibility for the CBC's broadcast content, as well as its other archival materials, was ambiguous and appears, sometimes, to have been disputed.

One contentious issue between the CBC and NAC, cited repeatedly in early 1990s documents, concerns philosophical differences having to do with competing understandings of broadcast content's value. As a public archive, NAC's concern was to heritage discourses, whereas the CBC's was to its immediate broadcasting needs. Viewed in this way, it is easy to see how their priorities with respect to broadcasting content would differ. Broadcasting and archival "worlds" were described as having "diametrically opposing assumptions and operational practices."[9] One characteristic example of this discourse contends that broadcasters "are preoccupied with the immediate future and cannot afford to be distracted by the past."[10] From a broadcaster's perspective, "tomorrow's program slot will arrive exactly on schedule and cannot be delayed," meaning that, to broadcasters, archival initiatives are thought to be indulgent uses of resources, and are, therefore, routinely deprioritized.[11] If, according to this logic, a broadcaster's future-oriented priorities are premised on the creation of *new* content to broadcast, archives and archival projects would be considered "distraction[s]."[12] By contrast, a public archive, such as NAC, premised on heritage discourse and providing the public and researchers access to materials, was, therefore, understood at the time to be in conflict with the CBC's archival priorities as a broadcaster.

Considering these conflicting priorities, the materials the CBC and NAC valued were bound to differ. One CBC document produced explains that the purpose of a broadcast archive:

> Is to preserve and provide access to selected records to meet the future requirements of a broadcasting corporation ... [I]t does not exist outside of the corporation and access is normally restricted to the corporation. Future requirements for material in the broadcast archive are generally defined in terms of re-use value, measured particularly in financial terms. Methods of access, records management, storage, and preservation are tailored to meet the corporation's normal operation and projected future requirements.[13]

This definition reinforces that, despite the CBC's status as a *public* broadcaster, the mandate of its broadcast archive was (and still is) not to serve the public.[14] Understandably, then, its preservation priorities were not based on cultural and historical merit or on public access to content. Rather, the mandate of a broadcast archive as articulated here is to preserve materials that are projected to serve the future requirements of the broadcaster. Such requirements are understood to be the production of new content or the use of existing content for revenue generation, which the CBC was under increasing pressure to pursue. One assessment of broadcasting archives accuses broadcasters of saving too much material. Due to "pride in their productions," and the legal requirement to retain "ancillary research and files," this argument is that broadcasting archives can retain an "impractical" amount of material of different priority than other sorts of archives would want.[15] One result is that broadcast archives are typically at cross-purposes with public archives particularly with respect to the value placed on materials, including certain types of broadcast content – a point to which I will return.

An *archive* is defined more broadly as "an institution responsible for the acquisition, permanent preservation, and communication of records."[16] The "nature of the records acquired ... is defined by the mandate of the individual archive."[17] While, in theory, this means that archives such as NAC should determine their own priorities, in the early 1990s NAC lacked the autonomy necessary to set priorities for archiving CBC materials.[18] This meant that although NAC and CBC mandates conflicted, the federal *public* archive was "sporadically, unhappily, and unsatisfactorily" functioning as the CBC's *broadcast* archive.[19]

Not surprisingly given these constraints, assessments of the CBC's archival situation were sometimes bleak. One such evaluation remarks on the "poor perception of CBC archival collections and a lack of credibility for an organization that enjoys a high reputation in other broadcasting aspects." [20] Another expresses disappointment that the CBC had "done very little beyond warehousing past programming," and even this was done inconsistently.[21] The CBC "looked to Canadian archives to preserve its heritage," says one, but "frustration is mounting ... over perceived lack of a systemic and rational approach by the Corporation with respect to its archives."[22] It further explains that under the current conditions, "records deposited cannot always be warranted as worthy of preservation in the accepted archival sense."[23] Pragmatic issues are cited, such as problems with processing and indexing content, along with changing technologies and financial and spatial constraints, as obstacles that "easily paralysed" archivists dealing with CBC materials.[24] In particular, the volume of broadcasting content housed on magnetic tape was considered to be a problem in devising useable archives that served both broadcaster and public/heritage interests. I will now turn to why medium specificities were understood to be of concern at the start of the 1990s.

Since the 1930s, the CBC had used a variety of formats of magnetic media to record radio broadcasts, a practice that was later adopted for television to produce short-term broadcasting records. Until the advent of digital video, magnetic formats were the dominant medium on which broadcast television was recorded and permanently stored. At the same time, because of the expense of some magnetic formats, there was pressure to recycle tapes rather than archive their content. On one occasion, Dick, as the CBC's corporate archivist, remembers seeing bathtubs full of CBC tapes waiting to be erased and reused; a telling image of potentially archive-worthy content about to go down the drain.

By the mid-1980s, the shift to smaller, less expensive tape formats significantly reduced the need to recycle. One might think that this would make content housed on magnetic formats more secure, but, at this point, another problem emerged. Tapes were accumulating at the CBC in dozens of different collections – both random and purposeful – in closets, basements, and transmitter sites, as well as in vaults at both the CBC's network and regional centres. Producers who wished to prevent their working tapes from being recycled sometimes kept caches of tapes in their offices or homes (deliberately away from the broadcast archive). The CBC's inconsistent policies in dealing with magnetic formats had obvious implications for collection and preservation.

Following the shift to smaller tape formats in the 1980s, an overabundance of materials presented problems for the CBC's archives and collections. As one report characterizes the situation:

> There are far too many tapes being stored, many of which are inappropriate. This also puts excessive strain on physical storage needs. As thousands of hours of television and radio programs are being produced every year, the amount of space required to store them increases. If no decision is taken to prune them, the vaults will continue to overflow, new storage locations will be requested, manual card indexing systems will overflow and storage cost will keep on increasing.[25]

While such documents call for archival self-selection to triage materials of value, others warned of the risks of curated collections. One report identifies existing ad hoc methods of self-selection as a main factor that inhibits the "survival" of broadcasting content.[26] Since preservation is not possible for every broadcast record, and in the absence of a formal archival strategy to determine key priorities, "self-selection" was seen as a process whereby biases toward (or away from) particular types of programs and media deem certain materials worthy of saving over others. "Self-selection," the authors warn, "has already eliminated 50%, or more, of CBC-originated network programming."[27] Considering the discursive nature of self-selection, the study implies that archives are symptomatic of discourses about which broadcasting materials were considered valuable at the time. In drawing attention to the existence of qualitative discourses at work at the CBC to determine the kind of programming that typically "survived," they contend that while "many agree that an adequate proportion of CBC programming should survive for posterity," the ways to facilitate "survival" are "not clear and self-evident."[28] Using the figurative language of survival in the study to characterize the effect of the archival process on broadcasting materials suggests that all archival gestures are determined by qualitative assessments that value and privilege certain types of texts, making some less ephemeral than others.

While an overabundance of materials is cited as one outcome of the format shift to smaller, less expensive magnetic formats, in the context of substantial funding cuts to the CBC, archivists still noted, "programming budgets [were] being scrutinized" to such an extent that still "some program areas may [have been] recycling tapes to stretch their program resources."[29] Despite these new formats, then, critics still warned that the life expectancy of content on magnetic media continued to "remain in flux."[30]

Although more content was technically being saved from the mid-1980s than previously, the volume of material and the lack of systematic methods to formally deposit, catalogue, track, and preserve magnetic media at the CBC and across the seven divisions of NAC's Archives Branch caused those concerned to remark that some of this content was inadvertently being made irretrievable. This means that the CBC's broadcasting archive, while providing much needed storage for magnetic media, was sometimes paradoxically contributing to its ephemerality.

SOLUTIONS PROPOSED

Although motivated by different reasons, colleagues at the CBC and NAC understood that archiving content was of no use if it could not be retrieved, and by the mid-1980s they were becoming aligned in common concerns about the consequences of "fragment[ing] the records."[31] To function as a finding aid for artefacts, in 1987, NAC published a *Guide to CBC Sources (1936–86)*, which listed the CBC's materials held in what was then known as the National Film, Television and Sound Archives (NFTSA) division.[32] In addition to including indexes of names, subjects, and program titles, the guide also lists the medium and formats of moving images in the collection, such as videotape dating from the early 1970s. The guide's approach is notably non-proprietary, as it encourages readers to conceptualize the CBC's artefacts even beyond those listed in NAC's collection, as a grouping that includes additional works housed in other international and regional archives.[33]

In 1989, following the guide's publication, Dick, its author, was brought from NAC's Moving Image and Sound Division on assignment to review the CBC's efforts in preserving its past.[34] According to Dick, this project was a direct response to CBC management's objectives to research and question the potential "future of its heritage."[35] Monetizing the archives cannot be overlooked as a possible motivation for management's archival concern and appointment of a dedicated corporate archivist.

Dick was well positioned to assess the CBC's archival holdings, which was his first undertaking in the position. As well as working as an archivist at NAC from 1974 to 1989, in the late 1970s Dick had been part of the

Association for the Study of Canadian Radio and Television (ASCRT), an advocacy group that brought together academics, archivists, and broadcasters concerned about audiovisual history in Canada. He was also active with US film and television archivists who were moving toward a professional organization.

Upon joining the CBC, Dick was charged with conducting a national audit of the institution's archival collections and practices. This involved travelling to the CBC's network and regional centres, assessing their collections, and drafting reports toward establishing best practice policies for the corporation's holdings. He also consulted with all provincial and university archives that had CBC materials in their collections, reviewing with them their hopes for ongoing relations with the CBC. Dick's findings helped to inspire an informal and collaborative rhetorical campaign whose purpose was to confirm that broadcasting content, particularly that which was found on magnetic media, had value. His gestures against broadcast content's ephemerality ensured that content's survival.

Dick's findings were published as two reports.[36] In these reports, his commentary and critique is notably informed by his experience at NAC. A main factor that he felt was exacerbating broadcasting content's ephemerality were the competing priorities of broadcasters and archives. Dick interpreted his role as corporate archivist as negotiating such polarities. His main task, as he articulates it, was to "understand ... opposing tendencies" in order to "propose appropriate linkages."[37] Dick bridged interests by outlining rationales for why archival strategies for magnetic media should matter, and why collaboration among constituencies was needed. For instance, Dick's 1990 review of the CBC's archives mentions colleagues and departments who were working on archival initiatives long before he arrived.[38] In retrospect, he sees his main contribution as corporate archivist as "creating a community of archival activities" throughout the institution that ultimately facilitated even greater collaboration.[39]

Dick's tenure as the only corporate archivist in the CBC's history represents a particularly self-reflexive period of archival networking when the institution took stock of its holdings and drafted corrective policies to determine what and how broadcast materials should be preserved. During the time of Dick's leadership, archival interventions into the ephemerality of the CBC's magnetic media had two apparent thrusts. One was in animating the development of pragmatic policies and best practices for the physical preservation of magnetic media. Although Dick insists that he did not propose policy, his work contributed important groundwork that led to pragmatic technical improvements. The second thrust for which Dick was directly responsible was in launching a discursive campaign that engaged in general rhetorical combat against the ephemerality of broadcasting materials and encouraged the broadcaster to realize, in Dick's words, "how much [it] relied on [its] own archives, whether [it] wanted to admit it or not."[40]

Dick's experience at both NAC and the CBC gave him a unique vantage point from which to offer commentary on not only the inherent challenges of archiving broadcasting material in general, but also the challenges specific to the CBC's unique archival culture. Articulated in a series of presentations, corporate documents, and essays, Dick's commentary on magnetic media offers insight into how archival gestures are necessarily discursive and, in effect, how efforts to collect and preserve broadcasting materials are premised on biased and shifting understandings of which materials have value. Dick knew, however, that to receive archival support for magnetic media, he would need to provide reasoning to show the effort was worthwhile.

In one example, Dick demonstrated the potential cost of neglect by pursuing an archival project that involved one of the first magnetic media formats to record CBC radio in the 1940s. These broadcasts, intended to be ephemeral, survived unintentionally since they were the last to be recorded on the medium before it became obsolete. Dick found twelve thirty-pound reels of magnetic tape that had been recorded on a device known as a Blattnerphone. The CBC was among a small group of broadcasters worldwide to have made Blattnerphone recordings. Intended only to last a short time, when they were discovered it was not known what content they recorded. Listening to the ends of the reels, Dick could hear fragments of the longest recordings – buried layers, which turned out to be radio broadcasts previously thought to have disappeared. Dick wrote and spoke publicly about the value of these and other broadcast findings believed to be ephemeral such as baseball broadcasts from the 1960s, which were later transferred to the Cooperstown baseball museum.[41] Such projects functioned to raise awareness about the various merits of broadcasting content – especially that which was thought to have disappeared – as a way of advocating for preservation.

Dick understood that much of the CBC's broadcast content had been made ephemeral due to practices and discourses that either debased magnetic media or were overwhelmed by its volume. With his colleagues in ASCRT and in archives across Canada, as well as at the CBC, he attempted to promote and safeguard existing collections as well as improve their functionality. One of Dick's interventions in this regard was to represent the CBC at the International Federation of Television Archives, hosted in 1990 at NAC.[42] In retrospect, Dick's recognizes that the "international comparisons [generated at the meeting] were most useful in changing the CBC [archival] mindset and practice."[43] Among its many successes, the symposium formalized archival debates and helped to foster collaboration. A publication of the symposium's proceedings, aptly titled *Documents that Move and Speak: Audiovisual Archives in the New Information Age*, signals anxiety about emerging digital formats. Notably, it includes a contribution by Canada's preeminent scholar of CBC programming, Mary Jane Miller.[44]

In describing an ideal archive, in which researchers are "recognized and made welcome as the ally [not the adversary] of the archivist," Miller advances the position that archives have a responsibility to make broadcasting content functional and accessible for users.[45] Advocating for the "legitimate researcher's" right to access materials, Miller writes, "in my dream archive, it is understood that the preservation of any artifact is meaningless without access and study."[46] In order to implement change for archives, Dick knew that he first needed to argue, as Miller did, why change was necessary. His discursive campaign in support of magnetic media took the form of other such platforms to do so, which ultimately extended the CBC's archival discussions to wider national and international audiences.

Following this discursive campaign in support of archival practices, specific policies and best practices developed for caring and handling magnetic tape at the CBC. The ways in which these policies and practices were articulated show a perceptual shift in how the CBC thought about and treated its broadcast content housed on magnetic media. In 1992, the CBC's Engineering Operation Department reviewed practices for archiving magnetic media, and in 1993 it made recommendations for its care, handling, and storage. Both documents call for improved, pragmatic best practices. These practices were to be followed at the broadcasting archive and, by extension, at NAC. These documents were written to update two CBC corporate policies on magnetic tape: "Preservation of CBC Programs and Documents" (27 June 1980) and "Retention of Recorded

Videotapes" (3 August 1978).[47] According to these documents, there had been no official CBC policy developments since 1980 dealing with magnetic tape, and even these outdated policies were not followed consistently. Recommendations were made in 1993 to "fill the existing void" of CBC archival practices.[48] These recommendations appear to be symptomatic of a shift at the CBC in conceptualizing magnetic media and its content as being considered worthy of systemic archival initiatives, warning, "tapes are being stored in less than optimum conditions, thus endangering the long-term preservation of the magnetic media."[49]

The CBC's Engineering Operations Department recommendations outline a series of environmental controls and guidelines for the physical care of magnetic media. Policies to be implemented regarding storage, tape handling, and inspection together constituted "recommended practices" for the care of magnetic media that had been distilled from the advice of "major tape manufactures, standards bodies, tape experts and archivists, and the practical experience of many tape users."[50] The intended audience for the recommendations is identified as "technical managers, archivists, and technicians for the care, handling, and storage (both medium and long term) or magnetic media and the audio-visual records they contain."[51]

While a few recommendations explicitly address habitual behaviours of tape handlers, such as the instruction that "no smoking, eating or drinking is to be allowed in operating or storage areas," most are intended to encourage compliance with storing magnetic media in appropriate locations.[52] In prescribing the optimum conditions for operations, shipping, and long- and medium-term storage, these recommendations could have been intended to curb practices mentioned in the section above related to stockpiling, wherein caches of magnetic materials were kept in unofficial storage locations, such as offices or homes. The prescriptive quality of many of the recommendations would have made it possible to empirically measure whether existing facilities were suitable to function as archives for magnetic media storage. Prescribing acceptable gradients of temperature, humidity, and magnetic fields in both operations and storage facilities would have provided quantitative assessment criteria to determine compliance of an archivist or facility. As a result, one contribution of these recommendations was to make an attempt at unifying divergent practices across the regional offices of the institution, the implementation of which became the responsibility thereafter of the Corporate Committee for Tape Purchases, "the de facto standards body of the CBC in all matters concerning magnetic media."[53] This group would also be charged with "immediately" evaluating the "backlog of material within CBC holdings store on obsolete formats" in order to determine what content should be archived.[54]

The Engineering Operations Department also recommended that "a single, unified and integrated records management system should be developed for use between National Archives and all CBC operating centres," and that "universal cataloguing and indexing system" be implemented to make content on magnetic media more retrievable.[55] These recommendations tasked archivists with exploring what improvements emergent digital media offer to enhance the archive's "information storage system," as well as "cataloguing, indexing and records management" for magnetic media. In proposing these changes, the report recommends an archival overhaul for magnetic media – specifically, "a total re-examination of the system architecture and design of the technical and administrative systems now in use ... to address the needs of the Archives well into the next century."[56] Explicitly and implicitly, the recommendations outlined in the document ascribe value to magnetic media.

In addition to offering the pragmatic recommendations mentioned above, the 1992 report addresses archival problems of a qualitative nature and specifically mentions the CBC's obligation to help fulfill NAC's "heritage" mandate. Encouraging the CBC to address "the long-term role it must play in conjunction with the National Archives of Canada in the conservation of Canadian heritage materials," the report implies that internal archival mandates at the CBC should be more expansive and cooperative, and should take heritage into account. In response to the question of what the CBC should do with tapes that "have successfully represented life in Canada and have become part of our Canadian heritage," the report states, "CBC has neither a policy nor uniform and effective procedures for the archiving of video and audio tape," and, "there are no selection criteria to guide decision-makers as to when a tape should be archived."[57] "The decision to archive a specific program," it indicates, "has to be made by an archivist," and "there are no comprehensive criteria for the selection of records or administrative directives for the practical implementation of video and audio tape storage and eventual archiving."[58]

In calling for a set of best practices, the Engineering Operations Department recommends that value be assigned to material outside the purview of the broadcast archive's priorities, which are assumed to ascribe different values to content than those of public archives. Not surprisingly given the controversial nature of identifying broadcasting material deemed important to Canadian heritage, the procedure of how best to select material from the broadcasting archive is left fairly ambiguous. News and information programs, which are, according to the document, "known to contain Canadian heritage material," are presumed to be of "high archival value," as is "historical drama," such as *Les filles de Caleb* and *Road to Avonlea*.[59] For these examples, which are considered (problematically) to be of indisputable merit to heritage, the report mandates, "every episode ... will be archived." Other more heritage-ambiguous programs, it suggests, should be left to a practice known as representative sampling: "keeping only one, two or three episodes," the document states, "might be enough."[60] The archival value placed on "heritage" programming is noteworthy, since what constitutes heritage functions here rhetorically but is never defined. This suggests that within the politics of such discourse, TV dramas about the past were seen to have lasting heritage value and were given greater archival weight than other types of content that might have significance in the future.

While Dick appeared to agree with the Engineering Operations Department's desire that the "CBC should establish and maintain a proper broadcast archive as well as an unambiguous archiving policy that includes objective selection criteria and administration procedures," he acknowledges that the way to do so remained unclear.[61] Unlike the Engineering Operations Department, Dick's advocacy tends to take the form of rhetorical questions when considering how to address archival challenges. "Of all of this broadcasting that is available to the citizen of the late twentieth century," he writes, "whatever does posterity need to be able to reconstruct? How much will future generations want to see and hear ... ? How much do we need to preserve in archives and how do we know when we have enough? ... How should [archives] appraise, preserve and catalogue broadcasting records?"[62]

As documents produced during this period show, a common motivation for devising and adopting best practices for magnetic media appears to have been anxiety about emerging digital formats. Such documents characterize the digital turn as both a potential opportunity for archives and a threat that could render content on obsolescent analog formats inaccessible. The shift, however, was perceived to be inevitable.

As the Engineering Operations Department argued, "the CBC will have no choice but to introduce digital component recording as a recording format in the future."

ASSESSMENTS AND CONCLUSIONS

As an unusually self-reflexive period for the CBC's archival practices, one contribution of this early 1990s archival culture was to produce documents that made underlying archival discourses themselves less ephemeral. As a result, it is now possible to glean arguments that were made in support of the value of broadcast content, as well as contentious archival issues, and initiatives that were undertaken to resolve them. In what follows, by way of conclusion, I offer a few brief assessments of subsequent outcomes and indicate, in the spirit of Mary Jane Miller's 1990 article, from the perspective of a "scholarly user," how archiving and accessing broadcasting content that was produced on magnetic media has fared.

The CBC's adoption of digital platforms throughout the 1990s for both production and preservation resulted in both gains and losses for migrating forward broadcasting content initially produced on magnetic media. To be clear, I distinguish analog content that was migrated to digital from content that was made using digital formats. Digital video production (in which Digital Betacam and digital SX video formats were used) ushered in built-in digital archival practices for content resulting in more predictable archival and collection practices, such as the immediate depositing of two digital copies of a show: one to be archived for preservation, and one to be accessed for "reuse, rebroadcast, or licensing to outside clients."[63] The process of migrating content to digital, however, had mixed results for broadcast content produced in the era of magnetic media. Key indicators for the type of content that benefited from the digital turn had to do with discursive perceptions of re-use value, and also with genre.

Considering the amount of broadcasting content that had been stored on magnetic formats, and the time and expense that it takes to make digital transfers (taking archivists and technicians away from other duties), it was understood at the outset of the shift to digital formats that not all of the CBC's holdings could be transferred. Content was cued for transfer based on expectations of what would be considered valuable as future CBC broadcast material or as an asset that was likely to generate revenue in external program or stock-shot sales. Content that migrated forward was a consequence of discursive and pragmatic assessments used to determine a program's use-value. These determinations tended to be made from the market-driven perspective of the broadcaster. This meant that the transfer of certain types of programming tended to be prioritized over others. For example, documentary news footage, which was deemed likely to be valuable on the stock-shot market, has apparently fared particularly well under these triage conditions.

From the perspective of a scholarly user, however, dramatic production has fared less well within the narrative of value's relation to ephemerality. I base this assessment on surviving accessible copies of materials for viewing purposes, and prospects for their potential circulation and re-use value. Arguably, the same pragmatic reasons that secured the success of stock-shot material have contributed to dramatic programming being in danger of obsolescence. Lapsed licensing agreements on many of the dramatic productions made during the magnetic era mean that, unlike with news footage, the CBC is currently unable to reuse or sell the shows without renegotiating rights with actors and writers union and securing music clearances. As this is a prohibitively complicated and expensive process, it tends not to happen and contributes to waning incentives to preserve and maintain these holdings. Gaining access to dramatic content produced on magnetic media has also proved more challenging than other types of programming after the digital turn. The CBC's Digital Archives project, for example, is a web-based curated project that gives the public access to a portion of its digital archives.[64] Created in 2008 with a one-time grant from the Canadian Culture Online Program Fund administered by the Department of Canadian Heritage, visitors can view clips from subject categories that the editorial board considers to denote key aspects of national culture. The site has thousands of clips of documentary, sports, and news footage, for which the CBC owns the rights, but while arts and entertainment is named as a category, there are no examples given of dramatic programming because of rights issues and lapsed agreements mentioned above.[65]

In the absence of such broadcasting content, the CBC's Digital Archives appears to be a project that is less about memorializing television shows than about memorializing the CBC's role in facilitating and consolidating the sense of a national community. The CBC is the object being archived here, not its broadcast content. The project's slogan, "relive Canada's history through CBC archives," emphasizes television's indexical function, but ultimately does not provide sufficient access to it. While master tapes of this content presumably exist in the CBC's broadcasting archives, with researchers being permitted less access to the CBC's broadcast collections and with no other mechanism to view dramatic content of the analog period, the prognosis for its survival within the public memory is waning, as is its use-value to the broadcaster.

Arguably, the situation for "scholarly users" at LAC has fared little better overall. With even more holdings to digitize, understandably, viewing copies of CBC content on magnetic media in its collection seem not to have been especially prioritized. I am likely not the only researcher who has travelled to NAC/LAC to find that the magnetic formats I had come to view had deteriorated to the point of being unwatchable.[66] For me, this made content indexed and housed in the public archive no more accessible than the broadcaster's production collection, to which I was denied access. This experience is a reminder that archival deposits are useless to the public unless are routinely assessed and maintained. Such undertakings are especially complicated for archives as there are still no internationally recognized standards for archiving magnetic media. Added to urgency brought about by deterioration of the CBC's holdings (a situation in which the LAC is certainly not alone) are new restrictions on accessing material. Recent developments in applying Canada's Access to Information Act has significantly restricted access to content housed at LAC, as well as other archives. Additionally, in 2012–13, restrictions were placed on LAC archivists' ability to speak publicly. Collaborations such as the conferences, symposia, and joint archival projects of the early 1990s seem less possible under these current conditions, which could potentially have ill effects for both broadcasting content and scholarly users of archives.

While the position of the CBC's corporate archivist was relatively short lived, documents generated during the time it existed witness and articulate challenges that are still relevant in a digital context for archiving broadcasting ephemera. While medium specificity plays a role in the pragmatics of preservation, determining what broadcasting content has value is also a perennial challenge for archives. With the production of broadcasting (and web-based) ephemera ever increasing, discourses used to perform triage on archival materials are determining what content will be preserved and remain accessible, and to whom. Since empirical criteria cannot determine merit, archives use discourse to do so. Dick's call in 1990 to place "new [internal] emphasis" by the CBC on its archives seems to have occurred and resulted, perhaps for different reasons than Dick had hoped, in "an appreciation of CBC's heritage in Canada by the Corporation itself."[67]

Concerns about magnetic tape established in the early 1990s have since been echoed in documents prepared by, for example, the Canadian Broadcast Museum Foundation, a non-profit charitable organization. Since 2001, the group has been lobbying to receive funding in the form of "per-subscriber fee-for-carriage" to preserve "broadcast heritage," much of it currently on magnetic tape. Calling for a "Made-in-Canada Solution" to "Canada's long-term failure" at preservation, the foundation recommends, "as we move from the analog to the digital era, Canada must act to preserve its broadcast legacy because this is an essential component of its national history."[68] This call to action suggests that even as digital storage offers new possibilities for archiving content, since all content housed on magnetic media is not migrating forward, in practice, it is becoming increasingly volatile as magnetic formats move toward obsolescence.

The 1990s witnessed a discursive shift for broadcasting content housed on magnetic media at the CBC and NAC. As I have shown, attempts to ward off broadcasting's ephemeral tendencies during this period – to ensure, "the future of its past" – required generous cooperation amongst a group of people, departments, facilities, and institutions, sometimes with divergent and conflicting interests.[69] During this period, the broadcaster and national archive, despite their divergent mandates, appear to have been momentarily aligned in their common anxiety about the future of magnetic media and the self-interested assertion that broadcasting content had value. The CBC's new market-driven mandate saw value in archival initiatives because of potential revenue that its content would generate. And, in a climate of funding cuts, the CBC also seemed anxious to justify its role as a public broadcaster by playing up cultural nationalism, which neatly aligned with its justification of archival initiatives around heritage discourse with NAC.

In making the case to adopt archival and preservation policies for magnetic media in common at the CBC and NAC, as well as across the CBC's regional production centres, the documents produced during this period are symptomatic of tensions between broadcasters and archival mandates – recycling the medium versus archiving its content, as well cautioning against practices of ad hoc stockpiling and self-selection. In facilitating steps toward the development of archival strategies for the care, handling, and storage of magnetic media, this body of evidence suggests, perhaps optimistically considering the outcomes mentioned above, that interventions for intervening on content's behalf are possible. These initial gestures at the CBC in the 1990s demonstrate the important role that advocacy can play in reorienting archival discourse toward best practices in caring for the heritage of broadcast content. As this history shows, it is possible to shape these always political discourses and, in terms of magnetic media, archivists and other interested parties have taken pragmatic and meaningful steps toward ensuring that content from the past will be preserved for the future.

NOTES

1 For an overview of this context, see Zoë Druick, "Continuity and Change in the Discourse of Canada's Cultural Industries," in *Cultural Industries.ca*, ed. Ira Wagman and Peter Urquhart (Toronto: Lorimer, 2012), 131–46.

2 CBC Engineering Operations Department's "Recommended Practice for the Care, Handling and Storage of CBC A/V Magnetic Media" states: "At the time of the writing of this document a clear and comprehensive Recommended Practice for the care and handling of magnetic media did not exist to guide technical operations managers, archivists, and technicians ... This Recommended Practice attempts to fill the existing void" (CBC, 20 April 1993): 3

3 Ernest J. Dick, "An Archival Acquisition Strategy for the Broadcast Records of the Canadian Broadcasting Corporation," *Historical Journal of Film, Radio and Television* 11, no. 3 (1991): 254.

4 Ernest J. Dick (CBC) and Jana Vosikovska (NA), "Survival of CBC Network Programming in Archives 1936–1984," (CBC and National Archives of Canada, 1994), 1.

5 Ibid., 2.

6 Michele Byers and I make this point in "Trafficking (in) the Archive: Canada, Copyright, and the Study of Television," *English Studies in Canada* 36, no. 1 (2010): 109–26 and "What Was Canada? Locating the Language of an Empty Archive," *Critical Studies in Television: Scholarly Studies of Small Screen Fictions* 5, no. 2 (2010): 105–17.

7 Tom Cavanagh, Marc Lapierre, and Marv Nolan, "Technology and the Practices Governing the Archiving of CBC Program Material on Magnetic Media" (CBC Engineering Operations Department, September 1992),15.

8 Ernest J. Dick, *Guide to CBC Sources at the Public Archives* (Public Archives of Canada. Minister of Supply and Services Canada, 1987), SA2-165/1987, vii.

9 Dick, "An Archival Acquisition Strategy for the Broadcast Records of the Canadian Broadcasting Corporation," 254.

10 Ibid.

11 Ibid.

12 Ibid.

13 CBC Engineering Operations Department, "Recommended Practice for the Care, Handling & Storage of CBC A/V Magnetic Media," 20 April 1993, 4.
14 Making holdings accessible to the public or to researchers is not considered a priority of the broadcast archive, and diverting resources to that end may, in fact, be perceived to impede its "normal operations" and "future requirements."
15 Dick, "An Archival Acquisition Strategy for the Broadcast Records of the Canadian Broadcasting Corporation," 257.
16 Cavanagh, Lapierre, and Nolan, "Technology and the Practices Governing the Archiving of CBC Program Material on Magnetic Media," 1.
17 Ibid.
18 Ibid., 1–4
19 These are the adjectives of Ernest Dick, who was acting in a position to characterize the relationship.
20 Ernest J. Dick, "The Need For a Review of CBC Archives," in *The Future of CBC's Past: A Review of Archives. Presentation for Senior Management* (1990), CBC: 2.
21 Dick and Vosikovska, "Survival of CBC Network Programming," 1.
22 Dick, "The Need for a Review," 2.
23 Ibid.
24 Dick and Vosikovska, "Survival of CBC Network Programming," 2.
25 Cavanagh, Lapierre, and Nolan, "Technology and the Practices Governing the Archiving of CBC Program Material on Magnetic Media," 14.
26 Dick and Vosikovska, "Survival of CBC Network Programming," 3.
27 Ibid.
28 Ibid., 1.
29 Ibid., 8.
30 Ibid.
31 This phrase appears in Dick, *Guide to CBC Sources at the Public Archives*, vii.
32 The guide was published in 1987 under the old name, Public Archives Canada.
33 This list includes Concordia and York Universities as well as the University of Quebec at Montreal. Dick, *Guide to CBC Sources at the Public Archives*, viii.
34 Dick worked as an archivist at NAC from 1974 to 1989.
35 Ernest J. Dick, email to the author, 5 July 2013.
36 Ernest J. Dick, "Background Paper" and "Presentation for Senior Management," in *The Future of CBC's Past: A Review of Archives* (CBC, 1990).
37 Dick, "An Archival Acquisition Strategy for the Broadcast Records of the Canadian Broadcasting Corporation," 254.
38 It mentions, for example, Radio Archives, Videotape Library, Film Library, Television News Library, Newsworld, SRC (CBC's French-language network), NAC, its Records Centre, Regional Broadcast Operations, the Historical Archives Section at CBC Head Office, Corporate Program Services Department (Business Affairs), the Central Registry System and staff, Management Information Systems, Engineering, Radio Canada International, CBC Reference Libraries, National Museum of Science and Technology, artefact committees, and York and Concordia Universities.
39 Ernest J. Dick, email to the author, 5 July 2013.
40 Ibid.

41 Ibid.
42 Ibid.
43 Ibid.
44 Mary Jane Miller, "Archives from the Point of View of the Scholarly User: Or If I Died and Went to a Platonic Archetype of a Sound and Moving Images Archive This is What I'd Find," in *Documents that Move and Speak: Audiovisual Archives in the New Information Age* (London: K.G. Saur, 1992). Michele Byers and I discuss other aspects of Miller's article in "Trafficking (in) the Archive: Canada, Copyright, and the Study of Television." *English Studies in Canada* 36.1 (2010): 109–26.
45 Miller, "Archives from the Point of View of the Scholarly User," 254.
46 Ibid.
47 Cavanagh, Lapierre, and Nolan, "Technology and the Practices Governing the Archiving of CBC Program Material on Magnetic Media," 13.
48 CBC Engineering Operations Department, 3.
49 Cavanagh, Lapierre, and Nolan, "Technology and the Practices Governing the Archiving of CBC Program Material on Magnetic Media," 3.
50 CBC Engineering Operations Department, 3
51 Ibid.
52 Ibid., 7.
53 Cavanagh, Lapierre, and Nolan, "Technology and the Practices Governing the Archiving of CBC Program Material," 4.
54 Ibid.
55 Ibid.
56 Ibid.
57 Ibid., 13.
58 Ibid., 14.
59 Ibid.
60 Ibid.
61 Ibid., 4.
62 Dick, "An Archival Acquisition Strategy for the Broadcast Records of the Canadian Broadcasting Corporation," 253.
63 CBC states, "the goal of the video archives is to have two copies of every program ever broadcast on the CBC – one "untouchable" master and one available to CBC staff to copy for reuse, rebroadcast or licensing to outside clients such as filmmakers and foreign networks. But as long as tapes decay and technology changes, the video archives will always be something of a work in progress." CBC, "A Visit to the Archives: Video," accessed 18 July 2013, http://www.cbc.ca/archives/about.
64 I discuss aspects of licensing agreements and other issues related to CBC Digital Archives in "(Who Knows?) What Remains to Be Seen: Archives and Other Pragmatic Problems for Canadian Television Studies," in *Canadian Television: Text and Context*, ed. Marian Bredin, Scott Henderson, and Sarah Matheson (Waterloo: Wilfrid Laurier Press, 2012), 39–57. See also Michele Byers and Jennifer VanderBurgh, "What Was Canada? Locating the Language of an Empty Archive," in *Critical Studies in Television: Scholarly Studies of Small Screen Fictions* 5, no. 2 (2010): 113.
65 See also Jennifer VanderBurgh, "(Who Knows?) What Remains to Be Seen:

Archives, Access, and Other Practical Problems for the Study of Canadian 'National' Television," in *Canadian Television: Text and Context*, edited by Marian Bredin, Scott Henderson, and Sarah A. Matheson (Waterloo: Wilfrid Laurier University Press, 2012) and Byers and VanderBurgh, "What Was Canada?," 112–13.

66 Byers and VanderBurgh, "What Was Canada?," 118.

67 Dick, "Scope of the Review of Archives" in *The Future of CBC's Past: A Review of Archives* (CBC, 1990).

68 Canadian Broadcast Museum Foundation, "Introduction" and "A Made-in-Canada Solution," *Newsletter Archive* no. 2, 2 (2009).

69 This quotation refers to the title of Dick's 1990 background paper and report, *The Future of CBC's Past.*

13 SEEING THEN, HEARING NOW

AUDIOVISUAL COUNTERPOINT AT THE INTERSECTION OF DUAL PRODUCTION CONTEXTS IN LARRY KENT'S *HASTINGS STREET*

Randolph Jordan

LARRY KENT'S FIRST film, *Hastings Street* (1962/2007), stands as a unique marker of the shifting dynamics of Vancouver as a major filmmaking centre, drawing the line from its roots in the ephemeral bouts of foreign production in the early twentieth century, through the emergence of local independent filmmaking in the 1960s and '70s, and into its current and relatively stable identity as Hollywood North. Originally titled *The Street*, Kent financed the short film out of his own pocket, shooting silent on location in 1962 with help from his theatre classmates at the University of British Columbia. Lacking resources for post-production, the uncompleted film was shelved and left for dead as Kent moved on to a series of feature films that would first gain him significant recognition and then plunge him into late-century obscurity. Happily, the early 2000s brought renewed interest in Kent's work, which parlayed into some grant money that allowed him to make digital transfers of *Hasting Street*'s original negative, re-edit the film, and construct a soundtrack from scratch.[1] Kent entrusted the new soundtrack to Marc Benoit and the students of his post-production audio class at the Art Institute of Vancouver in 2006/07. Under Benoit's supervision, new actors dubbed the dialogue for scenes shot forty-five years earlier, a music track was recorded, and sound effects were produced. Rich in location shooting of a Downtown Eastside now significantly changed, the images in *Hastings Street* stand alongside the photographs of Fred Herzog in offering a distinctive glimpse into the city's neon past. Yet the soundtrack functions differently, tasked with reconstructing the ephemeral soundscape of the world presented in the images while operating within the institutional context of a twenty-first century audio post-production class designed to feed into a bustling Vancouver media industry that did not exist when Kent was initially working in the city. The image and sound tracks in *Hastings Street* thus bracket major shifts in Vancouver as a city, its relationship to the film industry, and Kent's position within that industry.

The simultaneity of contrasting production contexts and their resultant aesthetics position *Hastings Street* at the nexus point of the overlapping spaces for media production that have been made manifest in Vancouver. In so doing, the film establishes an intriguing variation on the notion of "contrapuntal" relations between sound and image. As the writings and filmmaking of the Soviet Montage school of the late 1920s and early '30s articulate, the term "counterpoint" was used as a loose descriptor of approaches to sound/image synchronization that did not contribute to the naturalism or redundancy of information that these filmmakers (rightly) feared would dominate cinema with the coming of synchronized sound.[2] The soundtrack produced for *Hastings Street* operates according to long-established principles of realism and continuity, so it would seem to be ineligible for consideration as an example of any of the varied approaches to counterpoint that have been explored. Further, the film is not constructed with the overt reflexivity characteristic of works that make conscious use of contrapuntal strategies to pair sound and image. Yet the realist impulse of the sound design for *Hastings Street* is situated within the inevitability of the soundtrack's reinterpretation of images now decades old, a situation that offers avenues for the construction of meaning opened up by the interplay between sound and image that would not be possible when considering either the sound or image tracks in isolation. As I will demonstrate, thinking about the sound/image interaction here as a variation on audiovisual counterpoint opens the door to considering how *Hastings Street* enacts a concretization of the ephemeral qualities of Vancouver and its film industries, and audiovisual media in general.

In this chapter, I will focus on three dimensions in which this intriguing interaction between sound and image in *Hastings Street* engages with various levels of the cinematic ephemeral. As a "found footage" film that reassembles and sonorizes lost visual material from decades past, these images of Vancouver's Downtown Eastside in the early 1960s are brought to the world's attention in a way they wouldn't have been had the film been completed at that time. As a period piece in which the soundtrack attempts to evoke an authentic sense of the world depicted in the vintage imagery, the film raises questions about cinema's role in engaging with the ephemeral nature of the past. As a hybrid independent and industrial production, a duality inscribed on the image and sound tracks respectively, the film is in a unique position to speak to the intersections between these modes of practice, marking the shift from Vancouver-based

13.1 Charlie walks Hastings Street. Images shot on location in 1962 with studio sound constructed in 2007.

filmmaking as an ephemeral endeavour to an entrenched mainstay of the city's industry. In short, the contrapuntal space between sound and image in *Hastings Street* is the site at which the ephemeral becomes concrete and the film achieves a dimension of meaning that well surpasses the intention of the filmmakers both past and present.

THE CITY AND ITS RESOURCE INDUSTRIES IN LARRY KENT'S *HASTINGS STREET*

Twenty minutes long, the film charts the transition of small-time crook Charlie (Alan Scarfe) from penitentiary to civilian life as he wanders the streets of the Downtown Eastside, Vancouver's skid row area, visiting old contacts in search of a legitimate source of income. His only real shot is to get work at the Powell River lumber mill well north of the city, the kind of work that was once centrally located but has since moved away. But a strike has shut down operations at the mill, so Charlie is out of luck. With nowhere else to go, shunned even by his own mother over the phone, he falls back into a life of crime at the invitation of a local gangster. And so it ends, a bleak commentary on the effects of evacuating the industrial core of a city built around the hard labour of resource extraction.

This simple narrative line is traced through extraordinarily rich location shooting in Vancouver's poorest neighbourhood, which forms the centre for the city's low-incoming housing and ground zero for its homeless and/or drug-addicted population. The film is structured around a series of meetings between Charlie and his various contacts: a friend with union connections, an old girlfriend turned prostitute, a pool shark who uses all of his considerable earnings to stave off junk sickness, and old partners in organized crime. Between each are extended sequences in which Charlie walks between meeting points, observing the life of the street as he goes, smoking all the way. And the street life is rich. The 1950s and '60s were a notable time for this area, the peak of the city's proliferation of neon signage that also reflected vibrant commercial activity and marked a point of serious contention with Vancouverites who disliked the gaudiness and its associations with the neighbourhood's unseemly character. Though it was known as skid row even then, this was the era of the Woodward's flagship department store, a shopping mecca for people from across the city. Woodward's was the centerpiece of commercial activity in the area and helped ensure a diversity of class in the street population that has disappeared since the store's closure in 1993, the main event in a decade of commercial evacuation from the Downtown Eastside.[3] Charlie strolls with searching eyes as he continually shifts his attention around the busy environment, enhanced with POV shots that focus on specific details: a flashing restaurant sign, a trolley bus pulling away from the curb, an ambulance arriving to carry away an elderly drunkard. The soundtrack follows suit with heightened emphasis on the details of individual loci of attention: the distinctive crackle of neon, the plucking of high tension lines as trolleys pass through the overhead grid of wires at each intersection, the moan of a vintage ambulance siren as it arrives on the scene of a call. These sounds are set within an evocative din of bustling crowds and dense traffic, sometimes with an accompanying acoustic guitar score that evokes the folk music of the day (and at one point, with the help of delay effects, points to the psychedelic movement to come). In cataloguing the artefacts of post-war Hastings Street, Kent's film is unparalleled – even in comparison to Allan King's well known documentary *Skidrow* (1950) that, though shot on location, emphasizes interview subjects rather than the audiovisual details of the environment in which they live.

Charlie's plight is indicative of the lives of so many in Vancouver's skid row area in that era, named after its original function as a run for logs that would pass through town on the "skid road" heading for the mill, now populated with folks left in the gutter carved out by industry's increasing departure from the city. The film's narrative concern with an individual caught between the different worlds that overlap in the Downtown Eastside mirrors the film's own status as both harbinger and product of the intersections of independent and industrial filmmaking in the city. What we see and what we hear belong to separate times: the image reflects a 1960s with no substantial filmmaking industry in town, a hole left by ephemeral ventures like the "quota-quickies" of the 1930s that saw foreign production boost the local economy only to vacate once the circumstances for profit-making had vanished; the sound, on the other hand, reflects a Vancouver now established as Hollywood North where the presence of the filmmaking industry has been stable enough to give rise to a local network of institutions feeding talent into the market. Vancouver was once a place that filmmakers would have to leave to get work, just as traditional resource industry workers would have to do. Now, filmmaking in the city has marked a return of industry to the downtown core, making Vancouver a place to which people go for work, and where locals can remain. In turn, this industrial presence has made a vast array of resources available to independent production as well, creating a rich (if not perfect) set of relationships between very different worlds of local media production.[4] These relationships are made apparent in the interactions between the image and sound tracks in *Hasting Street.*

HASTINGS STREET AS FOUND-FOOTAGE FILM

Hastings Street doesn't quite fit the usual categories for classifying found-footage films:[5] since Kent is refashioning his own material, there isn't the level of appropriation often found in such work, and since he takes material only from one source – his original negatives for the shoot – it isn't a collage or compilation film either. And yet, because of the forty-five-year gap between shooting and the final editing and sound production, there is plenty of room for Kent and his collaborators to reinterpret the material. While overt commentary on Kent's original footage is not the goal of his twenty-first century picture montage or soundtrack, there is nevertheless an important dimension of reimagining at work in the finished film.

At the heart of the film's position as found footage is Kent's retitling of the film from the generic *The Street* to the more regionally specific *Hastings Street.*[6] When Kent shot the film, recently arrived from South Africa in 1957, his interest in the fine line between poverty and the working class in the Downtown Eastside was a meditation on a reality far from specific to Vancouver. Indeed, the film was shot in such a way that the signature visual elements with which the city is associated today are absolutely invisible: no water, no mountains, and no Hotel Vancouver. Although the film is rich in Vancouver's famous mid-century neon signage along with street names that give the location away, this was meant to be a film about the kind of skid row area that most cities have. As such, the film handles setting largely the way that many foreign productions do: as an ephemeral space, of interest only as appropriate backdrop for the demands of narrative. Although Kent does not have much to say about the new title,[7] his decision to retroactively brand the film with regionally specific connotations can be productively interpreted as a function of the area's current notoriety, bringing with it a powerful set of associations that prompt contemporary audiences to read the film's period narrative through the lens of hindsight about what that area would become in the decades after it was shot.

Indeed, there is a big difference between the Vancouver of 1962 and the Vancouver of 2007. While the Downtown Eastside has long been viewed as the city's gutter, its character has changed significantly. Visually, one of the most dramatic changes came with the massive reduction of downtown neon in the 1970s. The bright signage was once an important aspect of the city's urban character at a time when it was trying to prove its urbanity by distancing itself from the surrounding wilderness. But the 1970s saw the city rebranding itself with an emphasis on nature, and passed a by-law to drastically reduce the amount of signage on the streets as it was seen to interfere with the architecture and natural setting that were now considered essential to the city's identity.[8] Kent's choice to obliterate the city's natural setting in favour of emphasizing neon-lit street life speaks to the Vancouver of 1962 as a city aspiring to the likes of New York and Los Angeles rather than the more current public relations strategy of playing up eco-minded urban planning in the context of spectacular natural surroundings. So the Vancouver of 1962 was complicit with Kent's aim to tell a more or less generic tale of urban plight. The retroactive region-specific branding of the film speaks to the twenty-first century image of Hastings Street in the public consciousness as a particularly notorious area in a city that now defines itself in opposition to what is on display here, a situation enhanced by the gentrification of surrounding neighbourhoods.[9]

Like Hastings Street, the name Larry Kent is also understood differently now than it was in 1962. While his career is peppered with ups and downs, today Kent is recognized as Canada's first independent feature filmmaker and the father of Vancouver's emerging local scene dedicated to a regional specificity absent from the transnational productions that would eventually brand the city as Hollywood North. However, when he shot *Hastings Street* he was a student in the drama department at UBC setting out to make a short film out of his own pocket and with absolutely no experience. Kent maintains that he was unaware of the Vancouver cinema scene of the 1940s and '50s, which consisted of filmmakers like Stan Fox, Allan King, Arla Saare, and others working within Vancouver's Film Society and the CBUT Film Unit,[10] and thus he had no region-specific school of filmmaking in mind as either influence or market (though certainly those involved in filmmaking elsewhere in town were quickly made aware of Kent's work upon completion of his first feature, *The Bitter Ash*, in 1963). So there is logic to Kent's desire to make a film that could appeal to a wide variety of audiences by way of a generic theme. And while his subsequent Vancouver films are more region-specific, they tend to represent what Browne calls "the darker zeitgeist of their times,"[11] positioning Vancouver as a place that aspiring individuals want to leave, and using location shooting as a means for tying setting to characterization in these narratives of escape.[12] Indeed, after shooting three features in Vancouver, Kent ultimately made the move himself and went to Montreal in the late 1960s to take a short-lived job at the National Film Board. But his time in Montreal led to a series of frustrating production experiences that yielded several films but little success. Although he continues to live in Montreal, Kent's recent return to relatively prolific filmmaking in the twenty-first century has found him back in Vancouver for his most recent films *The Hamster Cage* (2005), *Exley* (2011), and *She Who Must Burn* (in post-production at the time of writing). No longer needing to prove he can make it out of Vancouver with his films, as character Colin so wanted to do with his plays in *The Bitter Ash*, Kent now actively celebrates the city as a place to go for work – fuelled by the new resources available to independent producers fostered by Hollywood setting up permanent shop during his absence – rather than a place to escape. The newly Vancouver-specific title attached to his first film speaks to his own personal trajectory as a filmmaker moving through different spatio-temporal geographies.

While *Hastings Street* is not particularly overt in its commentary on the original 1962 footage shot as *The Street*, and certainly is not using montage to call attention to its reinterpretation forty-five years after the fact of shooting, the final film is most definitely the product of an appropriation

13.2 Colin and Laurie argue near the Pender Street rail yard in *The Bitter Ash*. Images shot on location with sound dubbed in studio.

of material from another time, rethought by way of contemporary realities. Importantly, this twenty-first century sensibility guides the film's 2007 sound design as well. As I will discuss now, the soundtrack takes a generally realist approach to bringing sound to these vintage images. As such, the film is decidedly not in the same vein as any number of possibilities in the found-footage filmmaking realm that might take sound samples from 1960s Vancouver films or other archival material and play these off the images for dialectic effect. Yet, there is something about the sound design that provides ample room for understanding the realist impulses of the film as a marker of a different dialectic that exists between the vastly different production contexts of Kent's 1962 shooting and the 2007 sound production, each of which speaks to the film's engagement with region-specific elements of Vancouver in ways that would otherwise be impossible.

HASTINGS STREET AS PERIOD PIECE

A useful way to think through the soundtrack's reinterpretation of the 1962 footage is to consider the film's status as a period piece. Like any period film, *Hastings Street* is charged with taking the ephemeral qualities of a world past and making them concrete. The difference here is that it is largely up to the soundtrack to rethink the past from a contemporary perspective. There are certainly aspects of the image track that speak to the film's reinterpretation of the vintage images, particularly in the editing domain where shot selection, cutting style, and digital workflow are all informed by twenty-first-century filmmaking practices (along with a claustrophobic crop designed to conform to today's widescreen standards). However, the fact that these images were shot in the time the film is set makes them of an entirely different order than the elements of the newly produced soundtrack, which begs questions about the approaches available for such a project. All films that feature location shooting stand as documentaries of a kind, contributing to potential research into the geographically specific aspects of times past. Film soundtracks have the potential to act the same way, and here an interesting hypothetical question emerges: if Kent had succeeded in producing a soundtrack for the film back in 1962, would this soundtrack have offered a documentation of the area as rich as the visual track? Listening to Kent's following two features offers differing possible answers to this question.

On *The Bitter Ash* absolutely no sync sound recording was conducted, and the final soundtrack consists almost entirely of dubbed dialogue recorded by the actors in post-production paired with a continuous jazz music soundtrack composed for the film. There is practically no attempt at rendering environmental sound effects of any kind. The important exception here is an early shot of the Canadian Pacific Railway yard with accompanying location sound recording used to establish the "down by the tracks" poverty of a couple living on the adjacent Pender Street. Following the lingering shots of trains milling about the yard, we are introduced to Colin and Laurie, new parents to an infant boy whom Colin seems to view only as impediment to his dream of writing an avant-garde play that will put him on the world stage. Laurie is left in a proto-feminist bind as both housewife and sole breadwinner for the family. Their fraught interpersonal dynamic is made clear during their first conversation in the film, which takes place on their balcony overlooking the rail yard. As Colin complains that Laurie hasn't pressed his scarf in time for him to leave for a meeting with his peers, we hear nothing of the train sounds that were prominent just before, creating a strange sense of artificiality to which the awkward dubbing also contributes. At the end of the film,

13.3 Girl-watching on Kits Beach in *Sweet Substitute.* Images and sound recorded on location.

however, Kent brings the train sounds back to fill in for the lack of any sound effects accompanying a fight scene between Colin and Des, a frustrated factory worker who beds Laurie at the couple's rent party. With only these minimal instances of location recording, the film as a whole does not offer much access to the Vancouver soundscape apart from the voices of a few local actors and musicians.

On the other hand, Kent's next feature, *Sweet Substitute* (1964), includes direct sound in almost every scene, much of which was recorded outdoors, and is augmented again with a music track. An exemplary moment comes when two high school boys are at the beach discussing a lady of interest they see nearby, their conversation strained against the sound of ocean waves and audible wind distortion on the microphones – the nightmares of location sound recording that Kent's team endured on its first attempts at capturing synchronous sound. Here the film does stand as an auditory document of the city's environmental soundscape.[13] As a result, Kent's first two features must be handled differently as objects of potential research into the sound of Vancouver in the early 1960s. And the differing possibilities for audiovisual treatments on display in these films point to the vagaries that must be negotiated as part of any consideration of a film's engagement with place.

Critical assessment of a film soundtrack's value as marker of geographical space must take the problems of representational practice into account. Film sound theory has long been concerned with the flawed thinking at work in any notion that a sound recording can faithfully *reproduce* the recorded event to offer unmediated access to it.[14] Nevertheless, interest in location sound recording persists both in documentary and fiction filmmaking circles, reflecting the continuing belief in the indexical relationship that a recording has to reality that offers the potential for authentic engagement with place not afforded by post-production reconstructions (an attitude common with respect to location shooting as well).[15] This fundamental belief drives work such as that being conducted by the World Soundscape Project (WSP) in its continuing use of field recordings as both records and tools for soundscape analysis.[16] Yet as Karin Bijsterveld argues, any appeal to sound recordings as documents of geographical specificity must account for how these soundscapes are "staged," an approach that situates the ideological implications of sound design choices within the cultural and historical contexts of production along with the technical and conventional norms that govern particular forms of media.[17] The value of *Hastings Street* as document of Vancouver depends on our understanding of how the sound design has been staged, and in how we account for the issues this staging raises.

The unusual situation of the film's double context poses two essential questions about how sound designers might approach such a project. First, should the goal be to produce a soundtrack equivalent to what might have accompanied the film in 1962, or to follow present-day sensibilities instead? Second, should the soundtrack attempt to accurately reflect the soundscape of the locations in which the film was shot, regardless of when and how the sounds are produced? As *The Bitter Ash* indicates, nothing says that a film produced in a specific place at a specific time will offer the kind of geographical specificity associated with location recording or post-production rendering of location-specific sound elements. Further, most Vancouver productions (both local and foreign) are less interested in the specificities of place than they are in the concerns of narrative.[18] The result is a frequent desire to downplay the city's distinctiveness and produce a soundtrack free of anything identifiably local, such as the keynote sounds, signals, and sound marks that have so interested the World Soundscape Project in its research into Vancouver's characteristic soundscape.[19] There are myriad issues to navigate when assessing the staging of a film's sound design, ranging from practical production issues through the norms of convention and on into the politics of representation.

What ideologies govern the staging of sound in *Hastings Street*? Even if the filmmakers had wanted it to, the film's new soundtrack could not reflect the environmental soundscape of 1962 Vancouver the way it could have if location sound recording had accompanied the film's shooting. While there was potential to appeal to archival sound recordings and/or vintage recording equipment in the production of the new soundtrack, Benoit's approach was to focus on the visual cues contained in the images and draw from his memory of growing up in Vancouver to reimagine what kinds of sounds the pictured environments would have contained. Yet at the same time, Benoit took a current approach to the production of the soundtrack itself, drawing on material recorded specifically for the film along with a few stock tracks from sound effects libraries that offer newly produced recordings of vintage items. He brings the norms of twenty-first century industrial practices to bear on the film's attempts at authenticity.[20] Thus, as with any period piece, there are tensions at work in the degree to which the film engages with realities of time and place.

What if Benoit had treated the film as a historical research project? The use of visual cues to access soundscapes of the past is an approach familiar to many sound historians who have appealed to paintings and other visual art as indicators of past soundscapes, a practice familiar to the WSP as well (and in particular the writings of R. Murray Schafer).[21] Further, listening for sounds from the past that continue to resonate in present-day environments is one of the functions of the longitudinal case studies undertaken by the WSP and related research all over the world. Thus, Benoit's approach to the period reconstruction of Vancouver's sonic environment shares some strategy with academic soundscape research. Building from these connections, we could assess the film's value as cultural heritage by listening to its sonic details through the WSP's research and archival recordings. Here we would begin with its very first tape made on 13 September 1972 on the corner of Hastings and Columbia,[22] the same intersection at which Charlie disembarks a bus at the beginning of *Hastings Street*. A few months later, on 3 June 1973, the WSP recordists enacted this very process, exiting a trolley bus that then departs from the stop, followed by the recordist moving in to close-mic the buzzing of a neon sign (a sound that occurs in the film as well, shortly after Charlie begins his first Hastings Street walk).[23] Although made a decade or so after Kent shot his film, these recordings are still closer to what would have been recorded on location in 1962 than to 2007, and are similar in texture to the location recordings in *Sweet Substitute*.

When comparing Benoit's soundtrack to WSP recordings of the same area, or even to Kent's own recordings made for *Sweet Substitute*, it is clear that *Hastings Street* does not display the same limitations and distortions of field recording equipment or the inexperience of its operators evident in the material gathered for the WSP archive and for Kent's second feature. Instead, the sound design in *Hastings Street* has a distinctly current aesthetic. Here, the overall din audible in the actual location recordings, marked by a flattening of three dimensional space that increases competition between elements of similar frequency,[24] is replaced by clearly defined component parts – footsteps, passing vehicles, doors opening and closing – which are individually recorded in controlled circumstances and built up with careful spectrum management to minimize interference between the various elements. Though this is a standard approach to mixing in the digital age, the result is an odd feeling of emptiness despite the dense layering, a sanitized approximation of the environment rather than the down and dirty clutter of the earlier location recordings.[25] Indeed, the buzzing of neon in the film sounds closer to what we can hear of such signage isolated in the quiet confines of the *Neon Vancouver, Ugly Vancouver* exhibition room at the Museum of Vancouver, put on display for us to ponder their sociocultural significance safely removed from the density of their original context of the street. A similar distantiation is at work in the sound design for *Hastings Street*, the result of strategies for recording and mixing very different from what Kent practiced in the 1960s.

To consider a single sound example from the film in more detail: the passing fire truck with blaring siren used to emphasize Charlie's frustration during a phone call to his mother. As it becomes clear to Charlie that she will not give him the fifty dollars he says he needs to "see me straight," he raises his voice in anger as the truck speeds past, its siren dominating the soundtrack for a moment before receding into the distance as Charlie exits the phone booth and stands briefly motionless in dejection. The use of siren sounds to augment narrative tension is com-

13.4 A fire truck with siren blaring underscores Charlie's anxiety in *Hastings Street.*

monplace, but how do we know if this particular siren is akin to what would have actually been heard on the streets of Vancouver in 1962, and why would that matter?

As a starting point we could compare the siren sound with archival recordings from that era, such as those contained in the WSP archive. As it happens, the WSP recordists captured a passing fire truck on their first reel at Hastings and Columbia.[26] One major difference between the two recordings is that the WSP tape features a rich spatial signature that documents the interaction between the siren and the space around it as it reverberates through the buildings, changing dynamics as it goes. There is also a rough quality to the recording, a product of inexperience evident in the earliest WSP recordings, which would be considered unsuitable for use in the context of professional film sound design. In the film, the siren is crisp, free of distortion, and very dry with no sense of spatial context. Further, to evoke a sense of the truck's approach and recession the siren simply rises and falls in amplitude with no adjustments to the ratio of direct to reflected sound that guides real-world assessments of depth.

The WSP recording also features the alternation between different siren modes, whereas in the film the mode remains constant. This detail reveals an issue in the soundscape politics of the day: by the early 1970s, certain of the more piercing siren modes were being outlawed due to noise complaints, such as the faster yelping we hear in the film which, on the WSP tape, alternates with a milder oscillating sound. The move to ban the more intense mode was unpopular with fire fighters who felt that switching modes regularly was much more effective at getting the public's attention about oncoming vehicles, as explained in a conversation between WSP recordists and a fire fighter at the Burnaby Fire Hall in their 20 June 1973 recording.[27]

While the siren sound effect used in the film might well reflect one siren mode of the early 1960s, it lacks several dimensions specific to the physical and social space of Vancouver. In an assessment of the film's value as document of 1962 Vancouver, such cross-media comparison can reveal both the strengths and weaknesses of the new soundtrack's attempts at authenticity. Of course, in work like this I would also have to assess the approaches to staging sound in the WSP recordings themselves rather than simply treat them as unmediated documentary evidence of a past to be compared with rendered constructions like in *Hastings Street*, a task that falls beyond the purview of this chapter.[28]

As a period piece, the staging of sound in *Hastings Street* bears its ideological traces: as the case of the siren exemplifies, an attempt at authenticity is made with respect to the type of sound heard, but cleanliness and clarity are privileged over spatially defined acoustic naturalism and at the expense of the social dynamics of that space. However, the kind of cross-media investigation I have suggested here opens a rich environment for assessing how the film engages with Vancouver's changing dynamics over the last four decades. The long gap between the shooting and sound production opens up a contrapuntal space in which the twenty-first century experience of the city contributes to the auditory interpretation of these images of the past, providing every dimension of sound/image interaction with the potential to foster a form of audience engagement with Vancouver as defined by the dialectic between the film's two moments of production. As such, the film presents more than a simple narrative of one man's difficulties in the face of Vancouver's changing relationship to the resource industry; it threads this narrative through a very legible difference in modes of production on the image and sound tracks that bring Charlie's plight through to the level of the film's construction. *Hastings Street* thus moves beyond the representation of Vancouver-specific relationships between people and industry and becomes an enactment of these relationships. As I will now discuss, the most potent counterpoint comes in extending this reading of dual production moments to a consideration of the cultural implications of the difference between those moments: the conditions of production between the fierce independence of Kent's work in 1962 and its intersection with the industrial practices that governed the creation of the soundtrack in 2007.

HASTINGS STREET AS INDEPENDENT/INDUSTRIAL HYBRID

Aside from issues in the authenticity of the chosen sound effects and their implementation, there is another layer present in which the film's sound design is very much the product of a geographical specificity: Vancouver as centre for a Hollywood industry with its own aesthetic standards taught to locals who want to feed the Vancouver-based production houses. As a vehicle for industry professionals in training, *Hastings Street* needs to sound up to the standards of Hollywood's highly rendered products, and classes like those offered at the Art Institute of Vancouver reflect this reality. While we may listen to the soundtrack and know right away that there is no location recording from 1962, we also hear an earnest Vancouver spirit of rising to the challenge of industry professionalism set by a foreign market, resulting in the kinds of aesthetic details described above.

One of the most significant aspects of Vancouver's industrial status is that once the film industry was established, its resources became available to independent productions as well, making for a much more viable independent film culture (one reason why Kent returned to Vancouver in later years). These aspects of the film's sound design mark it with a regional specificity that plays very well off these images shot at the dawn of Vancouver's new era as a film production centre. Kent's impetuous do-it-yourself spirit is often cited as the catalyst for the local filmmakers that followed. "The guy was a madman to think he could do what he did," says Jack Darcus, "but none of us would be making films in Vancouver if he hadn't gotten up off his arse and made the first one."[29] Darcus shot *Great Coups of History* (1969), his first of many Vancouver features, shortly after Kent left town for Montreal – around the same time Robert Altman arrived to shoot *That Cold Day in the Park* (1969). This was the era that Hollywood rediscovered Vancouver while Vancouver filmmakers were discovering themselves, a situation that eventually led to the cross-pollination between industry and independent production that blossomed with the Pacific New Wave or West Coast Wave of the 1990s and that continues to the present day.[30] Thus, the sound/image relationships in *Hastings Street* move beyond the realist strategy of having the sources of sounds implied within the visual diegesis to a different level of cause

13.5 Charlie is shunned by his mother over the phone in *Hastings Street*, voiced forty-five years later by Nicholas Lea.

and effect: that of the image track's status as the beginning of the modern era of filmmaking in Vancouver that would go on to create the conditions for the effects on the soundtrack.

In the end, the outstanding sound mark of Vancouver's relationship to the film industry is the voice of Nicholas Lea dubbing Alan Scarfe's lines. Lea is a Vancouver actor who made his name as a regular on *The X-Files* playing Alex Krycek, a double agent who served as foil for Mulder (David Duchovny) and the Cigarette Smoking Man (William B. Davis) alike. *The X-Files* has become the quintessential example of foreign production in Vancouver. As such, the show acts as the site of many arguments for how geographical specificity can shine through Hollywood's consistent attempts to render the city as a stand-in for someplace else, yielding the type of insider readings of industrial product that Sarah Matheson identifies in Toronto-based television shows like *Night Heat*.[31] No doubt, the rain, lush greenery, and Gastown footage of early episodes of *The X-Files* mark the show with a visually distinctive Vancouver flavour. Yet there are myriad ways in which the regular involvement of local talent, both in front of and behind the camera, give the show a regional quality (such as when Vancouver actors reappear in multiple productions as part of a talent pool that is distinctly local). When listening to Lea's voice in *Hastings Street* I can't help but have Krycek's image in my mind, particularly in the above-mentioned scene where Charlie calls his mother for help, a moment recalling so many tense phone calls between Krycek and his associates over the many seasons of *The X-Files*.[32]

At the same time, focusing on the dialogue in *Hastings Street* brings us closest to the audiovisual character of Kent's first feature. As noted above, *The Bitter Ash* was marked by clunky dubbing, something Kent and his team got better at in subsequent outings. *Hastings Street* also has clunky dubbing, here the result of different actors trying to synchronize lines of dialogue without the original script. Lip reading and memory can only yield so much after forty-five years, and there are plenty of moments in the film where the lines we hear simply do not line up well with the lips we see moving on-screen. The experience can distance audiences used to a tighter and more spatially conscious approach to the synchronization of voices and the images of speaking bodies. Here the gap between voice and body offers the greatest experience of counterpoint between production contexts in the film.

An intertextual reading of Lea's presence in *Hastings Street*, linking the film both to Kent's early feature filmmaking and the products of Hollywood North in the 1990s, speaks powerfully to the film's unique position as both a herald of Vancouver's independent scene and a beneficiary of the industry that would eventually move in. Lea stands as evidence of the fact that actors, and other industry professionals, no longer have to leave Vancouver to get work.[33] For those who are home in the city, Vancouver has become a place to stay. For those who left, it has become a place to return to, just as Kent has returned to continue his filmmaking in recent years. To hear Lea dubbed over images of Scarfe playing Charlie is to follow a narrative about a man who cannot find work in the resource industry in Vancouver voiced by a man who, four decades later, has made his living in the latest incarnation of industry setting up shop within the city limits. And the fact that Lea can make a living on the industrial side of the equation means that he, like the various production service institutions that have opened up, is available for work on independent productions as well, creating an environment of rich interplay between different modes of filmmaking practice in Vancouver.

CONCLUSION

Counterpoint in *Hastings Street* is the space opened up by the lengthy gap between the production of the image and sound tracks, a space positioned at the nexus point of the overlapping contexts for media production in Vancouver. Though realist in aesthetic and not particularly reflexive in execution, the inevitability of the soundtrack's reinterpretation of images from a time past nevertheless offers avenues for the construction of meaning opened up by the interplay between sound and image that would not be possible when considering either the sound or image tracks in isolation, or if the sound and image had been produced at the same time. This contrapuntal space is the site at which *Hastings Street* pins down the ephemeral qualities of the city and its industries that form the subject matter of the film as well as the contexts for its production. As a found-footage period piece that intersects independent and industrial practices, the film makes concrete the lost worlds, lost footage, and shifting modes of production that speak as much about changes in the Vancouver film-making scene as they do about Kent's involvement in it.

Finally, *Hastings Street* bookends the birth of independent cinema and its current incarnation within Vancouver as industrial film centre, tracing Kent's trajectory through these different spatio-temporal realities. The film's twenty-first century completion also marks a new beginning for Kent in the city as he completes his third Vancouver feature since the 2003 retrospective that brought him back into the limelight, while acting as executive producer on a feature-length adaptation of *Hastings Street* to be released in 2014.[34] The story of Kent's ongoing participation in the Vancouver scene continues, a testimony to the vibrancy of independent filmmaking in the city since his debut in the early 1960s. In the end, the interaction between sound and image in *Hastings Street* offers a high level of engagement with place as a result of the odd situation of its staggered production, making it a valuable example of how the cinema can crystallize the ephemerality of shifting dynamics in a city and its film industries. The film stands as an important document of the histories of independent and industrial filmmaking in Canada and their development through to the present day, while also serving as an excellent example for how soundscape research can open up new ways to address issues in the cinematic documentation of specific geographical locales.

ACKNOWLEDGMENTS

Research for this project has been partially supported by a post-doctoral fellowship from FRQSC (Le Fonds de recherche du Québec – Société et culture).

NOTES

1 This renewed interest was fostered, in part, by a 2003 retrospective of Kent's work held at the Pacific Cinematheque in Vancouver, and by the efforts of Montreal-based film scholar Dave Douglas, who was instrumental in the process of getting Kent's early work digitized for DVD distribution. The twenty-first century has also seen Kent return to feature filmmaking after more than a decade on hiatus, and he is now in post-production on his third film since 2005. The finished version of *Hastings Street* is available for public screening on Kent's Vimeo account at http://vimeo.com/19191802.

2 See "A Statement," in *Film Sound: Theory and Practice*, edited by Elizabeth Weis and John Belton (New York: Columbia University Press, 1985), 83–5, in which Sergei Eisenstein, V.I. Pudovkin, and G.V. Alexandrov call for the use of "asynchronous sound" that would contribute to the dialectical approach to montage espoused by these filmmakers, often associated with jarring juxtapositions that force the audience to engage in active interpretation. But as Michel Chion rightly points out, the idea of counterpoint as jarring juxtaposition does not do justice to the concept's origins in Western classical music theory in which counterpoint functions as a form of melody rather than the dissonant harmony that better describes popular uses of the term in film sound theory. And as Kristin Thompson and Robert Robertson explore, the term "counterpoint" did not carry a precise prescription for the use of asynchronous sound. Many variations on counterpoint emerged in the practice of these filmmakers, the common goal being to create reflexive sound/image relationships that open up new avenues for meaning construction that would not be possible on the sound or image tracks alone, or if the sound and image were too similar in the information they carried. I argue that certain realist approaches to synchronization rejected by the Montagists can be productively included in the umbrella of counterpoint – if there is an accessible way of negotiating meaning from a tension between the two channels of transmission. Such is the case in *Hastings Street*. Michel Chion, *Audio-Vision: Sound on Screen*, trans. Claudia Gorbman (New York: Columbia University Press, 1994), 36–7; Kristin Thompson, "Early Sound Counterpoint," *Yale French Studies* special issue, no. 60 (1980): 115–40; and Robert Robertson, *Eisenstein on the Audiovisual: The Montage of Music, Image and Sound in Cinema* (London: Tauris Academic Studies, 2009).

3 See Jeff Sommers and Nick Blomley, "The Worst Block in Vancouver," in *Stan Douglas: Every Building on 100 West Hastings*, ed. Reid Shier (Vancouver: Arsenal Pulp Press, 2002), 18–58.

4 Colin Browne, Mike Gasher, Peter Morris, and David Spaner all discuss the history of foreign production in British Columbia prior to World War II, the peak being the period of the "quota quickies" in which American companies produced films in Canada, which, as a Commonwealth country, made them eligible for the British market during the years of its quota system to promote films made by British nationals. All acknowledge that this period whetted the

appetite of the provincial government for more foreign filmmaking business to set up shop in British Columbia, but the question was how to attract such business without the threat of sudden evacuation leaving the province high and dry. The governing argument in Gasher's book *Hollywood North* is that the BC government has always thought about filmmaking as a resource industry akin to logging or mining, and that its successful incentives to establish a northern branch of Hollywood in the late 1970s built on the experiences of fifty years prior to create a more stable local industry that it envisioned as part of the province's broader network of resource-based industries. Dennis Duffy provides a thorough account of the fits and starts of feature film production between the 1930s and '70s, and Gasher and Spaner offer excellent (although very different) accounts of the new intersections between industrial and independent filmmaking in the city created by the long-term presence of foreign production houses in Vancouver since the 1980s. Colin Browne, "Afterword: Fugitive Events," in *Cineworks 2000: Twenty Years of Independent Filmmaking in British Columbia*, ed. Justin MacGregor (Vancouver: Cineworks Independent Filmmakers Society, 2001); Colin Browne, *Motion Picture Production in British Columbia: 1898–1940 – A Brief Historical Background and Catalogue* (Victoria: British Columbia Provincial Museum, 1979); Mike Gasher, *Hollywood North: The Feature Film Industry in British Columbia* (Vancouver: University of British Columbia Press, 2002); Peter Morris, *Embattled Shadows: A History of Canadian Cinema, 1895–1939* (Montreal: McGill-Queen's University Press, 1978/1992); David Spaner, *Dreaming in the Rain: How Vancouver Became Hollywood North by Northwest* (Vancouver: Arsenal Pulp Press, 2003); and Dennis J. Duffy, *Camera West: British Columbia on Film, 1941–1965* (Victoria: Provincial Archives of British Columbia, 1986).

5 For example, William C. Wees identifies compilation, collage, and appropriation as three main strategies in found footage filmmaking (see *Recycled Images: The Art and Politics of Found Footage Films* [New York: Anthology Film Archives, 1993], 32–47).

6 This discussion follows from a point about the film's retitling made by my student Sacha Orenstein during his presentation on the film as part of a graduate seminar on Vancouver film that I taught at Concordia University in Montreal during the 2011 fall semester.

7 I asked Kent about the retitling during a private interview conducted in person on 30 January 2012, and he said simply that it seemed "appropriate" to call the film *Hastings Street* upon its resurrection.

8 The controversy over the neon signage is the subject of the permanent "Neon Vancouver, Ugly Vancouver" exhibition at the Museum of Vancouver (opened 13 October 2011), which features a selection of the signs that have been removed since 1974. See Nancy Noble and Mari Fujita, *Neon Vancouver, Ugly Vancouver* (Vancouver: Museum of Vancouver, 2012).

9 See Neil Smith and Jeff Derksen, "Urban Regeneration: Gentrification as Global Urban Strategy," in *Stan Douglas: Every Building on 100 West Hastings*,

ed. Reid Shier (Vancouver: Arsenal Pulp Press, 2002), 62–92; and John Punter, *The Vancouver Achievement: Urban Planning and Design* (Vancouver: University of British Columbia Press, 2003).

10 Browne, Duffy, and Newman chronicle the work of the Film Society and CBUT filmmakers during this period, arguing that their output has had a lasting influence on the Vancouver film scene. Browne, "Afterword: Fugitive Events"; Duffy, *Camera West*; Timothy Newman, "Mediating Collaborations: Arla Saare, the CBUT Film Unit, and the Emergence of the 'West Coast School'" (paper presented at the annual meeting of the Film Studies Association of Canada, University of Victoria, 5 June 2013).

11 Browne, "Afterword: Fugitive Events," 111.

12 See Dave Douglas, "Exile on Hastings and Main Street: The Vancouver Films of Larry Kent," *Canadian Journal of Film Studies* 5, no. 2 (1996): 85–99.

13 Although plainly evident in the listening, these details of sound production on Kent's early films were confirmed to me during the above-mentioned interview.

14 In "The Material Heterogeneity of Recorded Sound," Rick Altman argues that there is no such thing as an "original" sound that can be reproduced by a recording since any sound event is subject to the acoustic properties of the space in which it is heard (what he calls "spatial signature") and the position of the listener in that space. Thus any attempt to reproduce a sound event in a recording always reflects only one position in an endless array of variables, further complicated by the sounds introduced by the recording technologies themselves. In the "Sound Theory" chapter of his book *Sound Technology and the American Cinema*, James Lastra extends this argument to emphasize that all sound recording is merely representation, and he develops a model for understanding how strategies of representation have been used in American films. In chapter five of Michel Chion's *Audio-Vision: Sound on Screen*, Chion distinguishes between "the real and the rendered" in addressing the ideological and aesthetic implications of direct sound recording versus post-production fabrication, concluding that each has the potential to offer as authentic a representation of place as the other. And in his chapter "The Social Genesis of Sonic Fidelity" from *The Audible Past*, Jonathan Sterne positions the myth of reproducibility within the discourse of "vanishing mediation" that posits the possibility that a recording can transport the listener to the space of the recorded event. With this rich discourse in mind, any interrogation into how a film's soundtrack engages with a particular geographical locale must take these issues of fidelity into account as a starting point for understanding cinematic representation of space.

15 Charles O'Brien's book *Cinema's Conversion to Sound* offers one excellent account of the differing ideologies governing direct sound recording in the United States and France.

16 The World Soundscape Project began at Simon Fraser University in Vancouver in the late 1960s under the direction of R. Murray Schafer. Its

objective has been to study the relationships between people and the sonic environments in which they live. The investigators began with a study of the city of Vancouver that included extensive field recording in 1972–73 that yielded the publication of a booklet and LP, and this has since turned into a longitudinal investigation with new recordings added to the archive regularly over the following forty years. R. Murray Schafer, ed., *Document no. 5: The Vancouver Soundscape*, World Soundscape Project (Burnaby: Sonic Research Studio, Dept. of Communications, Simon Fraser University, 1973). Extensive documentation on the WSP and its activities can be found at http://www.sfu.ca/~truax/wsp.html.

17 See Karen Bijsterveld, *Soundscapes of the Urban Past: Staged Sound as Mediated Cultural Heritage* (Bielefeld: Transcript Verlag, 2013).

18 Mike Gasher has an excellent analysis of the role of Vancouver as location in local film production in chapter 5 of his book *Hollywood North.*

19 See Schafer, *Document no. 5*.

20 Again, although fairly clear in the listening, these details of sound production on *Hastings Street* were confirmed to me in private interviews I conducted with Marc Benoit in person and by email in 2012 and 2013.

21 See R. Murray Schafer, *The Tuning of the World* (Toronto: McClelland and Stewart, 1977) and *Voices of Tyranny, Temples of Silence* (Indian River: Arcana Editions, 1993).

22 Written documentation of the WSP recordings is available online at www.sfu.ca/sonic-studio. Access to the sound files is available upon request to Professor Barry Truax at Simon Fraser University. Details for this first Vancouver recording (reel 1) can be found at the World Soundscape Project Tape Library, "Reel 1," Vancouver/BC Collection, http://www.sfu.ca/sonic-studio/srs/Van1.html.

23 This WSP recording can be heard in the Vancouver collection, reel 100, side A, track 3. World Soundscape Project Tape Library, "Reel 100," Vancouver/BC Collection, http://www.sfu.ca/sonic-studio/srs/Van100.html.

24 This is one of the many ways in which sound recording affects our perception of real-world space, as discussed by Rick Altman, "The Material Heterogeneity of Recorded Sound," in *Sound Theory, Sound Practice*, ed. Rick Altman (New York: Routledge, 1992), 15–31.

25 Now, it can be argued that such a highly rendered approach to the construction of the film's soundscape might reflect perceptual reality better than location recordings, particularly in the context of the narrative situation that finds the character actively interrogating his environment with shifting attention. Film sound designers have long been in search of strategies for creating psychological realism that can account for the kind of filtering we all do within our sonic environments, the kind of selection that microphones do not do on their own. This is why Michel Chion argues that location recording and studio rendering are equally capable of providing either a realistic or expressionistic

portrait of space. However, as a document of a particular spatio-temporal location, the image track in *Hastings Street* is not of the same order as the soundtrack. Chion, *Audio-Vision,* 95–6.

26 The siren can be heard on reel 1, side A, track 2.

27 This conversation can be heard on reel 106, side B, track 4. World Soundscape Project Tape Library, "Reel 106," Vancouver/BC Collection, http://www.sfu.ca/sonic-studio/srs/Van106.html.

28 Karin Bijsterveld calls for such critical assessment of the WSP's work in her book *Mechanical Sound: Technology, Culture, and Public Problems of Noise in the Twentieth Century* (Cambridge, MA: MIT Press, 2008), 42, and is the substance of my broader postdoctoral research into the sound of Vancouver-based film and media currently in progress with Barry Truax at Simon Fraser University.

29 Quoted in Á. Ibrányi-Kiss, "Filmmaking West Coast Style: Jack Darcus," in *Canadian Film Reader,* ed. Joyce Nelson and Seth Feldman (Toronto: P. Martin Associates Limited, 1977), 269.

30 See David Spaner, *Dreaming in the Rain,* and Diane Burgess, "Charting the Course of the Pacific New Wave," *Cineaction* no. 61 (2003): 29.

31 See Sarah Matheson, "Projecting Placelessness: Industrial Television and the 'Authentic' Canadian City," in *Contracting out Hollywood: Runaway Productions and Foreign Location Shooting,* ed. Greg Elmer and Mike Gasher, 117–39 (Maryland: Rowman and Littlefield, 2005).

32 A particularly good example is when Krycek calls the Cigarette Smoking Man to inform him that the latter's attempt on the former's life had failed ("The Blessing Way," 1995). The restrained tension and hushed anger in his voice is very similar in performance style to Lea's interpretation of Charlie in the phone call to his mother in *Hastings Street.*

33 See Spaner, *Dreaming in the Rain,* chapter 9.

34 Details of the new *Hastings Street* feature directed by Andrew Moxham can be found at CineCoup, "Hastings Street," http://www.cinecoup.com/hastings-street.

14 PRESERVING EPHEMERAL ABORIGINAL FILMS AND VIDEOS

THE ARCHIVAL PRACTICES OF VTAPE AND ISUMATV

Katherine Quanz

> Unlike the freedom to express Aboriginal individuals are accustomed to, society as a whole has stifled a powerful voice ... until now. For the past 3 years I've had the honour of watching an incredible collection of Aboriginal cultures breath [*sic*] life. By that I mean; [*sic*] films and videos created by Aboriginal peoples about Aboriginal people (a relatively new concept).
>
> Cynthia Lickers-Sage, Vtape's Aboriginal Outreach Coordinator, 1998[1]

ABORIGINAL FILMMAKING IN Canada underwent a massive transformation in the early 1990s when a series of programs was developed to promote the production of media by Aboriginal peoples.[2] This movement changed the definition of "Aboriginal film" from films about Aboriginals to films created by Aboriginals. While the National Film Board (NFB) of Canada's involvement in the movement through the creation of Studio One has been well-documented elsewhere, equally important, but less well known, are Vtape and ISUMATV's efforts to collect, preserve, and exhibit Aboriginal ephemeral films and videos. By overlooking the contributions of these two organizations to Indigenous filmmaking in Canada, inaccurate conclusions regarding the prominence of the NFB within the Aboriginal film community have been formed. For example, Maria de Rosa touts the more than twenty films produced by the Aboriginal Filmmaking Program at the NFB between 1996 and 2000 as significant achievement.[3] While this was indeed impressive, during that same period Vtape collected over eighty Indigenous films and videos, yet this collection has received minimal scholarly attention. An exploration of Vtape's and ISUMATV's role as archives of Aboriginal experimental and ephemeral films and videos, areas that are doubly marginalized in their status as both Indigenous and ephemeral, corrects this oversight in scholarship of Canadian Aboriginal filmmaking.[4]

Although neither Vtape and ISUMATV can be classified as film archives in the traditional sense, as the first is a distributor and the second is a web portal, both function as exemplary repositories for Aboriginal media. They are exemplary in that they both target works produced by a specific population and do not actively curate the works in their respective collections. Without either of these organizations functioning as de facto archives, the majority of the works in their Aboriginal collections would not otherwise be preserved and there would be no central collection of independent Canadian Aboriginal produced moving images; additionally, both Vtape and ISUMATV have adopted practices to make the works accessible and to insert Indigenous filmmaking into the ethos of Canadian cinema. They have worked to broaden awareness of Aboriginal filmmaking in Canada and expand the focus of Aboriginal filmmaking and preservation beyond the NFB.

ABORIGINAL FILMMAKING AT THE NATIONAL FILM BOARD

The NFB has a long history of producing Aboriginal films. As early as the 1940s, documentaries on Aboriginal cultures in Canada were created from an ethnographic point of view.[5] Noel Starblanket summarizes these NFB produced documentaries as constructions by "*outsiders* looking in on the situation" (emphasis in original).[6] This changed in 1968, when the board trained a crew of all Aboriginal young adults to produce Aboriginal documentaries as part of its Challenge for Change program. The NFB held two training sessions for Indian crews from 1968 to 1970 and from 1971 to 1973.[7] While this resulted in the production of a handful of films, the NFB did not continue the training program or create an autonomous unit for Indigenous filmmakers, and as a result many of the filmmakers pursued other career paths outside of media arts.[8] Following this initial training period, the NFB had no formal plan for Aboriginal film until it launched Studio One, an Aboriginal production unit, in 1991.[9]

Studio One was founded on the same premise on which the NFB had developed Studio D, "the world's first production unit dedicated to women."[10] The creation of the unit was partly the result of the efforts put forth by the newly formed Aboriginal Film and Video Arts Alliance (AFVAA). This group was formed with the goal of promoting Aboriginal films made by Aboriginal filmmakers in Canada. To address AFVAA concerns for the adequate training of Indigenous filmmakers, Studio One developed a three-part, two-year program that included apprenticeships and training, the production of vignettes, followed by documentary film production.[11] In 1996, Studio One became the Aboriginal Filmmaking

Program, which had an increased budget and a wider production policy. In 1997, Shirley Cheechoo directed the first dramatic short for the studio, entitled *Silent Tears*. Maria de Rosa highlights the important contributions of this studio to Aboriginal filmmaking in Canada: "Without a doubt, Studio One, which has now developed into the Aboriginal Filmmaking Program at the NFB, has been a catalyst for a renaissance that is taking place in the Aboriginal film and television community – a renaissance of storytelling ... stories are finally being told by Aboriginal peoples, for Aboriginal peoples, *in their own voices*" (emphasis in original).[12] While Studio One's impact was indeed widespread, it was not the only initiative developed during the 1990s to promote Aboriginal productions in Canada. Equally significant to the renaissance of Aboriginal production of the 2000s was the partnership between AFVAA and Vtape.

VTAPE AND THE FORMATION OF A CENTRALIZED COLLECTION

While Studio One at the NFB was working to support filmmakers, some members of the Aboriginal community felt that the NFB was not meeting the needs of filmmakers. As de Rosa explains: "Some Aboriginal filmmakers felt the Studio was ghetto-izing filmmakers and not addressing the diversity of the Aboriginal film and video community across the country."[13] In 1994, Zachary Longboy approached Vtape on behalf of AFVAA Ontario with the goal of forming a partnership to promote and distribute independent Indigenous films and videos.[14] Vtape's distribution director Wanda Vanderstoop remembers that Vtape was selected to partner with the Aboriginal Film and Video Alliance because of the distributor's non-institutional practices.[15] As an established not-for-profit artist-based distributor founded in 1980, Vtape provided stability for AFVAA's collection. Furthermore, Vtape's mandate complemented AFVAA's objectives. Run by artists for artists, Vtape's primary goal was to promote video art and to compensate artists fairly for their work. Additionally, artists who worked with Vtape maintained full ownership of their work and could have their films and videos with multiple distributors, such as Video In Video Out in Vancouver and Videopool in Winnipeg.[16]

Once Vtape decided to distribute Aboriginal works, it quickly became an important vehicle for Indigenous artists. Its first step was to hire an Aboriginal outreach coordinator to create a centralized database of Aboriginal works. This position was briefly filled by Longboy, but when he moved out West Cynthia Lickers-Sage, who had been working with AFVAA

Ontario, took over the role. During her tenure at Vtape, Lickers-Sage oversaw the publication of multiple catalogues publicizing the collection, the launch of the imagineNATIVE Film Festival in 2000, and the programming for the second season of *imagineNATIVE: The Television Series* on the Aboriginal Peoples Television Network (APTN) in 2000.[17] All of these initiatives increased awareness of the collection and promoted independent Aboriginal filmmaking. Even though AFVAA was dissolved in 1999 as a result of government cutbacks and Lickers-Sage has moved on to other ventures Vtape continues to build the collection and preserve the works.[18]

The Aboriginal collection is the only specialized collection in Vtape's holdings. While Vtape also has a significant body of works that address sexuality and LGBT issues, these works have not been separated to create a second specialization, even though they form a larger portion of Vtape's overall collection than the Indigenous works. By only having one special collection, Vtape has signalled its devotion to Aboriginal works. Vtape's dedication to this collection is also apparent in its special projects designed to promote Aboriginal media, such as the launch of imagineNATIVE and the Aboriginal Digital Access Project discussed later in this chapter. The emphasis placed on the collection enabled Vtape to become the largest distributor of Indigenous films and videos in the world.[19]

THE LAUNCH OF A DIGITAL ABORIGINAL ARCHIVE: ISUMATV

ISUMATV is the brainchild of Igloolik Isuma Productions, best known for its independently produced *Fast Runner Trilogy*. This collective of Inuit video artists rose to international acclaim with the release of *Atanarjuat The Fast Runner* in 2001 (the first film in the trilogy was followed by *The Journals of Knud Rasmussen* in 2006 and *Before Tomorrow* in 2009). The film received accolades at Cannes, the Edinburgh International Film Festival, and the Toronto International Film Festival, among others. Prior to its international breakthrough, the collective produced several series of experimental documentaries, which were distributed by Vtape. With its newfound popularity, Igloolik Isuma Productions discovered that audiences were seeking new modes of "distribution" through the Internet.

Launched in 2007 as an "interactive network of Inuit and Indigenous multimedia," ISUMATV provides artists with Internet distribution.[20] ISUMATV quickly became the preferred portal for Indigenous productions in a multitude of languages with films continuously uploaded to the site by self-identified Aboriginal filmmakers. Fifteen months after its launch, the website had reached 7.5 million hits, fulfilling its mandate to increase the visibility of Indigenous filmmaking.[21] ISUMATV serves as an ever-expanding digital collection of Aboriginal media that is globally accessible.

Isuma's new method of distribution came into existence when Norman Cohen, a filmmaker with Igloolik Isuma Productions, checked to see how many people were illegally downloading *Atanarjuat The Fast Runner* at ten o'clock in the morning. He found that twelve people were in the process of stealing the film at that particular moment, and since films shared illegally over the internet are often compressed at higher bitrates than a standard DVD's MPEG-2 compression setting, much of the image quality would be lost.[22] While the film was reaching an audience because of its success at various film festivals, easy illegal downloading limited profits for the production company. To counter this, Cohen and the rest of the Igloolik Isuma Productions team devised a solution: create a place where audiences could stream Indigenous films in high resolution at no cost, with all the credit and distribution information at their fingertips. Additionally, Isuma made *Fast Runner Trilogy* available in high definition as a pay-what-you-can or "fair trade download" option. By taking advantage of the Internet, Isuma developed a new way to distribute, exhibit, and archive Aboriginal works. This model, however, failed to produce new revenue streams and Igloolik Isuma Productions was forced to declare bankruptcy in the summer of 2011. Now run as an independent entity through government sponsorship, ISUMATV continues its regular operations.[23]

Both ISUMATV and Vtape's collections of Aboriginal media can be viewed as archives with an agenda to preserve and promote Indigenous films and videos. In the remainder of this chapter, I will examine how these two collections are exemplary archives for works that would otherwise most likely be lost or forgotten. Nevertheless, these centralized collections, which indiscriminately accept and provide access to works by Indigenous creators, are not without problems. First, though the collections accept all moving image media by Aboriginal artists, those artists curate the collections by deciding which works to submit or upload. Second, both organizations endeavour to provide access to the works in their collections, but access to the videos is limited through archival practices: Vtape restricts access to the collection through a password-protected website in order to maintain control of the works, while ISUMATV's rapid growth has resulted in the burying of videos in its collection, with older and less popular videos hidden from view. Despite these issues, Vtape and

ISUMATV preserve a doubly marginalized group of moving images and in so doing, maintain the legacy of Aboriginal filmmaking in Canada.

CREATING A COLLECTION THROUGH FILMMAKER CURATION

Of critical importance to the practice of film archiving are debates over complete inclusion versus curation, as archives generally have inadequate budgets with which to acquire their desired films and limited space in which to store them. Due to such restrictions, archivists adopt strict selection criteria to ensure that the films in their collection are adequately maintained. For example, MoMA's Film Library, the British Film Institute's National Film Archives, and the Library of Congress's National Film Registry have all established curatorial practices with committees that select and propose films for inclusion in the collection, and exclude others.[24] For these archives, this has typically meant that a set of criteria was laid out to be followed by a committee. Ernest Lindgren, the head of the British Film Institute's National Film Archives, reportedly views selection as essential to the creation of the archive: "When it came to acquiring films, Lindgren did not see a selection policy as something to be grudgingly accepted because there was no possibility of taking everything. Far from it: he believed in selectivity as a principle, would have seen little point in an omnivorous archive."[25] For the majority of archivists, selecting a limited number of films and videos for preservation is a necessary component of archival practice.

As the film archiving movement grew in the 1970s and 1980s, the majority of national film archives developed policies to collect and preserve their national products.[26] The preservation of national films became a priority in part because UNESCO acknowledged that if the national archives did not preserve the film, no one would.[27] The curation practices of the majority of national archives, however, underscore a bias toward the preservation of narrative and documentary feature-length films, and include only a limited number of experimental, industrial, and amateur films.[28] The exclusion of these films by national film archives has left room for the development of smaller archives, such as regional, city, specialized, "programming," and university film archives; this exclusion has also spawned the orphan film movement in the United States.[29] While neither Vtape nor ISUMATV can be considered archives in the traditional sense, they can be classified as a cross between specialized and programming archives, since they focus on collecting Aboriginal productions and creating avenues for the general public to view them. Importantly, Vtape and ISUMATV house the only collections focused on Indigenous moving images in Canada and form the world's largest repositories of Aboriginal-produced media.[30]

Equally significantly, both organizations have adopted all-inclusive policies for collecting films or videos created by Aboriginal-identified filmmakers. Vtape's acceptance of all Aboriginal films and videos runs counter to its regular practices, as due to the costs and time involved in adding an artist to its catalogue Vtape otherwise only accepts works from established video artists. In relation to Aboriginal media, however, Vtape accepts films and videos from first-time filmmakers, so that the works can be documented and protected.[31] Similarly, Vtape's general collection is focused on video-based media, leaving film-based works to the Canadian Filmmakers Distribution Centre. However, for Aboriginal works Vtape does not distinguish between media, and catalogues films alongside videos in order to create a centralized collection.[32]

Even though Vtape has an open policy for Aboriginal films and videos, Vtape's general collection is focused on experimental videos and its Aboriginal collection has followed this trend. Since its inception in 1980, Vtape has primarily distributed contemporary media art with an emphasis on video-based media. This means that the vast majority of the works Vtape distributes are experimental, in that the videos work against mainstream cinema by playing with the form and content presented in the work.[33] Despite Vtape's openness to accepting all Indigenous moving image works, its Aboriginal collection remains heavily oriented toward the experimental. Vtape's history with video art appears to have drawn like-minded artists to the collection, as artists with other foci have found different homes for their works.[34] Even though Vtape provides no curation to the collection to create a comprehensive body of Aboriginal media, its reputation acts as a curatorial guide.

Vtape's focus on Aboriginal independent media has attracted a number of high profile Aboriginal artists to the collection, such as Shelley Niro, Zacharias Kunuk, and Dana Claxton. These three artists, in particular, have pioneered non-documentary Aboriginal filmmaking in Canada. As the first Indigenous narrative feature-length filmmaker in Canada, Niro paved the way for Aboriginal artists with *Honey Moccasin* (1998), which combines genres such as the detective film, melodrama, cable access television show, comedy, and experimental film. For instance, embedded in this multi-vocal work is a piece of performance art and an experimental film made by the lead character's daughter, Mabel. The first piece demonstrates the degree to which the film's villain, Zachary John, has ostracized himself from the community, as he openly dislikes Mabel's performance by referring to it as "a little on the weird side ... such depressing stuff." Mabel's second piece, a short experimental film entitled *Inukshuk*, reintegrates Zachary into the community as he plays the lead role. After the screening, his father, who was previously embarrassed by Zachary's actions, embraces him. By ending *Honey Moccasin* with Mabel's film school experimental film, Niro highlights the manner in which filmmaking brings Aboriginal communities together. This ending also acknowledges the rapid growth in the practice of experimental film by the new generation of Aboriginal filmmakers in Canada. Her feature was followed in 2001 by Kunuk's *Atanajurat*, the first Inuit-produced feature length narrative. Like *Honey Moccasin*, *Atanajurat* contains elements of experimental practices, such as long, reflective pauses not usually found in narrative features. While it is not explicitly classified as experimental, aspects of this video, such as the long takes, jump cuts, and images without synchronized sound, depict Igoolik Isuma Productions's adherence to the traditions of Inuit culture and video art, both of which fall outside of mainstream production conventions.[35] For example, a four-minute section comprised of long takes without sync sound occurs during Atanajurat's separation from his wife, Atuat, to represent their connection across the distance and over time. Finally, Claxton focuses on the production of experimental and performance art. Her work challenges mainstream concepts of "Indianness" and Western narratives of historical events. For example, in *Gun Play* (2004), Claxton questions the violence of the appropriation of the image of the Indian Chief on a toy gun, and in *I Want to Know Why* (1994), she investigates cultural genocide in her own family by highlighting the traumatic events that led to the premature deaths of her female relatives, such as her great-grandmother's forced walk to Canada with Sitting Bull. In acknowledgement of her contribution to the arts, Claxton has received a VIVA award and an Eiteljorg fellowship sponsored by the Ford Foundation. Niro, Kunuk, and Claxton's films and videos have raised the profile of Aboriginal filmmaking in Canada and have demonstrated an alternative to documentaries produced by the NFB. Even though this is just a tiny sample of the breadth of work in Vtape's collection, the three artists' range of work foregrounds Indigenous film and video's strength and focus on experimental modes of expression.

While Vtape stretches the concepts of the archive by functioning as both an archive and a distributor, the explosion of digital-video websites, such as YouTube, has further challenged traditional notions of the archive. Similarly, user uploads drive ISUMATV's content, and the only requirement is that the filmmaker must identify as Aboriginal and hold the rights to the video. ISUMATV allows users to upload their own content to the site and create their own mini-archive and exhibition channel for anyone to access. Since the site's wide accessibility diminishes the videos' profitability, ISUMATV primarily appears to attract ephemeral films. These films range from professionally produced documentaries and experimental works that are no longer in high demand and thus no longer generate revenue for the filmmaker to timely activist documentaries, amateur productions such as video recordings of class presentations and workshops, recordings of live performances, and home movies. Additionally, ISUMATV uses technology to connect people. For example, workshops and conferences can be taped and instantly streamed to the Internet to allow those unable to attend in person to watch in real time. For instance, ISUMATV live-streamed the closing screening of the 2011 imagineNATIVE Film + Media Arts Festival in Toronto, complete with a Skype setup for the question and answer period so that those unable to attend could participate. This availability is especially important for artists in remote areas, as access to these resources would otherwise be cost prohibitive. However, this easy access appears to have resulted in ISUMATV becoming a repository for videos with cultural currency rather than capital value. By this I mean that while the videos on the website do not generate revenue for the filmmakers, they preserve Aboriginal culture by documenting important events, traditions, and interviews. Even though ISUMATV set out to be an alternative avenue for the distribution of Aboriginal media already in circulation, it seems to have evolved into a repository for ephemeral works that would no doubt otherwise be lost.

Whether or not a film or video appears in either Vtape or ISUMATV's collection is driven by the filmmakers, and as such the collections are "curated" by filmmakers who opt to find the best venue for their work. Thus, Vtape's Aboriginal collection mirrors the organization's focus on experimental video, while ISUMATV's videos tend to highlight daily life, language preservation efforts, activism, interviews with elders, and traditional teachings.

EASY ACCESS AS A FORM OF PRESERVATION

As digitization has made film preservation an even more pressing issue within the archival field, archivists have developed competing approaches to building, maintaining, and managing archives. On a basic level, two opposing approaches to preservation characterize the spectrum, and each had an early champion: Ernest Lindgren, head of the British Film Institute's National Film Archives, limited access to the films in the collection to maintain them, while Henri Langlois, director of the Cinémathèque Française, screened the films in his collection frequently so they would be remembered.[36] Since Lindgren's policies for film preservation formed standard archival practices, Clyde Jeavons and Penelope Houston argue that his approach ultimately triumphed as the strict policies for preservation yield a larger, more stable collection in the long term.[37] However, the moving images in question in this study, independent and amateur Aboriginal films and videos, typically fall outside of the domain of established Canadian film archives such as the National Archives of Canada or Cinémathèque québécoise. As a result, the collection and preservation of these works has been left to nontraditional archives, namely an artist-based distributor and a web-based collection. In the context of distributors acting in a dual role as archivist and a web-based platform functioning as a collective archive, Langlois's approach of showing and sharing films and videos ends up being privileged over preservation through restricted access. For both of these organizations, making works accessible to viewers through film festivals and the Internet is the dominant form of preserving both the works and their messages.

Vtape became an exhibitor in 1998, four years after starting the Aboriginal collection when Cynthia Lickers-Sage, Vtape's Aboriginal outreach coordinator, established the imagineNATIVE film festival to promote the works in Vtape's Aboriginal collection; imagineNATIVE was started in response to the difficulties that Vtape had in finding venues to exhibit the Aboriginal short videos. During the 1990s, two Aboriginal film festivals had emerged in Canada, IMAGENation in Vancouver (1998 to 2006) and Terres en vues in Montreal (1990 to present), but both primarily screened feature-length films with a focus on documentaries rather than experimental works.[38] In order to ensure its films and videos found an audience, Vtape launched the imagineNATIVE Film Festival in its small screening room in downtown Toronto.[39] Even though the festival quickly grew into an independent organization, Vtape maintains a strong partnership with the festival and has organized special curated programs from its collection, such as "Culture Shock" (2008), "Aboriginal Screen Culture: Celebrating 10 Years of imagineNATIVE" (2009), and "Unsettling Sex" (2012). In addition to the film festival, Lickers-Sage also produced a catalogue of Indigenous moving images to highlight Vtape's collection and the *imagineNATIVE* television show for APTN, and the thirteen episodes of its second season were partially comprised of videos from Vtape's collection.[40] By actively seeking out an audience for its collection, Vtape has raised awareness of its films and videos, attracted new artists, and increased the profile of its collection and Aboriginal media in Canada. The creation of venues to exhibit non-documentary Indigenous films in Canada secured and promoted Vtape's collection as the videos became known to the public.

In 2012, Vtape updated access to its collection by launching the Aboriginal Digital Access Project. With this project, an increasing portion of the Aboriginal collection has been uploaded to a password-protected website for temporary access by curators, scholars, and programmers. Lisa Steele, Vtape's creative director, describes the important work carried out by Vtape archivist Kristie MacDonald:

> To date, over 300 titles by Indigenous artists produced from 1978 right up to the current year have been entered onto the Vtape preview website ... For the first time, programmers in Australia or Taiwan or Vancouver can have access to full-length versions of Aboriginal titles in the Vtapes collection on their own computers ... Utilizing her pre-existing knowledge of video formats, migration, and condition assessment, Kristie worked independently to contact artists, patch the racks, upload content and distribute press releases.[41]

While a large section of the collection is available online, Vtape strictly monitors access to the site to maintain control of how the works are used and to prevent theft. Limited online access is also vital as many film festivals have a policy of not accepting works that are readily accessible on the Internet.[42] Even though Vtape has made this digital archive available to interested parties free of charge, admission is reminiscent of the restrictive access policies other archives implement to preserve their collections, as prospective users must provide Vtape with their credentials to gain access for a limited time.

On the other hand, ISUMATV, which was based on the YouTube model, gives users full and open access. In a discussion of YouTube, Rick Prelinger contends that while the site is not technically an archive, the general population has viewed it as such since its inception in 2005: "YouTube might as well be an archive; that in the public mind it is not simply an archive but an ideal form of archive; and that it problematizes and threatens the canonical missions of established moving-image archives throughout the world [*sic*]."[43] Since YouTube created the illusion that every media clip is only a click away, web users have come to expect easy access to media and ISUMATV meets this expectation for Aboriginal media.

By supplying direct and easy access to videos of interviews, performances, and daily life, ISUMATV preserves the memory of these events. The use of video to protect cultural memory has been one of the fundamental goals of the Isuma collective.[44] Igoolik Isuma Productions's early videos, such as *Qaggiq* (1989), *Nunaqpa* (1991), and *Saputi* (1993), fundamentally aimed to record traditional Inuit customs and stories.[45] By providing easy access to the videos, ISUMATV maintains cultural memory through the retelling of traditional stories, the depiction of traditional ways of life, and the recounting of personal and cultural traumatic events (such as residential schools).

The plethora of videos available on ISUMATV, however, hampers accessibility. Like YouTube, ISUMATV organizes videos based on the name of the video, keywords, tags, and description, all provided by the producer. Viewers navigate the site by selecting tags (which include language, genre, area of interest, and location) or by searching for key terms, titles, or filmmakers. While these labels help to organize the uploaded videos into distinct categories, the broadness of the terms and the sheer number of available videos make the site difficult to traverse, not unlike YouTube. Videos can easily become buried in the site; after a few years, some videos can only be retrieved by searching for a work's title or filmmaker. While these works are technically still accessible, they are effectively relegated to obscurity. The lack of strict organizational practices, combined with the continuous stream of new works, has resulted in the website becoming a maze of information for would-be viewers.

The concealment of videos within the website points to the ephemeral nature of web-based archives. With the rapid proliferation of media, user curation is beginning to challenge traditional archival practice. Giovanna

Fossati reflects on the implications of sites such as YouTube for the role of the curator: "Film Archives curators are now being confronted with a community of users who are taking the selection process upon themselves … the chaperone mode [of curation] is no longer the only appropriate way to provide access to audiovisual content, as a community of users is eager to establish an alternative and more open access mode."[46] Fossati illuminates how the growth in online video content has given rise to website users who act as the curators of the content they watch. He goes on to advocate for a dual model: a curator "chaperoning" users by suggesting key videos and unrestricted user exploration. Even though ISUMATV has attempted to curate its collection through user-created channels, viewers are left to manoeuvre their own way through the mass of material available on the site. Access to the works is freely granted, but there is minimal guidance for viewers on what to watch.

ISUMATV and Vtape have both created methods for providing access to their respective collections; however, their approaches to granting access to digitized material are fundamentally different. For ISUMATV, the Internet allows for the preservation of traditions, important cultural events, teachings by elders, forgotten works of art, and records of daily life. Unrestricted access to video recordings keeps these works alive in cultural memory, but the sheer number of videos paradoxically hampers accessibility. For Vtape, restricted access is essential to preserving the video creators' rights. Although this demands greater resources at the front end, it protects artists' intellectual property. While access to the works through film festivals, television programs, and password-protected Internet sites promotes the films and videos while maintaining control over their use, restrictions result in a smaller audience.

CONCLUSION

Even though Vtape and ISUMATV did not set out to be archives, they both contribute to the maintenance of the heritage of otherwise ephemeral Aboriginal cinema through the creation of collections with inclusive selection policies and vigorous exhibition schemes designed to embed the videos and films into the history of Canadian cinema. The manner in which both Vtape and ISUMATV spotlight Aboriginal media for preservation in centralized collections has been vital to the promotion of the independent Indigenous cinema. It is important to note that both organizations rely on ongoing government funding to maintain their collections – Vtape is supported through the Canada Council for the Arts, the Ontario Arts Council, and the Toronto Arts Council, and ISUMATV is sponsored by the Department of Canadian Heritage through the Canadian Culture Online Strategy and Telefilm Canada. While government funding is essential to both not-for-profit organizations, these funding schemes change over time and are not always reliable, as demonstrated by the dissolution of AFVAA in 1999 after cuts to its funding. While there are limits to the collections, if these organizations were not devoting significant resources to the collection, preservation, and exhibition of Aboriginal audiovisual expression, the majority of these works would be lost.

Scholars who work in this area have often overlooked the significant impact made by these independent organizations in favour of highlighting the contributions made by the NFB. By taking into account this rich history of Aboriginal productions outside of the NFB, a vast legacy of Canadian Aboriginal videos and films covering a wide variety of topics and genres can inform a new understanding of Indigenous media in Canada. For instance, Vtape's and ISUMATV's collections have fostered a community of Indigenous filmmakers by providing outlets for the films and videos to be exhibited. While Aboriginal filmmakers working at the NFB, such as Alanis Obomsawin, Loretta Todd, and Gil Cardinal, were breaking new ground in redefining Aboriginal cinema, they were not working alone, but rather were part of a growing community of Aboriginal filmmakers in Canada seeking to have their voices heard. The renaissance of Indigenous filmmaking in the 2000s, to which Maria de Rosa refers, needs be attributed in part to the network of filmmakers established by Vtape. Additional research into the relationships among the NFB, Vtape, and ISUMATV will further illuminate the factors behind the rapid growth of Aboriginal cinema in Canada. While the history of Aboriginal cinema in Canada is relatively short, over the past two decades Indigenous filmmakers have revolutionized concepts of what Indigenous cinema might be. The creation of centralized archives has played an essential role in the growth of Aboriginal cinema by documenting the movement and preserving the works. Without these two organizations functioning as de facto archives, these works would not be preserved and the history of this overlooked component of the Aboriginal cinema movement in Canada would be lost. However, as the organizations are reliant on government funds, the future of Vtape's and ISUMATV's collections remains unstable.

ACKNOWLEDGMENTS

The research for this chapter was funded by the Film Studies Association of Canada's 2009 Gerald Pratley Award. The author would like to thank Zoë Druick, Gerda Cammaer, Ute Lischke, Katherine Spring, and the anonymous readers for their comments on earlier versions of this chapter. A special thank you to Wanda Vanderstoop, Erik Martinson, Cynthia Lickers-Sage, and Vtape for providing interviews and access to the films and videos.

NOTES

1 Cynthia Lickers, "imagineNATIVE: Images Create Stories: Or Is It the Other Way Around?" in *imagineNATIVE: Aboriginally Produced Film & Video*, ed. Cynthia Lickers (Toronto: Vtape, 1998), iii.

2 In this chapter I use the terms Aboriginal and Indigenous interchangeably to encompass First Nations, Inuit, Métis, and non-status Indians.

3 Maria de Rosa, "Studio One: Of Storytellers and Stories," in *North of Everything: English-Canadian Cinema since 1980*, eds. William Beard and Jerry White (Edmonton: University of Alberta Press, 2002), 337.

4 This chapter relies on interviews by the author and information published on Vtape's and ISUMATV websites due to the dearth of published materials on these two organizations.

5 Jennifer L. Gauthier, "Dismantling the Master's House: The Feminist Fourth Cinema Documentaries of Alanis Obosawin and Loretta Todd," in *Native Americans on Film: Conversations, Teaching, and Theory*, ed. M. Elise Marubbio and Eric L. Buffalohead (Lexington: University Press of Kentucky, 2013), 89.

6 Noel Starblanket, "A Voice for Canadian Indians: An Indian Film Crew (1968)," in *Challenge for Change: Activist Documentary at the National Film Board of Canada*, eds. Thomas Waugh, Michael Brendan Baker, and Ezra Winton (Montreal: McGill-Queen's University Press, 2010), 38.

7 Michelle Stewart, "*Cree Hunters of Mistassini*: Challenge for Change and Aboriginal Rights," in *Challenge for Change: Activist Documentary at the National Film Board of Canada*, eds. Thomas Waugh, Michael Brendan Baker, and Ezra Winton (Montreal: McGill-Queen's University Press, 2010), 181.

8 de Rosa, "Studio One," 330; and Stewart, "*Cree Hunters of Mistassini*," 181.

9 de Rosa, "Studio One," 331.

10 Ibid.

11 Ibid., 332.

12 Ibid., 329.

13 Ibid., 335.

14 Lisa Steele, "First Views a Partnership in Progress: Vtape and AFVAA," in *imagineNATIVE: Aboriginally Produced Film & Video*, ed. Cynthia Lickers (Toronto: Vtape, 1998), iv.

15 Wanda Vanderstoop, Vtape's distribution director, in discussion with the author, 21 April 2009.

16 For further information on video distributors in Canada see Jennifer Abbott, *Making Video "In": The Contested Ground of Alternative Video on the West Coast* (Vancouver: Video in Studios, 2000); Jenny Lion, ed., *Magnetic North* (Minneapolis University of Minnesota Press, Video Pool Inc, and Walker Art Center, 2000).

17 APTN, the first Aboriginal television station in the world, began broadcasting across Canada on 1 September 1999 as a CRTC-mandated cable station. For more information on APTN see Valerie Alia, *Un/Covering the North: News, Media and Aboriginal People* (Vancouver: University of British Columbia Press, 1999); Jennifer David, *Original People, Original Television: The Launching of the Aboriginal Peoples Television Network* (Ottawa: Debwe Communications, 2012); Lorna Roth, *Something New in the Air: The Story of First Peoples Television Broadcasting in Canada* (Montreal: McGill-Queen's University Press, 2005); Hafsteinsson Sigurjón Baldur and Marian Bredin, eds., *Indigenous Screen Cultures in Canada* (Winnipeg: University of Manitoba Press, 2010).

18 AFVAA production-based activities, such as workshops and training programs, have been incorporated into the Banff Centre for the Arts Indigenous Arts Program.

19 Vanderstoop, in discussion with the author, 21 April 2009.

20 ISUMATV, "About Us," accessed 22 June 2013, http://www.isuma.tv/about-us.

21 Nunavut, Independent Television Network, "NITV on ISUMATV" (Igloolik: ISUMATV, 2009), 4.

22 ISUMATV, "Distribution Panel," online video, 21:50, from a live stream recorded in 2008, accessed 22 June 2013, http://www.isuma.tv/lo/en/imaginenative08/distribution-panel.

23 CBC News, "Igloolik Isuma Productions Going out of Business," 8 July 2011, http://www.cbc.ca/news/arts/story/2011/07/08/isuma-productions-business.html.

24 Caroline Frick, *Saving Cinema: The Politics of Preservation* (New York: Oxford University Press, 2011), 4–5.

25 Penelope Houston, *Keepers of the Frame: The Film Archives* (London: BFI Publishing, 1994), 40.

26 Frick, *Saving Cinema*, 89, 111; Houston, *Keepers of the Frame*, 41.

27 Frick, *Saving Cinema*, 111.

28 Ibid., 179.

29 Paolo Cherchi Usai, *Burning Passions: An Introduction to the Study of Silent Cinema* (London: British Film Institute, 1994), 28–30.

30 Vanderstoop, in discussion with the author, 21 April 2009.

31 Ibid.

32 Ibid.

33 For more information on experimental cinema, see Michael Hoolboom, *Inside the Pleasure Dome: Fringe Film in Canada* (Toronto: Coach House Books, 2001); A.L. Rees, *A History of Experimental Film and Video: From Canonical Avant-Garde to Contemporary British Practice* (London: BFI Publishing, 1999); P. Adams Sitney, *Visionary Film the American Avant-Garde, 1943–2000*, 3rd ed. (Oxford: Oxford University Press, 2002); and Michael Zryd, "A Report on Canadian

Experimental Film Institutions, 1980–2000," in *North of Everything: English-Canadian Cinema since 1980*, eds. William Beard and Jerry White (Edmonton: University of Alberta Press, 2002).

34 Cynthia Lickers-Sage, Vtape's former Aboriginal outreach coordinator, in discussion with the author, 24 May 2013.

35 Michael Robert Evans, *Isuma: Inuit Video Art* (Montreal: McGill-Queen's University Press, 2008), 6–7, 70–2.

36 Frick, *Saving Cinema*, 170; Houston, *Keepers of the Frame*, 6.

37 Houston, *Keepers of the Frame*, 6; Clyde Jeavons, "The Moving Image: Subject or Object?," *Journal of Film Preservation* 73, no. 4 (2007): 27.

38 Vanderstoop, in discussion with the author, 21 April 2009.

39 Vanderstoop, in discussion with the author, 21 April 2009; and Lickers-Sage, in discussion with the author, 24 May 2013.

40 Vtape, "History of Organization," accessed 22 June 2013, http://www.vtape.org/contact.htm.

41 Lisa Steele, "Vtape's Aboriginal Digital Access Project," in *Aboriginal Digital Access Project*, ed. Vtape (Toronto: Vtape, 2012), 1.

42 For example, Kevin Lee Burton wanted to upload his video *Nikamowin* (*Song* 2007) to ISUMATV, but Vanderstoop advised Burton to wait. The video was then selected as part of Canada's Top Ten Short Films of 2008 and was acquired by the National Gallery of Canada in 2011. If he had uploaded his film to ISUMATV, it would have ineligible for inclusion in the Canada's Top Short Film program and the value of the work would have been diminished.

43 Rick Prelinger, "The Appearance of Archives," in *The YouTube Reader*, eds. Pelle Snickars and Patrick Vonderau (Stockholm: National Library of Sweden, 2009), 268.

44 Evans, *Isuma*, 26–7.

45 Ibid., 22–3.

46 Giovanna Fossati, "YouTube as a Mirror Maze," in *The YouTube Reader*, eds. Pelle Snickars and Patrick Vonderau (Stockholm: National Library of Sweden, 2009), 459.

15 PRESERVING/BURNING
KARL LEMIEUX'S FILM PERFORMANCES

André Habib

> les films sont
> des marchandises
> et il faut brûler les films
> je l'avais dit à Langlois
> mais attention
> avec le feu intérieur
> matière et mémoire
> l'art est comme l'incendie
> il naît
> de ce qu'il brûle[1]
>
> Jean-Luc Godard

MY FOCUS IN this chapter is on the performances and film works of Montreal-based artist Karl Lemieux, but I wish to begin with a long preamble in order to better frame the context, pertinence, and originality of his work, which in many ways is both a symptom of his time and of film history writ-large.

We usually acknowledge that the history of film preservation is closely tied to the reality of film's disappearance, of film's material decay and the long history of its neglect and destruction. It is well-known that the urgency of archiving film on a large scale only burgeoned in the early 1930s, once the silent era had come to a close and it became apparent that its history was in peril. Until then, and for many years after, film had been perceived as a commodity. Once its commercial lifespan had ended, it was to be stripped and repurposed, either as raw stock, lampshades, nail polish, hair brushes, or anything else its matter could become. As film culture proper slowly emerged in the 1920s (in France, Germany, the United States, and elsewhere) and certain milieus began to recognize cinema as an art form, the urge to rediscover and preserve early film expressions became stronger, albeit limited to small circles of aficionados.[2]

The well-known heroics of Henri Langlois and Georges Franju running across Paris to try to buy copies of films – often worn out, decaying, and lodged in humid attics or garages – from collectors in flea markets and bankrupt film companies have become part of the legend of archival history and have often shadowed thousands of other stories of films salvaged from destruction. In this chapter, I am interested in the idea that film preservation was born from the blunt fact of film's destruction, its potential disappearance. With the paradoxically poignant fascination with film's loss and decay, the gesture of archiving, structurally, historically, always points toward an *anarchiving* principle – a "death impulse," as Derrida would have it[3] – that precedes and commands it: ultimately, both preservation and destruction are intimately locked within a same passion for film. Indeed, part of the seduction, the "fetishization," of film material is tied to its very destructibility and self-destructiveness. This can easily be witnessed in Paolo Cherchi Usai's *Burning Passion* and *The Death of Cinema*, or in the Fédération internationale des archives du film (FIAF) anthology of texts, *This Film Is Dangerous: A Celebration of Nitrate Film* (the titles already tell everything), which are not only a plea for film preservation, but also an elegiac celebration of its inevitable fleeting nature ("cinema is the art of destroying moving images," as Cherchi Usai's famous adage goes).[4] Film was, and still is, although for different reasons, ontologically – and paradoxically, since it is born out of the age of mechanical reproduction – ephemeral, although this only became apparent fairly recently. Consider three major pivotal moments: in the 1930s, at the end of the silent era (tons of silent films, 80 per cent of everything made, had by that point disappeared); in the 1950s, after the production of nitrate films stopped and films were transferred en masse to safety prints (tons of nitrate film were then destroyed); and in the 1980s (and through the 1990s), with the "memory boom" that brought with it a massive patrimonial recognition for film preservation and restoration, in part due to the discovery of "vinegar syndrome" (tons of films have since been preserved, although many more tons are still being destroyed or are on the verge of disappearance partly because institutions believe they are digitally "safe").

In a sense, could one argue that it is through a certain redoubling of its ontology – and up to a certain extent of its history – that "ephemeral films" are the subject of such curiosity and attention today? Is it because ephemeral films are, by essence, always almost on the verge of disappearance, and also because they recast and remind us of the uniqueness and singularity of every film print (the copy I hold in my hand is always unique) in a world where the supposed infinite sameness of digital reproduction has made this idea more and more obsolete (but infinitely more precious)? Seen in this light, could the interest in ephemeral films, orphan works, and home movies that has grown in the last fifteen to twenty years be seen as a symptom of the digital age: an urge to recapture the lost aura of film?

There has been interest in the fragility or the decay of the film material in general, including as a mode of expression and allegory, since the 1980s, in the works of avant-garde artists such as Angela Ricci-Lucchi and Yervant Gianikian, Jürgen Reble, Peter Delpeut, Gustav Deutsch, Éric Rondepierre, Bill Morrison, Louise Bourque, and many others. This interest also coincides with a "turn toward the archives" on the part of early cinema academics and scholarship, the development of silent film festivals, and a much greater general public interest in images from the past, often fragmentary, anonymous, amateur (home movies, early newsreels, industrial cinema, etc.). As I show elsewhere,[5] this aesthetic reinvestment of filmic ruins is interesting to analyse in the face of – and possibly in reaction to – digital culture's utopia of immaterial transmissions, immaculate reproduction, of a world devoid of scratches and time wear. What I have tried to argue is that through these filmic ruins, one is invited to experience time's passing and the effect of singularization, or the "production of aura" it generates on every single shard of film. With time, every copy becomes an original: it bears, on its very flesh, traces of its little history, and through it we can capture a sense of time's fleeting memory.

These questions are too vast to discuss in this chapter alone, but offer a larger context to discuss the films and performances of Montreal-based artist Karl Lemieux, whose work opens fascinating perspectives on this dialectic between destruction and preservation. A founding member of the film collective Double Negative, created in 2004, Lemieux has explored various forms of experimental filmmaking: hand-painted films (*Mouvements de lumière*, 2004, and *Trash and No Stars*, with Claire Blanchet, 2007), experimental fiction (*Passage*, 2007), digital/analog animation (*Mamori*, 2009), re-photography off the screen (*Western Sunburn*, 2007), and, since 2003, 16 mm live film and music performances. Lemieux makes and/or performs all his works with the intimate collaboration of musicians: in the same way the musicians, in his films and performances, become image-makers, Lemieux's conceives his work, in a certain respect, as that of a musician.[6] One cannot go without the other. His films and performance draw their inspiration from those of Jürgen Reble and

Pierre Hébert, the art of Pierre Soulages and Franz Kline, and the music of numerous artists and groups, of which many are frequent collaborators: David Bryant, Roger Tellier-Craig, Jonathan Parant, Alexandre St-Onge, Hyena Hive, Godspeed you! Black Emperor, Radwan Moumneh (Jerusalem in my Heart), Sam Shalabi (Shalabi Effect), Francesco López, Olivier Borzeix, and others. Characterized by a deep involvement in the film material and its physical, organic properties, Lemieux's films and performances have a sensuous, tactile quality and provide a sense of being live, of experiential engagement with what seems to be unfolding for our eyes.

Lemieux's first live performance was a collaboration with filmmaker Daïchi Saïto in 2004. Both were invited to provide visual material for dancers performing a choreography on a piece by Olivier Borzeix at Studio 303 in Montreal. The 16 mm film loops and strips were all originals, cameraless, and abstract hand-painted or collage films. Some of the material Lemieux used paralleled his 2004 *Mouvements de lumière* (a powerful abstract animation, made by applying china ink directly to the film strip, to which Borzeix provided an intense soundtrack). Many, if not most, of Lemieux's performances since then have consisted of images he shot or made himself, either live action, optical printed, re-photography off a cinema or computer screen, hand-processed, hand-printed, hand-painted, etc. Alongside his own images, he has also used a wide variety of found images, documentary, industrial footage, trailers, newsreels, and animation that he received or bought in markets (he made some of his first films with found strips of super8 films that he bleached, scratched, or painted). Most of this footage, compared to other found-footage artists (e.g., Matthias Müller, Peter Tscherkassky, Christian Marclay, Craig Baldwin, Martin Arnold, etc.), does not rely on a certain degree of recognition on the part of the audience (actor, time period, etc.) and almost never relies on the kind of classical Hollywood or B-movie iconography many artists work with. Most often, the images he uses are unidentified, anonymous, impossible to date, and generically hard to define.[7]

Lemieux's first use of found material during a performance was in 2004. He was invited to perform for an event revolving around spaghetti Westerns. A couple of weeks before the performance, he had received a 16 mm print of a silent (or a silent version of an) unidentified black and white Western – the images suggest a 1950s film, but it is very hard to be sure (see figure 15.1). During the performance, he projected short loops of that film using four 16 mm projectors and proceeded to modify the

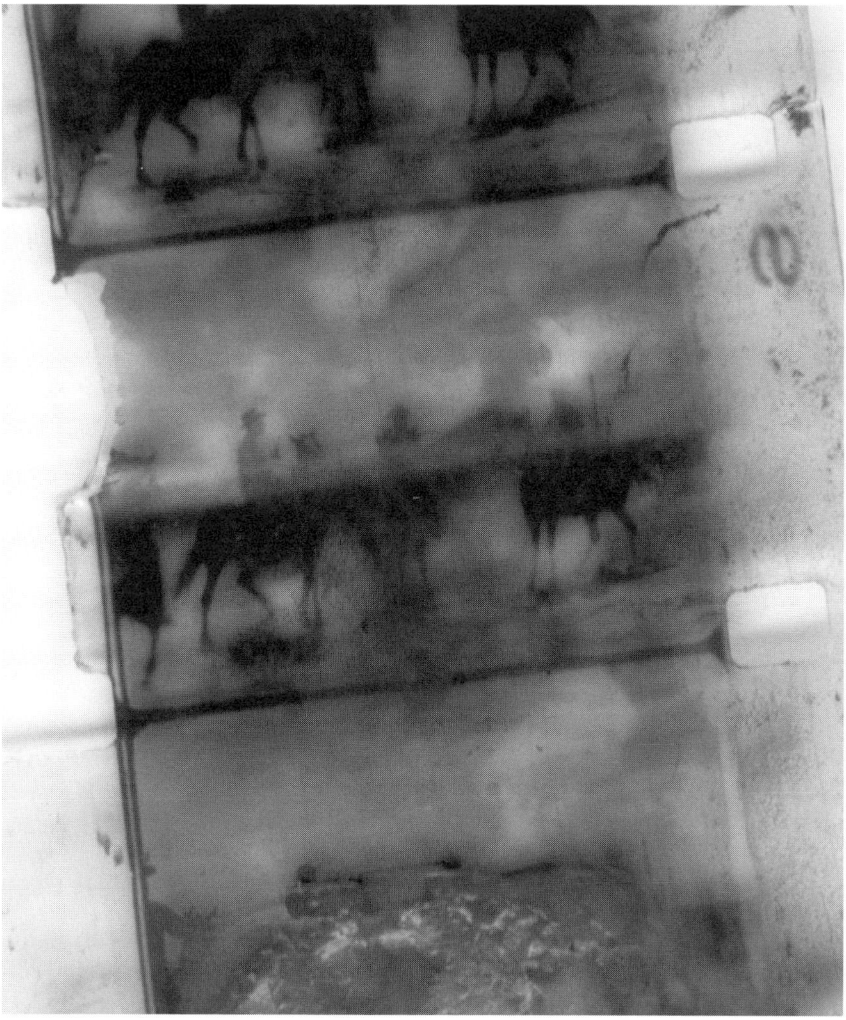

15.1 A digital scan of the original film strip used to make *Western Sunburn*.

material through various techniques, applying bleach, tearing the film strip with a small blade, painting over it with ink. He also stalled the movement of the film in the projector and let each image glide slowly in front of the light, so that eventually the heat of the bulb created spots of burning film (often enhanced by the tears on the celluloid), as he continued to move the film in order for it to burn without fully breaking. The result is a wondrous *pas de deux* between the rapid motion of the film as the loop is pulled across the gate (the frames fly before our eyes) and its flaming stasis:

15.2 A can of 16 mm film strips used in Lemieux's performance.

when the images on the frame become visible, they shortly begin to bubble and dissolve in a golden ring of burning celluloid. The incredible awe these images create, particularly in a live performance, draws comparison with many contemporary art forms or performances (Reble's film alchemy performances comes to mind), where chance operations are at the core of what the audience sees; a work in progress happens before our eyes. But the best comparison is probably found in the ecstatic game children play with magnifying class in the sun, drawing lines of fire on sheets of paper.

Although Lemieux seems to have been dissatisfied with the performance itself, he believed there was something there that needed to be explored further: he has done, since then, over a hundred film performances of the sort, and he continues to explore the possibilities of this type of multi-projector performance, varying the screens, the length of the loops, using filters, diffracting the flow of the light with a crystal bowl, etc.[8] But shortly after this first performance, in his workshop, he placed a HD camera in front of a screen and proceeded to project and perform for the camera, using the strips of film of the Western (most of it had not been yet fully destroyed).

15.3 The first of three generations of the same British newsreel footage used during Lemieux's performance, photographed off a Steenbeck screen.

He ended up with over three hours of raw stock that he, with Daïchi Saïto's help, edited into a ten-minute film, to which Radwan Ghazi Moumneh added a poignant and melancholic drone-guitar soundtrack. *Western Sunburn* was finished in 2007.

On the one hand, *Western Sunburn* can be seen as a film documentation of a performance, much in the same way *Tom, Tom the Piper's Son*, Ken Jacobs's 1969 masterpiece, can be seen as a film-version of a New York apartment performance using Billy Bitzer's 1905 film.[9] On the other hand, it is also an incredibly haunting, sensuous film experience in its own right, and it alternates textures of image, oscillating between motion and stillness, stasis and decomposition, the black and white footage and the sudden appearance of gold and brown sunburns on the film strip (both the title and the film itself have a pun-like dimension). *Western Sunburn* also offers a paradoxical meditation on the dialectic between preservation and destruction. In a way, Lemieux's re-filming preserves, through the same gesture that it burns and destroys, the images of this anonymous, unidentified, discarded Western.[10] As a scholar once suggested to me after a conference I was giving on this film, hypothetically, it is possible that *this* is the only remaining trace of this Western (it is

15.4 The second of three generations of the same British newsreel footage used during Lemieux's performance, photographed off a Steenbeck screen.

impossible to know how rare it is); hypothetically, a historian could end up having to use *Western Sunburn* to analyse this film if it was discovered no other copy existed in the world.[11] In turn, this Western might now have value and appear beautified precisely because it is destroyed and only fragments of opaque burned plastic remain.

One of the fascinating aspects of Lemieux's practice is, on the one hand, his eagerness to *sacrifice* – as he once suggested to me – these films for the sake of the performance;[12] and, on the other hand, his obsession with archiving his performances and material. He has carefully preserved, identified, and archived every single strip and frame of film he has used in a performance in his workshop (see figure 15.2). He knows exactly which films he used (and eventually abused) for which performance. The archivist and the arsonist coexist in the same artist.[13]

An interesting instance of this is a series of British newsreel images he has used in many instances (the first one was during a *Jerusalem in My Heart* performance opening for a Guy Sherwin screening/performance, in 2006 – among other images, there was a shot of Winston Churchill and the Queen saluting from a balcony that burned under Sherwin's disconcerted gaze). A sequence of the newsreel shows an

15.5 The third of three generations of the same British newsreel footage used during Lemieux's performance, photographed off a Steenbeck screen.

incredibly powerful black and white image of firefighters trying to put out a fire (possibly from incendiary bombs dropped by the Germans during World War II). During Lemieux's performance, the film itself soon began to burn, as if ruining by advance the firefighters' efforts.[14] The original footage was burned but the images were powerful enough that he wanted to reuse them. He contact printed the film, including the burned sections, to produce an inter-negative that he then used to produce more performance material. This footage was again burned, reprinted, etc. (see figures 15.3, 15.4, and 15.5). He has now reached the fourth successive generation of optically reprinted burned footage, each one documenting a fossilized version of a previous performance.

Lemieux's intuitive, hands-on way of working with film seems to provide a concrete edge to discussions around ephemeral films. In his performances, the ephemeral orphan films (anonymous, industrial, newsreel, documentary) he uses are shown – i.e., revealed – as ephemeral films, re-disappearing before our very eyes, evolving and transforming every instant, wearing off at every loop, at every imprint of burning light: Lemieux, in a way, performs their ephemerality in a performance that is itself ephemeral, fleeting, on the spot. What he preserves, archives, and carefully stows away in properly identified cans are the many remains of these film-actions, waiting to be resuscitated by the same light that will maybe destroy it. This dialectic between preserving and burning re-enacts, in a way, the ephemeral quality of the film experience itself, its fragility, its fleetingness, reactivating a lost aura of film in the wake of its current disappearance.

NOTES

1 Translated, this reads, "films are / trade goods / and they must be burned / I said as much to Henri Langlois / but beware / with its inner flame / matter and memory / art is like a conflagration / it is born / from what it burns." Jean-Luc Godard, "A Poem by Jean-Luc Godard," in *This Film is Dangerous: A Celebration of Nitrate Film*, ed. Roger Smither (Bruxelles: Fédération internationale des archives du film, 2002), 30.

2 For a history of cinémathèques and film culture in the 1920s and 1930s, see Raymond Borde, *Les cinémathèques* (Lausanne: L'âge d'homme, 1983); and Christophe Gauthier, *La passion du cinéma: Cinéphiles, ciné-club et salles spécialisées à Paris de 1920 à 1929* (Paris: Association française de recherche sur l'histoire du cinéma, 1999).

3 Jacques Derrida, *Mal d'archive: Une impression freudienne* (Paris: Galilée, 1995). Mary Ann Doane also analyses, although on different grounds, this double dimension of cinema between a desire for the rational, obsessive tension toward control and containment, and a desire for the irrational irruption of the contingent, the destructive, the irreversible. See Mary Ann Doane, *The Emergence of Cinematic Time: Modernity, Contingency, the Archive* (Cambridge, MA: Harvard University Press, 2002).

4 Paolo Cherchi Usai, *The Death of Cinema. History, Cultural Memory and the Digital Dark Age* (London: British Film Institute, 2001); *Burning Passions: An Introduction to the Study of Silent Cinema* (London: British Film Institute, 1994); and Roger Smither, ed., *This Film is Dangerous: A Celebration of Nitrate Film* (Bruxelles: Fédération internationale des archives du film, 2002).

5 André Habib, "Ruin, Archive and the Time of Cinema: Peter Delpeut's *Lyrisch nitraat*," *Substance* 35, no. 2: 120–39.

6 I am aware that this is not a new idea and that musicians, painters, and experimental filmmakers have very often collaborated throughout history. Avant-garde art and performance have always fed on the interaction between music and cinema, from Dada to Fluxus and beyond. What interests me here is the originality of Lemieux's performances in the context of a discussion on ephemeral films.

7 I recall a sequence he has used a few times that shows a funeral procession, and it is very hard to pinpoint whether it is a newsreel, a semi-professional home movie, or a documentary; whether it was shot in the 1930s or 1950s; whether it was shot in Europe or in America, etc. What is fundamental is the ghost-like quality of the image, the gazes of the people on the screen, and their black wear.

8 Karl Lemieux, personal conversation with the author.

9 As the story goes, Ken Jacobs had rented a roll of Paper Print films (which included Billy Bitzer's 1905 *Tom, Tom the Piper's Son*) in preparation for a class he was giving at St John's University in Queens. The print would have been obtained via Audio/Brandon Films, who in 1967 or 1968 started to distribute a 16 mm compilation entitled *In the Beginning*, a selection of one hundred paper print films put together by Kemp Niver (on this topic see my recent article: André Habib, "Archives, modes de reémploi: Pour une archéologie du *found footage*," *CiNéMAS* 24, no. 3 [Spring 2014]: 97–124.). Bewildered by the film, Jacobs screened it over and over on a "versatile" Kalart-Victor projector, and soon began "playing" with it by slowing it down, stopping the projector on certain frames, changing the focus, etc. He would invite friends to his loft and "performed" for them (Ernie Gehr, Hollis Frampton, Michael Snow, Joyce Wieland, and John Koos). It was Koos who suggested: "'Ken, that was wonderful. You should be filming it.'" (See Scott MacDonald, "Ken and Flo Jacobs," in *A Critical Cinema 3: Interviews with Independent Filmmakers* [Berkeley: University of California Press, 1998], 380). See also "Ernie Gehr Interviewed by Jonas Mekas, March 24, 1971," *Film Culture*, no. 53–5 (Spring 1972): 33.

10 More dramatically, Lemieux once used a roll of film he had been given showing various images of the cosmos and space exploration (he simply thought it was an educational documentary, without much value). These images were used and burned during a Shalabi Effect musical performance in 2006. The image of planets burning live on the screen was one of the highlights of the show. He only later found out that this film was actually a copy of Roman Kroitor and Colin Low's 1960 *Universe*, the film that inspired in part the special effects of Stanley Kubrick's *2001: A Space Odyssey*. Karl Lemieux, personal conversation with the author.

11 This recalls Serge Daney, discussing the documentary potential of film, who gives the example of pornographic films being used by a research group in an American university to "document" certain interior design fashion trends.

12 He is admittedly much more careful with his material now, and once he comes across a film he plans to use in a performance he contact prints it and produces an internegative that he then uses to strike material for other performances.

13 The famous film historian Kevin Brownlow explains in an article how, as a boy who had begun collecting 9.5 mm films, he received a 35 mm nitrate fragment from a film called *Rupert of Hentzau* (1915) and, since he was told it was dangerous and he had no way to project it, sacrificed it in a warfare game he was playing with a friend: "The last vestiges of *Rupert of Hentzau* were destroyed on a bomb-site in Swiss Cottage by a boy who was destined to become a film historian and to regret his action again and again." This was in fact the only surviving fragment of the film. (See Kevin Brownlow, "Dangerous Stuff," in *The Film is Dangerous: A Celebration of Nitrate Film*, ed. Roger Smither (Bruxelles: Fédération internationale des archives du film, 2002), 177–8.)

14 A similar kind of image occurs in Bill Morrison's *Decasia* (2002), where a boxer (who was probably, in the initial film, training against a punching bag) is seen fighting against blobs of decay that are mushrooming across the film strip. The mushrooms eventually win and swallow the boxer.

16 FILMS COLLECTING DUST AND DUSTY FILM COLLAGES

EPHEMERALITY AT WORK

Gerda Cammaer

> Our understanding of all sorts of plot – fictional plots and social plots – our understanding of how things happened indeed, is bound up with this understanding: that there is sequence, event, movement; things fall away, are abandoned, get lost. Something emerges, which is a story.
>
> Carolyn Steedman, *Dust: The Archive and Cultural History*[1]

LOOKING AT FILM history by focusing on the materiality of film, its ephemerality, and the trace it leaves behind is a fairly new approach. These ideas stem from the period when, coinciding with the one hundredth anniversary of cinema in 1995, the debates about the latest so-called death of film became a central concern in film scholarship, a period that began with the digital revolution. In hindsight, this "revolution" was nothing more than a technical "evolution"; that is, while it did not necessarily cause major changes in film language, the arrival of the digital age has resulted in a major shift in our thinking about film and cinema. The end of film or cinema was foretold many times prior to the introduction of digital technologies, yet this latest technological change has, generally speaking, been considered a breaking point that has caused many film scholars turn their attention to the very nature of film and its origins. In turn, media archaeology, a relatively new field in media studies that looks at material media cultures in a historical perspective, has gained a lot of prominence.

While it is still a challenge to provide a clear and definitive account of what media archaeology stands for, one of the areas of interest to the field is dead media or failed technologies that can be of as much relevance for the history of media as those technologies that survived and have been universally adopted. Hence with the possible (imminent?) shift of film's status to that of dead medium, it is not surprising that there is a growing interest in doing "media archaeological" work in film studies. As with the many other types of media archaeology, this work is characterized by the use of heterogeneous methods – more as a set of instruments and inspirations film historians use than a coherent theory. Generally speaking, media archaeology reminds us of the persistence of the material object (e.g., film), something that has become even more important in our digital culture of predominantly virtual and immaterial realities. Collecting media objects serves an important methodological function as part of this theory, and this object-centered focus sets media archaeology apart from cultural history. It is less about telling stories or counter histories, and more about how stories are recorded and in what kind of physical media, and even about analysing old media "as an amateur engineer who opens, checks physically, tests, and experiments to learn how media function."[2] In short, understanding current digital culture through a media-archaeological lens is done in different ways, but always with an enthusiasm for the object.

Prompted by the most recent claim that film is dead, film historians and theorists have developed a keen interest in media archaeology and have embraced the study of film as a material object (in demise). One development that this new approach has brought about is the use of the "ephemeral" as a category of study and as a critical methodology, making scholars rethink the notion of film as film and reconsider various film and media histories at once. The various meanings of ephemera and ephemerality offer interesting intersections for research, from the study of the impermanence of the moving image itself to the critical situation of ephemeral films existing in archives and as part of film collections, or to their use as found footage in films that function as virtual archives with imaginative narratives.

Media archaeology also promotes doing research that is literally archaeological and practical in nature; as methodology and process we attempt to recover facts and episodes in the history of film that are usually disregarded, while by excavating old media we hope to uncover relics, fragments, and traces of their former existence. It is also easy to see why media archaeology is such an interesting field for doing practice-based research and research creation, and its growing popularity has strengthened the interdisciplinary ties between media, technology, and art, as well as among film theorists, archivists, and artists. Parallel to the death of film and a new theoretical interest in the ontology of film, there has been a resurgence of "archaeological film art," that is, artworks that use references to the materiality of film as their major aesthetic and structural strategies.

Most of the debates about the death of film centre on the production and distribution of film, focussing on whether the transition to digital is either a revolution (a rupture) or an evolution (a transition). The use of digital technologies has also had a great impact on the archiving of film, and its use in teaching film history and theory, which began with the dramatic shrinking – or in some cases, the total disappearance – of celluloid teaching collections at universities and other institutions across Canada. For instructors and librarians alike, digital technology (e.g., DVDs, online video) is just easier to use: it is more flexible to access, it is a lot lighter to handle, and it takes up little if any shelf space. But it was actually the explosive growth of digital technology in the archival world that directed the attention of scholars to the materiality and ephemerality of film, and that has also revealed the need to examine the link between film theory and archival practices. As Giovanna Fossati states in her 2009 book *From Grain to Pixel*:

> There is very little theoretical work in the field of film and media studies with explicit reference to archives and archival practice. In a way, reading film and media literature one might think that the materiality of film, the significance of film as material artefact has very little importance for theory, and that the objects of the scholars are not necessarily the same of the archivists ... in a theory of archival practice the film as artefact, in its different possible meanings, is central.[3]

While it is true that the concern for film as the material object was previously the purview of film archivists who made it their task to preserve film, this is now changing. If the focus of film scholars for the film as artefact has only recently shifted, Fossati overlooks the fact that many filmmakers, especially found-footage filmmakers who work with archival films, have long specialized in this. In fact, Fossati later recognizes this oversight somewhat by introducing the concept "film as state of the art" as one possible framework for theorizing archival film. This framework looks for examples of filmmakers who push the limits of technology in order to translate their ideas into moving images. Fossati rightly categorizes this drive as not solely artistic. Rather, she recognizes that innovations in film can be the result of a variety of "inspirations": they can be market-driven, studio-based, or part of small independent productions. They can also happen in film laboratories or be the result of an archivist trying to resolve a specific film restoration problem. Key here is that for Fossati, film as state of the art is, as she puts it:

> The only theoretical framework that does not directly relate to the theoretical discourse, and it brings in close relation filmmaking and film restoration. This relation, namely the will to create, for filmmakers, and the will to recreate, for film restorers, is not only a conceptual, but also a practical one. The equipment, the laboratories, the available techniques and the technicians involved in filmmaking (especially for post production), and in film restoration, are often the same.[4]

This kind of recognition of the close ties between filmmaking and film archival work is truly refreshing. Indeed, film archivists and filmmakers share not only their interest in the materiality of film; they also share similar practical problems (especially faced with the constant decline in the availability of film stocks and film equipment), the same technology, and in some cases even the same (ephemeral) films. For instance, many experimental and found-footage filmmakers who are by trade specialists in handling film materials are also avid film collectors who often have to make similar decisions as film archivists working in major institutions, such as whether to digitize their entire collection and/or how accessible to make it. Moreover, some of the films institutional archives discard end up being the treasured goods of filmmakers who rescue them because they represent a goldmine of images that they can use in their own films, despite the material's sometimes deteriorated state. And digital technology has made it easier than ever to make found-footage films; the film copies do not need to be reprinted anymore, but can be transferred and reworked during editing (for example, by doing colour correction). Digital technology has also in one way or another entered most film archivists' workspaces (e.g., for film restoration, or for film archiving), and they now do work similar to filmmakers in post-production, albeit with a different purpose.[5] In other words, if there have not been many references to archival practices in film and media studies, there has always been a strong (albeit unrecognized) affinity between the work of found-footage filmmakers and film archivists, and there is also a strong affinity

16.1 A double-exposed image combining footage from *Canada at War* with dusty film leader.

with the work historians do in general, though perhaps in a less practical way. The acuteness of a possible disappearance of film in the wake of the digital revolution (or the death of film) brings these affinities to the fore.

For the remainder of the chapter, I will focus on the growing interest in the materiality and ephemerality of film by exploring how this has come to the foreground in concurrence with the recent discussions about the death of film. As I have previously suggested, the so-called digital revolution has caused major changes for film archivists and found-footage filmmakers alike, as they share more and more of the same problems *and* methods when dealing with ephemeral films in the digital age. In the latter part of this chapter, I present some practical examples selected from notes on the making of my film *Stardust* (digital video, 15 min., 2009).[6] After all, I made *Stardust* to illustrate the issues at hand in a playful way, by freely borrowing lines, images, and traces from the scrapheap of film history. The film is mainly composed with various images of film "dust" – any type of superficial film damage, such as embedded dirt particles and small scratches – which represent both the materiality and ephemerality of film (see figure 16.1).

Stardust is a personal manifesto of two film lovers tackling the recurrent claims that film is dead; indeed, it is a militant film essay that tries to raise awareness for the need to preserve ephemeral, 16 mm non-fiction films that is similar to what campaigns such as "nitrate can't wait" and "save an orphan" did for related causes. My aim in this chapter, and in the film *Stardust,* is to explore the growing interest in the material ephemerality of film as film and the increasing cultural ephemerality of film as its importance as part of our collective memory diminishes – phenomena that are also occurring at a time in which the way we communicate and preserve moving images is changing tremendously.

EPHEMERALITY AT WORK: FILMS GATHERING AND/OR BECOMING DUST

When we reach rock bottom, there is nowhere to go but up. The public profile of film preservation and archiving has never been higher. Film scholars are increasingly aware that a huge part of our film heritage is gathering dust, crumbling to dust, or already lost forever. As is generally accepted in film preservation circles, only 25 per cent of all films produced in the 1910s and 20 per cent of the films produced in the 1920s are still with us. Many of these films were destroyed by the industry itself (to protect copyrights and for other trivial reasons) or went up in flames (nitrate film is highly flammable).[7] Of the early films that remain, many are disintegrating due to nitrate degradation. In the 1990s, the celebrations of one hundred years of cinema generated a renewed interest in early cinema, and especially nitrate films, which in some cases were fetishized.[8] Since then, any copy of an early nitrate film that is rediscovered is treated as a treasure. For these films, the slogan "nitrate can't wait" and the Nitrate 2000 campaign were effective.[9]

In the United States, Martin Scorsese has been championing the cause of film preservation on behalf of *all* cinema treasures, fiction and non-fiction, feature and shorts, with some impressive successes. Yet in the United States, as elsewhere, there are still thousands of films that are physically, commercially, and historically neglected. Most of these films are on small (non-commercial) formats such as 16 mm, and on acetate film, which is also subject to chemical decay, and at an even faster rate than nitrate stock despite its label "safety film." A process called "acetate degradation" causes the film to shrink, curl, and turn brittle (see figure 16.2). It has been dubbed "vinegar syndrome" after the distinctive odour that the decaying film emits when you open the can. There are also numerous

16.2 Close-up of film deterioration in a Super-8 home movie image.

Eastman colour films, some only a few years old, that have turned rosy pink, a recurrent feature of many images in *Stardust*.[10] Scorsese was one of the first to blow the whistle on colour fading as early as the 1970s. All these film-deteriorating phenomena actually are (and have been) *the* justification to trash films, especially each time a new (video) format has come along. Getting rid of film in favour of video, both analogue and digital, is the major historical difference between commercial and non-commercial films, and between fiction and non-fiction films.

Commercial feature fiction films are much less prone to become obsolete than non-commercial and/or non-fiction films, and they are for the most part still preserved on film. For example, since the boom of the DVD market, many film classics of the studio system era have been restored and reissued. The industry swiftly started to follow the commercial model of Roger Mayer, general manager of MGM, who in the 1960s had already made his studio a bastion of film preservation and film restoration. He pitched the need to preserve the company's films to his board of directors as "asset management" and simply asked them if they really wanted "their assets to deteriorate?" That got their attention.[11] Indeed, now the label "restored print" is presented as an added-value feature that can help seduce the general public to come see a film or buy a DVD. But we still need to shift this positive attention for film preservation to work on those non-commercial historical treasures that only public funds can pay for, namely "orphan films." These are films of various lesser-known genres that are not backed by big directors, big producers, or big institutions with an immediate financial interest in seeing them restored. Despite the fact that these films are mostly forgotten, many of them (mostly 16 mm) were once produced in large numbers and widely distributed on the home market. Thus they form a significant chapter in our celluloid past that deserves critical attention.

In Canada, the National Film Board (NFB) was a production leader in this 16 mm home market. Making most of the film collection available to the Canadian public has always been an institutional mandate for the NFB as part of the wide accessibility and democratic engagement of this organization. Currently, most NFB productions are available through various online and digital platforms, such as DVD box sets,[12] while before the NFB films used to be widely distributed to educational institutions and public libraries on 16 mm. In the 1980s, the NFB launched a major distribution campaign to make its films more directly available to the public by teaming up with fifty-one libraries across the country. This method of getting NFB films to Canadian audiences is based on another much earlier but highly effective distribution network: in the 1940s and 1950s, the NFB brought its 16 mm films directly to communities as a form of travelling cinema.

The massive 16 mm distribution system of the NFB in the 1980s contributed to another complex issue in film preservation: because for most titles there were multiple prints in circulation, several film copies of the same, more popular, NFB titles keep turning up (in the garbage or to be recycled in some way). When tracing the genealogy of a film print, it becomes clear how easily multiple prints of one film can be orphaned. But this successive orphaning does not necessarily result in the total loss of the film, because as long as *one* print survives – and of course as long as someone cares for it or retains the original negative, which hopefully the NFB is doing consistently – a new print can be struck and redistributed. What we know for sure is that since the late 1990s, all the 16 mm prints that the NFB widely distributed to various libraries have been taken out of circulation, and many were trashed. An important reason for this widespread dumping of film prints is that library finances are based on the number of loans for the items in their collection. The past twenty years has also seen a huge decrease in the use of 16 mm film in classrooms, and even more so at home, in club houses, or in church basements. Hence, as these films have become dead weight in public libraries and university libraries alike, they have more often than not ended up in the junkyard.[13] While the NFB continues to make some of its films available online in what Tom Perlmutter called "the NFB's virtual church basement," the vast majority of the 16 mm films that formerly screened in real church basements have simply disappeared.[14]

EPHEMERALITY AND THE MANY DEATHS OF FILM(S)

The death of film has been announced from its inception as a new medium, with Antoine Lumière trying to convince George Méliès that it was an invention without a commercial future. Since then, every introduction of a technological innovation or new invention intended to improve the film medium (e.g., sound, video, digital technology) has meant that film history presents itself as an ongoing series of traumas and deaths. From this perspective, one should not merely question the most recent announcement of the death of film, but consider it as one of the medium's many deaths and explore why it is perceived or promoted as a death. A good place to start to unravel the mystery of film's demise is to look at the work of Jean-Luc Godard, who has actively and creatively invoked the spectre of death in cinema in a very persuasive apocalyptic fashion. As Michael Witt describes, Godard does this by giving cinema a human body and a life cycle: "to claim that the cinema can die assumes that it is, or was, alive. Cinema, an industrial art form, is thus inherently romanticized and accorded a 'life.'"[15] Besides a life and a body, Godard regularly attributes other human qualities to cinema. He even goes as far as to presumptuously link the death of the cinema to his own mortality, thereby limiting the lifespan for cinema: "I think that I'll probably die at the same time as the cinema, such as it was invented ... The existence of cinema can't exceed, roughly, the length of a human life: between eighty and 120 years. It's something that will have been transitory, ephemeral."[16] It is worth underscoring that Godard declares all cinema to be ephemeral, not just the films that we usually consider to be transitory such as industrial or educational films and home movies. The degradation of cinema and visual culture in general that Godard laments is just a typical provocation on his behalf akin to the drama he creates and the critiques he voices in his own films, but it is an influential one. Witt actually goes as far as to say that discussion of the death of cinema can be traced back to Godard himself and his hyperbolical statements about the lamentable state of cinema as an art form since the early 1960s: "much of the recent talk on the deterioration, decay and death of cinema can be traced back to Godard."[17]

Coming from a very different world, Roger Mayer, founding member and chair of the National Film Preservation Foundation, has also heard the song that film is dead many times before:

> Ever since I started in the movie business in 1952, I have been hearing that film would not be around very much longer. It was always just about to be replaced by something electronic. First broadcast television, then cable television, than videocassettes and DVDs, then the Internet – all have lined up for the role of movie-killer. The difference now may be that all of these threatening mediums are united by a single characteristic: they are all digital, or rapidly becoming so.[18]

Indeed, it is important to recognize that the "new" media threatening film now are all digital. The fact that in the last two decades digital media have become very visible and accessible for the public at large probably has contributed to creating a much more general and persuasive perception that film is dead. As Paolo Cherchi Usai states, "the much-noted benefits of the digital revolution have quickly shifted towards a subtle yet persuasive ideology. There is something inherently reactionary in how worldwide consensus has been gathered around this new myth of scientific progress. What is worse, denouncing its excesses will make you feel like the latest anti-technologist on the block."[19] In other words, digital technology is so present that we are not prompted to question the myths that come with it, created by technologists who champion novelty, change, and progress, but who rarely critique (imposed) changes, let alone prompt users to be critical of a new technology or hold onto one that has already proven its value as a moving image carrier for more than a century.

Despite its still excellent qualities, the industry itself relentlessly presents film as a medium that represents the past. A grainy black-and-white image, the look of reversal film or of a faded colour film, is constantly used (and imitated) to represent history and memory. Earlier this role was attributed to photography, as Roland Barthes explains in *Camera*

16.3 Analogue incomplete film burn.

Lucida (1981),[20] a book that retroactively can be seen as announcing the death of analogue photography (while exploring the relationship between photography and death). Before, the photograph was coded as the past, as the "what has been." Now this characteristic has been attributed to film. As Catherine Russell explains, digital image processing has opened up the possibility of infinite manipulation so, "in light of the TV monitor, the cinema is reinvented as a site of disappearance, loss and memory."[21] Indeed, various digital effects allow users to create "filmic" effects such as scratches, grain, colour fading, film flicker, and even always perfect frame burns (not the case in analogue film, see figure 16.3).

The way these effects are used (for example in commercials) promotes and enhances the general idea that film is about memory, the past, and, in a best case scenario, "the good old times." Whatever their particular usage, these effects reinforce the general idea that film is history, that film is dead. The irony is that these effects refer to something that is not so evident anymore: the actual film prints that have these characteristics are disappearing and decaying at a fast rate so that these filmic effects have become ever more purely digital and virtual. Indeed, the only true current "death of film" we need to worry about, besides the trashing of film prints, is the shrinking, breaking, fading, deteriorating, and ultimately, crumbling of our cinematic past. That deathly process is very active and present. But, film being film, even its material death – the most destructive process of all – is always a beautiful one.

FOUND-FOOTAGE FILMS AS ARCHIVAL PRACTICE

Found-footage filmmakers have made films with ephemeral and orphan films for decades. This process of freely and creatively recycling film is actually how my interest in ephemeral cinema began. As I became more interested in film history, especially the small and forgotten stories, my appreciation of found-footage films changed: it shifted from an emphasis on the content of the images used in relation to the new film to the origins of the source material used. I started to consider found-footage films as an alternative film archive of ephemeral cinema and to focus on to what extent the filmmaker is celebrating or deconstructing the images used. In his book *Recycled Images, The Art and Politics of Found Footage Films,* William C. Wees explores the different methods of using found-footage. He cites Ken Jacobs to remind us "that a lot of film is perfect left alone," which permits us to see the original footage as the filmmakers and their contemporaries saw it.[22] This way, "we observe the passage of time, how it has invested the film footage with nostalgia, historical and sociological interest, and an aesthetic value that is apparent only because [the filmmaker] left the footage intact, rather than re-editing it to suit his own formal and thematic concerns."[23] Thanks to found-footage filmmakers who work this way, we get to see the whole film as it is: the found-footage filmmaker has not only made it available to us for study, but has also preserved it and given it a second life and a new audience.

In his blog, Rick Prelinger, a prominent example of a filmmaker turned film archivist, takes a similar position. He actually laments the use and abuse of a lot of found footage to construct histories that emphasize personal experience, particularly in documentary, which seems to be a more prominent practice since films have been digitized and made available online. According to Prelinger:

> Many of us who collect or take care of moving images and sounds feel that original material tell pretty good stories on their own. Aside from some courageous DVD collections of uncut archival films, a supplement here and there, and several sketchy sites

> presenting downloadable archival materials, most original materials don't reach the public without being run through the storytelling Cuisinart ... Bits and pieces from our collections are being woven into works that don't really speak to the value of their components. [24]

As a solution, Prelinger pleads for making all ephemeral films available online as they are, because for him film archives are part of the cultural production system. He also suggests that more archivists should become filmmakers and consider production as part of their archival mission. Addressing his colleagues, he says: "As more and more archivists become curators and preservers of digital files, and as working with physical moving image materials becomes an unjustly underfunded artisanal speciality, we may have to figure out what exactly it is that we do. I suggest we consider becoming moving image authors too."[25]

As Prelinger states, most compilation and found-footage filmmakers do not present their material uncut in order to pay respect to the unrecognized gems of cinematic art that they are. These are exceptions. More often, filmmakers use the found films because "their very artlessness exposes them to more critical – and more amusing – readings than their original makers intended or their original audiences were likely to produce."[26] To create new meaning is also why most experimental filmmakers will rework their original film material in some way, so that its richer implications become apparent, and combine images from different films. By intercutting the found images, they build a new narrative that demonstrates their personal concerns, often themes far remote from the original content of the found film.[27] The genre is called "found-footage films" and not "found-film films" for a reason.

Some filmmakers, besides cutting and pasting, also use technical tricks such as repetition and slow motion, or layering (superimposition), or they attack the footage itself by scratching and painting over it. The more the material is intercut with other source material and the more the images are reworked, the more the original images disappear into the background and lose the connection with the source film and its message. Yet, despite the entirely new context of the footage, and consequently the loss of its historical value and meaning, these found-footage films still remind us of the "wealth" of neglected non-commercial films in general, even if they are used to show off their oddity rather than to show concern for their survival as films in their own right.

Insofar as some orphan films indeed shine for their artlessness, others actually impress by their professional quality and artfulness, as well as their interesting and at times intriguing content. That is why I suggest the possibility of restudying found-footage films as moving picture compilations of hidden treasures and vanished media: creative catalogues of bits and pieces of films that deserve to be recognized as part of our cultural heritage. This will not be easy. A lot depends on filmmakers' approaches, and on whether they use the source films anonymously or credit them at the end of the film.[28] Generally speaking, the latter goes against the premise that collage films are a form of underground or counter culture, and most filmmakers, concerned about copyrights, try not to call attention to the fact that they are using the footage "illegally."

THE DUSTY TRACES AND FORGOTTEN STARS OF *STARDUST*

Stardust[29] is an imaginative (and ironic) plea to preserve our dying celluloid past and to fight digital technologies' total takeover. I intended it to be a compilation film with no other content than film dust and scratches, a collage of various parts of films that are not really part of the film itself yet a necessary element for projection: the film's countdown or academy leader, and the white or coloured leader at the beginning and end of every film print used to safely thread the film through the projector (see figure 16.4). My original idea was to make a film that would display the liveliness of real film dust and scratches, contrary to the repetitive and unrealistic film dust and scratches available as a digital filter used to try make any high-definition video appear aged and historical.

Given the unusual (and very abstract) images I intended to work with, I reversed the workflow by creating the soundtrack first, and then edited the images to the sound. The soundtrack for *Stardust* is composed by Randolph Jordan (artist name Gerstyn Hayward) who is, given the narrative significance of the soundtrack, credited as co-author of the film. Similar to work he had made previously as a sound artist, he created a sound collage with lines of films and TV series that refer to dust, death, ephemerality, and the fleetingness of time. The use of all these popular culture references in *Stardust* is meant as an antidote to Godard's and other critics' comments on the life and death of cinema and their rather pessimistic interpretations of film's life expectancy as a medium and as an art form. Once the soundtrack was completed, the film became a collage with the abstract images of dust and scratches intercut with different

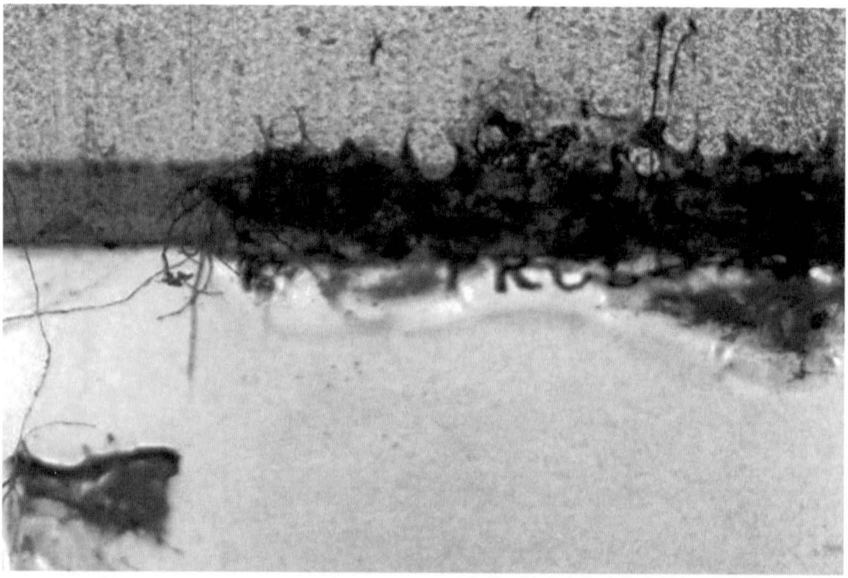

16.4 Dense film dust on Academy leader (origin unknown).

images from various orphaned films that were needed to carry the multilayered narrative Jordan had created for the film (e.g., clips of NFB films, CBC footage, Canadian educational or publicity films, etc.).

The title *Stardust,* besides being a direct reference to film dust, evokes the theme of space travel and the exploration of the universe that is an important part of the narrative of the film. This theme comes to a large extent from the film *CN Turbo* (Canadian National, 1970) of which the original opening is used as a prologue in *Stardust.* This film and its life story illustrate the issues at stake here. I first rescued this orphaned film copy from the dusty shelves of an antique shop in Montreal for $20. I then "killed" the film by cutting it up so that I could reprint some of its discoloured images on the optical printer for my film *Struggling in Paradise* (2004),[30] damaging the original print beyond repair by doing so. Years later I re-spliced the film, putting it back together in the order I found it, bringing it back to life so to speak, albeit badly scarred and scratched (in addition to the discolouration already present when I acquired it). I also transferred it to digital video while recording the optical sound separately, re-syncing both and improving the film's muffled sound as much as possible. Hence, the

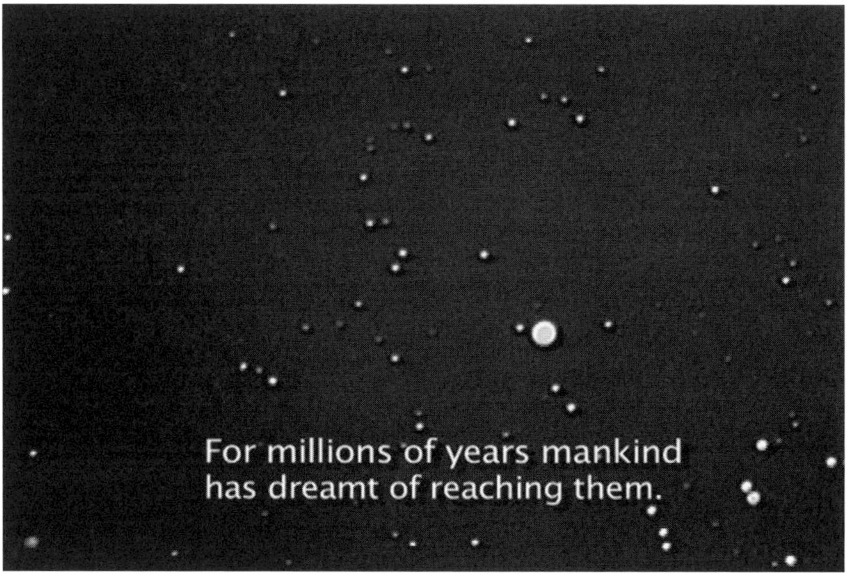

16.5 The fake starry sky (original footage from CN *Turbo).*

film exists now as a damaged film print, and as a more or less restored digital video of which I could make new copies and if needed migrate to new video formats. That the film print I used is damaged (by my own doing) makes the image shakier than originally intended. When in the latter part of *Stardust* the film's constant dust storm takes on more dramatic proportions the voice-over warns, "when it arrives, it will shake the universe."[31] The wobbly opening of the film is a sneak preview of what such a major shake of the universe might look like, also reminding us that navigating our celluloid universe has become more hazardous in these times of peril for film.

From the beginning, the opening of this 1970 CN film amazed me with its (ab)use of space travel as a sales argument to promote a new train model. Close-up images of the train's motor are presented as if they are parts of a spacecraft. The fact that they used the original sound of Apollo 11's launch from the Kennedy Space Center on 20 July 1969, including the actual countdown to take-off, gives this idea a lot of credibility, especially since the train leaves the frame vertically instead of horizontally. In the spirit of the times, the film's French voice-over reminds us how mankind has always dreamt of exploring the stars and space, and that this now (in 1970) has become an attainable goal: all this is illustrated with images of a huge space telescope in an observatory that gradually opens its roof to reveal a sky full of stars. And this is where it all falls apart, as what we get to see is a rather amateurish maquette of the firmament (see figure 16.5), a useful reminder that there were times before Google Earth and high-resolution stock footage from NASA available on the Internet, or sophisticated digital motion graphics and other special effects.

This fake firmament reappears in *Stardust* toward the end of the film, when the trip through celluloid space has taken a dramatic turn and suggests that we are now preparing for an intergalactic battle to save the world of film. The launch of a second space trip in the film is evoked with images of a canon shot, a flight simulator, an airplane cockpit, and quickly moving dust strips, all concocted as a fast and delirious trip of characters and parts travelling at light speed.[32] The actual travel through space happens on the sound of a damaged film, which was introduced earlier as the sound of film dust.[33] This space trip ends as the sky opens up with an actual frame burn (not a digital effect) of a deep blue sky at night with a full moon, a sky speckled first with the large white dots that in the old days were used to label a film print, and then with a digital dust effect that imitates the stars (another allusion that is embedded in the title). When the frame burns, it looks for a brief moment as though there is a second full moon, or simply a hole in the sky, but because the projector quickly caught the next sprocket hole, a new frame appears with the sky whole again: the frame burn does not come to full fruition and thus does not wipe out the entire image. This illustrates not only the regenerative powers of the film medium, but also, when performed non-digitally, how beautiful and unpredictable its glitches and so-called flaws are.[34]

This second space trip in *Stardust* heads into the fake night sky of the CN film to end with a harsh landing in a place that is all too familiar to anyone involved in film preservation: a vault full of films crumbling to dust.[35] All of a sudden the voice-over has a much more serious tone as it addresses the risks and perils of nitrate film stock, rhetorically asking if "we will ever know what's on a lot of these reels: they are so far gone you can't project them or even save them in a lab. Are there any jewels left amongst all this dust and debris?"[36] While the question resonates over the images of crumbling film material, it gradually sinks in that we may have landed in the future.[37] A voice we have heard before urges us to get a broom,[38] quickly followed by a repeat of various brief statements about

16.6 Maria Schneider (*The Passenger*, 1975) staring across a slug-film scratch at film dust and a troubled future for film.

dust from earlier in the film: they all sound much more serious and less playful now that we know more about the imminent and actual death of film, its own material fragility and ephemerality. *Stardust* ends with the only moment in the entire film that sound and image are reconnected true to the original film: silent slug-film images of *The Passenger* (Michelangelo Antonioni, 1975) are briefly re-synced with their sound (taken from the newly restored version on DVD). As Maria Schneider states the obvious that "it is very dusty here" (see figure 16.6), we look forward to more dust at the other side of the frame, across that conspicuous slug-film scratch,[39] and to a troubled future that reads "end." After the credits listing all the individual film images and sounds used, *Time Life Films* is listed as a second distributor for *Stardust*, a precaution since this film stirs up so much dust and death.

Ironically, all the so-called flaws of film (the grainy images, the scratches, dust and frame burns, and, ultimately, decay) that are directly or indirectly responsible for the death of film are exactly what make the medium so lively: no two prints of a film are ever the same, and every print carries its own life-story on its celluloid face.[40] The more a film is used, the more it shows dust, scratches, and other signs of aging. This particular quality of film – that every print has its own life and death, and that every print goes through a particular aging process – was my initial impetus to make the film *Stardust.* The film reiterates some of the drama present in the texts about the death of film mentioned above, in particular the many deaths of film Jean-Luc Godard orchestrates, by making similar links with our own mortality (dust to dust), including cremations and burials. A key moment in the film (at around six minutes) is when this formerly implicit link between the death of film and our own mortality is made explicit, in *Stardust* initially visually represented by the image of a collision test technician carrying the dummy of a child. This particular shot is taken from *A School Bus Collision Test Film* (Transport Canada, Ministry of Supply and Services, 1984), of which I obtained a print from the Atlantic Filmmakers Cooperative in 2002. I recently discovered another copy of this film as part of the 16 mm film collection of the Ontario Safety League I have adopted, which illustrates that of some industrial and educational films so many copies were in distribution that collectors have the luxury to keep (or use) the best-preserved one. This was actually one of the parts in the making of the film where it was extremely difficult to find images to accompany the soundtrack – how do you show dead people if there are no zombies or corpses in your footage? – a problem I solved by also using two "china girls" as images of "dead" persons.[41] It is one of the many allusions in *Stardust* to film practices that now definitively belong to the past, such as the use of a porcelain mannequin or a heavily made-up live model to print an image that can be used for calibration purposes when processing film: as many other specialized skills, film timing is a dying art in an increasingly digitized film industry.

The sound bits used to evoke this "death and dying" theme in the film all come from popular TV series and films, the kind of mainstream media that Godard accused of affecting and ultimately killing cinema. But *Stardust* goes beyond this kind of lament, as it reminds the audience of the urgency to come to the rescue of the many "orphans of the storm" (as the first orphan film symposium was called in reference to D.W. Griffith's 1921 film. The film achieves this with a narrative that brings to mind various disaster films and by using war images from the famous NFB documentary series *Canada at War* produced by Donald Brittain in 1962 (more specifically from the second part of the series, *Days of Infamy*). These shots were all found in a university editing room, where an entire collection of 16 mm NFB film prints was used as teaching material for

16.7 General mobilization for the pending dust storm (original footage from *Canada at War*, CBC, 1962).

exercises in flatbed editing. This is one example of what the NFB did with all redundant film copies once it started to digitize its collection in the 1990s: it donated them to be used by film students as found footage. By the time I got to these reels, most of the prints were already heavily plundered for interesting shots, with as a consequence that the films were reduced to take-out reels rather than actual films. It is from the remaining fragmented images of one single *Canada at War* film reel that *Stardust* acquires its militant tone as a manifesto against the general death sentence for 16 mm film. Halfway through the film, the story goes that a storm is coming, "our storm," and, "when it arrives, it will shake the universe."[42] In a quick succession of events, a CBC reporter announces "an impeccable storm has descended," a sailor warns with light signals that there is a "dust cloud ahead," and images of a general mobilization (all taken from *Canada at War*) illustrate the seriousness of the emergency at hand (see figure 16.7).

In the midst of all this, Hitchcock keeps his regular cool. When asked what he knows about dust, he tells us that we should not be too hasty and that "there is no need for a dust-up."[43] Yet he addresses us from a tiny snippet of film rescued from a trim-bin, his portrait only a fragment, scratched, dusty, and orphaned, no longer a part of the original CBC feature interview it belonged to because a filmmaker of a new generation that no longer recognizes Hitchcock used it as fill film for 16 mm sound editing.[44] This is one film scenario that the master of horror and suspense did not imagine (for) himself: to be cut to pieces, edited to lines spoken by characters from other films, and, even worse, to be swept up as a dust particle by a crew of eager rescue workers who were answering the call to "go fetch a broom."[45]

Whereas *Stardust* is a trip into the strange universe of film and its material qualities, it is as much a mental trip into the imaginative powers of cinema, and of the Kuleshov effect[46] in particular. In this film, instead of a bowl of soup, dust is the central concept-image that ties all the images and sounds together. Used in both literal and metaphorical ways, dust effectively unites the micro and macro, from minute (film-)dust particles to a cluster of stars so distant they resemble a luminous cloud of dust. For the makers of *Stardust*, the central drive to work with found-footage and found-sound is exactly this possibility of making connections between things found and collected separately so that they can all be understood as part of a larger system. Here, "stardust" is the guiding concept to convey not only that all films are bound together, but also that the film medium is bound up with humanity in a physical way. We are all literally made of stardust, each one of us containing molecules that were once found in extraterrestrial objects – that is the living connection between all things that the entire film alludes to. This idea is very present in the CN film that opens *Stardust*, which evokes terrestrial train travel with extraterrestrial references, but also in all the connections between dust, stars, life, and death that follow.

Although conceptually *Stardust* is clearly following in the footsteps of found-footage filmmakers such as Arthur Lipsett who evoke a doomsday image of the world, the film is also in tune with several recent works that show a fascination with the material qualities of film and/or concern for the so-called death of film.[47] Whereas it plays on the seriousness and darkness of the disaster thinking that was present in a lot of the work of the 1960s and '70s, the film offers relief with its irony and popular culture references, which also relates it to the found-footage films of the 1980s and '90s that reworked footage much more freely into new narratives about personal concerns or into fictional stories. Thematically, the film is aligned with the current need to reaffirm the authenticity and specificity of film in a time when there is an overproduction of images and powerful new tools to create and manipulate still and moving images; even if a large part of that task is now to show film's fragility and fleetingness and actual crumbling to dust. But just like dust, film or film history will never totally go away or be erased. Any archive, whether an actual film archive or a film that functions as a living film archive, is as much a record of the past as it points to the future. The end – be it of *a* film or of *film* – is always just *an ending*.

"SO MANY WORLDS, BUT CONNECTING THEM ALL IS DUST"[48]

Long after making *Stardust*, I discovered a small book by Carolyn Steedman titled *Dust: The Archive and Cultural History* (2002), a rather original introduction to the work of archivists and historians that I probably read more eagerly because I had made this film. Steedman offers a set of meditations on the act of deriving meaning from the past (the task of historians) written very much in the style of an historical compilation film, with a flair that I can only describe as "archive fever" (after Derrida), a central theme in the book. An important thread in *Dust* is the fascinating story of French historian Jules Michelet, who made it his task to make the dead come alive by finding the meaning of their brief existences – every social historian's dream. Doing this work in various French archives, he actually breathed in so much dust that he first had severe headaches – a particular type of archive fever – and in the end he died of it. Reading this story reminded me of the times I have opened a rusty can of film only to find snippets and lots of dust in it, or when I smelled a whiff of vinegar on a rapidly disintegrating film. Archival work can indeed be physically dangerous, especially for someone with severe dust allergies like me. But on the other hand, nothing is more mentally thrilling than discovering lost histories – on or about film – and being able to make work that integrates both. It is very close to how Steedman describes doing social history: "in strictly formal and stylistic terms, a text of social history is very closely connected to those novels in which a girl flies, a mountain moves, the clocks run backward, and where the dead walk among the living. If the archive is a place of dreams, it permits this one, above all others, the one that Michelet dreamt first, of making the dead walk and talk."[49] Letting dead films (re)run and speak is at the core of a lot of found-footage filmmaking, and of *Stardust* in particular, as the film directly addresses issues linked to the material and cultural death of film, including the impermanence of film archives and film collections.

Steedman actually follows in the steps of others, building on the work of Foucault and Derrida and recognizing that the archive is a creation that covers as much as it reveals. For Steedman, archives are impossible to imagine without considering history as a mass of material that needs to be ordered according to a certain narrative. And that is where lies the (creative) task of the historian. As Steedman puts it: "There is everything, or Everything, the great undifferentiated past, all of it, which is not history, but just stuff. The smallest fragment of its representation (nearly always in some kind of written language) ends up in various kinds of archive and record office (and also in the vastly expanded data banks that Derrida refers to in 'Archive Fever'). From that, you make history, which is never what *was* there, once upon a time. (There was only stuff, Everything, dust)."[50] Oddly enough, this sounds similar to what media archaeology theorist Wolfgang Ernst proposes as a method to get away from textual analysis: "If we redeploy the analytical tools developed by the so-called 'new historicism' in literary studies from textual analysis to material cultural studies, we find not merely archival data on history (the symbolic regime of sources for historians) but also – as opposed to the textuality of (narrative) history – the otherness (even resistance to interpretation) of the material fragment, the relic."[51]

Hence, for the antiquarian/media archaeologist who intends to achieve a *monumental* relation to the past, "this method aims to avoid prematurely interpreting archival or archaeological evidence as documents of history but rather isolates this data into concrete series in order to rearrange them and open them up for different configurations."[52] Both statements illustrate how the attention of historians and archivists has shifted. In film history, digital technology has brought the materiality and ephemerality of film to the foreground as a common concern of film archivists and film historians, both in their own way now rethinking their work by focussing more on the presence of film fragments, by including small films, and by writing "small history." I hope to have proven here that filmmakers whose work and activities also deal with ephemeral films and the ephemerality of film often operate in very similar ways as film archivists and film historians, however different the outcome. Indeed, both descriptions can easily be read as a description of combining found footage in a new context in order to construct new meaning. As creative archives, found-footage films are made with carefully selected and con-

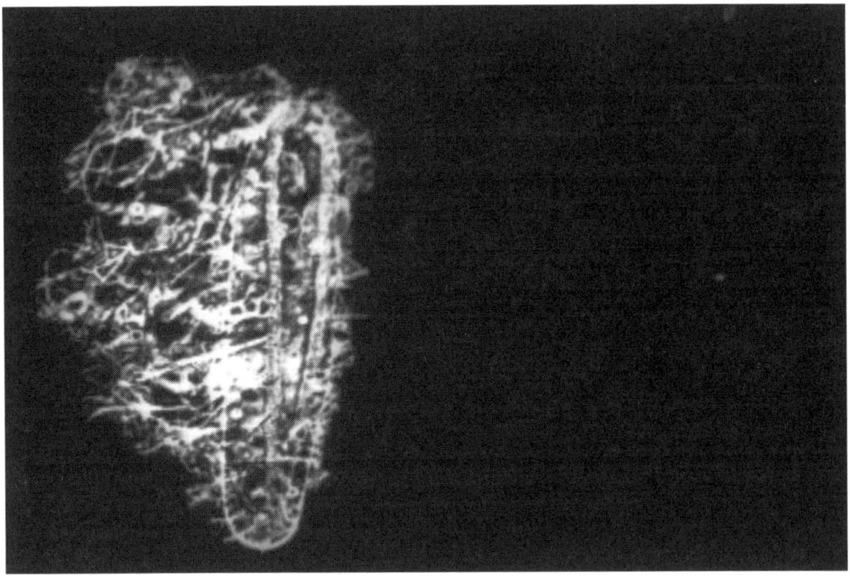

16.8 An extreme close up of film dust particle (optically printed). A voice-over says: "This is the essence of what they were ... distilled down into these compact shapes."

sciously chosen film fragments, often film material that no one intended to preserve, and they can even include the most ephemeral material of all: film dust (see figure 16.8).

NOTES

1 Carolyn Steedman, *Dust: The Archive and Cultural History* (New Brunswick, NJ: Rutgers University Press, 2002), 166.

2 Jussi Parikka, "Archival Media Theory: An Introduction to Wolfgang Ernst's Media Archaeology," in Wolfgang Ernst, *Digital Memory and the Archive* (Minneapolis: University of Minnesota Press, 2013), 7–12.

3 Giovanna Fossati, *From Grain to Pixel: The Archival Life of Film in Transition* (Amsterdam: Amsterdam University Press, 2009), 104.

4 Fossati, *From Grain to Pixel*, 130–1.

5 Rick Prelinger actually goes so far as to encourage film archivists to become filmmakers themselves, which I discuss in more detail later.

6 The soundtrack for *Stardust* is composed by Randolph Jordan (artist name Gerstyn Hayward) who is, given the narrative significance of the soundtrack, credited as co-author of the film. The film is available for viewing on Vimeo at https://vimeo.com/24885958.

7 Roger Smither and Catherine A. Surowiec, eds., *This Film is Dangerous: A Celebration of Nitrate Film* (Brussels: FIAF, 2002).

8 Dominique Païni, "Reproduction, Disappearance," in *This Film is Dangerous*, ed. Roger Smither and Catherine A. Surowiec (Brussels: FIAF, 2002), 173.

9 Several filmmakers also helped this cause by making compilation or collage films with nitrate films, disintegrated or not. Two well-known examples are *Decasia* by Bill Morrison (US, 2004) and *Lyrical Nitrate* by Peter Delpeut (The Netherlands, 1990).
10 For more information about this process, see Chute, "Film Preservation at The (Digital) Crossroads," *Film Comment* (unpublished article), 5, accessed 1 May 2008, http://www.geocities.com/Tokyo/Island/3102/f-prez.htm.
11 Ibid., 3.
12 See Druick in this collection.
13 Ryerson University rescued the entire film collection of the Thompson Public Library in Manitoba, which contains almost exclusively NFB titles. I was able to rescue sixty-four 16 mm films from the North York public library, including several Arthur Lipsett films, a complete 16 mm print of *Nanook of the North* (Robert Flaherty, 1922), and several NFB documentaries. Other film fanatics adopted some of the surviving 16 mm NFB prints for free by simply taking them out of a garbage dump. One can find several more for sale on eBay, craigslist, and film vintage sites.
14 The NFB donated many film prints to film schools, either as screening collections or to be used as editing material by students. This is how I obtained the images of the *Canada at War* series that are an important visual theme in *Stardust.*
15 Michael Witt, "The Death(s) of Cinema According to Godard," *Screen* 40, no. 3 (Autumn 1999): 332.
16 Jean-Luc Godard, as cited in Witt (his translation), 333.
17 One of the more original theses about the death of cinema explored by Godard is the one linked to the Holocaust: the failure of cinema to deal with the horrors of the Nazi genocide of Jews. Witt, "The Death(s) of Cinema According to Godard," 334 and 345.
18 Roger Mayer, cited in David Chute, "Film Preservation at The (Digital) Crossroads," *Film Comment* (unpublished article), 1–2, accessed 1 May 2008, http://www.geocities.com/Tokyo/Island/3102/f-prez.htm.
19 Paolo Cherchi Usai, *The Death of Cinema: History, Cultural Memory and the Digital Dark Age* (London, British Film Institute, 2001), 3.
20 Roland Barthes, *Camera Lucida: Reflections on Photography*, trans. Richard Howard (New York: Hill and Wang, 1981).
21 Catherine Russell, *Experimental Ethnography: The Work of Film in the Age of Video* (Durham, NC: Duke University Press, 1999), 7.
22 William Wees, *Recycled Images: The Art and Politics of Found Footage Films* (New York: Anthology Film Archives, 1993), 6.
23 Ibid.
24 Rick Prelinger, "Taking History Back from the 'Storytellers,'", Blackoystercatcher, blog post, 22 June 2009, http://blackoystercatcher.blogspot.ca/2009/06/taking-history-back-from-storytellers.html.
25 Ibid.
26 Ibid., 8.
27 Arthur Lipsett was a master in using news footage and other found images to create witty narratives that offered a sarcastic critique of modern society. See

also Gerda Johanna Cammaer, *Lipsett's Legacy: Recollecting Collage Films from the NFB and CFMDC*, published in conjunction with a film screening at the Art Gallery of Nova Scotia, and at Saw Gallery in Ottawa (Halifax: Atlantic Filmmakers Cooperative, 2007).

28 I really understood the complications of a more historical approach to found-footage films from comparing Peter Delpeut's film *Lyrical Nitrate* (1990) and Bill Morrison's *Decasia* (2004): see Gerda Johanna Cammaer, "Film Reviews: *Lyrical Nitrate.* Directed by Peter Delpeut, the Netherlands 1990. Decasia. Directed by Bill Morrison, USA 2002." *Convergence* 15, no. 3 (August 2009): 371–3. In some cases, films do not have credits and then it is not possible to list the origin of the found-footage used. This is especially the case with early films.

29 The film is available for viewing on Vimeo at https://vimeo.com/24885958.

30 I effectively enhanced the discoloured look of the film by reprinting it using an orange filter, thus making them look more monochrome and saturated. See https://vimeo.com/24893431.

31 Audio from David Lynch's film *Dune* (1984), line spoken by Paul Atreides, played by Kyle MacLachlan.

32 Audio for this part includes lines and sound from *Dune* (1984), *The Golden Compass* (2007), and the original *Star Wars* film (1977).

33 The sound is from a silent German film on beekeeping that was damaged by water, creating stains all along the strip that usually is reserved for the optical soundtrack. By recording the white patches as if it was sound, a crackling soundtrack was created. It can be heard in its entirety in the film *The B-Film Keeper* (2010, https://vimeo.com/24790941), an experimental found-footage-film about film decay and film preservation.

34 At another time in the film, a brief appearance of a partial frame-burn of this same image of the night sky with the full moon is used: the partial burn there looks as though under the full moon there is a full brain is hanging in the sky.

35 This scene is accompanied by audio from the documentary *The Race to Save 100 Years*, directed by Scott Benson (US, 1997). Although this documentary mentions a film vault in Hollywood, California, the images are from my film about the National Film Institute in Maputo, Mozambique, filmed on location in 1999.

36 Voice-over from *Stardust*, taken from the documentary *The Race to Save 100 Years* (1997).

37 I filmed these images in the National Film Institute of Mozambique on my visit in 1999. They are video images of a pile of damaged films left behind after the institute burned down in 1991. I applied a solarisation effect to the images so that they would look less "video-like" and to make the grain of these analogue video images come to life as if the films are actively crumbling to dust.

38 Audio from Werner Herzog's *Nosferatu* (1979), character Jonathan Harker played by Bruno Ganz.

39 Slug film was previously made by film labs of duplicate copies of commercial films on 16 mm that had had their best days in small independent theatres. After retrieving these copies, the lab made them "unusable" by scratching the image midway through and then sold the films as slug film at negligible

prices. The practice of scratching the images in the middle (stripping the films in the middle of about a three millimetre strip of information) was common practice to make sure the images could no longer be used for projection or to be optically copied. Working with slug or fill film is, to a large extent, a lost and forgotten practice because it belongs to the technique of cutting film and sound tracks on flatbed editing machines, which has been almost completely replaced by editing on computer. In any computer-editing program, users can insert "slug" with a click of the mouse. Slug is a "blank" picture without sound, to fill the spaces where there are, usually temporarily, no images or sound; places where the film needs a short break or breather; or to facilitate editing A and B rolls together. In sound, which when edited on a flatbed was cut on 16 mm magnetic film, slug was used where silence was needed. The editor used strips of 16 mm images, because over time blank magnetic sound film picks up dust and that would gradually become a (rather noisy) sound track in itself. This is the original purpose of the scratched images. Black leader and magnetic film were more costly than slug film, so there was also an economic reason to use it. This is how I obtained the last reel of Michelangelo Antonioni's film *The Passenger* (1975), which was hidden in a batch of duly scratched and discoloured 16 mm slug film I bought over a decade ago. Besides this brief appearance in *Stardust*, I also used this particular film footage from *The Passenger* to make two short videos that illustrate the double life most feature films on 16 mm lead these days: digital and restored or analogue and discoloured. See *Double Identity* (2009, https://vimeo.com/24890966) and *Jack Hits a Wall* (2009, https://vimeo.com/24891216).

40 As David Rodowick points out: "Often criticized in the history of the aesthetic as a medium of mechanical copying, the aesthetic experience of cinema is in essence non-repeatable. No two prints of the same film will ever be identical – each will always bear its unique traces of destruction with a specific projection history; thus each print is in some respects unique. And for similar reasons, there will never be identically repeatable viewings of the same print." Rodowick, *The Virtual Life of Film* (Cambridge, MA: Harvard University Press, 2007), 20.

41 In film, the term "china girl" refers to a model used in a series of frames at the beginning of the film, whose skin and apparel contain all the primary and complementary colours. Her colours, along with various patches in the frame, are used by the grader for colour correction during processing.

42 The audio is from David Lynch's film *Dune* (1984), line spoken by Paul Atreides, played by Kyle MacLachlan.

43 Audio also from the film *The Golden Compass* (2007), line spoken by Lee Scorseby played by Sam Elliot.

44 I already used this image to add suspense in my first found-footage film *Struggling in Paradise* (2004, https://vimeo.com/24893431).

45 This is a line from Werner Herzog's *Nosferatu* (1979). It is used twice in *Stardust*, once in the first part of the film, and then here again at the climax of the fight against dust.

46 The Kuleshov effect lies at the basis of a style of editing known as montage,

which gained importance in the 1910s and 1920s as a key concept of the Russian montage theory. This technique consists of assembling fragments of pre-existing films that are quite distinct, so that it is no longer the content of the images that is important, but the way they are combined: the film gets its power from the way the artist has disassembled and reassembled the images into new juxtapositions.

47 See Habib in this collection.

48 Line from *The Golden Compass* by character Serafina Pekkala played by Eva Green.

49 Steedman, *Dust*, 150.

50 Ibid., 146.

51 Wolfgang Ernst, "Let There Be Irony: Cultural History and Media Archaeology in Parallel Lines," in *Digital Memory and the Archive* (Minneapolis: University of Minnesota Press, 2013), 43–4.

52 Ibid., 44.

17 SAMPLING HERITAGE
THE NFB'S DIGITAL ARCHIVE

Zöe Druick

ACROSS THE COMPUTER screen lurch digitized images of the jumpy edits of an aged 16 mm black and white film. Identified as a part of the Faces of Canada series of the 1950s, the film features a mad scientist/artist, an immigrant to Canada, who is working on a machine that broadcasts "organic television" that will show Canada to itself. Nothing seems quite right. Are we in a dream? A man keeps repeating "aurora" and "Ademi" as we learn about his invention of a new Theremin-like electro-musical machine, a combination of the Internet and the Telharmonium called the Telemelodium. It can "show Canada to itself, the sum of ordinary things ... Ordinary things combined and made miraculous." Along with the "faces of Canada" reference, this phrase asks viewers to reflect on the original mandate of the National Film Board of Canada (NFB). Yes, it must be, for there in the montage we discern flickers from 1940s NFB films about life on the prairies. And, although he is never mentioned, in Ademi's accented English, his age, and his location in nocturnal Winnipeg we feel an affinity to the main character in Roman Kroiter's film *Paul Tomkowicz, Street Railway Switchman* (1953). And then there is the fact that we are watching the film on the NFB website.

The short film by Guy Maddin described above, *Night Mayor* (2009), is a "fable about the NFB" in which the director set out to "invent someone who's a tribute to the NFB and make a documentary about that person."[1] It cannot possibly be mistaken for a conventional NFB documentary, but it requires them all the same. Paul Tomkowicz, the reference for *Night Mayor*, is a humble man who cleans snow and ice off the streetcar rails in nocturnal Winnipeg. Ademi is an inspired inventor (played by a Bosnian artist and refugee of the same name) who has a mad dream to find "the peculiar truth which comes from the false" and whose operation to send and receive images and sounds from across the nation is soon shut down by the police. Maddin's tribute to the NFB's seventieth anniversary may well be the most idiosyncratic the institution received. However, as I will explore in this chapter, it engages with an archival project becoming increasingly dominant at the board.

The NFB, established in 1939, has been in transition since it began to face funding cuts in the early 1990s. While production is still part of the organization's mandate, increasingly it has been surpassed by the goal of preserving and presenting its archive of Canadian filmmaking. Since 2007, the agency has made considerable efforts to digitize its collection for web access, spending 5 per cent of its annual budget on this objective and also launching applications for watching films on mobile devices in 2010. At the same time, since the retirement of its long time in-house archivist Bernard Lutz in 2007, access to the archives by scholars and researchers has been severely curtailed. The NFB has no formal archival reading room or viewing area, and, since 2011, researchers have been required to submit official Access to Information requests to gain access to the archive.[2] At the same time, all over the country, 16 mm film prints of NFB films, once widely available, have been jettisoned by schools and libraries no longer willing or able to maintain these aging media artefacts and their requisite projector equipment. So, as with much of the transition to digital, the new archive is making certain things visible even while it contributes to the demise of other possibilities. In this chapter, I will explore the ways in which new platforms for and creative uses of the NFB archive are paradoxically related to some of the roadblocks to research and filmmaking that have been constructed. I will sketch out how these developments might be situated in relation to current discussions about film archiving, sampling style filmmaking, and historical cinema scholarship.

In her study of the politics of film preservation, *Saving Cinema*, Caroline Frick points out that archiving is a practice that simultaneously both defines and limits the range of material deemed worthy of preservation. She writes: "Those involved in moving image preservation have not merely preserved movie history; they have, instead, actively produced cinematic heritage."[3] Under the new digital regime, the audiovisual archive has most often come to be seen as a valuable image bank.[4] Furthermore, the neoliberal turn in the archival world is toward conceptualizing digital access through the language of the marketplace. We speak now of "content" and "users" in a move that arguably devalues the specificity of the texts in question, and certainly renders their materiality irrelevant.[5] In order to generate income, more and more film archives are curating and releasing their holdings on DVD or making them available for streaming. But doing so often puts archives squarely in the midst of intellectual property issues for which they are often under-resourced. Once released, they are quickly shared online and the films circulate without the care the archivists took to render them in high quality and provide context and interpretation. This is the more general context in which the NFB is trying to preserve its slice of Canadian cinema history.

CANADIAN FILM ARCHIVES

Unlike Britain and the United States, both of which have long-standing film archives, and even countries of more comparable size like Australia that have made great efforts to preserve and circulate their cinema history, Canada has never had a stand alone media archive and has a spotty record of preserving audiovisual texts.[6] The Canadian Film Institute, established in 1935, maintained a large archival collection of some 7,000 films (not all Canadian) until financial difficulties forced it to deposit its materials with the National Film Archives (part of the National Archives, now Library and Archives Canada [LAC]) in 1975.[7] The Audio-Visual Heritage Trust was established in 1996 on the recommendation of the Department of Canadian Heritage and the National Archives. During its lifetime, its programs advocated and supported preservation and aimed to make Canadians aware of their audiovisual heritage. The trust preserved and promoted "master works," restoring and re-releasing important Canadian feature films and sound recordings. In 2008, the Conservative government cut the trust's $300,000 budget, which led to its demise in 2009. In June 2010, the Academy of Canadian Cinema and Television announced that it would continue the trust's mission to carry out film and television preservation and restoration, although its accomplishments in this quarter are difficult to track.[8] In 2012, following a slew of cuts to the arts and public sector, cutbacks to LAC's film section risk making that archive less accessible.[9]

There are 250,000 objects in the NFB's film and video archives, including 13,000 original productions of various lengths; its website provides access to 2,000 films (through streaming, short-term rental, and purchase) and several thousand stock shots (which must be purchased).[10] Curatorial selection has been made at a number of levels. There appear to be two overriding factors that currently determine selections: marketability and rights clearance. Two full-time analysts work with marketing and sales to determine which new productions should go on the web and which older films are of interest due to their relation to current events or their status as classics. You can sometimes find the analysts' "picks" on the site, although they don't tend to provide more than ties to recent events or even times of year to justify their choices.[11] The most apparently accessible contacts in the NFB office work in the research and rights clearance support department, are named on the website, and are available by phone during business hours.

Over the years, the NFB has made many strategic distribution choices. The release of films on 16 mm to film clubs, schools, and libraries from the 1940s to the 1980s was comprised of curatorial choices. The decision to version films from French to English and vice versa, as well as into other languages, was based on a will to find larger possibilities of circulation for certain titles and topics (see Christine York's chapter in this collection). The CinéRobothèque in Montreal (1992–2012) and the Mediatheque in Toronto (opened in 2002) only ever supplied certain titles for their visitors to choose from, as did the intra-net library subscription service Cinéroute (1993–2008), which provided access to 600 titles deemed useful in educational settings.[12] When the NFB went to video distribution in the 1990s, only certain titles were made available and currently 6,000 DVDs are available for sale. On the website, less than 20 per cent of the total number of films are available for streaming and even fewer (1,000) are available on the NFB YouTube channel, which launched in 2006. In short, the NFB has always made choices about which of its films would have longer shelf lives and which would fade into obscurity.

Certainly, no one can fault the NFB, an underfunded institution trying to produce films and maintain its archive with dwindling resources, for making curatorial choices when considering any distribution strategy. Presumably such choices are welcome arbitrations of value, information, and entertainment for the majority of viewers who, when faced with YouTube-like viewing situation – a plethora of unknown titles – may well gratefully click on the most viewed options. As with many projects at the NFB over the years, digitization began when an envelope for funding, the Canadian Memory Fund, was made available in 2005–06. Answering to the question of priority, the first films to be digitized were those that were by and about Aboriginals, as well as those about World War I and II.[13]

While there are plans to digitize more of the collection, the NFB has run up against the issue of rights. Up to the late 1970s, the NFB controlled rights to all of its productions in perpetuity, and since 2000 Internet rights have been included in all contracts with producers. However, during the 1980s and 1990s, rights reverted to the creators. This means that the NFB must buy back or extend the rights for productions it wants to make available through its website, which has led to resource issues, both the expense of paying for copyright and for hiring staff to track down creators. Often music rights are simply too expensive to justify, and so certain films will most likely remain categorically excluded from the site.

Despite these issues, the NFB has plans to have its entire archive digitized by 2020 (a goal that can only be reached with its current capacities and may be affected by recent cutbacks). This is an important objective because, of course, the complete NFB archive consists of much more than its most popular films or those without copyright issues. The archive is an invaluable record of both filmmaking in Canada and visions of Canadian society with films going back to the NFB's founding in 1939. Researchers working on many areas of scholarly inquiry, including film history, social and political history, sociology, anthropology, art history, and communication studies, seek out the films and the written files that accompany them, as well as other footage, in order to pursue original research on the events and representations of the twentieth century. This, too, is an essential and irreplaceable feature of the archive.[14] As the 16 mm prints formerly available at a multitude of lending institutions are jettisoned, the digital archive becomes an incomplete source for researchers who are otherwise compelled to travel to Montreal North in order to seek out the prints at the physical archive, if they are permitted to do so. While some video transfers are available at the LAC, its collection is far from complete. (The NFB office in Montreal houses the physical film vaults for the preservation copies with a small percentage of materials, including nitrate prints, interpositive and internegative elements, and early video, held at the LAC's Gatineau facility.) The capacity at both sites is limited and the NFB is currently determining the best options for preserving the collection.

The NFB also keeps production files on many of the films produced under its auspices, but unfortunately, given the large amount of material, there is no overarching finding aid. In the years leading up to his retirement in 2007, archivist Bernard Lutz transferred aspects of the print archives on commonly requested topics into virtual search files. These include the Aboriginal studio in Edmonton; John Grierson; Norman McLaren; Arthur Lipsett; itinerant projectionists; Challenge for Change; and Studio D. In 2008, some restructuring at the NFB moved the archives under the administrative umbrella and away from the production side. At that point, they came under stricter interpretations of the privacy act and over a three-year period numerous researchers were denied access to the archives.[15] Since 2011, document requests must be filed under the Access to Information guidelines that regulate all government documents and a list of requests and outcomes since August 2011 is listed on the NFB website. (All documents that postdate 1969 need Access to Information requests because of these new policies.) Rather than visit the archive, requested documents (or a certain portion of them) are duplicated and sent to scholars. However, because there is no finding aid, researchers rely on NFB archivists to interpret their requests.

From its earliest days, the NFB has operated a stock shot library, which was famously used as the basis for wartime films in the 1940s and experimental film essays by Arthur Lipsett in the 1960s.[16] Today, the stock shot service offers access to thousands of short clips and photographs organized by topic, from the NFB and other archives, such as National Geographic, Framepool, and Gaumont Pathé. Highlighted NFB topics are: "classic and contemporary material on war and conflict, industrialization, rural and urban lifestyles, celebrities, wildlife and a treasure trove of film footage on the Arctic." Stock shots are an essential way to monetize a collection of historical images and an important means of income generation for the NFB. However, stock footage by definition is decontextualized, made ready for any new context in which it might be placed. The circulation of Canadian historical images as stock footage is most certainly not part of the interpretation of Canadian audiovisual heritage.[17]

INTERPRETING HERITAGE

Given the extremely restricted access to the archives and the lack of a comprehensive record of what is in them, it is somewhat ironic that the NFB's current mission is organized around the concept of heritage. The organization's five-year plan for the period of digitization (2008–13) notes, "The NFB is the steward of one of the world's great audiovisual collections; it is an invaluable heritage for Canadians and for the world."[18] The report calls for the animation of the archive through increased access by Canadians. The NFB website elaborates:

> The NFB is the steward of a historically and culturally significant collection of thirteen thousand productions, as well as five hundred thousand still images, an extensive sound library and almost six

> thousand teacher guides – with more works being added each year. This publicly owned collection is one that we're committed to digitizing, to make our work available to Canadians as never before while preserving it for future generations. The NFB has reallocated resources to meet the demands of digitization, offering content across a range of digital formats. We have launched a new web destination for stock footage professionals. We have also developed a unique DVD on-demand service, making over five thousand more productions available in this format. These digitized assets yield significant economic benefits, enabling the NFB to better leverage our brand visibility while exploiting the "long tail" economics of productions that appeal to a wide range of niche markets. Through digitization, the NFB is transforming a heritage collection into a vital cultural and economic asset for all Canadians.[19]

In the above quotation the heritage discourse is intertwined with the neoliberal market discourse in complex ways. With the heritage angle, the NFB is positioning itself in relation to an increasingly common framing of the value of records and art of the past. According to Frick, the discourse of "cultural heritage" that has taken hold in cinema preservation projects since the 1980s has been a survival strategy for archives that have become beholden to government and industry for support.[20] In Canada this relationship is especially overdetermined given the NFB's reliance on the state. Along with other cultural agencies, such as the CBC and LAC, the NFB has been in the Canadian Heritage portfolio since that ministry's creation in 1995. Yet over the past couple of decades, we have seen that heritage can be a slippery term, mobilized to foreground certain stories and marginalize others, levelling the past to an apolitical assemblage of historical facts. The NFB, which has always struggled to balance a mandate of sponsored and socially oriented filmmaking with the desire to be recognized internationally for its contribution to film art, is vulnerable to the problems of the "heritage" framework. The NFB archive is in a myriad of ways an excessive body of texts, many made to address pressing contemporary issues, which in some terms might not be justified as worthy of preservation. The framework of "heritage" in some ways remedies that issue, rendering the collection of historical significance despite many of the films' dated or aesthetically indifferent content. Yet the selective curation of the archive through the website often means that while NFB films have never been so readily available, the archive itself is being pre-screened and thereby less available for a more thoroughgoing analysis. Restriction of this sort means that the archive arguably serves a certain vision of history, rather than the researchers and artists who make it meaningful through their analyses. While there is nothing wrong with making curatorial choices for the public, these should not be at the expense of more in-depth research.

What does the NFB's vision of its past look like? In the following sections I consider a number of ways in which the NFB presents its past: through the website and DVD releases; a variety of remix film contests supported under the auspices of the board; and the archival filmmaking it has recently commissioned, such as Maddin's *Night Mayor* (2009), discussed above, and Luc Bourdon's *The Memory of Angels* (2008).

WEBSITE AND DVD RELEASES

The NFB's website organizes the films into eleven genres (animated, children, documentary, experimental, feature-length fiction, fiction, interactive materials, interview, making of, news magazine, and promotional material) and four formats (short film, feature, trailer, and clip).[21] There are fourteen channels on which to watch preselected playlists, including arts, kids' movies, the green channel, biography, hot topics, animation, outside the box, world, history, and Aboriginal peoples. Registered users can also create their own playlists and personal homepages on the site, discuss individual films on bulletin boards, and stay connected to the NFB through social media. In January 2012, the NFB introduced the "Campus" feature, which makes certain content available to viewers who are registered members of educational institutions. (Presumably, this opens the door to pay-per-use for other users.) As a result, the streaming options currently make distinctions between home viewers and educational subscription holders. The films are organized alphabetically by title, and can also be searched by director, key word, or series title.

The DVD releases are geared toward the most marketable titles for home and institutional sales, and most of them are feature documentaries. There are also digital downloads available for purchase or forty-eight-hour rental (at the time of writing, streaming is still free). The board has recently focused on a few of its historical auteurs, releasing compilations and interpretive documentaries about Arthur Lipsett and box sets of the work of Denys Arcand, Michel Brault, Gilles Groulx,

Norman McLaren, Alanis Obomsawin, and Pierre Perrault. Upon entering the NFB online store, the user is prompted to choose between a number of categories: Canada for home use; Canada for schools, libraries, and companies; United States for home use; United States for schools, libraries, and companies; and international (for which there is not an online purchasing option). The home use categories are different from the institutional ones, and place a greater emphasis on current events, family viewing, and Oscar winners. The institutional categories are more detailed, and allow for more focused and technical use of the site.[22]

Remix Films

In this category I put Jean-François Pouliot's commissioned anniversary film, *NFB 70 Years* (2009), Brett Gaylor's *RIP: A Remix Manifesto* (2009), and the numerous short films made as part of the remix projects the NFB has promoted in the past few years. In these films, the archive is often stripped of its historical and aesthetic context and made to stand in fairly simplistic way for either "great moments" in Canadian history or cinema, or generic images of Canadiana: beavers, RCMP officers, and the like. Often in these films the NFB takes some flack for producing boring or official visions of Canada, a story that greatly undermines the rich variety of work produced under its auspices. One of the projects for youth – Minus 40 – required that filmmakers work with images from World War II (films from before 1957 are in the public domain).[23]

La Mémoire des anges/The Memories of Angels

The NFB commissioned three films to commemorate its seventieth anniversary in 2009, the most high profile of which was Luc Bourdon's *La Mémoire des anges/ The Memories of Angels* (the other two were *NFB 70 Years* and *Night Mayor*, previously discussed). To their credit, and in very different styles, the films engaged the NFB as an ambivalent and suggestive archive that hides as much as its reveals. Bourdon's film uses the archive quite differently than Maddin, Pouliot, or the remix films. Drawing on images and sounds of Montreal found in the NFB archive – from both films and out-takes – Bourdon examines the tumultuous post war decades (1947–67) as Quebec's Quiet Revolution transformed Montreal. A self-proclaimed musical that presents a historical city symphony, Bourdon and his editor create a series of tableaux of Montreal at work, at home, and at play, across the seasons, on the streets, in the clubs. Cutting between black and white and colour and between the more stagey style of the earlier films and the more observational work of the 1960s, the film maps the shift over these twenty years from a city with dominant rural and religious roots to one that has entered the ambit of global capitalism. Although Bourdon denies the film's romanticism, there is an overriding elegiac tone made apparent, for instance, in the sequence about Parc La Fontaine, which is accompanied by a nostalgic song about childhood. The song continues over a montage of images of the city's skyline seen from Mount Royal, clearly linking the city to themes of loss and mortality. Even the nationalist folk songs of the 1960s, though accompanied by a brief sequence of rioting, are presented with nostalgia rather than outrage, another signifier of Quebec along with the Montreal Canadiens and the neon signs of rue Sainte-Catherine. Moreover, the film ends ambiguously by returning to the images of a lost Montreal. Working-class communities and tenements sacrificed to visions of a new and modern metropolis.

In his study of the film's take on urban heritage, James Cisneros argues that Bourdon's poetic style poses a fundamental challenge to the current discussion of urban heritage in Montreal and says, "the past is not a collective museum or an archive for everyone, but an ongoing social confrontation with winners and losers."[24] However, while acknowledging the changes to Montreal and the many angels of the departed, the film is ultimately ambiguous on its politics about the past, ending with a sequence from that most modern Montreal moment, Expo 67.

Although made to correspond to the NFB's anniversary and related to the NFB's heritage strategy, the film was proposed by Bourdon in the 1980s and arguably exceeds the NFB's official position on heritage.[25] Indeed, it is very different from the in-house contest for "Montreal lovers" called Montreal Remix that the NFB ran in 2011. In that contest, participants, who had the opportunity to win an opportunity for more film training in France, were given access to forty-eight videos about Montreal and asked to create their own five-minute mash-ups in what amounted to an audition tape. Unlike Pouliot, Maddin, or the remix contests, Bourdon took the opportunity granted to him through the heritage orientation to provide his own extremely personal and somewhat subversive take on heritage.

CONCLUSION

In this chapter, I have tried to indicate some of the paradoxes of the transition to digital archiving as they are playing out at the NFB. In the past five years, austerity measures have meant drastic cuts to public spending on the arts in Canada and public institutions housing audiovisual (and other) historical materials have been hit hard. In cinema, this has meant the end of the Audio-Visual Heritage Trust and ever more cuts to the LAC and NFB. In part, these cuts are justified by the very fact of digital archives, which seem to solve issues of access once and for all. One worrisome by-product of this assault on the public sphere is that, while the NFB grapples with its changing roles, scholarly archives are being made less accessible at the same time that popular archives are gaining greater profile. Using the heritage discourse to justify its preservation and digitization mandate, the NFB has perhaps unwittingly succumbed to the federal government's current attempt to restrict public discussions of Canadian history and thereby constrict visions of our collective future.

The NFB is a fundamentally public archive in two senses: it has been paid for by the public and it is an archive of the public. The digitization of the NFB archives seems on the surface to offer renewed and expanded access to the past, but may be doing so at the expense of the critical interpretive frameworks that scholarship and art practice can provide. In addition, by controlling the artists who have access to the archive for remix purposes, and turning the archive into a market through the pedaling of more or less decontextualized stock footage, the number of filmmakers who can lawfully use the NFB archive has dwindled.[26]

These images and sounds ought to be considered more than just "content" to be made available to users on a variety of platforms. Nor are they heritage in any simple sense. Certainly, they do represent a vast repository of filmmaking that has the potential to reward sustained investigation. Although the digital interface offers the potential to find and stream thousands of hours of archival material, as with other digital databases, the problem is potentially one of framing and contextualization. The idea for this chapter stemmed from the realization that scholars and filmmakers who use and value Canadian cinema archives should be entering into dialogue with the archivists who work there and the policymakers who determine budgets and objectives. Film scholars and archivists should be engaging the NFB – and the public – in discussion and debate that transcends the question of accessing content. We should encourage our students to see the NFB as more than a repository of kitsch images ready for remixing. The archive we need has to do more than offer us the discourse of heritage – it needs to support work that sharpens our perceptions of cinema in Canadian history and the vital role of such an archive in imagining our future.

FILMOGRAPHY

Bourdon, Luc. 2008. *La Mémoire des anges/The Memories of Angels.* National Film Board of Canada.

Gaylor, Brett. 2009. *RIP: A Remix Manifesto.* National Film Board of Canada.

Maddin, Guy. 2009. *Night Mayor.* National Film Board of Canada.

Pouliot, Jean-François. 2009. *NFB 70 Years.* National Film Board of Canada.

NOTES

1 "The NFB's *Night Mayor*, An Interview with Director Guy Maddin," 17 March 2009, http://www.onf-nfb.gc.ca/eng/news/index.php?id=1910. See also Julie Matlin, "Behind the Scenes of Guy Maddin's *Night Mayor*," 3 February 2010, http://blog.nfb.ca/2010/02/03/behind-the-scenes-of-guy-maddins-night-mayor/?ntpg_src=links&ntpg_sid=jm_cr_20110414.

2 In 2012, the NFB's funding was cut again by $6.68 million, approximately 10 per cent. "The NFB Announces the Measures that Will Be Implemented under the Deficit Reduction Action Plan," 4 April 2012, http://www.onf-nfb.gc.ca/eng/press-room/index.php?id=20712.

3 Caroline Frick, *Saving Cinema: The Politics of Preservation* (Oxford: Oxford University Press, 2011), 5.

4 Paolo Cherchi Usai, D. Francis, A. Horwath, and M. Loebenstein, eds., *Film Curatorship: Archives, Museums, and the Digital Marketplace* (Vienna: Österreichisches Filmmuseum, 2008), 81.

5 Cherchi Usai, Francis, Horwath, and Loebenstein, *Film Curatorship*, 79.

6 For information about Australia's national media archive, see Ray Edmondson, "The National Film and Sound Archive at Twenty-Five," *Metro Magazine*, September 2009, 142–7.

7 See Piers Handling, "Canadian Film Institute," *Cinema Canada* 19 (May/June 1975), 14. My thanks to Sanja Obradovic for this reference.

8 See Paul McCormick, "Preserving Canada's Cultural Heritage: The AV Trust," *Feliciter*, December 2007, 158; "ACCT to Continue AV Trusts' Efforts to Preserve and Promote Canada's Film and Television Heritage," 1 June 2010, http://www.academy.ca/press/release_acct_20100601en.pdf.

9 On 1 May 2012, following an austerity budget, Library and Archives Canada announced plans to cut 20 per cent of its workforce of 1,065 over the next three years, replacing in-person consultation with self-service through an augmented website. See Bill Curry, "Visiting Library and Archives in Ottawa? Not without An Appointment," *Globe and Mail*, 1 May 2012, http://www.theglobeandmail.com/news/politics/ottawa-notebook/visiting-library-and-archives-in-ottawa-not-without-an-appointment/article2418960.

10 James Roberts provided most of the information about the contemporary organizational situation at the NFB in this chapter. The NFB website is misleading in that it promises "over 13,000 Canadian productions at your fingertips," although this may be coming at some point.

11 For instance, in summer 2012, *King of the Hill* (1974), characterized by Albert Ohayon, collection analyst, as "Donald Brittain's terrific baseball documentary ... a look at the greatest Canadian baseball player of all time, Ferguson Jenkins" is listed as an "expert's viewing suggestion" apparently due to the concurrence of baseball season. These choices are also emailed to NFB subscribers.

12 "Cuts Lead NFB to Lay off 37 Montrealers, Close Cinerobotheque," CTV, 5 April 2012, http://montreal.ctvnews.ca/cuts-lead-nfb-to-lay-off-37-montrealers-close-cinerobotheque-1.792459.

13 One of the results of this was the 2011 launch of the Unikkausivut – Sharing Our Stories site and DVD collection of the many films made about and sometimes by Inuit peoples at the NFB.

14 See, for instance, the work published in *Challenge for Change: Activist Documentary at the National Film Board of Canada*, ed. Thomas Waugh, Michael Brendan Baker, and Ezra Winton (Montreal: McGill-Queen's University Press, 2010), much of which relied on original archival research.

15 Personal communications with numerous scholarly researchers, 2011 to 2014.

16 Celebrating Arthur Lipsett's work has taken on a particular resonance of late. The NFB has recently released three films that consider his life and work: *Remembering Arthur* (Martin Lavut, 2006), *The Arthur Lipsett Project* (Eric Gaucher, 2007), and *Lipsett Diaries* (Theodore Ushev, 2010).

17 Films made up almost entirely of stock footage, such as Adam Curtis's trilogy *All Watched Over by Machines of Loving Grace* (2011), are one way to catch sight of Canadian audiovisual heritage.

18 Tom Perlmutter, "NFB Strategic Plan, 2008–2009–2012–2013," (Ottawa: National Film Board of Canada, April 2008), 13.

19 NFB, "Collective Memory," accessed 28 May 2014, http://onf-nfb.gc.ca/en/about-the-nfb/the-nfb-today/collective-memory.

20 Frick, *Saving Cinema*, 55.

21 Note that there are two websites: www.nfb.ca, on which one can browse the film collection and create online playlists, and www.onf-nfb.gc.ca, which uses the Canadian government template and hosts the online store and the stock footage collection as well as providing educational resources and institutional history.

22 The home use categories (of which there are eighteen) are: new releases; newly available on DVD; Oscar winners and nominees; bestsellers; box sets and series; animation for the family; animation cutting edge; youth and family; sports and recreation; health and psychology; arts; history and politics; Canada; world views; spirituality; environment; catalogues and collectibles; and Alanis Obomsawin. The institutional categories (of which there are twenty-four) are: new releases; global issues; newly available on DVD; bestsellers; catalogues/brochures; Aboriginal people/Aboriginal studies; animation; arts; biographies; children/family; conflict resolution; drama/dramatization/fiction; economics; environment and conservation;

food and agriculture; geography; government/citizenship/politics; health and medicine; history; religion and spirituality; science; social issues; social studies; and collectibles.

23 However, using war as heritage is potentially problematic. In the bicentennial year of the War of 1812, the Conservative government's emphasis on war as a basis of Canadian identity received a mixed reaction. Meagan Fitzpatrick, "Conservatives Draw Fire for War of 1812 Spending," CBC News, 15 June 2012, http://www.cbc.ca/news/politics/story/2012/06/14/pol-war-of-1812-bicentennial-federal-events.html.

24 James Cisneros, "The NFB's Turn to Heritage: Revisiting Montreal in Luc Bourdon's *La Mémoire des anges*," *TOPIA: Canadian Journal of Cultural Studies* no. 27 (2012): 40.

25 Ibid., 32.

26 Compare, for example, the BBC Creative Archive and the Prelinger Archive, both of which allow filmmakers to use historical footage for free as long as the project is not profit-driven.

18 MEMORY, MAGNETIC TAPE, AND *DEATH BY POPCORN: THE TRAGEDY OF THE WINNIPEG JETS*

Andrew Burke

THE WORK OF THE the art collective L'Atelier national du Manitoba (2005–08) springs in part from the fortuitous discovery of a cache of de-accessioned tapes in a dumpster outside the offices of CTV Winnipeg. These tapes, jettisoned as the station was in the process of moving to its new downtown location, contained hours of footage of local news events, commercials, and current affairs programming stretching back to the late 1970s. The collective, spearheaded by core members Matthew Rankin, Mike Maryniuk, and Walter Forsberg, used this discarded archive material, along with other scraps gleaned from yard sale VHS discoveries and newly shot material, to make *Death by Popcorn: The Tragedy of the Winnipeg Jets* (2005). The film predates Guy Maddin's *My Winnipeg* (2007), but shares many of its preoccupations, particularly the fascination with the dialectic of attraction and repulsion the city exerts on its inhabitants. Whereas Maddin's film is deeply Freudian, with its absent but mythologized fathers and the monstrous femininity of its many mothers and maternal figures, L'Atelier national's work is less melodramatic and more methodical. *Death by Popcorn* sifts through the video remains of an earlier era and constructs a turbulent and trenchant video portrait of the city.

The hour-long video collage resists categorization. In this chapter, I will frequently refer to it as a film, despite its medium and format, in part to distinguish the overall work from its source video material, but also because the concept of "film" somewhat counter-intuitively includes video of many sorts, particularly long-format works like *Death by Popcorn* that offer a story or argument or document something. If format introduces a whole set of terminological problems, so too does genre. *Death by Popcorn* is a historical documentary about Winnipeg's hockey franchise, but it is also an essay film about the city itself, especially its economic decline and the onset of civic malaise in the 1980s and 1990s. The film's extensive use of archival material connects it to found-footage filmmaking, but its reliance on degraded and decaying analogue sources also makes it a kind of meditation on video specifically and on the medium's connection to history and to memory.[1] The film has a sharp satirical edge in the way that it pokes fun at the commonplace perception that the fate of the city is inextricably linked to the fortunes of its hockey team. Yet at the same time, it approaches the operatic and overblown presentation of paranoid conspiracies about the Jets' departure from Winnipeg in 1996 with great seriousness. In order to do justice to the generic and aesthetic complexities of the work, I will talk a little bit about Winnipeg and a little bit about videocassettes, ultimately connecting the two in order to argue that the work of L'Atelier national du Manitoba is specifically about *video-era* Winnipeg, that period stretching from the late 1970s to the late 1990s. The cultural memory of this era is mediated by magnetic tape and *Death by Popcorn* reworks and reconfigures those video memories, drawing on abject and forlorn jettisoned cassettes to present, as an intertitle near the beginning of the film puts it, history as written by the losers.[2]

After months of rumours and eager speculation, Mark Chipman, the chairman of True North Sports and Entertainment, announced on 31 May 2011 that professional hockey would return to Winnipeg, with confirmation that the team once again would be called the Jets coming just weeks later. The new Jets played their first game against the Montreal Canadiens at home on 9 October 2011, losing 5–1. The redesign of the Jets' logo and jerseys combined with the existence of a new, modern downtown arena renders the images of the old Jets in *Death by Popcorn* all the more uncanny, remnants of a past that is now firmly past, but which somehow still cannot be forgotten and shape the civic character. They are no longer traumatic reminders of unimaginable loss, but catalysts for a kind of civic righteousness grounded in the idea that recent historical wrongs have now been righted. Nevertheless, the pain of the memory still remains and is often conveyed in the most melodramatic of terms. For instance, in conversation with the *New York Times* about the return of the city's hockey franchise, Winnipeg's mayor Sam Katz describes the Jets' departure in strikingly gruesome terms: "When we lost the Jets, it was like someone smashed their fist through your rib cage, and while you were still conscious, pulled your heart out."[3] Katz's effort here to convey the city's psychic pain in terrifying, yet at the same time tremendously camp, physical terms is a testament to the central place that the loss of the Jets retains in the city's cultural imagination. This makes *Death by Popcorn* an even more valuable document in the sense that it captures a city in the throes of a deep and profound melancholia and in the darkest night of its civic soul, fixated on the lost object and waiting for a new dawn that does not seem to be on the horizon. It reveals the civic psychic scars that even the return of the Jets, the happy ending no one for a long time thought imaginable, has not healed.[4]

The film begins with an extraordinary montage sequence that draws its soundtrack in part from the opening lines of Michael Radford's adaptation of George Orwell's *Nineteen Eighty-Four* (1984). As Big Brother speaks of a "land of peace and plenty, harmony and hope" under perpetual threat from the "dark armies" of elsewhere, the film presents a series of images of the Jets and their fans, and of local commercials for furniture stores, fast-food chicken outlets, and pierogi makers that satirically represent Manitoban cultural specificity. The dark armies are represented by two figures, National Hockey League (NHL) president Gary Bettman and now retired hockey superstar Wayne Gretzky. The force of these images derives from the civic animosity Winnipeg harbours toward these men, both of whom play a key role in the various conspiratorial fantasies that seek to explain the Jets' departure from Winnipeg in 1996.

The conventional understanding of the Jets' exit is that the city was betrayed by Bettman, who orchestrated the team's move to Phoenix as part of a larger effort to secure a greater share of the lucrative American sports market. But this corporate conspiracy is grounded in the fact that the Jets' unsustainability as a big league franchise had everything to do with the city's status as a small market with a sentimentalized but antiquated arena incapable of generating sufficient revenue through ticket sales, the leasing of corporate boxes, or the licensing of television rights.[5] The team's failure throughout its history to capture the league's top honour, the Stanley Cup, is often explained as a direct consequence of this lack of a strong and significant revenue stream. Unlike their bitter rivals, the Edmonton Oilers, who won a series of league titles throughout the 1980s and early 1990s, the Jets seemed destined to always fall short of success, to be plucky but ineffectual, and to inevitably exit the league playoffs in the opening round. This failure on the ice seemed to manifest itself in a kind of provincial malaise, even resentment, as well. The Oilers' domination of the Jets, subjecting them to year after year of heartbreak and humiliation, came to represent Manitoba's position vis-à-vis the oil-rich and politically powerful province of Alberta in the provincial cultural imagination. The use of Big Brother's speech in the film points to the proximity between provincial *ressentiment* and a more full-blown fear of and hostility toward outsiders. The film does not assert that there is some fundamental xenophobia that defines Manitoba or Manitobans. Nevertheless, its satiric force does have a diagnostic edge in that it identifies in the collective anxiety about the province's status in the world, and about what others think of it, and documents the transformation of these anxieties into both resentment toward successful neighbours and a perverse and lacerating self-hatred.

These are topics to which I will return, but for now I will move on to the second bête noire in the story of *Death by Popcorn*. The film's demonization of Gretzky and obsession with his role in the Jets' downfall are at the core of what it has to say about the contemporary corporatization of professional hockey, the place the game occupies in the national cultural imagination, the importance of television and video in the Canadian 1980s and 1990s, and the contemporary function of the videocassette as the vehicle for the cultural memory of that time. Part of the film's humour derives from its elevation of Gretzky to a position of absolute evil, as the icon and embodiment of "the dark armies" that aim to destroy Winnipeg. Gretzky is shown throughout the film working his magic on the ice, he and his fellow Oilers scoring goal after goal on a series of demoralized Jets teams throughout the 1980s and 1990s, but the key images in the opening sequence are not from a highlight reel, but from a commercial for Pro Stars, a breakfast cereal created in 1984 to capitalize on Gretzky's overwhelming popularity (see figure 18.1).

A probable source for the commercial is an aging videocassette most likely recorded by some young hockey fan that laid dormant in a basement or attic for many years only to be thrown out, given to Goodwill, or sold at a yard sale after the kid had gone off to college or university. The static on the tape suggests this story, or one like it, but it also fits with the paranoid and apocalyptic tone that the film establishes. The snow might be the result of poor reception during taping, partial demagnetization while in storage, or the degradation of tape that occurs over time, but the film transforms this visual noise into a signifier for otherness, as if these images of a feather-haired superstar are the intercepted transmissions of an enemy nation, recorded and retransmitted as part of a propaganda campaign. Gretzky, in both the media reality of 1980s Canada and also in the dystopian fantasy the film constructs, is "the Great One."

18.1 Wayne Gretzky, seen here in an ad for Pro Stars breakfast cereal, is at the heart of the conspiratorial fantasies about Winnipeg's failure to keep the Jets.

His deification everywhere else stands in stark contrast to his demonization in Winnipeg. When the film cuts between images of a young Gretzky on the ice, his talent already visible at the pee-wee level, and those of a frenzied crowd, the clip drawn from a Hollywood film but meant to represent impassioned Jets fans confronted with the image of their sworn enemy and baying for his blood, it shows the city, to its own detriment, to be isolated, out of sync, and out of step with the course of history.[6]

Following this dystopian prologue that establishes the basic parameters for the film's satiric analysis of recent history, *Death by Popcorn* settles into its investigation of Winnipeg's civic disposition, from its desperate search for saviours, both on the ice and in the boardroom, to its tendency toward melancholia and fatalism. Video mediates this investigation, and so I want to say more about the specificity of video as a medium, and particularly the experience of watching an analogue format in a digital era. My sense is that video now signifies a particular era in a precise way, with its formal attributes and the signs of its wear and tear situating it historically. What I call the "video era" names that portion of history stretching from the late 1970s to the late 1990s when the lines of the video image rather than the grain of the film image or the clarity of the digital image signified the texture of the real. Of course, video itself has a longer history than that, with early recordings dating back to the immediate post-war period and its residual use continuing today. Despite this longer history, I argue that the look of video is now inextricably associated with the 1980s and 1990s, in the same way that desaturated 8 mm colour stock immediately invokes an imagined 1950s and 1960s or over-cranked monochromatic silent images conjure a sped-up 1910s and 1920s.[7]

The video era is a periodizing category that relies not simply on the visibility of technology and format that comes with the passing of time, but on their aestheticization as well. The look of video generates nostalgia, but there is something deeply uncanny about it as well, the lines of resolutions estranging us from a past that is relatively recent yet is starting to feel shockingly distant. There have been a handful of studies in recent years that have sought to think through the dynamics of social change and cultural memory in terms of both materiality and mediality.[8] The videocassette has played a significant role in several of them. Will Straw's "Embedded Memories" stands out as a key contribution to what might be called "videocassette studies" in its assessment of how they serve as a vehicle for the circulation of "cultural knowledges"[9] at the same time that they, due to their tendency to pile up and accumulate, also function as the storage containers of, and triggers for, cultural memory. As Straw explains: "Like any container, the videocassette may serve to both transport and stockpile the cultural knowledges held within it. It will transport these across geographical and demographic boundaries, and, through such transportation, contribute to the mobility of contemporary cultural life. At the same time, in stockpiling these knowledges, the videocassette, like any medium of storage, allows them to pile up and to persist."[10]

While the videocassette may be, as Straw says, like any other container in its ability to circulate and its tendency to accumulate, it does stand, alongside its companion the audio cassette, as the privileged media container of the 1980s and 1990s.[11] As a consequence, the videocassette, and perhaps the VHS tape in particular, stands as a key symbol of the era not because it remains the primary vehicle via which the sounds and images of the period circulate, but because, even once digitized and distributed online or via DVD, its material retains some textural trace of its source medium. Because of this, even in a digital age, the analogue consistency of video still filters our cultural memories of the 1980s and 1990s. The texture of video can even trigger these memories, as format and feel becomes as much as a marker of the past as of content.

VHS was not primarily a format designed for the creation of home videos. It was used for this, but, as Lucas Hilderbrand argues in *Inherent Vice*, it was a dependent technology principally used to tape broadcast television off the air.[12] As a consequence, there exists an incredible material archive of television from the 1980s and 1990s on videocassette that is now in danger of disappearing and being destroyed. This is perhaps not so catastrophic in terms of the endless number of primetime network television programs and marquee events that were taped, labelled, stored, and perhaps never watched again, but for the paratelevisual material that surrounded the programs themselves. Charles Acland uses the term "vernacular moving image library" to describe these video-captured remnants of broadcast television and points to their value:

> Buried in the shallow grave of those vernacular archives of video recordings are an extraordinarily rich, if haphazard and idiosyncratic, assembly of broadcasting oddities. One-time broadcasting events and anomalies, rare local commercials, station identifications, and sign-off notices. Bumpers, news inserts, and weather alerts announce that one is not just watching, for instance, *Force of Evil* (1948), but a specific late-night broadcast by a particular station of that classic noir.[13]

This material sadly lies beyond the purview of most institutional archives, but has become something of a YouTube phenomenon as enthusiasts sift through their video libraries for bits and pieces that are now in many ways far more interesting than the programs they were originally thought to have interrupted.[14]

The members of L'Atelier national are clearly collectors and archivists of this material. They collaborated initially with Winnipeg artist Daniel Barrow on a series of screenings that focused on local public access programming titled *Garbage Hill: A Showcase of Discarded Winnipeg Film and TV* (2005).[15] This was followed by a video compilation that unearthed a rich history of local television advertising, *Kubasa in a Glass: The Fetishised Winnipeg TV Commercial 1976–1992* (2006). *Death by Popcorn* manipulates and redeploys much of the material from these compilations and special screenings, interspersing it with the footage from the dumpster cassettes and supplementing it with home recordings of Jets games. While the content historicizes the images in the film, making it a eulogy not simply for a hockey team but for a bygone era, however recent, so too does the texture of their technological reproduction. The dropouts, rainbow flares, skew-errors, noise bars, and tracking interference likewise historicize the film, generating as much as the content does a sense of the age of the images and of the world being presented.

Death by Popcorn in particular, and L'Atelier national's work more generally, uses format historicity and medium specificity to demarcate, investigate, and, to a certain degree, celebrate the video era. The ads and local programming feature all kinds of oddballs and eccentrics of a sort rarely seen on television today, and that in itself is perhaps something to celebrate. As much as the poor production values and lack of ease in front of the camera define much of this material, there is also a good deal of inventiveness, playfulness, and wit. Above and beyond this, however, I want to follow Hilderbrand, who argues that video has an aesthetic dimension that is frequently overlooked and disregarded. Far from merely being a sign of technological failure or the format's limitations, these flaws represent "an aesthetics of access" in that they are "historical records of audiences' interactions with the media objects."[16] What was taped is of interest, as are the signs that what was taped was watched. Part of the force of *Death by Popcorn* is that the poor quality of some of its material is precisely the index of its importance: skew lines at the top and bottom of the image, for instance, points to something rewound frequently and played repeatedly (see figure 18.2). This tape stress suggests both passion and pathology. In *Death by Popcorn*, moments of triumph bear these signs of repeated viewings, but so do sequences of failure, suggesting a compulsion not simply to figure out what went wrong but also to dwell on it in an almost pathological way.

The bizarre richness of 1980s and 1990s Winnipeg television is what will return me to the tragedy of the Jets. One way to explain the efflorescence of local programming during that time is the city's size. Winnipeg was large and isolated enough to need and demand its own in-house productions, but small and peripheral enough to allow for a modicum of creative freedom and experimentation for those working in the field, including such local filmmaking luminaries as John Paizs and Guy Maddin,

18.2 The analogue technology of the VHS tape registers the stress and strain of repeat viewings and, as such, is a sign of the spectator's attachment to, even obsession with, the images it contains.

who were affiliated with the vibrant Winnipeg Film Group.[17] This mixture of necessity and opportunity generated a televisual culture that would largely disappear when the Canadian Radio and Television Commission changed the regulations governing locally produced programming in the mid-nineties and with the disappearance of local television advertising more generally as costs increased and viewership dwindled.[18] The Jets' tenure in the NHL coincided with this moment of odd and extraordinary local televisual production. The history of the team, as well as the history of the city itself in that era, is not simply *on* video, but is primarily accessible *as* video. Video mediates, but it also becomes the texture and format of cultural memory itself, even for those who were there. This connection between medium and memory is, to my mind, as much the substance of *Death by Popcorn* as is the desire to tell the tragic tale of the Jets and the city they left behind.

I should reiterate at this point that the film is no simple exercise in soft or celebratory nostalgia, either for the 1980s and 1990s or for Winnipeg during that time. Even as the film explores the aesthetic and cultural possibilities that opened up in that era due to the development of video technology and the particular fertility of Manitoba visual culture, it is also diagnostic in its assessment of the province's collective anxieties and the city's civic failures. One of the most striking features of *Death by Popcorn* is its incisive analysis of Winnipeg's desire for a saviour, a player who might have counteracted the force of Gretzky or led the Jets to a Stanley Cup victory. Over the years, three figures emerged who nearly fit this bill: Dale Hawerchuk, Thomas Steen, and Teemu Selanne.

Hawerchuk is the earliest of these figures, selected by Winnipeg as the first overall pick in the 1981 NHL entry draft. The team at this point was desperate for a player who could turn its fortunes around. Though they won the World Hockey Association's AVCO Cup in 1979, the Jets struggled immensely after joining the NHL for the 1979–80 season. The film makes much of the Jets' 1979 victory in a league that was about to be dissolved. In a montage sequence set to Screamin' Jay Hawkins's "I Put a Spell on You," *Death by Popcorn* imagines the AVCO Cup as a poisoned chalice, drinking from which doomed the team to failure during their existence in the NHL. The victory, ironically, was over the Oilers and their eighteen-year-old phenomenon Wayne Gretzky, and the film suggests that he takes revenge throughout the 1980s for the disappointment of this early, traumatic loss. But the most resonant element of the clip is the observation from the play-by-play announcer that, if victorious, "Winnipeg will get permanent possession of the Cup." The film loops and repeats this fragment, intensifying its force and transforming it into a terrifying prophecy that Winnipeg will suffer because of its success, that the city's golden age is over, and that it will not be able to succeed or survive in the harsher, more fiercely competitive NHL.

A dreadful first two years in the NHL followed this victory, and upon his arrival Hawerchuk did seem to be the saviour of the team and the city. He won the Calder Trophy for rookie of the year in his debut season and lifted the Jets from the bottom of the standings to a respectable finish and a place in the play-offs. The film does not dispute Hawerchuk's formidable talent on the ice, but does take aim at the pressure the team and city placed on him as Winnipeg's answer to Gretzky. While Gretzky exemplified the ease and charm of a sporting superstar and seemed wholly comfortable with his role as the league's pre-eminent player, Hawerchuk seemed altogether less comfortable in the spotlight. *Death by Popcorn* reduces the speech Hawerchuk delivered when he was inducted into the Hockey Hall of Fame in 2001 to a string of conjunctions and hesitations that stands in stark contrast to Gretzky's polished media fluency seen everywhere else in the film. Such an editing tactic is undoubtedly harsh on Hawerchuk, but also humanizes him. Hawerchuk represents a humility and awkwardness of talent that was beloved in Winnipeg (and elsewhere) specifically because it is so different from Gretzky's crafted, polished, and marketed superstardom.

This ironic celebration of Hawerchuk as the anti-Gretzky continues in a newly filmed sequence that sees Rankin, as L'Atelier member Matthew Rankin is called the few times he appears in the film, speaking by telephone to Sylvain Séguin, the lead singer of the Québécois indie rock group Les Dales Hawerchuk. Séguin tells Rankin that the band got its name because when he was young his friends told him his style of play was reminiscent of the Jets player. The name is a sincere tribute, as is its song "Dale Hawerchuk," the music video *Death by Popcorn* absorbs and manipulates. The song is a tribute to Hawerchuk from the perspective of a weekend hockey player who fully embraces the comparison with the Jets' star and imagines that it gives him potency on the ice and in the bedroom. The video has the band members in hockey gear, as if they just arrived home from the arena, parked in front of their television watching hockey highlights. *Death by Popcorn* augments the original video with footage of the Jets in action and other bits and pieces of Winnipeg-specific imagery.

The music video concludes with a tape auto-ejecting from an old top-loading VHS player. This is significant since both sports and music videos were staples of VHS culture and the subject of much home taping.[19] The most significant connection between the VCR and the NHL is *Don Cherry's Rock 'em Sock 'em Hockey* franchise, a video series that compiles highlights from the league with a particular focus on spectacular goals and savage checks. A perennial bestseller in Canada, the first instalment of the series was released on VHS in 1989.[20] In its montage sequences, *Death by Popcorn* participates in an ironic dialogue with the Cherry franchise. But it specifically engages with one volume in particular. During the making of the film, the members of L'Atelier national followed a list of seven rules. One of these rules identified the editor of *Rock 'em Sock 'em 5* as an influence and inspiration:

> This unsung film genius is the veritable Walter Murch of direct-to-video bargain-basement hockey tapes. Mark Devitt is the subversive editor behind Don Cherry's only cinematic masterpiece, *Rock 'em*

> *Sock'em V* (1993). While other works in the Rock'em Sock'em canon might more accurately be termed as "procedural exercises," its fifth permutation is a highly-stylized work of early-1990s formalist wonder. In it, cloaked in red and obscured by dark glasses, Cherry is shown to preside over a sinister hockey underworld, rapping out his strict commandments from the eye of a swirly, analogue vortex of magnetic Brakhage-gasms. In one sequence, the dazed and devastated Winnipeg Jets spontaneously burst into frames in the middle of the ice as a cackling Cherry leaves them to writhe and scream in this punishing fibre-optic agony. With *Rock'em Sock'em V*, Devitt made the very idea of hockey look like a horrible, conspiratorial nightmare.[21]

Death by Popcorn's highlight sequences have much of the same energy that attracts hockey fans in general to the *Rock 'em Sock 'em* series, and adheres to the Devittean model L'Atelier national themselves cite and explain. They interlace the action on the ice with an array of other images, from crying Jets fans to chopped and re-sequenced Kern Hill Furniture Co-op commercials, in order to parallel arena combat with the city's ongoing fight for survival in the face of an anticipated apocalypse. With both hockey highlights and music videos now having essentially relocated to YouTube, the collective social practice of watching tapes of this sort has receded into memory. The music video for "Dale Hawerchuk" captures the enthusiasm and electricity of watching something on tape, whether the experience of seeing something grabbed off the air and played over and over again or that of viewing a professionally assembled compilation as part of a pre- or post-game ritual.

The interview with Séguin also confirms a fascination with Québécois culture evident in the very name L'Atelier national du Manitoba. For the interview Rankin wears a Québec Nordiques jersey and sits in a room decorated with the fleur-de-lis and a Montreal Expos batting helmet alongside a Jets pennant. The mixing of this paraphernalia points to an imagined fraternity between the two provinces and a solidarity between Quebec City and Winnipeg as the two small-market Canadian cities that lost their NHL franchises in the 1990s. At the same time, it suggests a kind of provincial envy or admiration. While Quebec City may have lost its franchise, the province still had its beloved Montreal Canadiens. Furthermore, the strength and robustness of Québécois culture means that such a loss, while disappointing, was not as traumatic as it was for Winnipeg. This envy is not expressed by the ordinary Jets fans *Death by Popcorn* shows on-screen, but rather is something in the construction of the film itself and in the iconography that L'Atelier national adopts. Indeed, in "The Horizontalist Manifesto," the founding document of L'Atelier national that was composed in January 2005, the group claims, "Notre lutte est une lutte de liberté et de l'indépendence. Notre pays, la vraie patrie de notre Manitoba, c'est le Québec, pas le Canada."[22] The film offers a kind of reading of Manitoban political and cultural history by contrasting the province with Quebec, but also by adopting Quebec as a model for cultural independence. *Death by Popcorn* suggests that Manitoba's contemporary malaise and anxiety is due in part to the fact that it did not experience a cultural revolution of the Québécois sort and as a result retains a provincial, rather than national, identity.

In *Death by Popcorn,* this comparison between Manitoba and Quebec plays out, oddly enough, through the story of Teemu Selanne, another one of the promised franchise saviours, who arrived in 1992. Selanne's choice to stay in Winnipeg even though he had an offer from the Calgary Flames endeared him to Jets fans. The video clip of the news report on Selanne's decision to play for the Jets conveys both pride and incomprehension, once again pointing to the collective uncertainty of why anyone, if they had the opportunity to go anywhere else, would choose Winnipeg. Like Hawerchuk, Selanne had an immediate impact in his first season and set the record for goals by a rookie. The Jets' fans nicknamed him "the Finnish Flash," but *Death by Popcorn* creates the fiction that Selanne was known as "Général du Goal" for the purposes of a montage sequence that imagines him as the European leader who would inspire the team and the province to new heights.

After showing the highlights of a game in which Selanne almost single-handedly defeated the Oilers, the film switches to an extended clip of Québécois nationalist Pierre Bourgault speaking at a rally in the wake of General de Gaulle's visit to Montreal in 1967. Subtitles translate the speech, but transform its meaning entirely by substituting "Winnipeg" for "Quebec." As a result, the film forces us to consider Winnipeg as "fundamentally colonized" and a "ruined city." The force of the clip resides in Bourgault's assault on the sentimentalization of defeat. There is a spectacular moment when Bourgault tells the crowd that Quebec has no heroes, only martyrs. There are murmurs of disagreement from the audience, but he continues in the face of these jeers to argue that the lionization of martyrs can result only in an ongoing culture of defeat. General de Gaulle's speech, he argues, catalyzed a sense that Quebec could overturn its history of defeat, subordination, and colonization and become the winner of history. Bourgault names Montcalm, Papineau, and Riel among the martyrs of French Canada, the memory of whom must be overcome if Quebec is to move forward, but the subtitles substitute their names with those of legendary Jets players MacLean, Domi, and Hawerchuk. Just as Bourgault paraphrases General de Gaulle's inspirational message to the people of Quebec as "never give up," so too does the film imagine that, in the early to mid-nineties at least, Selanne would inspire Winnipeg and help transform its perception of itself from loser to winner.

However absurd the comparison between General de Gaulle and Général du Goal seems, it provides insight into the complexities of *Death by Popcorn*'s political commitments and fantasies. While it may on the face of it seem ridiculous to suggest that Manitoba could or should have a Quebec-like cultural revolution, the comparison reiterates the film's overall premise that there is a self-destructive aspect to Manitoban culture. Rankin takes this up in a film that he made after *Death by Popcorn*. *Hydro-Lévesque* (2007) is an experimental film essay that speculates on how the revolutionary energies of Quebec in the 1960s and 1970s might be transferred to and reanimated in contemporary Manitoba. As Rankin himself explains in an interview, the comparison between the two provinces comes out of the recognition that both "have something of a fetishized relationship with their own misfortune."[23] But whereas Quebec was able to harness the energies of discontent in a period of accelerated modernization and the growth of a sovereignty movement, modern Manitoba has thus far been unable to do the same. Rankin explains:

> In the 1960s and 1970s, Québec nationalism had a very heavy self-destructive streak to it. But, in large part because of René Lévesque, that electricity was re-channelled into a positive transmitter and today, in its best, most positive form, Québec nationalism is truly heroic and universal in its resilience. And I wanted that energy to be the force of good in my film. Winnipeg today is much like Québec was in the 1950s, except we are far more apathetic. Often we believe we are improving our city and affirming our collective worth as we commit the most profane acts of self-destruction. We demolish our

> icons, we vandalize our downtown with beautification projects, we curse the difficulty of our existence and long to be normal. To me, all of this is nihilism. So this was going to be the negative charge in my film. But in the end, I wanted Winnipeg to find its Lévesque. That's why, at the end, it is the electricity of Québec sovereignty that saves Winnipeg's life, like a transplanted heart.[24]

As such, *Hydro-Lévesque* offers a kind of solution to the intractable dilemmas sketched out in *Death by Popcorn*. Whereas the later film offers a kind of sci-fi-influenced political fantasy that imagines the reanimation of the province through the transplantation of energies from elsewhere, the former dwells satirically on the sense of imminent doom associated with the Jets' departure. *Hydro-Lévesque* follows the détourned footage of Bourgault with a terrifying clip of *Survival* (1982–87), a local Winnipeg public access show that purported to be a preparation guide for the coming apocalypse. A hooded figure warns viewers, "People are living their lives now, they're preparing for a future. But they are preparing for a future of nothingness and death if they are not preparing to survive cataclysm." *Death by Popcorn* juxtaposes this survivalist satire with video images of rallies held in a desperate effort to keep the Jets in Winnipeg and call-in programs that feature local fans almost in tears over the announcement of the team's departure. On the one hand, the film sets up the loss of the Jets as the cataclysmic event for which Winnipeggers have been sternly instructed to prepare, but on the other hand, it suggests the rallies of protest and ongoing efforts to save the Jets are precisely the fantasies of a future that will never be, the distraction from a cataclysm already in progress. That these rallies took place at the symbolic centre of Winnipeg, the much-mythologized intersection of Portage Avenue and Main Street, takes viewers to the heart of "the ruined city." Winnipeg's identity as a midwestern industrial city is marked by its history of suburbanization and the emptying out of its downtown. Successive city centre renewal efforts throughout the 1980s and early 1990s are distinguished by their complete misguidedness and almost total failure, and while Portage and Main remains the city's symbolic centre due to its historical importance, it had been transformed by the mid-1990s into a symbol of urban decline, with the bank towers that mark it quickly giving way on surrounding streets to parking lots, empty buildings, abject poverty, and other signs the urban core had been politically and socially abandoned. The clip from *Survival* extends the apocalyptic imagery that runs through *Hydro-Lévesque*, but it also invites viewers to see life in contemporary Winnipeg as already post-apocalyptic, with videotapes of Jets' past glory as the surviving remnants of life before cataclysm.

Selanne was a success during his time as a Jet, but was unable to lead the team to the victory it ultimately desired. He was traded to the Mighty Ducks of Anaheim in February 1996 as part of a fire sale the Jets management launched once it realized that the franchise's move to Phoenix was inevitable. An array of video clips from the time shows a city already in mourning for a team still on the ice, suffering through the remainder of the 1995–96 season in a kind of living death. *Death by Popcorn* draws on a local sports call-in show and on the street interviews to reveal the emotional and psychological impact the announcement of the team's departure had on the city. Mass exodus is a particular fear of many callers and interviewees. Without the Jets, they ask, why would young people choose to stay in Winnipeg? Such worries are expressed in an overblown and melodramatic manner, yet they nevertheless address the real fear of a provincial city that has long had to deal with outmigration. The Weakerthans' album *Left and Leaving* (2000) might be the exemplary expression of the melancholy of the abandoned, but *Death by Popcorn*, in its own satiric way, conveys a similar sense that for all the hysteria and handwringing the loss of the Jets caused, it was also a sign of Winnipeg's demotion or relegation to a lower level of urban desirability. As one tearful fan says, "I don't know what to do anymore. What can we watch in the winter, now? What is Winnipeg now? It's just nothing."

This fear of undesirability and emptiness explains Winnipeg's affection for Thomas Steen, who completes the film's trio of player case studies. While Steen's natural goal scoring ability may not have matched either Hawerchuk's or Selanne's, he was a leader on the ice and a consummate playmaker. Yet the primary reason Jets fans loved him so much seems to have been his attachment to the city itself. Steen spent his entire NHL career playing for the Jets, a commitment highly unusual in an era of free agency and the full marketization of sports labour. *Death by Popcorn* draws clips from the ceremony marking the retirement of Steen's jersey number in 1995. As Steen skates onto the ice for the award, the stadium announcer commends him for his commitment to the city itself: "This man and his wife and family embraced our city. Winnipeg became their home. They became involved in the community, spoke proudly about living here and passionately defended the quality of life in Winnipeg from the many outside our area who love to knock this great place in which we live." *Death by Popcorn* intensifies the disturbing weirdness of the commendation's mix of incredulity and resentment by replaying it repeatedly. The phrasing echoes the speech from *1984* that opens the film, but also establishes that Steen represents what a title card indicates is "Le rêve Winnipegois." That dream is less of victory, but of acceptance; for an outsider to come to Winnipeg and embrace the city. Steen, as such, counters fears of outmigration and abandonment, but does so as the representative of conservative domesticity. His professional afterlife as a Conservative candidate in the Winnipeg riding of Elmwood-Transcona in the 2008 Federal Election confirmed this symbolic status. He lost that election, but was elected to Winnipeg city council in 2010. Steen's foray into politics was the subject of great enthusiasm in the local press, but was also met with tempered criticism that had to dance around his popularity as a former Jet in order to criticize him as a candidate.[25]

With tongue planted firmly in cheek, *Death by Popcorn* presents a fourth possible saviour of the Jets. This fourth figure was not a player but a performer. Since its inception, L'Atelier national has had a fascination with Burton Cummings, the lead singer of Winnipeg's own the Guess Who, perhaps most famous for its hit "American Woman," the first single by a Canadian band to reach number one on the Billboard Top 100 (see figure 18.3). Its heyday coincides with the founding of the Jets as a World Hockey Association franchise in 1972. In his review of its *Live at the Paramount* LP that year, Lester Bangs announces, "the Guess Who is God," and explains, "they have absolutely no taste at all, they don't even mind embarrassing everyone in the audience, they're real punks without even working too hard at it."[26] Bangs's ironic enthusiasm for "Canuck creep" Cummings must have been short-lived since, by the mid-1970s, the Guess Who had disbanded and Cummings had transformed himself into a power ballad crooner. Key to this transformation was Cummings's image. The combination of his curly hair, bushy moustache, and toothy smirk became iconic, at once signifying a soulful sensitivity, a mischievous eroticism, and a bizarre goofiness. L'Atelier national seized upon this image in a postering and stickering campaign throughout 2005 and 2006, scattering a screen-printed image of Burton's face around Winnipeg with the title of his first solo hit, "Stand Tall," written underneath. In the midst of urban decline and dilapidation, this injunction seemed cruelly ironic, an impossible task

18.3 Burton Cummings, lead singer of the Guess Who, was drafted into efforts to keep the Jets in Winnipeg.

in a downtown that bore the scars of profound economic disenfranchisement and a city largely defined by its economic marginalization.

Death by Popcorn draws on video footage of Burton suiting up for a Jets practice, a cheap publicity stunt that took place in the midst of the departure crisis. Cummings, like Steen, is loved for remaining in Winnipeg despite his success, but ironically is also mocked for it, as if choosing to remain in Winnipeg is so inexplicable and embarrassing that it must be counterbalanced with ridicule and scorn. Cummings's own relationship with the city is understandably fraught. His endorsement of the Jets and his playful media appearances in the 1990s documented in *Death by Popcorn* show someone passionately committed to the city, as does his part ownership in Salisbury House, or Sal's, a local chain of burger restaurants. Yet Cummings is also known for his criticisms of the city, most notoriously his 1985 assessment that the Winnipeg he knew had been replaced by "Negativipeg" after a late night incident in which he was hit on the head with a beer bottle at a north-end 7-Eleven. This oscillation between passionate commitment to the city and frustrated and fed-up self-lacerating

18.4 "Winnipeg is losers. Winnipeg is the worst. Winnipeg is a shit-cake of broken dreams."

outbursts is what makes Cummings the local icon he is, embodying as it does some key aspect of Winnipeg's psychic disposition.[27]

Finally, the enigmatic title of the film itself refers to an incident from the 1990 Stanley Cup play-offs. The Jets led the Oilers three games to two in their opening round series, were up three goals to one in game six, and seemed assured of victory over their now Gretzky-less but still formidable arch-rivals. Then, late in the third period, a fan threw a box of popcorn on the ice. The moment is much mythologized and much lamented in Winnipeg hockey history, as it seemed to quash Winnipeg's momentum. The Oilers scored three quick goals to win the game, which turned the series around and saw the Jets once again eliminated from the play-offs by their arch-rivals.

Death by Popcorn dedicates a newly shot sequence to this incident. It stages a night-time back alley meeting in the depths of winter between Rankin and a man, played by local actor Rob Vilar, who alleges to have been the one who threw the fateful box of popcorn. Dressed entirely in Oilers garb and snacking manically on a box of Nutty Club popcorn, an iconic local Winnipeg brand, the man seems slightly unhinged and over the course of the interview grows incandescent with rage. He explains that he communicates telepathically with Gretzky on a daily basis and that the Great One has passed a divine message on to him. That message, he explains, is that "Winnipeg is losers. Winnipeg is the worst. Winnipeg is a shit-cake of broken dreams" (see figure 18.4). He proceeds to launch an assault on a series of cherished Winnipeg icons, from former provincial Liberal Party leader Sharon Carstairs to legendary the Guess Who members Burton Cummings and Randy Bachman to local television advertising staple furniture salesman Nick Kern. The punchline of the sequence comes when Rankin asks the man where he was born. The answer, of course, is "Winnipeg," satirizing and exemplifying the self-destructive self-loathing of Jets fans and Winnipeggers all in one fell swoop.

The comic ferocity of the self-loathing is combined in the sequence with the pathos-drenched, fatalistic assessment of Jets president Barry Shenkarow, who claims, "everything was going our way; if that fan hadn't thrown the popcorn on the ice, we probably would have beaten Edmonton that year." This deeply held conviction, shared by many, illuminates the second part of the film's title. The tragedy of the Winnipeg Jets is that their fate is understood as tragedy, as the result of some fundamental flaw that condemned them to years of agonizing defeat and eventual disappearance. The box of popcorn thrown on the ice symbolizes the civic sense that Winnipeg is the cause of its own failures. And as much as the film examines how this becomes a kind of self-fulfilling prophecy, it also quite ruthlessly pushes it even further, showing how such thinking is debilitating and comforting in equal measure. *Death by Popcorn*'s most tender moment comes when it returns to the conversation between Rankin and Sylvain Séguin from Les Dales Hawerchuk near its end. Asked if he has any message for Jets fans, Séguin says, "I'd tell them that they shouldn't give up their hopes of having an NHL hockey team again one day. You never know! And never think it's your fault for not having an NHL team. It is not Winnipeg's fault" (see figure 18.5) This is a clear echo of de Gaulle's message to Quebeckers not to give up that Bourgault passionately relates, but more importantly it is a compassionate message that recognizes the city's tendency for self-laceration and self-loathing and encourages healthy persistence rather than pathological fixation.

Video's role in all of this is as a medium for memory. The tragedy of the Winnipeg Jets was not the stuff of the stage or even of film, but of video, a format with which the team shares a lifespan and on which its highs and lows were captured. Piles of videocassettes archived the history of the team and the signs of their wear and tear, the decay and degradation of the video image, signifies the civic passion for the franchise, the

18.5 Sylvain Séguin of Les Dale Hawerchuk, a Québécois rock band, consoles Jets' fans who blame themselves for the city's loss of the team.

deep melancholy experienced upon its departure, and the passing of time itself. The Jets of the 1970s, 1980s, and 1990s are distinguished from the team's new incarnation not simply by new uniforms, a new arena, and a different set of players and management, but by the textural difference between the new high-definition video that will capture the on-ice action and the desaturated, low-definition VHS and Betamax that now dates its contents in a very specific way. *Death by Popcorn* salvages this forlorn material and in revisiting the recent past, shows the inextricability of memory, magnetic tape, and the Manitoba of the 1980s and 1990s.

NOTES

1 William C. Wees's *Recycled Images* remains the standard work on the subject. Wees's categorization of the various forms of found-footage filmmaking is helpful in understanding how L'Atelier national du Manitoba's work participates in a longer history of cinematic experimentation. The rescue of the tapes from a dumpster allies them with a filmmaker such as Ken Jacobs, whose *Perfect Film* (1986) consists of unedited material found in the trash. But their reworking of this salvaged material links them more concretely to found-footage filmmakers such as Bruce Conner and Craig Baldwin who, as Wees puts it, share "the ability to make others' images serve their own purposes through the transformative power of montage." William C. Wees, *Recycled*

Images: The Art and Politics of Found Footage Films (New York: Anthology Film Archives, 1993), 5, 14

2 The additional irony here is that the film itself was almost lost to history. After a sold-out run at the Cinématheque in Winnipeg and on the eve of a scheduled screening in Toronto, the filmmakers received a cease and desist order from lawyers representing CKY, the CTV affiliate that had jettisoned the material over a year earlier. The case was resolved not in court, but allegedly over clubhouse sandwiches at the Wagon Wheel, an iconic local Winnipeg restaurant, between the filmmakers and representatives of CKY. For more on how the experience of L'Atelier national exemplifies the fraught relationship between Canadian copyright law and the reuse and appropriation of existing media in the arts, see Val Ross, "Who's Killing *Death by Popcorn*? Artists Worry over Copyright Legislation as a New Film is Pulled from Harbourfront Program," *Globe and Mail*, 5 July 2006.

3 Jeff Z. Klein, "N.H.L.: Giddy Winnipeg Reclaims its Long-Lost Prairie Companion," *New York Times*, 8 October 2011

4 In the same *New York Times* article, Guy Maddin appeals to the conventions of epic and tragedy to convey his incredulity that Winnipeg once again has its Jets: "'So improbable is their return that I'm still convinced it hasn't happened,' said the film director Guy Maddin, likening the Jets' story to 'ghostly return in ancient texts' like Ulysses' journey in the 'Odyssey' and the shade of Hamlet's father strolling the parapet." The framing of *Death by Popcorn* as *The Tragedy of the Winnipeg Jets* captures the way in which the story of the team, the brutal economic realities of it disappearance, and the financial hopes staked on it return is best expressed in the form and language of fiction.

5 For a compelling reading of the political and economic context of the Jets' departure, see Jim Silver's *Thin Ice: Money, Politics, and the Demise of an NHL Franchise* (Winnipeg: Fernwood, 1996). Silver lays out how the Jets' survival could only have been accomplished with a massive injection of government funding, something that hardly seemed justified in a city renowned for its staggering level of child poverty and its more general economic precariousness. Silver himself was involved in a social justice group in the years prior to the Jets' departure that protested against the public subsidization of professional hockey, whether in the form of further tax breaks for the club or of municipal funding for the construction of a new arena. In his introduction, Silver contrasts the ascendency of the NHL as a desirable commercial product in the 1980s and '90s with Winnipeg's long economic decline from its heyday early in the twentieth century in a manner that resonates with, if not fully anticipates, the apocalyptic tone of *Death by Popcorn.*

6 Paranoia and conspiracy occupy a key place in found-footage filmmaking due, at least in part, to the genre's ongoing fascination with filmic material produced during the Cold War. Such material forms part of Bruce Conner's *A Movie* (1958), which is commonly identified as a key film within the genre. But perhaps the more striking antecedent for *Death by Popcorn*'s satirical reexamination of recent history is Craig Baldwin's *Tribulations 99: Alien Anomalies in America* (1991), a found-footage film that draws on a dizzying array of material to critique US foreign policy and the country's involvement in Latin America.

As Michael Zyrd argues, Baldwin's film illuminates the complex relationship between found-footage film and historical representation: "Found footage filmmaking is a metahistorical form commenting on the cultural discourses and narrative patterns behind history. Whether picking through the detritus of the mass mediascape or refinding (through image processing and optical printing) the new in the familiar, the found footage artist critically investigates the history *behind* the image, discursively embedded within the history of its production, circulation, and consumption." As a metahistorical form, found-footage filmmaking has the capacity not only to reveal history itself as constructed, but to expose the governing ideological fantasies and powerful social anxieties that shape that construction. Michael Zyrd, "Found Footage Film as Discursive Metahistory: Craig Baldwin's *Tribulation 99*," *The Moving Image* 3, no. 2 (2003): 42.

7 For further proof of these decennial associations, we need only look to the 8 mm Vintage Camera iPhone app, which offers "5 grainy, discolored, dusted and aged films from different eras," including the 1920s and the 1970s among others. There is now even an app, VHS FX Maker, that reproduces the look, feel, and resolution of 1980s-era videocassette recordings and promises to "make your videos look like old and retro VHS tapes."

8 The most significant of these – since it deals directly with the significance of videotape in all its analogue specificity, reproductive capability, and aesthetic opportunity – is Lucas Hilderbrand's *Inherent Vice*. I draw on and engage with Hilderbrand's study of videotape below. In addition to this key study specifically on videotape, several works have analysed the videocassette as a form of residual media. Articles by Will Straw and Kate Egan appear in Charles R. Acland's edited volume *Residual Media*, and Acland himself has written about "The Last Days of Videotape." Also important is Iain Robert Smith's "Collecting the Trash: The Cult of the Ephemeral Clip from VHS to YouTube" for the way that it situates the culture of VHS collectors and clip hunters within a larger history of cult film enthusiasts and found-footage filmmakers. In terms of a more broadly construed category of "format studies," Jonathan Sterne's *MP3: The Meaning of a Format* offers a model for thinking historically about media and format that potentially reveals all kinds of unexpected antecedents and extraordinary connections.

9 Straw, "Embedded Memories," in *Residual Media*, ed. Charles R. Acland (Minneapolis: University of Minnesota Press, 2007), 7.

10 Ibid., 7.

11 For more on the connection between the audio cassette, taping practices, and cultural memory, see essays by Bas Jensen, Michael Bull, and Karen Bijsterveld and by Annelies Jacobs in *Sound Souvenirs: Audio Technologies, Memory and Cultural Practices*, ed. Karen Bijsterveld and José van Dijck (Amsterdam: Amsterdam University Press, 2009).

12 Lucas Hilderbrand, *Inherent Vice: Bootleg Histories of Videotape and Copyright* (Durham, NC: Duke University Press, 2009), 35.

13 Acland, "The Last Days of Videotape," *Flow TV* 11, no. 2 (2009): 15 August 2012, http://flowtv.org/2009/11/the-last-days-of-videotapecharles-r-acland-concordia-university.

14 This is not to devalue the importance of the programs themselves, especially when rare or "missing, believed wiped" episodes, to use the BBC's phrasing for lost programs, turn up on videocassettes taped off-air. Videocassettes that contain programming taped off-air are especially important in Canada, which does not have a national television archive that houses older programs or collects current ones. For more on the consequences of this failure to archive and on the importance of VHS in accessing the Canadian televisual past, see Michelle Byers and Jennifer VanderBurgh, "What Was Canada? Locating the Language of an Empty National Archive," *Critical Studies in Television* 5, no. 2 (2010): 105–17.

15 Much of this material is on *Winnipeg Babysitter* (2009), a DVD compiled by Daniel Barrow and released by the Winnipeg Film Group.

16 Hilderbrand, *Inherent Vice*, 15.

17 In his article on L'Atelier national du Manitoba, Solomon Nagler provides a reading that situates its work in relation to both Paizs and Maddin. Nagler argues that the group continues the practice of "bargain basement filmmaking" Paizs exemplified and shares with both Paizs and Maddin a fascination with form and material: "L'Atelier's obsession with partially ruined visual materials can also be seen as a mannerism inherited from previous generations of prairie auteurs. Degraded celluloid that looks discovered rather than created and beaten Beta tapes that have lost most of their magnetic resonance are yet another means of expressing the ironic historicism of the prairie postmodern." Solomon Nagler, "Winnipeg Eats Itself: L'Atelier National du Manitoba's Scheme for Sovereignty," *Incite: Journal of Experimental Media and Radical Aesthetics* no. 1 (2008), http://www.incite-online.net/nagler.html.

18 For more on the institutional and regulatory factors that led to the rich fertility of Winnipeg cable access television in the 1980s and 1990s, see Allison Gillmor's article on Barrow's *Winnipeg Babysitter*. As she explains, unlike the CTV material the members of L'Atelier salvaged from a dumpster, the public access material had already been destroyed: "Original tapes of the shows were junked shortly after Shaw acquired local cable provider Videon in 2001, so Barrow's footage – which he has been hunting down for almost three years – was scavenged through informal channels, mostly from the private archives of show hosts or the stashes of packrat fans." Alison Gillmor, "Channeling Mayhem," CBC News, accessed 15 August 2012, http://www.cbc.ca/news/story/2006/04/12/winnipeg-babysitter.html.

19 I do not know of a comprehensive history of home taping practices and the culture of VHS, but in the absence of such a study, YouTube might serve as evidence that VCRs were used extensively to tape both music videos and sports events. Many of the clips on the site bear the traces of the material's broadcast origin and such digital remediations constitute evidentiary traces of a whole set of material practices of taping that existed in the 1980s and 1990s.

20 The history of the series neatly recapitulates the rise and fall of VHS. Volumes one to nine (1989–97) were released only on VHS, with the first DVD release coinciding with the tenth anniversary of the series in 1998. Volumes ten to eighteen (1998–2006) were released on both formats, with the VHS release being discontinued with volume nineteen released in 2007. Since 2007, *Rock 'em Sock 'em* has been available only on DVD.

21 L'Atelier national du Manitoba, "'The Seven Pillars of Atelier Aide-Mémoire on the Cinematic Form of the Winnipeg Jets' with Notations by Matthew Rankin," *Blackflash* 23, no. 3 (2006): 26.

22 My translation: "Our fight is a fight for liberty and for independence. Our country, the true homeland of our Manitoba, is Quebec, not Canada." L'Atelier national du Manitoba, "The Horizontalist Manifesto," *Incite: Journal of Experimental Media and Radical Aesthetics* no. 1 (2008), http://www.incite-online.net/manitoba.html.

23 Todd Brown, "A Conversation with Winnipeg Film Maker Matthew Rankin," interview conducted by Kier-La Janisse, *Twitch*, 15 April 2009, http://twitchfilm.com/2009/04/a-conversation-with-winnipeg-film-maker-matthew-rankin.html.

24 Ibid.

25 See especially Mary Agnes Welch's report on the 2008 election debates in the *Winnipeg Free Press*, 12 October 2008. She writes that Steen was "by all accounts and appearances a lovely and honourable gentleman," but concludes that he was "radically out of his depth, muzzled by his party and unfamiliar with the issues." Such an assessment points to the political capital that Steen brought to the election as someone associated with the Jets, even twelve years after the team's dissolution, while the care with which the criticism is worded, braced as it is for angry letters to the editor and ferocious online comments from Jets' fans and Steen supporters, points to the perceived hazards of challenging the team's legacy in any way.

26 Lester Bangs, *Psychotic Reactions and Carburetor Dung* (New York: Vintage, 1988), 112–13.

27 Although the 7-Eleven incident does not play a part in *Death by Popcorn*, it is the subject of a series of key post-L'Atelier films by its members. The Burton Cycle investigates the incident through interviews and re-enactments. The Cycle includes *Fahrenheit 7-Eleven* (Walter Forsberg, 2011) and *Negativipeg* (Matthew Rankin, 2011) with a third film slated to come.

ILLUSTRATIONS

1.1 One of the Kahnawake Mohawks performing in the *Hiawatha* pageant cinematographed by the Natural Colour Kinematograph Co in 1911. (Montreal *Daily Star*, 22 June 1911, 4.)

1.2 Montreal film exhibitors wishing to offer balanced programs frequently produced local topicals in the transitional era. (*The Standard*, 8 February 1913, 22.)]

2.1 A portion of "E" Division of the RCMP, assisting at the filming of *Policing the Plains*; Vancouver courthouse in the background, with Margaret Lougheed as Britannia. (British Columbia Archives, A.D. Kean collection, H-01266.)

2.2 "The Indians of the Blackfoot Confederacy were most intelligent, and gave serious heed to all details of the subject in hand – Treaty Number 7." (British Columbia Archives, A.D. Kean collection, H-01428).

2.3 The Royal Alexandra Theatre for the opening of *Policing the Plains* (1927). (British Columbia Archives, A.D. Kean collection, H-01428.)

3.1 This sequence from *Mighty Niagara* is reminiscent of early "phantom ride" films, which simulated travel by positioning the camera, and therefore the spectator, at the front or window of a moving train. (*Mighty Niagara* [Leslie Thatcher, 1933], courtesy Toronto Film and Video Club.)

3.2 *Mighty Niagara*: "Turbulent beauty found in the rapids above the Falls." (*Mighty Niagara* [Leslie Thatcher, 1933], courtesy Toronto Film and Video Club.)

3.3 *Another Day*'s modernist fragmentation and reconstruction is demonstrated in a sequence about Saturday morning at different kinds of work. (*Another Day* [Leslie Thatcher, 1934], courtesy Toronto Film and Video Club.)

3.4 In this sequence from *Another Day*, we see an increasingly abstract depiction of the events of everyday life, as a shower of coins represents commerce. (*Another Day* [Leslie Thatcher, 1934], courtesy Toronto Film and Video Club.)

3.5 An accountant at a ledger stands in for one kind of work. (*Another Day* [Leslie Thatcher, 1934], courtesy Toronto Film and Video Club.)

3.6 And a swinging hammer represents another. (*Another Day* [Leslie Thatcher, 1934], courtesy Toronto Film and Video Club.)

3.7 This sequence situates the fisherman in his milieu and shows his craggy features against those of the rocky landscape and the sky. (*Fishers of Grande Anse* [Leslie Thatcher, 1935], courtesy Toronto Film and Video Club.)

5.1 A flyer advertising Betty and Lewis Rasmussen, film lecturers from Racine, Wisconsin. Represented by the Redpath Bureau, the Rasmussens made a series of Canadian-themed film lectures, mostly about the North and the Arctic, in the 1940s and 1950s, including *Arctic Holiday*. (Flyer advertising Betty and Lewis Rasmussen. 1940/49. University of Iowa Libraries, Redpath Chautauqua Collection, MSC0150. digital.lib.uiowa.edu/tc.)

6.1 Whereas *La lutte* featured only the sportscaster's play by play, *Wrestling* was made more conventional by the addition of narration. (*La lutte/Wrestling* ©1961 National Film Board of Canada. All rights reserved.)

6.2 *The Bird Fancier* was one of the first NFB films to be translated through subtitles instead of voice-over. (*L'homme aux oiseaux/ The Bird Fancier* ©1952 National Film Board of Canada. All rights reserved.)

7.1 In a few moments Mary will see the world for the first time, thanks to the miracle of modern medicine. (*Barbara's Blindness*, 1965, Betty Ferguson and Joyce Weiland, *The Complete Works of Joyce Weiland*, vol. 1, DVD, Canadian Filmmakers Distribution Centre.)

7.2 A zombie woman emerges from the ground in a grotesque parody of Mary's emergence from blindness. (*Barbara's Blindness*, 1965, Betty Ferguson and Joyce Weiland, *The Complete Works of Joyce Weiland*, vol. 1, DVD, Canadian Filmmakers Distribution Centre.)

7.3 Young women enjoying themselves at a Job Corps retraining centre. The original black and white footage is tinted magenta in Weiland's film. (*Handtinting*, Joyce Weiland, 1967–68, *The Complete Works of Joyce Weiland*, vol. 2, DVD, Canadian Filmmakers Distribution Centre.)

7.4 Besides embodying the playful camaraderie of the young women at the retraining centre, this pose suggests a momentary liberation from the straitened circumstances of the women's everyday lives. (*Handtinting*, Joyce Weiland, 1967–68, *The Complete Works of Joyce Weiland*, vol. 2, DVD, Canadian Filmmakers Distribution Centre.)

7.5 In his film's next-to-last image, Lipsett sums up his view of the shallow and stupidly comic character of twentieth century Western culture. (*A Trip down Memory Lane*, Arthur Lipsett, 1965, The National Film Board of Canada.)

7.6 The film ends with a photograph of Einstein seemingly contemplating the sorry state of the world depicted in the rest of the film. (*A Trip down Memory Lane*, Arthur Lipsett, 1965, The National Film Board of Canada.)

7.7 As the film nears its end, a dandelion's full head of seeds suggests the continuance of the natural order of fertility and the renewal of life. (*The Eighth Day/Le huitième jour*, Charles Gagnon, 1967, *Charles Gagnon: 4 Films*, DVD, Spectral Media.)

7.8 Gagnon brings his film to a pessimistic conclusion with a negative image of a dandelion's full head of seeds, suggesting it has been burned black by the nuclear explosion in the immediately preceding shot. (*The Eighth Day/Le huitième jour*, Charles Gagnon, 1967, *Charles Gagnon: 4 Films*, DVD, Spectral Media.)

7.9 One of many archival images manipulated by Chambers to represent the fragile and insubstantial – yet still present – memories of the past. (*The Hart of London*, Jack Chambers, 1968–70, Art Gallery of Ontario.)

7.10 Chambers's home movie footage of one of his sons feeding a deer brings the film into the present while alluding to the past in which newsreel footage showed a deer leaping over fences in the backyards of London, Ontario. (*The Hart of London*, Jack Chambers, 1968–70, Art Gallery of Ontario.)

8.1 Yves Gaucher with the finished painting *R69* in his studio, 1969. (Film still, *R69 [unfinished/inachevé]* [Charles Gagnon, 1969–], 16 mm, colour, 53 minutes. Courtesy the Estate of Charles Gagnon.)

8.2 Yves Gaucher's studio, prepping canvas for *R69*. (Screen grab from *Archiving R69* [2011], made in Korsakow [interactive database film], created by Monika Kin Gagnon, www.archivingr69.ca.)
8.3 Yves Gaucher interviewed in front of his painting, *R69* (1969), by Klaus Fuchs, at the opening of *Grands formats* at the Musée d'art contemporain de Montréal, 1970. (Film still, *R69 [unfinished/inachevé]* [Charles Gagnon, 1969–], 16 mm, colour, 53 minutes. Courtesy the Estate of Charles Gagnon.)
8.4 Charles Gagnon checking the camera. (Film still, *R69 [unfinished/inachevé]* [Charles Gagnon, 1969–]. 16 mm, colour, 53 minutes. Courtesy the Estate of Charles Gagnon.)
8.5 Image of Wendy Michener (holding a Bolex film camera) and Joyce Wieland (with her back to camera), on a train between Toronto and Vancouver in the late 1960s. (Courtesy York University Libraries, Clara Thomas Archives & Special Collections, Joyce Wieland fonds. Photographer unknown. [ASC07123.])
8.6 Yves Gaucher mixing paints for *R69* in his studio, 1969. (Film still, *R69 [unfinished/inachevé]* [Charles Gagnon, 1969–], 16 mm, colour, 53 minutes. Courtesy the Estate of Charles Gagnon.)
9.1 One of Colin Low's arrangements of irregularly shaped multiple screens within the frame. (Courtesy of Colin Low and Library and Archives Canada.)
9.2 The nine-screen compositional palette. (Courtesy of IMAX Corporation, Graeme Ferguson, and Roman Kroitor.)
9.3 The three part vertical composition found throughout *Tiger Child.* In this case, what appears to be a single image is revealed to be three separate frames. (Courtesy of IMAX Corporation, Graeme Ferguson, and Roman Kroitor.)
9.4 Intellectual montage within the frame during the Ku Klux Klan sequence. (Courtesy of IMAX Corporation, Graeme Ferguson, and Colin Low.)
9.5 The "tiger child" juxtaposed with a desert landscape. (Courtesy of IMAX Corporation, Graeme Ferguson, and Roman Kroitor.)
9.6 The blind man amid the rioting. (Courtesy of IMAX Corporation, Graeme Ferguson, and Colin Low.)
13.1 Charlie walks Hastings Street. Images shot on location in 1962 with studio sound constructed in 2007. (*Hastings Street* [Larry Kent, 1962/2007]). Courtesy of Larry Kent.)

13.2 Colin and Laurie argue near the Pender Street rail yard in *The Bitter Ash.* Images shot on location with sound dubbed in studio. (*The Bitter Ash* [Larry Kent, 1963]. Courtesy of Larry Kent.)
13.3 Girl-watching on Kitsilano Beach in *Sweet Substitute.* Images and sound recorded on location. (*Sweet Substitute* [Larry Kent, 1964)]. Courtesy of Larry Kent.)
13.4 A fire truck with siren blaring (audio sourced from a sound effects library) underscores Charlie's anxiety in *Hastings Street.* (*Hastings Street* [Larry Kent, 1962/2007]. Courtesy of Larry Kent.)
13.5 Charlie is shunned by his mother over the phone in *Hastings Street,* originally played by Alan Scarfe and voiced forty-five years later by Nicholas Lea. (*Hastings Street* [Larry Kent, 1962/2007]. Courtesy of Larry Kent.)
15.1 A digital scan of the original film strip used to make *Western Sunburn.* (*Western Sunburn* [Karl Lemieux, 2007]. Courtesy of Karl Lemieux.)
15.2 A can of 16 mm film strips used in Lemieux's performance. (Personal collection of Karl Lemieux, photograph by André Habib, 2013.)
15.3 The first of three generations of the same British newsreel footage used during Lemieux's performance, photographed off a Steenbeck screen. (Courtesy of Karl Lemieux, photograph by André Habib, 2013.)
15.4. The second of three generations of the same British newsreel footage used during Lemieux's performance, photographed off a Steenbeck screen. (Courtesy of Karl Lemieux, photograph by André Habib, 2013.)
15.5 The third of three generations of the same British newsreel footage used during Lemieux's performance, photographed off a Steenbeck screen. (Courtesy of Karl Lemieux, photograph by André Habib, 2013.)
16.1 A double-exposed image combining footage from *Canada at War* with dusty film leader. (*Stardust* [Gerda Cammaer and Randolph Jordan, 2009]. Courtesy Syncope Productions.)
16.2 Close-up of film deterioration in a Super-8 home movie image. (*Stardust* [Gerda Cammaer and Randolph Jordan, 2009]. Courtesy Syncope Productions.)

16.3 Analogue incomplete film burn. (*Stardust* [Gerda Cammaer and Randolph Jordan, 2009]. Courtesy Syncope Productions.)
16.4 Dense film dust on Academy leader (origin unknown). (*Stardust* [Gerda Cammaer and Randolph Jordan, 2009]. Courtesy Syncope Productions.)
16.5 The fake starry sky (original footage from *CN Turbo*). (*Stardust* [Gerda Cammaer and Randolph Jordan, 2009]. Courtesy Syncope Productions.)
16.6 Maria Schneider (*The Passenger*, 1975) staring across a slug-film scratch at film dust and a troubled future for film. (*Stardust* [Gerda Cammaer and Randolph Jordan, 2009]. Courtesy Syncope Productions.)
16.7 General mobilization for the pending dust storm (original footage from *Canada at War*, CBC, 1962). (*Stardust* [Gerda Cammaer and Randolph Jordan, 2009]. Courtesy Syncope Productions.)
16.8 An extreme close up of film dust particle (optically printed). A voice-over says: "This is the essence of what they were ... distilled down into these compact shapes." (*Stardust* [Gerda Cammaer and Randolph Jordan, 2009]. Courtesy Syncope Productions.)
18.1 Wayne Gretzky, seen here in an ad for Pro Stars breakfast cereal, is at the heart of the conspiratorial fantasies about Winnipeg's failure to keep the Jets. (*Death by Popcorn: The Tragedy of the Winnipeg Jets* [L'Atelier national du Manitoba, 2005.])
18.2 The analogue technology of the VHS tape registers the stress and strain of repeat viewings and, as such, is a sign of the spectator's attachment to, even obsession with, the images it contains. (*Death by Popcorn: The Tragedy of the Winnipeg Jets* [L'Atelier national du Manitoba, 2005.])
18.3 Burton Cummings, lead singer of the Guess Who, was drafted into efforts to keep the Jets in Winnipeg. (*Death by Popcorn: The Tragedy of the Winnipeg Jets* [L'Atelier national du Manitoba, 2005.])
18.4 "Winnipeg is losers. Winnipeg is the worst. Winnipeg is a shit-cake of broken dreams." (*Death by Popcorn: The Tragedy of the Winnipeg Jets* [L'Atelier national du Manitoba, 2005.])

18.5 Sylvain Séguin of Les Dale Hawerchuk, a Québécois rock band, consoles Jets' fans who blame themselves for the city's loss of the team. (*Death by Popcorn: The Tragedy of the Winnipeg Jets* [L'Atelier national du Manitoba, 2005.])

BIBLIOGRAPHY

Abbott, Jennifer. *Making Video "In": The Contested Ground of Alternative Video on the West Coast.* Vancouver: Video in Studios, 2000.

Acland, Charles. "The Last Days of Videotape." *Flow TV* 11, no. 2 (2009): 15 August 2012. http://flowtv.org/2009/11/the-last-days-of-video-tapecharles-r-acland-concordia-university.

– *Movies, Multiplexes and Global Culture.* Durham, NC: Duke University Press, 2003.

– *Residual Media.* Minneapolis: University of Minnesota Press, 2007.

Acland, Charles, and Haidee Wasson, eds. *Useful Cinema.* Durham, NC: Duke University Press, 2011.

Alia, Valerie. *Un/Covering the North: News, Media and Aboriginal People.* Vancouver: University of British Columbia Press, 1999.

Altman, Rick. "From Lecturer's Prop to Industrial Product." In *Virtual Voyages: Travel and Cinema,* edited by Jeffery Ruoff, 61–78. Durham, NC: Duke University Press, 2006.

– "The Material Heterogeneity of Recorded Sound." In *Sound Theory, Sound Practice,* edited by Rick Altman, 15–31. New York: Routledge, 1992.

– *Silent Film Sound.* New York: Columbia University Press, 2004.

Armatage, Kay. "Kay Armatage Interviews Joyce Wieland." In *The Films of Joyce Wieland,* edited by Katherine Elder, 151–60. Toronto: Cinematheque Ontario, 1999.

Balcerzak, S., and J. Sperb, eds. *Cinephilia in the Age of Digital Reproduction.* London: Wallflower Press, 2012.

Baldur Hafsteinsson, Sigurjón, and Marian Bredin, eds. *Indigenous Screen Cultures in Canada.* Winnipeg: University of Manitoba Press, 2010.

Bangs, Lester. *Psychotic Reactions and Carburetor Dung.* New York: Vintage, 1988.

Banning, Kass. "Textual Excess in Joyce Wieland's *Handtinting*." In *The Films of Joyce Wieland*, edited by Katherine Elder, 129–35. Toronto: Cinematheque Ontario, 1999.

Barber, Theodore X. "The Roots of Travel Cinema: John L. Stoddard, E. Burton Holmes and the Nineteenth-Century Illustrated Travel Lecture." *Film History* 5, no. 1 (1993): 68–84.

Barthes, Roland. *Camera Lucida: Reflections on Photography*. New York: Hill and Wang, 1981.

Basen, Leila. "Translating the Reality." *Cinema Canada* (July 1982): 25–6.

Beauvais, Yann. *Found Footage/Films Retrouvé*. Paris: Galerie nationale du Jeu de Paume, 1995.

Beers, Clifford. *A Mind that Found Itself*. New York: Doubleday, 1908.

Berton, Pierre. *Hollywood's Canada: The Americanization of Our National Image*. Toronto: McClelland and Stewart, 1975.

Bertrand, Ina. "The Mystery of the Missing Director." *Film History* 12, no. 2 (2000): 215–25.

Bijsterveld, Karen. *Mechanical Sound: Technology, Culture, and Public Problems of Noise in the Twentieth Century*. Cambridge, MA: MIT Press, 2008.

– *Soundscapes of the Urban Past: Staged Sound as Mediated Cultural Heritage*. Bielefeld: Transcript Verlag, 2013.

Bijsterveld, Karen, and Annelies Jacob. "Storing Sound Souvenirs: The Multi-sited Domestication of the Tape Recorder." In *Sound Souvenirs: Audio Technologies, Memory and Cultural Practices*, edited by Karen Bijsterveld and Jose van Dijck. Amsterdam: Amsterdam University Press, 2009.

Bijsterveld, Karen, and Jose van Dijck, eds. *Sound Souvenirs: Audio Technologies, Memory and Cultural Practices*. Amsterdam: Amsterdam University Press, 2009.

Bobet, Jacques. "Les racines cachées." In *La production française à l'ONF: 25 ans en perspectives*, edited by Carol Faucher, 13–19. Montréal: Cinémathèque québécoise, 1984.

– "Survol Historique – Interview by Richard Gay." In *Les 50 ans de l'ONF*, 15–36. Montréal: Les Éditions Saint-Martin; Les Entreprises Radio-Canada, 1989.

Borde, Raymond. *Les Cinémathèques*. Lausanne: Editions l'age d'homme, 1983.

Bordeleau, Christian. "Les Bons Coups." *Sortie: Le Journal Gai* 1 (October 1982): 35.

Bottomore, Stephen. "From the Factory Gate to the 'Home Talent' Drama: An International Overview of Local Films in the Silent Era." In *The Lost World of Mitchell and Kenyon: Edwardian Britain on Film*, edited by Vanessa Toulmin, Simon Popple, and Patrick Russell, 38–40. London: British Film Institute, 2004.

Bouchard, Vincent. *Pour un cinéma léger et synchrone! Invention d'un dispositif à l'Office national du film à Montréal.* Villeneuve d'Ascq: Presses Universitaires du Septentrion, 2012.

Brakhage, Stan. "*The Hart of London*: A Document of the City." In *The Films of Joyce Wieland*, edited by Katherine Elder, 117–24. Toronto: Cinematheque Ontario, 2002.

Brody, Richard. *Everything Is Cinema: The Working Life of Jean-Luc Godard.* New York: Metropolitan Books/Henry Holt & Co, 2008.

Browne, Colin. "Afterword: Fugitive Events." In *Cineworks 2000: Twenty Years of Independent Filmmaking in British Columbia*, edited by Justin MacGregor. Vancouver: Cineworks Independent Filmmakers Society, 2001.

– *Motion Picture Production in British Columbia: 1898–1940 – A Brief Historical Background and Catalogue.* Victoria: British Columbia Provincial Museum, 1979.

Bruzzi, Stella. *New Documentary.* New York: Routledge, 2006.

Bull, Michael. "The Auditory Nostalgia of iPod Culture." In *Sound Souvenirs: Audio Technologies, Memory and Cultural Practices*, edited by Karen Bijsterveld and Jose van Dijck, 83–93. Amsterdam: Amsterdam University Press, 2009.

Burgess, Diane. "Charting the Course of the Pacific New Wave." *Cineaction* no. 61 (2003): 29.

Byers, Michele, and Jennifer VanderBurgh. "Trafficking (in) the Archive: Canada, Copyright, and the Study of Television." *English Studies in Canada* 36, no. 1 (2010): 109–26.

– "What Was Canada? Locating the Language of an Empty National Archive." *Critical Studies in Television* 5, no. 2 (2010): 105–17.

Cammaer, Gerda. "Film Reviews: *Lyrical Nitrate.* Directed by Peter Delpeut, the Netherlands 1990. *Decasia.* Directed by Bill Morrison, USA 2002." *Convergence: The International Journal of Research into New*

Media Technologies 15, no. 3 (August 2009): 371–3.

– *Lipsett's Legacy: Recollecting Collage Films from the NFB and CFMDC.* Halifax: Atlantic Filmmakers Cooperative, 2007.

Canada. *Report of the Royal Commission on National Development in the Arts, Letters and Sciences.* Ottawa: King's Printer, 1951.

Canadian Broadcast Museum Foundation. "Introduction" and "A Made-in-Canada Solution." *Newsletter Archive* no. 2 (2009).

Cavanagh, Tom, Marc Lapierre, and Marv Nolan. *Technology and the Practices Governing the Archiving of CBC Program Material on Magnetic Media.* Montreal: CBC Engineering Operations Department, 1992.

CBC Engineering Operations Department. *Recommended Practice for the Care, Handling & Storage of CBC A/V Magnetic Media.* CBC Engineering Operations Department, 1993.

Cherchi Usai, Paolo. *Burning Passions: An Introduction to the Study of Silent Cinema.* London: British Film Institute, 1994.

– *The Death of Cinema: History, Cultural Memory and the Digital Dark Age.* London: British Film Institute London, 2001.

– *Silent Cinema: An Introduction.* London: British Film Institute, 2000.

– "What is an Orphan Film? Definition, Rationale and Controversy." Paper presented at Orphans of the Storm: Saving Orphan Films in the Digital Age, University of South Carolina. University of South Carolina, Columbia, SC, 23 September 1999. http://www.sc.edu/filmsymposium/archive/orphans2001/usai.html.

Cherchi Usai, Paolo, D. Francis, A. Horwath, and M. Loebenstein, eds. *Film Curatorship: Archives, Museums, and the Digital Marketplace.* Vienna: Österreichisches Filmmuseum, 2008.

Chion, Michel. *Audio-Vision: Sound on Screen.* Translated by Claudia Gorbman. New York: Columbia University Press, 1994.

Chun, Wendy Hui Kyong. "The Enduring Ephemeral, Or the Future Is a Memory." *Critical Inquiry* 35, no. 1 (2008): 148–71.

Cisneros, James. "The NFB's Turn to Heritage: Revisiting Montreal in Luc Bourdon's *La Mémoire des anges.*" *TOPIA: Canadian Journal of Cultural Studies* no. 27 (2012): 29–46.

Clouzot, Claire. "Review of *Daisies.*" *Film Quarterly* 21, no. 3 (Spring 1968): 35–7.

Corbeil, Danielle. "Charles Gagnon, Painter, Filmmaker, 35 Years Old, Lives in Montréal." *Artscanada* 27, no. 2 (April 1970): 39–42.

Cornwell, Regina. "The Films of Joyce Wieland." In *The Films of Joyce Wieland*, edited by Katherine Elder, 51–6. Toronto: Cinematheque Ontario, 1999.

Craig, Estelle. *Under the Circumstances: How to Meet Celebrities without Leaving Home*. Bloomington, IN: Author House, 2005.

Cvetkovich, Ann. *An Archive of Feelings: Trauma, Sexuality, and Lesbian Public Cultures*. Durham, NC: Duke University Press, 2003.

David, Jennifer. *Original People, Original Television: The Launching of the Aboriginal Peoples Television Network*. Ottawa: Debwe Communications, 2012.

Dawson, Michael. *The Mountie from Dime Novel to Disney*. Toronto: Between the Lines, 1998.

de Kuyper, Eric. "Anyone for an Aesthetic of Film History?" *Film History* 6, no. 1 (1994): 100–09.

Delaney, Marshall, and Robert Fulford. "Film Technique at Expo 67." *Saturday Night*, July 1967. 33.

Demczuck, Irène and Frank W. Remiggi. *Sortir de l'ombre: Histoires des communautés lesbienne et gaie de Montréal*. Montreal: VLB Éditeur, 1998.

Derrida, Jacque. *Mal d'archive*. Paris: Galilée, 1995.

Dick, Ernest. "An Archival Acquisition Strategy for the Broadcast Records of the Canadian Broadcasting Corporation." *Historical Journal of Film, Radio and Television* 11, no. 3 (1991): 253–68.

– "Background Communication." In *The Future of CBC's Past: A Review of Archives*. 1990.

– "Presentation for Senior Management." In *The Future of CBC's Past: A Review of Archives*. 1990.

– *Guide to CBC Sources at the Public Archives 1936–1986*. Minister of Supply and Services Canada (Cat no. SA2-165/1987). Public Archives Canada, 1987.

Dick, Ernest, and Jana Vosikovska. "Survival of CBC Network Programming in Archives 1936–1984." National Archives of Canada, 1994.

Doane, Mary Ann. *The Emergence of Cinematic Time: Modernity, Contingency, the Archive*. Cambridge, MA: Harvard University Press, 2002.

Dorland, Michael. *So Close to the State/s: The Emergence of Canadian Feature Film Policy*. Toronto: University of Toronto Press, 1998.

Douglas, Dave. "Exile on Hastings and Main Street: The Vancouver Films of Larry Kent." *Canadian Journal of Film Studies* 5, no. 2 (1996): 85–99.

Drouin, Francois, and Yves Lille. "La taverne Québécoise: Histoire d'un commerce en voie de disparution." *Cap-Aux-Diamants: La revue d'histoire du Québec* 1, no. 2 (1985): 32–4.

Druick, Zoë. "Continuity and Change in the Discourse of Canada's Cultural Industries." In *Cultural Industries.ca*, edited by Ira Wagman and Peter Urquhart, 131–46. Toronto: Lorimer, 2012.

– *Projecting Canada: Government Policy and Documentary Film at the National Film Board of Canada*. Montreal: McGill-Queen's University Press, 2007.

Duffy, Dennis J. *Camera West: British Columbia on Film, 1941–1965*. Victoria: Provincial Archives of British Columbia, 1986.

Duffy, Dennis J., and David Mattison. "A.D. Kean, Canada's Cowboy Movie-Maker." *The Beaver* 69, no. 1 (1989): 28–41.

Duncan, Nancy, and James Duncan. "Doing Landscape Interpretation." In *Sage Handbook of Qualitative Geography*, edited by Dydia DeLyser, Aitken Stuart, Linda McDowell, Steve Herbert, and Mike Crang, 225–47. London: Sage Publications Limited, 2009.

Eberwein, Robert. *Sex Ed: Film, Video, and the Framework of Desire*. New Brunswick, NJ: Rutgers University Press, 1999.

Egan, Jennifer. "The Celebration of a 'Proper Product': Exploring the Residual Collectible through the 'Video Nasty.'" In *Residual Media*, edited by Charles R. Acland, 200–21. Minneapolis: University of Minnesota Press, 2007.

Eisenstein, Sergei, V.I. Pudovkin, and G.V. Alexandrov. "A Statement." In *Film Sound: Theory and Practice*, edited by Elizabeth Weis and John Belton, 83–5. New York: Columbia University Press, 1985.

Elder, Katherine, ed. *The Films of Joyce Wieland*. Toronto: Cinematheque Ontario, 1999.

Elder, R. Bruce. *Image and Identity: Reflections on Canadian Film and Culture*. Waterloo: Wilfrid Laurier University Press, 1989.

Ernst, Wolfgang. *Digital Memory and the Archive*. Minneapolis: University of Minnesota, 2012.

Evans, Gary. *In the National Interest: A Chronicle of the National Film Board of Canada from 1949 to 1989*. Toronto: University of Toronto Press, 1991.

Evans, Michael Robert. *Isuma: Inuit Video Art*. Montreal: McGill-Queen's University Press, 2008.

Featherstone, Mike. "Archive." *Theory, Culture & Society* 23, no. 2–3 (2006): 591–6.

Feldman, Seth, and Joyce Nelson, eds. *Canadian Film Reader.* Toronto: Peter Martin Associates, 1977.

Fossati, Giovanna. "YouTube as a Mirror Maze." In *The YouTube Reader,* edited by Pelle Snickars and Patrick Vonderau, 458–64. Stockholm: National Library of Sweden, 2009.

Fossati, Giovanni. *From Grain to Pixel: The Archival Life of Film in Transition.* Amsterdam: Amsterdam University Press, 2009.

Francis, David. "Hearing before the Panel of the National Film Preservation Board, United States Library of Congress." In *A Study of the Current State of American Film Preservation.* Washington, DC, 1993.

Fraser, Graeme. "Audio-Visual Education in Canada." *Crawley Commentary,* 10 December 1956.

Frick, Caroline. *Saving Cinema: The Politics of Preservation.* Oxford: Oxford University Press, 2011.

Froger, Marion. *Le cinema à l'épreuve de la communauté: Le cinema francophone de l'Office national du film 1960–1985.* Montréal: Les Presses de l'Université de Montréal, 2009.

Gagnon, Monika Kin, ed. *Charles Gagnon: 4 Films.* DVD and catalogue. Spectral Media, 2009.

– "The Christian Pavilion at Expo 67: Notes from Charles Gagnon's Archive." In *Expo 67: Not Just a Souvenir,* edited by Rhona Richman Kenneally and Johanne Sloan, 142–62. Toronto: University of Toronto Press, 2010.

– "Posthumous Cinema: On *Archiving R69.*" In *Charles Gagnon: 4 Films,* edited by Monika Kin Gagnon. Spectral Media, 2009.

Gasher, Mike. *Hollywood North: The Feature Film Industry in British Columbia.* Vancouver: University of British Columbia Press, 2002.

Gauthier, Christophe. *La passion du cinéma: Cinéphiles, ciné-clubs et salles spécialisées à Paris de 1920 à 1929.* Paris: Association française de recherche sur l'histoire du cinéma, 1999.

Gauthier, Jennifer L. "Dismantling the Master's House: The Feminist Fourth Cinema Documentaries of Alanis Obosawin and Loretta Todd." In *Native Americans on Film: Conversations, Teaching, and Theory,* edited by M. Elise Marubbio and Eric L. Buffalohead, 89–115. Lexington: The University Press of Kentucky, 2013.

Godard, Jean Luc. *Introduction à une véritable histoire du cinéma.* Vol. 22. Paris: Albatros, 1980.

Green, Charles. *The Third Hand: Collaboration in Art from Conceptualism to Postmodernism.* Minneapolis: University of Minnesota Press, 2001.

Gregory, D. *Change Your Underwear Twice a Week: Lessons from the Golden Age of the Classroom Filmstrips.* New York: Artisan Publishers, 2004.

Griffiths, Alison. "'To the World the World We Show': Early Travelogues as Filmed Ethnography." *Film History* 11, no. 3 (1999): 282–307.

Gunning, Tom. "'The Whole World within Reach': Travel Images without Borders." In *Virtual Voyages: Travel and Cinema,* edited by Jeffery Ruoff. Durham, NC: Duke University Press, 2006.

Habib, André. "Ruin, Archive and the Time of Cinema: Peter Delpeut's *Lyrisch Nitraat.*" *Substance* 35, no. 2 (Fall 2006): 120–39.

Habib, André, and Michel Marie, eds. *L'Avenir de la mémoire: Patrimoine, restauration et réemploi cinématographiques.* Villeneuve-d'Ascq, France: Presses Universitaires du Septentrion, 2013.

Hancox, Richard. "Geography and Myth in *Paul Tomkowicz*: Coordinates of National Identity." In *Candid Eyes: Essays on Canadian Documentaries,* edited by J. Leach and J. Sloniowski, 13–30. Toronto: University of Toronto Press, 2003.

Hand, Martin. "Lost in Translation: Authenticity and the Ontology of the Archive." In *Making Digital Cultures: Access, Interactivity, and Authenticity.* Burlington, VT: Ashgate, 2008.

Handling, Piers. "Canadian Film Institute." *Cinema Canada* no. 19 (May/June 1975): 14.

Hansen, Miriam. "The Mass Production of the Senses: Classical Cinema as Vernacular Modernism." In *Reinventing Film Studies,* edited by Christine Gledhill and Linda Williams. London: Oxford University Press, 2000.

Hilderbrand, Lucas. *Inherent Vice: Bootleg Histories of Videotape and Copyright.* Durham, NC: Duke University Press, 2009.

Hill, Michael. *Archival Strategies and Techniques.* Thousand Oaks, CA: Sage Publications, 1993.

Hoolboom, Michael. *Inside the Pleasure Dome: Fringe Film in Canada.* Toronto: Coach House, 2001.

Houston, Penelope. *Keepers of the Frame: The Film Archives.* London: BFI Publishing, 1994.

Huhtamo, Erikki, and Jussi Parikka. *Media Archaeology: Approaches, Applications, and Implications.* Berkeley: University of California Press, 2011.

Ibrányi-Kiss, Á. "Filmmaking West Coast Style: Jack Darcus." In *Canadian Film Reader*, edited by Joyce Nelson and Seth Feldman, 268–73. Toronto: P. Martin Associates Limited, 1977.

James, C.R. *Film as a National Art: NFB of Canada and the Film Board Idea.* New York: Arno Press, 1977.

Jansen, Bas. "Tape Cassettes and Former Selves: How Mix Tapes Mediate Memories." In *Sound Souvenirs: Audio Technologies, Memory and Cultural Practices*, edited by Karen Bijsterveld and Jose van Dijck, 43–54. Amsterdam: Amsterdam University Press, 2009.

Jeavons, Clyde. "The Moving Image: Subject or Object?" *Journal of Film Preservation* 73, no. 4 (2007): 19–32.

Jones, D.B. *Movies and Memoranda: An Interpretative History of the National Film Board of Canada.* Ottawa: Canadian Film Institute, 1981.

Kattelle, Alan D. "The Amateur Cinema League and its Films." *Film History* 15, no. 2 (2003): 238–51.

Keil, Charlie, and Shelley Stamp. "Introduction." In *American Cinema's Transitional Era: Audiences, Institutions, Practices*, edited by Charlie Keil and Shelley Stamp, 1–14. Berkeley: University of California Press, 2004.

Kelly, William A. *Educational Psychology.* New York: The Bruce Publishing Company, 1935.

Kinik, Anthony. "City of Contrasts: *Rhapsody in Two Languages* and the Politics of Modernity." FSAC Conference, 2009.

Koch, G., V. Pantenburg, and S. Rothohler, eds. *Screen Dynamics: Mapping the Borders of Cinema.* Vienna: Österreichisches Filmmuseum: SYNEMA-Gesellschaft für Film und Medien, 2012.

Kuter, Lois. "Take Me to Paradise: The Travel Film and the Real World." *Saying Cheese: Studies in Folklore and Visual Communication*, 63–75. Folklore Forum: A Communication for Students of Folklore and Bibliographic Series, 1975.

L'Atelier national du Manitoba. "The Horizontalist Manifesto." *Incite: Journal of Experimental Media and Radical Aesthetics* no. 1 (2008). http://www.incite-online.net/manitoba.html.

– "'The Seven Pillars of Atelier Aide-Mémoire on the Cinematic Form of the Winnipeg Jets' with Notations by Matthew Rankin." *Blackflash*

23, no. 3 (2006): 26.

Larouche, Michel. " Godard et les Québécois." *Cinémaction* 52 (1989): 158–64.

Lastra, James. *Sound Technology and the American Cinema: Perception, Representation, Modernity*. New York: Columbia University Press, 2000.

Lever, Y. *Le cinéma de la Révolution tranquille: De* Panoramique *à* Valérie. Montréal: Institut Québécois du cinéma, 1991.

Leyda, Jay. *Films Beget Films: A Study of the Compilation Film*. New York: Hill and Wang, 1964.

Lickers, Cynthia. "imagineNATIVE: Images Create Stories: Or Is It the Other Way Around?" In *ImagineNATIVE: Aboriginally Produced Film & Video*, edited by Cynthia Lickers, Aboriginal Film and Video Art Alliance of Ontario, and Vtape. Toronto: Vtape, 1998.

Lind, Jane. *Joyce Wieland: Artist on Fire*. Toronto: James Lorimer and Company, 2001.

Lion, Jenny, ed. *Magnetic North*. Minneapolis: University of Minnesota Press, Video Pool Inc, and Walker Art Center, 2000.

Lipsett, Arthur. "Notes and Proposals." *Canadian Journal of Film Studies* 7, no. 1 (1986): 46–62.

Löfgren, Orvar. *On Holiday: A History of Vacationing*. Berkeley: University of California Press, 2002.

Loughney, Patrick. "A Descriptive Analysis of the Library of Congress Paper Print Collection and Related Copyright Materials." George Washington University, 1988.

MacDonald, Scott. *A Critical Cinema 3: Interviews with Independent Filmmakers*. Berkeley: University of California Press, 1998.

MacKenzie, Scott. "Flowers in the Dustbin: Termite Culture and Detritus Cinema." *Cineaction* no. 47 (1998): 24–9.

– *Screening Québec: Québécois Moving Images, National Identity, and the Public Sphere*. Manchester: Manchester University Press, 2004.

Magder, Ted. *Canada's Hollywood: The Canadian State and Feature Films*. Toronto: University of Toronto Press, 1993.

Maltin, Leonard. *The Great Movie Shorts: Those Wonderful One- and Two-Reelers of the Thirties and Forties*. New York: Bonanza Books, 1972.

Marks, Laura. "Loving a Disappearing Image." *Cinémas: Revue d'Études Cinématographiques* 8, no. 1–2 (1997): 93–111.

Marsolais, G. *L'Aventure du cinéma direct revisitée: Histoire, esthétique, méthodes, tendances, textes des cinéastes, repères chronologiques, glossaire, index.* Laval, Quebec: 400 coups, 1997.

Matamala, Anna. "Teaching Voice-over: A Practical Approach." In *The Didactics of Audiovisual Translation,* edited by Jorge Díaz Cintas. Philadelphia, PA: John Benjamins, 2008.

Matheson, Sarah. "Projecting Placelessness: Industrial Television and the 'Authentic' Canadian City." In *Contracting out Hollywood: Runaway Productions and Foreign Location Shooting,* edited by Greg Elmer and Mike Gasher, 117–39. Maryland: Rowman and Littlefield, 2005.

Mekas, Jonas. "Ernie Gehr Interviewed by Jonas Mekas, March 24, 1971." *Film Culture* no. 53–5 (Spring 1972).

Miller, Mary Jane. "Archives from the Point of View of the Scholarly User: Or if I Died and Went to a Platonic Archetype of a Sound and Moving Images Archive This Is What I'd Find." In *Documents that Move and Speak: Audiovisual Archives in the New Information Age,* 252–7. London: KG Saur, 1992.

Morris, Peter. "After Grierson: The National Film Board 1945–1953." In *Take Two: A Tribute to Film in Canada,* edited by Seth Feldman. Toronto: Irwin Publishing, 1984.

– *Embattled Shadows: A History of Canadian Cinema, 1895–1939.* Montreal: McGill-Queen's University Press, 1978/1992.

– "The Years of the Quota." In *Embattled Shadows: A History of Canadian Cinema, 1895–1939.* Montreal: McGill-Queen's University Press, 1978/1992.

Musser, Charles. "Film, Propaganda and World War I: Images of War in the United States during the First Months of Neutrality." In *Cinéma sans frontière 1896–1918*, edited by Roland Cosandey and François Albera, 261–71. Lausanne/Quebec: Payot/Nuit blanche, 1995.

Nagler, Solomon. "Winnipeg Eats Itself: L'Atelier National du Manitoba's Scheme for Sovereignty." *Incite: Journal of Experimental Media and Radical Aesthetics* no. 1 (2008). http://www.incite-online.net/nagler.html.

National Film Board. *NFB Strategic Plan 2008–9–2012–13.* National Film Board, 2008.

Newman, Timothy. "Mediating Collaborations: Arla Saare, the CBUT Film Unit, and the Emergence of the 'West Coast School.'" Paper presented at the annual meeting of the Film Studies Association of

Canada, University of Victoria, 5 June 2013.
NITV on IsumaTV. Television. Directed by Nunavut Independent Television Network. Igloolik: Nunavut Independent Television Network, 2009.
Noble, Nancy, and Mari Fujita. *Neon Vancouver, Ugly Vancouver*. Vancouver: Museum of Vancouver, 2012.
Nolan, Brian. *Donald Brittain – Man of Film*. Toronto: DigiWire, 2004.
Nornes, Abé Mark. *Cinema Babel: Translating Global Cinema*. Minneapolis: University of Minnesota Press, 2007.
Nuss, Steve. "Music from the Right: The Politics of Toshiro Mayuzumi's Essay for String Orchestra." In *Locating East Asia in Western Art Music*, edited by Yayoi Uno Everett and Frederick Lau, 85–118. Middletown, CT: Wesleyan University Press, 2004.
O'Brien, Charles. *Cinema's Conversion to Sound: Technology and Film Style in France and the U.S.* Bloomington: Indiana University Press, 2005.
Païni, Dominique. *Le cinéma, un art moderne*. Paris: Cahiers du cinéma, 1997.
Papazian, Elizabeth. *Manufacturing Truth: The Documentary Moment in Early Soviet Culture*. DeKalb: Northern Illinois University Press, 2009.
Pendakur, Manjunath. *Canadian Dreams and American Control: The Political Economy of the Canadian Film Industry*. Detroit: Wayne State University Press, 1990.
Perron, Julie. *Mai en Décembre: Godard en Abitibi*. Office national du film du Canada, 2000.
Peters, John Durham. *Speaking into the Air: A History of the Idea of Communication*. Chicago: University of Chicago Press, 1999.
Peterson, Betty. *The Toronto Movie Club: Its First Fifty Years, 1934–1984*. Toronto: pamphlet, nd. [1984].
Peterson, James. *Dreams of Chaos, Visions of Order: Understanding the American Avant-Garde Cinema*. Detroit: Wayne State University Press, 1994.
Peterson, Jennifer Lynn. *Education in the School of Dreams: Travelogues and Early Nonfiction Film*. Durham, NC: Duke University Press, 2013.
– "Travelogues." In *Encyclopedia of Early Cinema*, 640–3. New York: Routledge, 2005.
– "Travelogues and Early Nonfiction Film Introduction." In *American Cinema's Transitional Era: Audiences, Institutions, Practices*, edited by Charlie Keil and Shelley Stamp, 191–213. Berkeley: University of

California Press, 2004.
Pierce, David. "The Legion of the Condemned: Why American Silent Films Perished." *Film History* 9 (1997): 5–27.
Prelinger, Rick. "The Appearance of Archives." In *The Youtube Reader*, edited by Pelle Snickars and Patrick Vonderau, 268–74. Stockholm: National Library of Sweden, 2009.
Punter, John. *The Vancouver Achievement: Urban Planning and Design.* Vancouver: University of British Columbia Press, 2003.
Rabinovitz, Lauren. "The Development of Feminist Strategies in the Experimental Films of Joyce Wieland." In *The Films of Joyce Wieland*, edited by Katherine Elder, 119–28. Toronto: Cinematheque Ontario, 1999.
– *Electric Dreamland: Amusement Parks, Movies, and American Modernity.* New York: Columbia University Press, 2012.
– *Points of Resistance: Women, Power, and Politics in the New York Avant-Garde Cinema, 1943–71.* 2nd ed. Chicago: University of Illinois Press, 2003.
Rees, A.L. *A History of Experimental Film and Video: From Canonical Avant-Garde to Contemporary British Practice.* London: BFI Publishing, 1999.
Register of Copyrights. *Report on Orphan Works.* Washington, DC: United States Copyright Office, 2006.
Riesman, David. *The Lonely Crowd: A Study in the Changing American Character.* Abridged ed. New Haven: Yale University Press, 1989.
Robertson, Robert. *Eisenstein on the Audiovisual: The Montage of Music, Image and Sound in Cinema.* London: Tauris Academic Studies, 2009.
Rodowick, David Norman. *The Virtual Life of Film.* Cambridge, MA: Harvard University Press, 2007.
Rony, Fatimah Tobing. *The Third Eye: Race, Cinema, and Ethnographic Spectacle.* Durham, NC: Duke University Press, 1996.
Rosa, Maria de. "Studio One: Of Storytellers and Stories." In *North of Everything: English-Canadian Cinema since 1980*, edited by William Beard and Jerry White, 328–41. Edmonton: University of Alberta Press, 2002.
Rosenbaum, Jonathan. *Goodbye Cinema, Hello Cinephilia: Film Culture in Transition.* Chicago: University of Chicago Press, 2010.
Ross, Melvin. "Cine Vagabonds." Unpublished manuscript. Vol. PR2004.0122/6 Provincial Archives of Alberta.
Roth, Lorna. *Something New in the Air: The Story of First Peoples*

Television Broadcasting in Canada. Montreal: McGill-Queen's University Press, 2005.
Rugh, Susan Sessions. *Are We There Yet?: The Golden Age of American Family Vacations*. Lawrence: University Press of Kansas, 2008.
Ruoff, Jeffery. "Around the World in Eighty Minutes: The Travel Lecture Film." *Cineaction* 47 (1998): 2–11.
– "Around the World in Eighty Minutes: The Travel Lecture Film." *Visual Anthropology* 15, no. 1 (2002): 91–114.
– *Virtual Voyages: Travel and Cinema*. Durham, NC: Duke University Press, 2006.
Russell, Catherine. *Experimental Ethnography: The Work of Film in the Age of Video*. Durham, NC: Duke University Press, 1999.
Schafer, R. Murray, ed. *Document no. 5: The Vancouver Soundscape*. World Soundscape Project. Burnaby: Sonic Research Studio, Dept. of Communications, Simon Fraser University, 1973.
– *The Tuning of the World*. Toronto: McClelland and Stewart, 1977.
– *Voices of Tyranny, Temples of Silence*. Indian River: Arcana Editions, 1993.
Sconce, Jeffrey. *Haunted Media: Electronic Presence from Telegraphy to Television*. Durham, NC: Duke University Press, 2000.
Secord, Jim. "Monsters at the Crystal Palace." In *Models: The Third Dimension of Science*, edited by S. de Chadarevian and N. Hopwood, 138–69. Stanford: Stanford University Press, 2004.
Sekula, Allan. "Reading an Archive." In *Blasted Allegories: An Anthology of Writings by Contemporary Artists*, edited by Brian Wallis. Vol. 2. Cambridge, MA: MIT Press, 1987.
Silver, Jim. *Thin Ice: Money, Politics and the Demise of an NHL Franchise*. Winnipeg: Fernwood, 1996.
Sitney, P. Adams. *Visionary Film: The American Avant-Garde, 1943–2000*. 3rd ed. Oxford: Oxford University Press, 2002.
Sjöberg, Patrik. *The World in Pieces: A Study of the Compilation Film*. Stockholm: Aura förlag, 2001.
Smith, Iain R. "Collecting the Trash: The Cult of the Ephemeral Clip from VHS to YouTube." *Flow TV* 14, no. 8 (16 September 2011): http://flowtv.org/2011/09/collecting-the-trash.
Smith, K. *Mental Hygiene: Classroom Films 1945–1970*. New York: Blast Books, 1999.
Smith, Neil, and Jeff Derksen. "Urban Regeneration: Gentrification as

Global Urban Strategy." In *Stan Douglas: Every Building on 100 West Hastings*, edited by Reid Shier, 62–92. Vancouver: Arsenal Pulp Press, 2002.

Smither, Roger, and Catherine Surowiec, eds. *This Film is Dangerous: A Celebration of Nitrate Film*. Bruxelles: Fédération internationale des archives du film, 2002.

Sommers, Jeff, and Nick Blomley. "The Worst Block in Vancouver." In *Stan Douglas: Every Building on 100 West Hastings*, edited by Reid Shier, 18–58. Vancouver: Arsenal Pulp Press, 2002.

Soukup, Katarina. "Banquet of Profanities: Food and Subversion in Vera Chytilova's Daisies." *Tessera* 24 (Summer 1998): 38–52.

Spaner, David. *Dreaming in the Rain: How Vancouver Became Hollywood North by Northwest*. Vancouver: Arsenal Pulp Press, 2003.

Spock, Benjamin. *The Common Sense Book of Baby and Child Care*. New York: Duell, Sloand and Pearce, 1946.

Starblanket, Noel. "A Voice for Canadian Indians: An Indian Film Crew (1968)." In *Challenge for Change: Activist Documentary at the National Film Board of Canada*, edited by Thomas Waugh, Ezra Winton, and Michael Brendan Baker, 38–40. Montreal: McGill-Queen's University Press, 2010.

Steedman, Carolyn. *Dust: The Archive and Cultural History*. New Brunswick, NJ: Rutgers University Press, 2002.

Steele, Lisa. "First Views a Partnership in Progress: Vtape and AFVAA." In *imagineNATIVE: Aboriginally Produced Film & Video*, edited by Cynthia Lickers, Aboriginal Film and Video Art Alliance of Ontario, and Vtape, iv–v. Toronto: Vtape, 1998.

– "Vtape's Aboriginal Digital Access Project." In *Aboriginal Digital Access Project*, edited by Vtape. Toronto: Vtape, 2012.

Sterne, Jonathan. *The Audible Past: Cultural Origins of Sound Reproduction*. Durham, NC: Duke University Press, 2006.

– *MP3: The Meaning of a Format*. Durham, NC: Duke University Press, 2012.

Stewart, Michelle. "Cree Hunters of Mistassini: Challenge for Change and Aboriginal Rights." In *Challenge for Change: Activist Documentary at the National Film Board of Canada*, edited by Thomas Waugh, Michael Brendan Baker, and Ezra Winton, 180–9. Montreal: McGill-Queen's University Press, 2010.

Straw, Will. "Embedded Memories." In *Residual Media*, edited by Charles

R. Acland, 3–15. Minneapolis: University of Minnesota Press, 2007.

Streible, Dan. "The Role of Orphan Films in the 21st Century Archive." *Cinema Journal* 46, no. 3 (Spring 2007): 124–8.

Teo, Stephen, and Vivian Lee. "Introduction: Placing Value in the Missing and the Lost." *Journal of Chinese Cinemas* 4, no. 2 (May 2010): 83–7.

Testa, Bart. "Chamber's Epic: *The Hart of London*, History's Protagonist." In *The Films of Jack Chambers*, edited by Katherine Elder, 141–73. Toronto: Cinematheque Ontario, 2002.

Theall, Donald. "McGill University Study of Audio-Visual and Multi-Media Aspects in Selected National and Theme Buildings at Expo 67: Prepared for the National Film Board." Unpublished report.

Thompson, Kristin. "Early Sound Counterpoint." *Yale French Studies* special issue, no. 60 (1980): 115–40.

Thompson, Nellie Z. "Arranging those Assembly Programs." *NASSP Bulletin* 35, no. 180 (October 1951): 65–7.

Van Dijck, Jose. *Mediated Memories in the Digital Age*. Stanford: Stanford University Press, 2007.

VanderBurgh, Jennifer. "(Who Knows?) What Remains to Be Seen: Archives, Access, and Other Practical Problems for the Study of Canadian 'National' Television." In *Canadian Television: Text and Context*, edited by Marian Bredin, Scott Henderson, and Sarah A. Matheson. Waterloo: Wilfrid Laurier University Press, 2012.

Vanstone, Gail. *D Is for Daring: The Women behind the Films of Studio D*. Toronto: Sumach Press, 2007.

Véronneau, Pierre. "De la féodalité à la fronde, de 1939 à 1964." In *La production française à l'ONF: 25 ans en perspectives*, edited by Carol Faucher, 5–11. Montréal: Cinémathèque québécoise, 1984.

– "Early Activities of the Francophone Group at the National Film Board." In *A Celebration of Canada's Arts, 1930–1970*, edited by G.B. Carruthers and G. Lazarevich, 165–73. Toronto: Canadian Scholars' Press, 1996.

– *Résistance et affirmation: La production francophone à l'ONF – 1939–1964*. Montreal: Cinémathèque québécoise, 1987.

Vincendeau, Ginette. "Hollywood Babel: The Multiple Language Version." *Screen* 29, no. 2 (1988): 24–39.

Waugh, T. *The Fruit Machine: Twenty Years of Writings on Queer Cinema.*

Durham, NC: Duke University Press, 2000.
– *Romance of Transgression in Canada: Queering Sexualities, Nations, Cinemas.* Montreal: McGill-Queen's University Press, 2006.
Waugh, T., M.B. Baker, and E. Winton, eds. *Challenge for Change: Activist Documentary at the National Film Board of Canada.* Montreal: McGill-Queen's University Press, 2010.
Wees, William C. *Recycled Images: The Art and Politics of Found Footage Films.* New York: Anthology Film Archives, 1993.
Whitney, Alison. "Labyrinth: Cinema, Myth and Nation at Expo 67." McGill University, 1999.
Witt, Michael. "The Death(s) of Cinema According to Godard." *Screen* 40, no. 3 (1999): 331–46.
– "Introduction. Jean-Luc Godard: *Histoire(s) Du CinéMa.*" *Screen* 40, no. 3 (1999): 304–15.
– "Paroles Non-Éternelles." In *Jean-Luc Godard: Documents*, edited by Nicole Brenez. Paris: Centre Georges Pompidou, 2006.
Zéau, Caroline. *L'Office national du film et le cinéma canadien (1939–2003): Éloge de la frugalité.* Vol. 10. Brussels: Peter Lang Publishing, 2006.
Zielinksi, Siegfried. *Deep Time of Media: Toward an Archeology of Hearing and Seeing by Technical Means.* Cambridge, MA: MIT Press, 2008.
Zyrd, Michael. "Found Footage Film as Discursive Metahistory: Craig Baldwin's *Tribulation 99.*" *The Moving Image* 3, no. 2 (2003): 40–61.
– "A Report on Canadian Experimental Film Institutions, 1980–2000." In *North of Everything*, edited by William Beard and Jerry White, 392–401. Edmonton: University of Alberta Press, 2002.

CONTRIBUTORS

ANDREW BURKE is an associate professor in the Department of English at the University of Winnipeg, where he specializes in critical theory and cultural studies. He has recently published articles on the cultural history of the Moog synthesizer, the installation work of Douglas Coupland, and the films made by the pop group Saint Etienne. He is currently at work on a project about cultural memory and the public service announcement.

GERDA CAMMAER is an associate professor in the School of Image Arts at Ryerson University in Toronto, where she teaches in the film studies (BA), documentary media (MFA), and film and photography preservation and collections management (MA) programs. Her films have been shown at various festivals in Canada and abroad, and her publications have appeared in journals such as *The Moving Image, Convergence, Camera Obscura,* and *Environmental Communication,* as well as in the collections *Challenge for Change: Activist Documentary at the National Film Board of Canada* (McGill-Queen's, 2010), *Beyond the Screen: Networks, Institutions and Publics of Early Cinema* (John Libbey Publishing, 2012), and *L'avenir de la mémoire: Patrimoine, restauration, réemploy cinématographiques* (Éditions du Septentrion, 2013).

JASON B. CRAWFORD holds a PhD in humanities from Concordia University in Montreal and teaches in the Humanities Department at Champlain College, Saint-Lambert, Quebec. He researches and writes on the geographies and histories of queer cultures with particular emphasis on community archives, memory, and the politics of Canadian gay and lesbian activist historiography. His work has appeared in the *Journal of Canadian Studies* and *Canadian Theatre Review.*

LIZ CZACH is an associate professor in the Department of English and Film Studies at the University of Alberta. Her research interests include Canadian and Québécois film, home movies and amateur film, film festivals, and star studies. She has been published in these areas in numerous journals and edited collections. Her current research project is a book-length cultural history of post-war travel film lectures.

ZOË DRUICK is an associate professor in the School of Communication at Simon Fraser University. Her monographs include *Projecting Canada: Documentary Film and Government Policy at the National Film Board* (2007) and *Allan King's* A Married Couple (2010). Her edited collections include *Programming Reality: Perspectives on English-Canadian Television* (2008, with Aspa Kotsopoulos) and *The Grierson Effect: Tracing Documentary's International Movement* (2014, with Deane Williams).

SETH FELDMAN is a professor of cinema and media studies at York University. His publications include pioneering collections of work on Canadian cinema, two books on the Soviet documentary filmmaker Dziga Vertov, and a monograph on Canadian director Allan King. He is also a prolific producer of radio and film documentaries.

MONIKA KIN GAGNON is a professor in communication studies at Concordia University. She is author of *Other Conundrums: Race, Culture and Canadian Art* (2000), and, with Richard Fung, *13 Conversations about Art and Cultural Race Politics* (2002). Recent work includes *Charles Gagnon: 4 Films* (2009), research on Theresa Hak Kyung Cha's unfinished *White Dust from Mongolia*, and *Reimagining Cinema: Film at Expo 67*, co-edited with Janine Marchessault, on the films and archives of Expo 67.

ANDRÉ HABIB is an associate professor of film studies at the Université de Montréal. He is the author of *L'attrait de la ruine* (Yellow Now, 2011). He co-edited the following works: *Chris Marker et l'imprimerie du regard* (L'Harmattan, 2008), *L'avenir de la mémoire: Patrimoine, restauration, réemploi cinématographiques* (Presses universitaires du Septentrion, 2013), and *Épopée: Textes, entretiens, documents* (Spirale/Nota Bene, 2013). He is also the co-director of the online journal *Hors Champ*.

RANDOLPH JORDAN is a postdoctoral research fellow in the School of Communication at Simon Fraser University. His research intersects film sound studies with acoustic ecology, and he is currently engaging in an intermedial historiography of Vancouver with a particular emphasis on how the city's soundscape has been staged across a variety of locally based film and media. He is now writing a book for Oxford University Press, provisionally titled *Reflective Audioviewing: An Acoustic Ecology of the Cinema.*

PETER LESTER is an assistant professor in the Department of Communication, Popular Culture and Film at Brock University, where he teaches courses in Canadian cinema. He has recently published articles in such venues as the *Canadian Journal of Film Studies*, *SCOPE*, *Film History*, and the *Quarterly Review of Film and Video.*

SCOTT MACKENZIE teaches film and media at Queen's University, Canada, where he is also a visiting research fellow cross-appointed to the graduate program in cultural studies. His books include *Cinema and Nation* (with Mette Hjort, 2000); *Purity and Provocation* (with Mette Hjort, 2003); *Screening Québec* (2004); *The Perils of Pedagogy: The Works of John Greyson* (with Brenda Longfellow and Thomas Waugh, 2013); *Film Manifestos and Global Cinema Cultures* (2014); *Films on Ice: Cinemas of the Arctic* (with Anna Westerståhl Stenport, 2014); and *The Cinema, too, Must Be Destroyed: The Films of Guy Debord* (forthcoming).

LOUIS PELLETIER is a SSHRC postdoctoral fellow at Université de Montréal and Concordia University. He has published on silent cinema, industrial films, and film exhibition in *The Moving Image*, *Film History*, *Living Pictures* (with Catherine Russell), and *Cinémas* (with Paul S. Moore). He is research coordinator of the Canadian Educational, Sponsored and Industrial Film Archive (www.screenculture.org/cesif).

KATHERINE QUANZ is a doctoral candidate at Wilfrid Laurier University. Her two primary research areas are Canadian Aboriginal experimental cinema and the development of the Canadian post-production sound industry.

MICKY STOREY is a graduate of St Andrews, Cambridge, and Concordia universities. He teaches English literature and film studies at New College, Pontefract.

CHARLES TEPPERMAN is an assistant professor of film studies at the University of Calgary. He is the author of *Amateur Cinema: The Rise of North American Moviemaking, 1923–1960* (University of California Press, 2014).

JENNIFER VANDERBURGH is an associate professor of film and media studies in the Department of English at Saint Mary's University. Her research on archiving and accessing Canadian television, as well as how films and TV shows relate to culture, citizenship, and collective memory, has been published in journals and edited collections. She is currently writing a book on the relationship between television and Toronto.

WILLIAM C. WEES is an emeritus professor at McGill University. He is the author of *Vorticism and the English Avant-Garde*, *Light Moving in Time: Studies in the Visual Aesthetics of Avant-Garde Film*, *Recycled Images: The Art and Politics of Found-Footage Films*, and numerous essays and reviews, most of which deal with experimental/avant-garde film and video.

JERRY WHITE is Canada Research Chair in European studies at Dalhousie University. His most recent book is *Two Bicycles: The Work of Jean-Luc Godard and Anne-Marie Miéville* (WLU Press, 2013).

CHRISTINE YORK is a lecturer in translation studies at Concordia University and recently completed her PhD at the University of Ottawa. Previously, she worked as a freelancer specializing in audiovisual translation. In 2012, she organized the Canadian Association for Translation Studies conference under the theme "Translation, Texts, Media."

INDEX

An italic *f* following a page reference indicates the presence of an illustration.